FOR R.V.P.

*The Adventures
of Conan Doyle*

By CHARLES HIGHAM

The Adventures of Conan Doyle

THE LIFE OF THE CREATOR OF

SHERLOCK HOLMES

W · W · NORTON & COMPANY · INC
NEW YORK
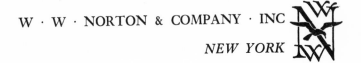

THE TEXT of this book is set in Linotype Janson. Composition, printing, and binding are by the Vail-Ballou Press, Inc.

Library of Congress Cataloging in Publication Data

Higham, Charles, 1931–
    The adventures of Conan Doyle.
    Bibliography: p.
    Includes index.
    1. Doyle, Arthur Conan, Sir, 1859–1930—Biography.
I. Title.
PR4623.H5   823'.9'12   [B]   76-20499

ISBN 0–393–07507–9

2 3 4 5 6 7 8 9 0

CONTENTS

Preface   9
Acknowledgments   13
1 . . . Edinburgh, London, and Moriarty   19
2 . . . Ghosts of the Arctic   39
3 . . . Holmes Is Born   65
4 . . . Phantoms and Detections   88
5 . . . America, Egypt, and Falling in Love   128
6 . . . Typhoid in Bloemfontein   150
7 . . . Holmes Is Reborn   174
8 . . . Conan Doyle as Sherlock   199
9 . . . Submarines and Science Fiction   223
10 . . . Adventures in Other Worlds   276
11 . . . The Greatest Journey   313
Epilogue: Séances, Mystery, and Murder   335
Appendix   345
Selective Bibliography   347
Index   355

Illustrations follow page 185

PREFACE

WHO, REALLY, was Dr. Watson? And who was
Sherlock Holmes? Both, I discovered in exploring the background
for this book, had their parallels in real life. There actually was a
Dr. John Watson, who lived in London, had served in the war in
India, and had been wounded. And it is well-known that Holmes
was very much like Dr. Joseph Bell, a skillfully deductive surgeon who taught at Edinburgh University. But I determined, as
I worked on, that in the last analysis, Dr. Watson and Mr. Holmes,
like Dr. Jekyll and Mr. Hyde, were really different aspects of the
same person, in this instance Arthur Conan Doyle.

Consider the parallels with Watson in terms of personality.
Going through the entire Holmes-Watson *oeuvre*, we discover
more and more resemblances. Watson was kindly, sensible, out-
wardly genial and composed. He enjoyed sea stories, and was
only casual about studying medicine. He liked sport, and played
Rugby and billiards expertly. He loved dogs, and kept a bull pup.
He loved Turkish baths. He had a kind of wild courage, and
tended to be romantic and gullible. He was loyal, a patriot, faithful to his friends and his wife. Self-effacing and considerate,
though capable of being rash and headstrong, he was the perfect
Boswell for Holmes.

Conan Doyle's resemblances to Holmes are numerous.
Holmes was descended from a family of squires, and he had some
French blood. He had gray eyes. He had one brother. He suffered from conflicting moods of excitement and depression. He
could be impatient and sharp. He had a bizarre sense of humor.
He loved to make subtle literary references. He was inordinately
excited by murder cases. He was familiar with an extraordinary

range of subjects, including ciphers, medieval manuscripts, and the structure of warships. He went out in society but was at heart a solitary. He could be weighed down by the monotony of existence, yet he was optimistic most of the time.

Conan Doyle found the highest assurance of the goodness of Providence in the existence of flowers. Holmes says in *The Naval Treaty*, ". . . our desires, our food, are all really necessary for our existence in the first instance. But this rose is an extra. Its smell and its colour are an embellishment of life, not a condition of it. It is only goodness which gives extras." (This is a curious reference to Conan Doyle's interest in spiritualism; the "extra" was the term used by spiritualists, by the time *The Naval Treaty* was published in 1893, for a psychic face in a photograph, the presence of which was regarded as demonstrative of survival after death.) He loved to reflect on philosophy and the course of history. Like Watson, he longed for the country while in London.

Holmes had an almost clairvoyant grasp of events, beyond that of any other detective. He made up his own mind about crimes, deliberately acting as an accessory, when necessary, for the ultimate solution of a case, assuming the roles of judge and jury, and sometimes releasing the apparently guilty. He could deduce details of people's lives simply by glancing at them. Conan Doyle's son Adrian wrote of his father that he could sit in a café and determine from the hats, coats, shoes, umbrellas, and walking sticks of those who came in virtually their whole life stories.

Sherlock Holmes refused a knighthood; Conan Doyle wanted to. Successive changes in the location of the cases Holmes solved reflect Conan Doyle's own changes of address. Although we find no mention of his birthplace, Edinburgh, in the Holmes stories, we find several references to Plymouth and Portsmouth, where he first lived as an adult.

In Montague Street, London, Holmes had his first rooms; Conan Doyle's London rooms were in Montague Place. By the time Conan Doyle moved to South Norwood, a suburb of London, he had already placed one of his characters in Upper Norwood. We see more of southeast England as we follow the author's eye down the railway from Charing Cross Station and Victoria Station into Surrey, Kent, and Sussex. In the stories written after Conan Doyle moved to Hindhead, we become more aware of the lovely countryside of that region, and three-quarters of the Holmes cases take place within a radius of seventy miles of London. Conan Doyle's further removal to Sussex is mirrored by Sherlock Holmes's own removal there to keep bees. In Sussex, Holmes is about five miles from Eastbourne, beyond the South Downs, which were visible from the windows of Conan Doyle's lovely house at Crowborough.

There are, of course, radical differences between Holmes and Conan Doyle. Holmes, by his own definition, was entirely cerebral, his body merely an "appendix" to his brain. Conan Doyle was by contrast earthily physical. Conan Doyle did not write a series of monographs on the subject of criminology, but instead —a rather subtle difference—wrote agitatory manifestoes about people falsely accused of crime. He did not receive a gold snuff-box from the King of Bohemia, a ring from the royal family of Holland, an emerald tiepin from Queen Victoria, or, the Légion d'Honneur.* Holmes coolly accepted these rewards.

Conan Doyle never did retire; but he could, in the last years of his life, enjoy something of the leisure which Holmes experienced. To the best of my belief, he did not emulate Holmes in robbing safes or breaking and entering premises without a warrant. He did not—some sensation seekers may be disappointed—take drugs, or assume disguises more than twice: once when he frightened the children by dressing up as a dragon at Christmas, and once when he appeared as one of his own characters, the irascible Professor Challenger, for a publicity photograph. Holmes, we know, assumed exactly thirteen disguises: as a seaman, a groom, a clergyman, an ancient man, a drifter, a priest, a deformed bookseller, a bearded plumber engaged to a housemaid, a French laborer, a nondescript ne'er-do-well, an old woman, a man on his deathbed, and a disaffected Irish-American spy.

In traveling through the complex maze of the mind of Conan Doyle–Holmes–Watson, I have traveled very far afield both physically and mentally, and in this book I have tried to unravel some at least of the tangled skein of fact and fancy which makes up

---

* Anglicized by Conan Doyle as "the Order of the Legion of Honour" in *The Golden Pince-Nez.*

the Sacred Writings of the Holmes canon. Endless odd coincidences, prophecies, quirks, cropped up during my research, revealing this author's intelligence to be of an astonishing richness. In my journeys, I was delighted to find that Sir Arthur's daughter Lady Bromet was a governor of the Star and Garter home for ex-servicemen which my father founded. Pleasanter still, she was living on the west side of Cadogan Square. Cadogan West is one of the characters in a favorite Holmes story, *The Bruce-Partington Plans*.

I spent many happy hours in that favorite haunt of Conan Doyle's, the British Museum, also a haunt of the naturalist and lepidopterist Jack Stapleton in *The Hound of the Baskervilles*. I was disappointed to find that Conan Doyle's rooms in Montague Place, facing an entrance to the Museum, had been replaced by an office building. But I was pleased to note that what were presumably Holmes's rooms in Montague Street before he moved to Baker Street were still intact. In Lausanne, Switzerland, I looked out of virtually the same window across Lake Geneva as did the Conan Doyle character Lady Frances Carfax at the National Hotel. Davos, where Conan Doyle and his first wife, Louise, lived, is not all that drastically changed.

Conan Doyle's house in Southsea, together with the adjoining church and the street canopied with elms in high summer, was destroyed by enemy action in World War II. The Edinburgh houses where he spent his childhood have, equally sad to say, all vanished in redevelopment projects, and so has his London residence of later years, the block of flats known as Buckingham Palace Mansions. Fortunately, his homes Undershaw, Windlesham, and Bignell House have been preserved, and so has his grandfather John's house at 17, Cambridge Terrace. His Uncle Richard's house at 7, Finborough Road has been divided into flats.

The immortality of this marvelous writer is fixed forever in the Holmes stories, today enjoying their greatest vogue. These perhaps more than any others in the detective-story genre can give irresistible pleasure to child and adult alike.

CHARLES HIGHAM

ACKNOWLEDGMENTS

MY GREATEST DEBT is to Robin Sanders-Clark, Sir Arthur Conan Doyle's only surviving close friend, who has also been a leading investigator of psychic phenomena and spiritualist mediums. He has read the book, supplying numerous suggestions for improvement in matters of detail, and has answered questions tirelessly. His enthusiasm for the book, and his general support, have been indispensable. Tony Rayns, in London, has with great expertise explored, described, and photographed the surviving homes of Conan Doyle, and interviewed his servants, Latter and Bassett, as well as Dr. R. K. McAll, present owner of Bignell House. Patrick Culliton provided many details relating to Houdini and psychic phenomena. Lady Bromet, the daughter of Conan Doyle's second marriage, has been extremely co-operative in supplying information about her father's life; and so has Mary Conan Doyle, the daughter of his first marriage, born shortly after Sherlock Holmes. Anthony Howlett of the Sherlock Holmes Society of Great Britain has been a mine of information. A list of institutions which have proved helpful in supplying unpublished or published written matter is given at the beginning of the Bibliography.

CHARLES HIGHAM

Los Angeles, March 22, 1976

"*My whole life is spent in a series of frantic endeavors to escape from the dreary commonplaces of existence.*"

—SHERLOCK HOLMES, in the play of the same name by Sir Arthur Conan Doyle and William Gillette, adapting a remark made in *The Red-Headed League.*

"*It has been the common ambition of mankind to set the whole world talking. To set the whole world screaming was the privilege of Challenger alone.*"

—WHEN THE WORLD SCREAMED

The Adventures
of Conan Doyle

1

EDINBURGH, LONDON, AND MORIARTY

IMAGINE THAT you are invisible, that you can move through doors and walls and ceilings at will. It is March, 1886, and you are in Portsmouth, a nice, gray little town on the Hampshire coast of England. Snow is swirling through the streets, in the last flurries of a great storm which is blowing itself out after several days. The street you are flying along is sheltered by elm trees, which are so heaped with snow that they look like anchored clouds. You see a church with a self-important steeple, and then you stop at a small house, nestled close to the church wall as though huddling for protection against the wind.

The front door, shut snugly against the cold, has an arched, ecclesiastical look. You don't bother with the brass door knocker, but pass instead through varnished oak into a narrow hallway, brown and cheerless, lit by a single gas lamp in the ceiling. Ahead of you is a cheap, purple-velvet curtain, draped in the Turkish style, pulled up on each side by tarnished, gilt-tasseled ropes. To your right, a door stands slightly ajar; you see a consulting room, furnished with a badly upholstered leather chair, a large table, a small red square of carpet, books and surgical instruments. Among the pictures on the walls are two strange paintings—one of a haunted house, and the other of a coach, white and eerie, hurtling through a sinister landscape. Upstairs, you discover a small dining room on your left, and on your right a sitting room, cramped and cheaply furnished, where a young, brown-haired woman with a pale face is knitting, her eyes filled with a sweet and touching expression.

You travel up yet another flight to a tiny study with a vaulted ceiling, the walls papered in robin's-egg blue. There, in a round-backed chair, before a small desk cluttered with sheaves of paper, framed photographs, books, an inkwell, and a pipe stand, a man is sitting. He is tall, well over six feet. He is in his late twenties, but looks several years older. His hair is brown, his gray eyes, screwed up in premature pouches of flesh, are secretive, but genial and bright. His cheeks are full, and tanned by sun and wind. A bushy mustache conceals the firm, determined Scottish-Irish line of his mouth. His shoulders are broad. His barrel chest fills out his heavy tweed jacket, and his waistcoat with the silver watch chain over it. He is apt to chuckle, or roar with laughter, or shout out dialogue to himself as he writes. Each quarter hour the church bell chimes over his head, vibrating the room and sometimes making him glance up. But he does not hesitate long; the pen is dipped into the black ink, the powerful hand gets to work, and five more words of a story are written—one of the most famous introductions of one person to another in the whole of fiction:

"Dr. Watson, Mr. Sherlock Holmes."

We journey back twenty-seven years, to Scotland in 1859. The city of Edinburgh resembles nothing so much as a dignified spinster with syphilis. For all the Athenian grandeur of Edinburgh's public buildings, the severe beauty of her Georgian square, the city is a national disgrace. By the mid-1850's, the corruption and extravagance of the Town Council have stripped the coffers bare. Extending the Leith Docks and erecting pseudo-classical monuments to civic vanity have been flamboyant and self-indulgent mistakes. Scottish thrift, like British colonial justice, has become a vaporous myth, and there is no provision for tolerable conditions for the poor.

Old Town, with its tenements and poorhouses, its befouled, cobbled streets filled with the cries of match-sellers and apple-hawkers, is a running sore on the prim, gray face of Scotland. Families of eleven and more live in rooms like sties; plumbing is primitive or nonexistent, and indoor baths are virtually unknown; most of the inhabitants relieve themselves in troughs or slop pails, which are emptied out into the streets at night. The gutters flow with a stew of black, sooty rain, vomit, and turds; staircases are strewn with garbage; prostitutes lift their skirts in unlit streets by the light of farthing candles. The death rate is thirty-seven per thousand per week, mainly from murder—strangling and knifing are the most popular crimes—but many die from rampant small-pox, typhus, and other varieties of fever. The Edinburgh Infirmary overflows with the sweating, coughing, vomiting, and cursing hordes of the sick and dying.

Together with the din of hawkers and the ceaseless rattle and scrape of carriage wheels on cobbles, Edinburgh echoes to the forlorn cries of stream trains, with their ironical suggestion of escape to greener pastures. Only the richest areas can afford the luxury of gaslight. And Auld Reekie, as it is known, can offer a variety of stenches which make London seem as sweet-smelling by comparison as the Vale of Kent. The tanning factories, the glue factories, and the establishments which make catgut from entrails, all exude a fume of decomposing animal flesh which spreads across the city like a pestilence; the new gasworks belches smoke from its chimney. The bad air reaches to the famous and elegant Princes Street, and on the frequent rainy days, refuse from the Caledonian Distillery flows through the streets even of the handsome New Town.

It was into this urban purgatory that Arthur Conan Doyle was born on May 22, 1859. Arthur was named almost certainly for King Arthur, and most definitely for his distinguished grand-uncle and godfather, Michael Edward Conan,* who had combined work as an artist with service as a foreign correspondent for the London *Morning Herald*. Later, Michael Conan had become liter-ary, music, and dramatic critic for the same newspaper, and in 1854, he had moved to Paris to free-lance. Ten years after that, when Arthur was five years old, Conan became Paris correspondent of *The Art Journal*. In his late teens, Arthur was to visit him at his house in the Avenue de Wagram in Paris. Arthur was born at 11, Picardy Place, since pulled down, but his family moved rest-

---

* Brother of Marianna Conan, the early-deceased wife of Arthur's grandfather John.

lessly, looking for an escape from the poisoned air, the sheer reek of the city. Wherever they went the atmosphere was unhealthy, and the windows usually had to be closed against the stench.

In his home life, Arthur was aware of the same unfairness of Fate that made Old Town what it was. His father, Charles, was the unlucky youngest son of a remarkable family. While the other members flourished, sunning themselves in public and critical esteem, Charles Altamont Doyle remained obscure.

The Doyle family was devoutly Roman Catholic. On his father's side, Arthur was descended from a long line of Irish gentry. His famous grandfather, John Doyle, had risen from a background of genteel Irish poverty to become one of the most gifted caricaturists of his generation. Beginning as a miniaturist, a student of the Italian landscape artist Gaspare Gabrielli, and later becoming a disciple of the miniaturist John Comerford in Ireland, he had arrived in London possessed of an entirely new conception of political caricature. James Gillray and George Cruikshank, his illustrious predecessors, had been harsh and cruel; he would be gently and considerately satirical. After making a contract with a London publisher, he hid behind the discreet cipher of "HB."* His drawings were delivered to the printer in a closed carriage, taken in by a go-between, and printed in secrecy. In this way, John Doyle ensured his anonymity and his freedom from pressure by political figures.

Tall and benign, he gently educated his five sons, James, Henry, Richard, Francis, and Charles, and his two daughters, Annette and Adelaide (known as Adele), with the aid of a tutor and a governess, in his cool, airy studio on the fourth floor of a handsome house at 17, Cambridge Terrace, Regent's Park. His wife had died young, and he was both father and mother to the children. He taught them the principles of draftsmanship, and he encouraged them to follow their own bent. Each Sunday they would bring their latest work to him. Richard might draw pictures of Alfred the Great in the Danish camp; James might make

* "H.B. is inscribed on a hat belonging to a Henry Baker in the Sherlock Holmes adventure *The Blue Carbuncle*. Also, Charles Doyle's middle name, Altamont, is used by Holmes as a pseudonym when he is pretending to be a disaffected Irish-American in *His Last Bow*.

delicate illustrations of Tasso; Annette might sketch a single flower. John Doyle would give his opinion, and the rest of the family would, in the friendliest spirit, comment on each other's work.

The great man's reputation flourished. His was a technique which his grandson Arthur would pass on to Sherlock Holmes. He was never content with a mere likeness. He insisted on a minutely concentrated observation of the subject's face and figure, a search for tiny revealing details which would disclose a personal history or a state of mind. A tic, a slight crease in clothing, the flush of a cheek, an eye that was dimmer than its neighbor—all were noted down. He did not, in the strictest sense, caricature in his drawings; he *characterized*. He was a detective of detail. He tackled the famous without fear. His artistic range encompassed everything from the tender charm displayed in a drawing of the child Victoria riding in the park, to the ferocity evident in a group portrait of litigants in a libel suit. He depicted the lowliest Bow Street runner as acutely as he limned George IV, William IV, the Queen, Palmerston, Melbourne, the Duke of Cumberland, and that greatest opponent of reform, the Duke of Wellington himself.

When, on the anniversary of Waterloo, Wellington was stoned on his way to the Mint, John Doyle showed the Iron Duke at home, looking sadly through a shattered window of his house, with the caption, "Taking an Airing in Hyde Park." Later, when the Duke was restored to favor, John Doyle showed Wellington arm in arm linked with John Bull, the caption reading, "Auld Lang Syne."

With gentle but firm strokes of his pen, he skewered the inept Lord John Russell and the even more clumsy Lord Chancellor, Lord Brougham; on a low flame, he simmered Sir Robert Peel. He dined with the Prince of Wales and visited the Queen. His home at 17, Cambridge Terrace, with its high ceilings, paneled walls, shining mahogany tables, and Chippendale chairs, was further adorned by the presence of the illustrious figures of the day.

To sustain this way of life without the income of an aristocrat, John Doyle went heavily into debt. His children, fortunately, were quite capable of supplementing the family income. Annette took over as family housekeeper when he became too poor to afford a maid. Richard, the most talented, began a career as a graphic artist, peopling landscapes with dancing elves, fairies, goblins in antic procession, designing the cover of *Punch* which was retained for one hundred and seven years. After resigning from the magazine in 1850 because of its attacks on the Pope, he pursued an equally remarkable career as illustrator to Ruskin, Dickens, and Thackeray. Henry Doyle was an accomplished painter and became director of the National Gallery of Ireland; James was a skilled portraitist, painter of religious subjects, caricaturist, and author of *The Chronicle of England;* Francis, who died at the age of fifteen, left behind some lovely miniatures.

Charles Doyle, Arthur's father, was a changeling in a family of charmers. The strain of artistic talent ran thin in the veins of this youngest child. Born when his mother was sick and failing, and when his father was over fifty years old, he suffered from epilepsy and emotional disturbances. He was so darkly overshadowed by his brothers that he developed an inferiority complex. He was the only one of them to abandon the intellectual world of his day, to talk about sailing to the gold fields in Australia, and to settle in Edinburgh.

About ten years before Arthur was born, he joined the Scottish Office of Works, as architect, designer and builder; he designed the fountain of Holyrood and a window of Glasgow Cathedral. In 1855 he married the diminutive, intense, and forceful Mary Foley, seventeen-year-old daughter of his Irish lodging-house keeper. Charles Doyle's income of £180 a year, gradually increasing to £200 by 1859, was just enough to sustain him, his wife, his three daughters, and young Arthur in shabby yet vaguely genteel circumstances in shared houses in run-down neighborhoods in New Town. He supplemented his income by sketching criminal trials for magazines and by illustrating fairy tales, books of rhymes, and books about heroes and heroines of England, among them *The Book of Ballads, Brave Men's Footsteps,* and *Three Blind Mice.* Spidery and delicate, reflective of his anemic character, his drawings lack the robust flair of his brother Richard's work. But his macabre water colors "The Haunted House" and "The Ghost Coach" have more originality, reflecting as they do his melancholy and morbid disposition. Gradually, Charles Doyle became an alcoholic; his condition deteriorated so drastically that he was finally committed to the Crichton Royal Institution, a mental hospital near Dumfries.

Life in the Doyle family when Arthur was a child was dismal and cloistered. In the cramped sitting room by dimly glowing gas lamps, Arthur's father made his fragile little etchings. His daughters—Annette, Connie, and Lottie—read or sewed, and Arthur, at that time the youngest, sat at his mother's knee or on a table swinging his legs, listening to her recitals of her complex ancestry. Obsessed with family, she could trace her lineage all the way back to the Plantagenet kings. She was distantly related to Sir Walter Scott, and she had spent the ten years since she had left her family in Ireland finding out the details of her original heraldic arms, her connections with branches of the Percy line, and her other noble ancestors.

Arthur wrote about her in his autobiographical work *The Stark Munro Letters* (1894):

You must remember her sweet face, her sensitive mouth, her peering, shortsighted eyes, her general suggestion of a plump little hen, who is still on the alert about her chickens. . . . Ever since I can remember she has been the quaintest mixture of the housewife and the woman of letters, with the high-bred spirited lady as a base for either character.

He always recalled her stirring the porridge with one hand and holding *Le Revue des Deux Mondes* before her eyes with the other; discussing the Goncourts, Flaubert, and Gautier with him for hours on end while darning socks, sewing up tears, knitting, scrubbing, or breast feeding one of her younger babies—Ida and Dodo. (Two more children, Julia and Innes, were born later.) One morning, while absorbed in an interesting chapter, she managed to put a small portion of rusk and milk into Dodo's earhole.

Arthur was very close to his mother, but he felt most acutely the lack of contact with his father. He revealed his feelings later in *The Stark Munro Letters*:

I admire him, yet I feel there is little intellectual sympathy between us. He appears to think that these opinions of mine upon religion and politics which come from my inmost soul have been assumed either out of indifference or bravado. So I have ceased to talk on vital subjects with him.

Worshiping, as he did then and later, muscular and intellectual force, this sensitive and most dutiful son must have been distressed by the remote, defeated, tragic epileptic who indifferently pecked his wife on her cheek each morning and walked to work, to save the carriage fare, shuffling along with bowed shoulders to his duties at the Office of Works in Holyrood Palace. But in later years, Arthur grew very affectionate and tender toward his father, whose medical condition was a scrupulously kept family secret.

Mary Doyle, tough and practical despite her obsession with chivalry and romance, must have found Charles Doyle disappointing also, for all her love of him. No doubt her romantic imagination lent color to much that she told Arthur in those years. Since the theater was too expensive to be visited very often, buying a new book was stretching a tight budget even tighter, and even a walk through Edinburgh at night was not advisable because the streets were more dangerous than in most big cities today, her tales of her ancestors must have been one of her few means of obtaining a feeling of release from her environment, from her unhappy husband, and from the strain of raising a family at a bare level of subsistence.

Arthur was steeped from birth in myths of heraldry, chivalry, honor, the dash and glitter of the English knights, the green of forests alive with crimson and gold flags, the clash of sword and shield and the soft touch of miniver, the splintering of lances and the rumble of hooves, the winning of ladies fair from villains foul: that whole rich, imaginative tapestry which he later rewove into the fabric of his historical novels. At the same time, the terror of Edinburgh, the constant threat of violence and the reality of squalor, shaped the sense of dread and darkness which underlay the Sherlock Holmes stories and which was to awaken in him most fully on his first visit to London at the age of fifteen.

Influenced by his father and his Uncle Richard, he developed the dreamy, visionary side of his character which later attracted him to spiritualism; and from his paternal grandfather, John, he inherited his benign good sense, sturdy forthrightness, and bedrock English decency. His character was strongly developed. He was at once reflective and practical, imaginative and down-to-earth, physically expert and tough, intellectually inquiring and acute. He could go into the neighboring streets and beat up a bully, then return home to read Sir Walter Scott's *Ivanhoe* with an impassioned but not entirely uncritical eye, identifying with its theme of knightly courage, the showy championship of the underdog.

His reading was typical for a boy of his age and his period, and certainly was encouraged by his mother. His Uncle Richard —whose first work in book form, written and illustrated by him at the age of fifteen, had been *The Eglinton Tournament; or, The Age of Chivalry Revived*, a graceful satire on the old romances— had been steeped in similar books as a child. Aware of the obsession of young boys with Empire and foreign adventure, successful authors of children's books created visions of fir forest and coral island, of dangerous peak and threatening deep, of white man against redskin or spear-wielding black man, colorfully limning a world of excitement that spread from the Arctic to Cape Horn.

Of the books by these writers, Arthur most loved those of Mayne Reid, and Irishman who had left his job as a tutor for the exciting life of a fur trapper and trader in the American wilderness. *The Scalp Hunters* (1851), was a special favorite of Arthur's. It is easy to understand its firm grip on his mind. The first-person narrative appealed at once; Arthur himself learned to use this technique of storytelling with great skill later on. Captain Reid buttonholed the reader, wrenching him from his secure hearth and firmly setting him down in the American wilderness. He provided the basis of Arthur's conception of God, not as a benign, bearded old presence, looking down from heaven, nor even as a being incarnated on earth through His son Jesus Christ, but as a force for good which permeates all nature. The first page of *The Scalp Hunters* awoke a responsive chord which vibrated through the rest of Arthur's life:

[God's] ambient spirit lives in the silent grandeur of the mountains, and speaks in the roar of its mighty rivers; a region redolent of romance, rich in the reality of adventure.

From Reid, the boy obtained his knowledge of botany; during journeys through the basins of the Platte and the Mississippi, the author had learned the name of almost every surrounding tree and shrub. The book awoke in Arthur a longing for America, which he later satisfied on numerous journeys. More than any work by Scott, it provided the basis for the fluid, eloquent style of his best fiction. And it supplied a scene which may well have floated up from memory when the time came to portray the fatal confrontation between Sherlock Holmes and Professor Moriarty at the Reichenbach Falls:

I stand upon beetling cliffs and look into chasms that yawn beneath, sleeping in the silence of desolation. . . . Dark precipices frown me into fear, and my head reels with a dizzy faintness.

Deeper even than the influence of the facts the book contained and the style in which it was executed, was its gospel of victory with honor. Like most authors of his day, Captain Reid was not above inserting a moral lesson into the midst of his narrative pages. He was intensely Victorian in calling for correct rules in a fight, manly endurance of suffering without complaint, tenderness to the fair sex, and courtly graciousness in dealing with social and financial inferiors.

The Doyle family's Roman Catholic convictions called for a Catholic education. After a brief stay at a preparatory school dominated by a teacher Arthur called "a pock-marked rascal," who sadistically punished his pupils, Arthur was sent, at nine years of age, to Hodder, the preparatory school for Stonyhurst, the famous Jesuit college near Preston, in Lancashire.

The best-known of the Jesuit schools in England, Stonyhurst had been established there after it was moved in 1794 from Belgium, where it had been known as St. Omer's. A run-down country house had been bought by the brothers and converted into a grandiose cluster of buildings, including a hall modeled on King's College, Cambridge, an observatory, a library, a mill to obtain water power from a nearby lake, an infirmary, and a church. The gardens were handsome and extensive, and the air brisk and clean. When Arthur was met at the train by the somber Jesuit brothers, and driven by a four-wheeler to his destination, he saw these buildings dominated by two tall towers, he felt considerably cheered. But life at the school was grim, and the unrelieved austerity quickly depressed him.

He stayed for two years at Hodder, where he was taught mostly by young brothers, under the stern guidance of Father Edward Ignatius Purbrick. At the age of eleven and a half, he graduated to Stonyhurst proper. Life at both establishments can only be described as a survival course. Each day began with the clanging of a bell, which awakened the boys in their long dormitory. They ran into a large, bare bathroom, unheated and consisting of damp stone walls and floors, with only a trough to carry away the dirty water. They dried themselves, shivering, dressed hastily, and ran back to change into uniforms that resembled prison garb.

Breakfast consisted of white bread soaked in milk. This meal was followed by a period of walking and praying in the corridors, to destroy (as an official school history would later put it) "the germs of nostalgia and homesickness, which even the healthiest may contract." Group prayers lasted more than an hour; lessons were conducted without humor or spirit; lunch usually meant a repellent stew; and only the afternoon games provided Arthur with any enjoyment. Big for his age, burly and broad-shouldered, he proved to be an expert at "Stonyhurst cricket." This was a peculiar version of the game played with homemade balls and oddly shaped alder-wood bats, employing underarm bowling exclusively. Instead of a well-mown green pitch, a gravel stretch was used. Soccer was another joy; his hefty physique proved invaluable for his team. This game, too, was played in a version peculiar to Stonyhurst: the number of participants was flexible, and they were allowed to punch the ball with a closed fist. The game was extremely violent, and often involved wild kicking and beating. Rugby, rounders, and hockey were all played with unique rules and attendant violence. On weekends, there was salmon and trout fishing along the Ribble and Hodder rivers. And billiards, a special enthusiasm of Arthur's in later years, was played.

His fondness for sport, his sheer size and courage, his tough decency and good humor, all made him popular with his school-fellows. But he was not popular with his teachers. He was ob-streperous and outspoken in his opposition to physical punish-ment. He constantly tried to bring about school reform. He was angered by the use of the "tolley," a strip of gutta-percha re-sembling the sole of a tennis shoe with which the brothers used to thrash an open hand until it was so swollen black and blue the owner could not turn a door handle with it. He deplored the custom of spying—the boys were watched day and night—though he noted in his memoirs that at least this surveillance had the merit of preventing any "immoral behavior" among the pupils.

In most English public schools, homosexuality was tacitly en-couraged, or at least not too strictly repressed. Prefects were like Roman emperors, distributing favors to the handsomest boys, scorning and bullying the weaker, less athletic, and less attractive ones. The nights were a rustle of passionate exchanges, shifting bedclothes, pattering feet, and sharp cries of relief. Not so at Stonyhurst; the nights were long—with lights out at 9:30, the wake-up bell at 5:30—and silent and dark. If desire arose in any-one, it was quenched by the fear of discovery, the threat of the tolley, or the punishment of solitary confinement without food for twenty-four hours.

This Dickensian hell did not entirely fail to please young Arthur Conan Doyle. One side of him enjoyed constraints, and no doubt his mother's idealized romantic teaching of the values of grace and chivalry resulted in his rejoicing at the chance to help the bullied and the oppressed. He was apparently one of those boys in whom sexuality is not predominant, and was able to work off his adolescent energies on the playing field. He was continually being punished, presumably for indulging in the popular Stonyhurst sins—smoking behind the shrubbery that enclosed the playground, slipping away from the vigilant prefects to buy "tuck" or tobacco at the local shops, Dick's and Ravelyea's, or going to Preston to smile at the pretty girls. These, we know, were the most favored adventures of the more daring boys, and Arthur later claimed to have been the leader in their escapades.

Somehow, in the dreary round of classical and scientific study, and between strenuous bouts on the playing field, Arthur managed to squeeze in a great deal of reading. He was even able to slip a small candle in a bottle under the bed sheets at night, and with knees humped high, to prop up a book and read it for a few minutes while a prefect nodded off on the watch. He relished Sir Walter Scott, Oliver Wendell Holmes (the small olive-green volumes smuggled under his pajama coat), and Thomas Babington Macaulay, whose essays were so glamorously filled with romantic detail. His leather-bound and increasingly tattered copy of Lord Macaulay, with its tarnished, gilt-edged pages, was a magic door to enchantment. He relished the roll of the sentences, rich with metaphor and simile, the purple coloration of adjective and adverb, the sheer dazzle of the ornate style. One individual sentence delighted him so much that he constantly quoted it to his fellow pupils, roaring with laughter as he did so: "Lady Jerningham kept a vase in which people placed foolish verses, and Mr. Dash wrote verses which were fit to be placed in Lady Jerningham's vase."

In addition to his reading, Arthur found writing and telling stories a source of diversion. At the age of six, in Edinburgh, he had completed his first story, a horror tale about a man eaten alive by a tiger. Now, at Stonyhurst, he kept his school friends enthralled on wet half holidays, sitting on a desk while they lay on the floor, their chins cupped in their hands, as he told hair-raising stories of adventure in foreign lands. He could easily be bribed with a jam tart to continue the next installment. (He wrote later, "I always stipulated for tarts 'down' and strict business, which

shows that I was born to be a member of the Authors' Society.")
When he got tired of jam tarts, apples could loosen his tongue.
He would end his narrative with words like, "With his left hand
in her glossy locks he was waving the blood-stained knife above
her head, when—" and only another jam tart could make him resume and disclose that a rescuer was on the way.

In his fantasies, either confided to his friends or simply
swarming in his head, he imagined himself setting a prairie on fire
to escape a pursuer, running down rivers to throw off blood-
hounds, slipping into moccasins to hide his tracks, slaying Indian
braves, and killing bears.

Perhaps the severest sorrow of Arthur's existence at Stonyhurst was the lack of Christmas holidays. Even his distracted
father had been present at the seasonal gatherings around the brick
fireplaces of the successive family homes, and on these occasions
his mother would tell more of her tales of knights bold and ladies
fair. But the Jesuit authorities rigidly forbade the seasonal vacation. It was not until 1874, when he was fifteen, that Arthur was
given special permission by the brothers to make a first visit to
London, to see his Uncle Richard, now living at 7, Finborough
Road, with Aunt Annette as housekeeper. His grandfather John
had died only a few weeks after Arthur first went to school, and
his Uncle Francis and Aunt Adelaide had died in a typhoid epidemic in their teens. But James and Richard were in London,
and so was Henry, on Christmas leave from his post as director of
the National Gallery of Ireland. Arthur was to stay with Richard,
and the family prepared to give him an especially good time.

Although the existing biographical accounts, and Arthur's
own memoirs, fix the date of his arrival in London at Christmas
week, he in fact came to town at the end of November. The
reason for the confusion is that he delayed almost three weeks
before writing his first London letter to his mother. The establishment of the date is possible because he spoke of arriving in a fog;
there was no other fog before Christmas. He reached London
after two accidents—not three as he said—on what he called the
"Lancashire railways" (the Lancashire and Yorkshire Line). The
collisions involving his train took place on Saturday, Novem-

ber 21. At one point, the train from Preston ran into another while passing through a goods yard; at another, it collided with a cart on a level crossing, crushing the driver.

Newspaper accounts make clear what the journey to London must have entailed. The yellow fog was so thick that men had to line up along the tracks outside of towns, holding oil lamps to guide the engineer on his way. Despite windows pulled tight with leather straps, the carriages were swirling with noxious fumes; the cold was so intense that it froze hands and faces. Arthur, big and bluff, wrapped in a red muffler, a heavy woolen coat, and the end of a fellow traveler's checked rug, clapping his mittened hands together in the chill, was enthralled by the trip. His Aunt Annette met him at Euston Station in London, and they drove in a hansom cab to Uncle Richard's house.

Richard Doyle had a robust, cheerful personality. When laughing, he had a famous trick of pulling his head down inside his high collar like a turtle into its shell, and then pushing it out again with a little twist and roaring loudly. Twinkling and Pickwickian, Uncle Richard made a happy impression on Arthur. His rooms were alive with cavorting goblins, fairies, and antic elves which the famous "Dicky" (his emblem a small, singing dickybird) had painted on the walls. Arthur was, of course, already familiar with Richard's work. He had sat for him at the age of five in Edinburgh. He was addicted to his drawings in *Punch*, and knew well the family diary which Dicky had written at fifteen, giving a rich account of theatrical occasions, riots, the Queen's wedding to Prince Albert, triumphal processions in Hyde Park, the jostle and excitement of Piccadilly and Oxford Street. The diary was heavily illustrated with his squat, witty, cheerfully knowing drawings. Undoubtedly, Arthur learned from this happy visit to respect his uncle's unique knowledge of the human face, his skill in noting the revealing details which later Holmes was to use in his detection. He also obtained the suggestion for another characteristic of his detective. We need look no further than Richard Doyle for the source of Sherlock Holmes's violin playing.

Although neither Arthur nor any of his memorialists ever referred to it, the fact is that Richard Doyle's obsession was playing a fiddle. He had begun as a child, writing in his diary:

Next to painting, music is the most delightful of pursuits, and as I am finding time to learn the violin, I find time to indulge pretty freely in it, though I am obliged to confess that the big pleasure consists in playing the gamut, and if I may judge from the awful countenance of anyone who is unfortunate to come into the room at such times I should certainly be led on to suppose that the sound resembled the singing of an asthmatic donkey or the conversation of an insane cat.

Later, Richard improved, and by 1874, he was playing with fair aptitude. We know that he fiddled cheerfully in his window seat at Finborough Road. Also, though optimistic by nature, he sometimes had moods of sadness, which playing the violin helped to ease.

Another great and so far neglected source of Arthur's inspiration can be found in the newspapers appearing during the second week of his arrival in London. In the first days of December, the *Times* and other newspapers recorded a lurid event which took place in Marylebone Police Court, only a step from Baker Street. A George Moriarty, described by the *Times* as "a strong, powerful looking man" was charged before Mr. D'Eyncourt under the following circumstances. The *Times* reporter wrote:

It appeared that the person was of an unsound mind, and had been sent to prison from this court several times during the last 15 or 20 years with drunkenness and assaults. He had also been committed from there several times as a lunatic. . . . On Monday afternoon he came [to court] to sign a declaration and was asked if he had got a witness. He said that he had not, and Amstead, the gaoler, told him he must get one. He then went to a shop in the neighborhood and purchased a large clasp-knife. He returned to the court, and on being asked by the gaoler if he got his witness said, "This is my witness!" He at the same time took out the knife and flourished it before the gaoler's eyes. Police Constable Stephen Sheaf . . . wrested the knife out of his hand. Mr. D'Eyncourt observed that the prisoner ought again to be placed in an asylum. Upon hearing that, the prisoner seemed to lose all control over himself in the dock. He screamed at the top of his voice, his eyes started from their sockets, he savagely tore up his felt hat . . . he afterwards ran across the room, dashed himself against the window, broke the glass, and endeavored to throw himself out.

This figure of primitive fury and violence must have affected Arthur—and we cannot doubt that he read this account, since he was an assiduous reader of the *Times* and indeed of anything he could get hold of, especially anything bearing on the dark and the sinister.

Another very influential event of his stay in London was a visit with Uncle Richard to Madame Tussaud's waxworks. The waxworks was situated on Baker Street, just off Portman Square, as part of a grand, glass-roofed arcade, the Bazaar; not far from the exact address at which, given the descriptions in the stories, "221B, Baker Street" would have stood. A waxworks catalogue for 1874 discloses the marvels and terrors that Arthur saw. Leafing through the pink and white pages of the brochure, he must have been impressed, too, by the variety of drugs offered for sale in the opening advertisements.

His interest in history must have been further stimulated, following his readings in Macaulay and Scott, by the first room he walked into, the Hall of Kings. According to articles in contemporary publications, a new and more elaborate exhibit opened the week of his arrival, and after he had paid his shilling entrance fee, Arthur must have been jostled by a large crowd gathering around the still, cold, corpselike figures of the great. Beyond the kings and queens lay the Napoleon Room, with the relics of the glorious monster, including his camp bed, for which the Tussauds had paid Prince Lucien Bonaparte £450; the Crown of Charlemagne, worn by Napoleon at his wedding to Josephine; and as described with grisly relish in the catalogue, "the most extraordinary and curious relic in existence, the counterpane used on the bed in which Napoleon died, STAINED WITH HIS BLOOD. (*Affirmed*)."

But for Arthur, as he wrote in a letter to his mother, the greatest delight of all was the Chamber of Horrors. It awoke in him that passion for the strange and the terrible which was so marked in his father and his Uncle Richard, and which became the force giving his best work its fascination and depth. Opened as a separate room in 1869, the Chamber of Horrors was the most popular attraction in the waxworks, so much so that the brothers Tussaud thought it necessary to put in the catalogue:

"They assure the public that, so far from the exhibition of the likenesses of criminals creating a desire to imitate them, experience teaches that it has a direct tendency to the contrary."

The stories of criminals recounted with relish in the catalogue emphasized the abduction and butchery of the young and innocent. This was to be a recurrent Holmesian theme. The subject of threats to the innocent appealed to Arthur, steeped as he was in his mother's tales of knightly valor; and Sherlock Holmes, for all his cold powers of deductive reasoning, was, of course, to become an incarnation of the chivalric virtues, helping the innocent victims of evil. The parade of murderers must have lodged in Arthur's subconscious mind, along with the look they all seemed to have, even in wax, of fierce concentration—glass eyes staring coldly. Dressed in the clothes in which they were hanged or guillotined, they appeared to be tense and ready to spring.

The catalogue, and contemporary photographs, give us a complete picture: Arthur observed Henry Wainwright ("of his biography," the catalogue says with prim good humor, "the less said the better"); Dumolland and his wife, who lured young girls on the pretext of getting them work, robbed and murdered them, and then buried them in shallow earth in the forests near Lyons; James Bloomfield Rush, who murdered his family; James Greenacre, with the knife he used to decapitate his victims—he carried a head wrapped in a cloth as he rode a horse-bus around London, and described it to the inquiring as "a healthy red cabbage"; Ravaillac, who stabbed to death Henry IV of France, and who suffered a grisly execution: first the flesh was pulled from his bones with red-hot pincers, then boiling oil, resin, and brimstone were poured into the wounds, and finally the wretched body was torn to pieces by wild horses; Courvoiser, the valet-murderer who had killed the inept Lord William Russell; Nana Sahib, the tiny Indian mass murderer echoed in Tonga, the villain in Conan Doyle's *The Sign of Four;* and Marat, shown stabbed in his bath, whose wax image was sketched by Richard Doyle. The spectators seemed more sinister than Marat himself, as they gazed morbidly at his likeness.

Emerging to a high gale and rain which whipped away the

fog but turned the dust of the city into a river of mud, Arthur and his uncle left Madame Tussaud's waxworks to enter a London no less alarming than the Chamber of Horrors itself. London was to become a central focus of Arthur's imagination, the gloomy setting of so many Holmes adventures. London enveloped them as the fifteen-year-old Arthur and his balding fifty-year-old uncle bowled along through the drenching rain and seventy-mile-an-hour wind, in their hansom costing sixpence a mile. In 1874 London was a city of almost four million people. The streets were paved with wood and asphalt, which had been ground to powder by half a million pairs of wheels and the iron-shod hoofs of horses. There was a thick layer of horse manure everywhere; and on days like this, the soot of millions of chimneys and the rain combined to blend the surface into a gruel called "London mud," of which, wrote one chronicler, "the watery and gaseous parts were evaporated into the air we breathed, while the solid particles swirled down the crowded streets."

Looking through the windows of their swaying, wind-swept, and rain-lashed conveyance, uncle and nephew must have seen countless similar vehicles, as well as broughams, carriages, and horse-buses (the men riding bravely in the uncovered area on top, the women huddled inside below). The streets on such a day were littered with umbrellas turned inside out, looking like bats' wings, and were filled with pedestrians futilely calling for cabs. Beggars huddled in rags under the inadequate protection of ledges and stone awnings, joining children with skull-like faces, forced by the rain to abandon their apple-selling or organ-grinding.

London was a city of accidents. In that winter of 1874, more than 1,600 mishaps were recorded, not all of them caused by the fog, the rains, and the gales: people were crushed to death, fell down steps or down a shaft at the Foreign Office, plunged off roofs, ledges, window sills. People were swallowed up in molten steel at a factory, run over by fire engines, dragged to death on the reins of runaway horses. There were numerous murders: the *Times*'s index for the period of Arthur's stay shows many packed columns of entries for crime. Garrotings and abductions of heiresses were especially rife. There was talk of the activity of more than one secret society; these, given the prejudice of the time, always seemed to emanate from Bohemia. And the recent state visit of the Czar still gave rise to killings, by militant anti-Czarists, of unfortunate immigrant Russians in the slums. There were over 36,000 known criminals in London, who had to report periodically and whose photographs were in police files, and a far larger army of the unknown; there were over 60,000 arrests a year, and the number would increase to 80,000 in the early 1890's; there were 134,000 summonses; the property loss in burglaries reached a million pounds; the Thames Police Force was as busy in 1874 as it was to be at the time of Conan Doyle's novella *The Sign of Four* (known in the United States as *The Sign of the Four*) in 1890.

It was a treacherous city. Ninety-six bodies were found floating in the river in December, 1874, alone, many of them with their throats cut or their necks still circled by the ropes or kerchiefs that had strangled them. Each morning, ragged street urchins, to become the models for Sherlock Holmes's helpers the Baker Street irregulars, flooded out into the streets, bent on robbery or tasks such as collecting garbage in wheeled carts and depositing it in great heaps along the banks of the River Thames. In the poorer districts, where there was sometimes no light at all, not even the cheapest of whale-oil lamps, the reeking courts swarmed with drunken, struggling women, children shouting obscenities, men bent on every kind of dangerous business, or fighting like hyenas for food. Fourteen years before the book publication of *A Study in Scarlet* and the advent of Jack the Ripper, the foundations for the greatest literary and criminal debuts of the late nineteenth century had been firmly laid down.

2

GHOSTS OF THE ARCTIC

A GREAT EXPERIENCE of Arthur's Christmas of 1874 was a visit to see Henry Irving in *Hamlet*, which had opened at the Lyceum on October 31. He and his Uncle James sat in a box, mesmerized by a performance which, predicted to be a disaster by all the critics in London, was now the talk of the city. Tall and lean, with aquiline features, wearing thick-ribbed black silk and a chain of gold, his complexion pale and his mood melancholy, Irving may have influenced Arthur's portrait of his famous melancholy detective; the boy had first seen the actor in Edinburgh at the age of eight.

At Westminster Abbey, Arthur stood capless before the funerary bust of Macaulay, who had died in 1859, the year Arthur was born; the accompanying gravestone bore the words, "His body is buried in peace, but his spirit liveth evermore." The boy saw the bust of Thackeray, who was buried at Kensal Green, and monuments to Ben Jonson, Samuel Butler, John Milton, and many others. He visited the Tower of London, which in that year had only two rooms open to visitors—the Armoury and the Jewel Tower; he marveled at the display of rifles, which appealed to his militaristic side; he was dazzled by the crown jewels. Best of all, he liked the instruments of torture, which a catalogue of 1874, the one he examined, describes as follows:

Thumbscrews; bilboes; the torture-cravat known as Skeffington's daughter after its inventor; and a Spanish collar of torture taken in the Armada; the Axe which is said to have beheaded the Earl of Essex; the Block used at (and made for) the executions of Balmerino, Kilmarnock and Lovat.

He wrote in a letter to his mother of "67,000 Martini rifles," but this was evidently an excess of the imagination, for in 1874 very few contemporary rifles were displayed, most of the guns being of the Tudor period. The walls and floors of the Tower were steeped in the blackness of England's past, making young Arthur more aware than any dry-as-dust Jesuit lesson could of the terror of history, of man's still dark and primitive nature.

He returned to Stonyhurst to find himself again repelled by the Jesuit teaching method, ready to reject Catholicism and all belief in Heaven and Hell. He makes it clear in his memoirs, *Memories and Adventures* (1924), that he no longer believed in Grace or the perfectibility of human beings. We can imagine how disgusted he must have been by a grisly Stonyhurst collection: a thorn from Christ's crown, the thumb of the Venerable Robert Sutton, taken from his martyr's gibbet, the shinbone of St. Thomas of Hereford, and a thong that bound the tortured body of Campion the martyr. Above all, Arthur was aware, even at fifteen, of morality; the stones of the Abbey had seemed to seal off life with a cold finality. He edited the school magazine, as he had promised to do, scraped through the Matriculation Examination, and traveled on to spend a final year at Feldkirch, the Stonyhurst school branch in Austria.

At Feldkirch, in a Gothic atmosphere of mountains and somber valleys, his sense of the strange undoubtedly increased. His fascination with Napoleon sharpened also, for Napoleon had marched across a nearby pass. Arthur had never forgotten the first impact of the Napoleon relics at Tussaud's. He played the bombardon horn, a massive brass instrument with thick coils like an anaconda's, in the school band, relishing his scarlet-and-gold uniform on performance days. He published a new version of the Stonyhurst magazine which he entitled *The Feldkirch Gazette,* but he made a mistake: he personally emblazoned on the cover the words, "Fear not, and put it in print," and began with a forceful editorial in which he condemned the brothers' practice of reading and censoring the boys' leters. As a result, his teachers held a kangaroo court, loosely described as a "court martial," and pronounced that the magazine must be banned. It was, and Arthur never forgave his judges. But he enjoyed two solaces: that year, he made a pleasant trip to his Uncle Michael in Paris, and he discovered the first source of his literary inspiration—Edgar Allan Poe.

His first readings in Poe were *The Gold Bug* and *The Murders in the Rue Morgue*. He had cast aside nearly all detective stories most impatiently, reserving a special place only for Wilkie Collins' novels *The Moonstone* and *The Woman in White*, both of which exerted an influence on him in later years. Poe really bowled him over. His experience of London had changed him from being an average, bluff young Victorian into a youth who was privately haunted; Poe added a few ghosts to his mental landscape. Poe was scarcely typical reading for a handsome, healthy young man who was good at games and whose rugged figure suggested the sportsman rather than the scholar or introspective dreamer; but clearly his Irish origins were beginning to be revealed.

The Gold Bug, with its story of hidden treasure and its mysterious cryptogram, excited him greatly; but there can be no doubt, based on the evidence of his work, that he was even more captivated by *The Murders in the Rue Morgue*. Just consider these sentences from the opening of Poe's story, a leisurely dissertation on the analytical approach to criminal investigation:

As the strong exults in his physical ability, delighting in such exercises as call his muscles into action, so glories the analyst in that moral activity which *disentangles*. He derives pleasure from even the most trivial occupations bringing his talents into play. He is fond of enigmas, of conundrums, hieroglyphics; exhibiting in his solutions of each a degree of *acumen* which appears to the ordinary apprehension præternatural.

Poe goes on to explain how the powers of observation and calculation, allied to a powerful intuitive sense, can bring about success in games of skill as in life; and he then proceeds to illustrate his point by the example of his master detective, Auguste Dupin.

The narrator is a man of average intelligence, who, in the first person, describes Dupin as a being possessed of superior intellectual powers. When he needed it some eleven years later,

Conan Doyle remembered this device and forged the framework for the telling of the Holmes stories by a narrator, Dr. Watson. After a collision of the narrator and a fruit vendor in a back street of Paris, Dupin is able to deduce the precise character of the train of thought set off in the narrator by the encounter. Later, when two women are brutally murdered in the Quartier St. Roch, the body of one of them stuffed up a chimney, Dupin, the embodiment of pure reason, is able to describe to his befuddled admirer precisely how the murder has been done: by an orangutan belonging to a sailor. The police, of course, have been quite unable to struggle toward the conclusions which Dupin, merely by examining tresses of gray hair wrenched from a scalp, a window, and a lightning rod, among other significant objects, leaps to instantly. Like Holmes, his descendant, he relishes the word *outré* in discussing the details of a bizarre crime. His promised investigation of a room full of charnel horrors is accompanied by the words, "An inquiry will afford us amusement." This seeming callousness masks a personality which gains its only pleasure from exposure of the guilty. Even Dupin's tone of voice is echoed by Holmes. Dupin tells his friend:

The wild disorder of the room; the corpse thrust, with the head downward, up the chimney; the frightful mutilation of the body of the old lady; these considerations, with those just mentioned, and others which I need not mention, have sufficed to paralyze the powers, by putting completely at fault the boasted *acumen* of the government agents. They have fallen into the gross but common error of confounding the unusual with the abstruse.

In page after page of the story, the parallels are very striking. While the narrator gazes at him "in mute astonishment," Dupin discloses a mass of almost clairvoyant knowledge of—among other things—the exact width of a certain kind of chimney toward its top; the nature of a certain species of shutter, called a *ferrade;* the character of the digits of the East Indian orangutan; the habits of sailors; and the fact that the tar who owns the beast, and whom Dupin has never met, belongs to the crew of a Maltese vessel.

In his earlier career, Conan Doyle was somewhat reluctant to admit the influence of Poe, making Sherlock Holmes dismiss Poe rather peremptorily in his first novel, *A Study in Scarlet*. It was only years later, in the story *The Cardboard Box* (and in some editions, in *The Resident Patient*), that Conan Doyle at last let Holmes acknowledge the impact of Dupin, indirectly but unmistakably. Holmes says to Watson:

You remember that some little time ago when I read you the passage in one of Poe's sketches in which a close reasoner follows the unspoken thoughts of his companion, you were inclined to treat the matter as a mere *tour-de-force* of the author. On my remarking that I was constantly in the habit of doing the same thing you expressed incredulity.

An even more potent source of inspiration was the French writer Émile Gaboriau, a former cavalryman, whose paper *feuilletons*, forerunners of serials in films, were circulating in Austria when Arthur was at Feldkirch. Conan Doyle, in his memoirs, dismissed Gaboriau very cavalierly, as simply having supplied the idea of "the well-knit plot." This is nonsense. Imitating Poe, Gaboriau developed the characters of the Master Detective and his bewildered admirer as adroitly as Poe himself. And in his best-written book, *Monsieur Lecoq* (1869), Gaboriau begins with a setting which gave Conan Doyle the idea of using his own memories of slushy, foggy London as the chief setting for the first Holmes stories. On Gaboriau's first page, we are in the midst of a night of mud and stifling fog in the wake of a snowstorm in Paris. We are introduced to Gevrol, of the Sûreté, the model for Conan Doyle's favorite policeman, Inspector Lestrade of Scotland Yard. Gaboriau writes of Gevrol:

His powers of penetration were not very great, but he thoroughly understood his business; its resources, labyrinths and artifices . . . he laid his hand upon the collar of the most dangerous criminal as tranquilly as a devotee dips his fingers in a basin of holy water.

We are plunged at once into an atmosphere of violence and terror. Gaboriau starkly evokes the drinking saloon in the murky Paris back street, with three men dead on the floor, a woman cowering on the stairs with her apron flung over her head, and a youth, drenched in blood, waiting like a wounded hyena for the police to seize him. Reminiscent of the great pioneer detective François Eugène Vidocq, also a model for Dupin, Monsieur Lecoq —young, pale, and black-haired, his eyes sparkling brilliantly when he is on a case but dull when he is not—has a monomaniac drive to find the story behind the murder. He chooses as his companion, his foil, and his captive audience, a former cavalry officer, the least intelligent man on the force, whom he calls Father Absinthe. Large and bumbling, Father Absinthe is the perfect prototype of Dr. Watson. A typical exchange between Lecoq and Father Absinthe goes as follows:

"To begin with, whom do you suppose the person we have just arrested to be?"

"A porter, probably, or a vagabond," Father Absinthe replied.

"That is to say, a man belonging to the lowest order of society; consequently, a man without education?"

"Quite so."

"And now," Lecoq continued, "what would you say if I should prove to you that this young man had received an excellent, even a refined education?"

Another characteristic passage has Lecoq and Father Absinthe exploring some suspicious footprints.

"Oh!" Papa Absinthe said. "A man's footprint!"

"Exactly. And this fellow wore the finest of boots. See that imprint, how clear and neat it is."

Worthy Father Absinthe furiously scratches his ear, this being his usual method of quickening his rather slow wits.

"But it seems to me," he ventured at last, "that this individual was not coming *from* this ill-fated hovel."

"Of course not; the direction of the foot tells you that. No, he was not going from here, he was coming here. But he did not pass beyond the spot where we are standing. He was advancing tip-toe with outstretched neck and listening ears; on reaching the spot, he heard some noise; fear seized him, and he fled."

"Or, rather, the women were going out as he was coming, and—"

"No, the women were outside the garden when they entered it."

And so on, for many pages of icily logical deduction which

in the end brings the criminals to book. *Monsieur Lecoq* and its companion works, written at great speed for the feuilletons by the poverty-stricken author, who died young from exhaustion, are filled with the glamor of detection. From Lecoq, Conan Doyle obtained the idea of giving his detective a mastery of disguise. The parallels from page to page, both in plot and in the treatment of plot, would themselves fill a book.

The Doyle family felt that since Arthur had not yet shown any of the artistic talent of his grandfather, uncles, and father, he should enter the priesthood, the legal profession, or medicine. He decided on the latter, for his interest in detective fiction had imbued him with a special fascination with the study, then in its infancy, of criminal types—and physical peculiarities.

Arthur graduated from Stonyhurst and went home to enter Edinburgh University in 1877. There he found a real-life Dupin or Lecoq, unknown to Poe and Gaboriau, who was to form yet another of the images on which Sherlock Holmes would be based: Dr. Joseph Bell.

The study of criminal psychology was a specialty of Dr. Joseph Bell, who was not, as he is so often said to have been, on the regular faculty at Edinburgh. He was a skilled surgeon, who gave extracurricular lectures on clinical surgery at the Edinburgh Infirmary. He liked Arthur, and to help him eke out the high cost of his studies, engaged him as his outpatient clerk. Arthur became Watson to Bell's Holmes. Gauche and clumsy in his late teens, his pocket a tangle of assorted objects, his clothes and desk and Edinburgh digs remarkably untidy, Arthur was a perfect foil for the detached, meticulously precise surgeon. Bell's high forehead, sharp nose, pronounced chin, and expression of cool self-absorption made him the physical embodiment of pure reason. He took great pleasure in hypothesizing about the biographies of patients whom he was seeing for the first time. In his memoirs, Conan Doyle recalled a typical statement of Bell's: "I see this man is from a Highland Regiment. Almost certainly he may be identified as a performer in a military band. He has been a deserter."

Like Dupin, Bell asserted that unexpected touches of detail provided sources of information for the deductive mind. He always maintained that whereas, of course, everyone had a head, eyes, a nose, a mouth, and a body with its limbs, the tiny variations from perfect regularity were endlessly revealing. Hands, with their scars—even fingernails—could disclose the occupations of certain tradesmen. Arthur would register an outpatient in his book, usher him in, and then see the tall, thin, bloodless figure before him delineate the particulars of career, profession, or craft to the astonished client. The inside of a trouser leg, frayed in a certain way, would indicate the presence of the lapstone of a cobbler; a worker's boots, with bits of clipped turf adhering to them, would reveal that he had been on a golf links. Conan Doyle never tired, in later years, of describing a tiny scene which epitomized Bell's deductive capacities. Discussing a patient in view of his class, Bell said:

"Well, my man, you've served in the Army?"

"Aye, sir."

"Not long discharged?"

"No, sir."

"A Highland Regiment?"

"Aye, sir."

"A non-commissioned officer?"

"Aye, sir."

"Stationed at Barbados?"

"Aye, sir."

Bell then turned to his students and said, his eyes twinkling with frosty amusement, his cheeks temporarily flushing with pleasure: "You see, gentlemen, the man was a respectful man, but he did not remove his hat. They do not in the army, but he would have learned civilian ways had he been long discharged. He has an aid of authority and he is obviously Scottish. As to Barbados, his complaint is elephantiasis, which is West Indian not British, and the Scottish regiments are at present in that particular island."

Bell was not the only influence upon Arthur at Edinburgh. Andrew Maclagan, Professor of Forensic Medicine, whose advice was called upon in many famous murder cases of the day, taught him how to observe the details of human corpses which disclosed the precise causes of death, invaluable knowledge for a detective-story writer. William Rutherford, with booming voice, squat, powerful figure and Assyrian black spade beard, was Professor of Physiology. His experiments were popular in class because of his macabre sense of humor. He became the basis for Conan Doyle's Professor Challenger in *The Lost World* and other novels. The name "Challenger" was that of the famous corvette which another member of the faculty, Sir Charles Wyville Thomson, had sailed aboard to collect the zoological specimens which Daniel Cunningham, Edinburgh Professor of Anatomy, had subsequently analyzed.

Arthur was an indifferent student. On his first day, one of a horde of pale and underfed young men, notebooks clutched in their hands, he hurried down the cobbled slopes from the University to the Infirmary, along an archway and down a gray stone corridor, to the demonstration theater, filled with an excited hubbub. From one of the high tiers of benches, he looked down in terror at the focus of everyone's attention: the dead white of the operating table. A length of dark-brown oilcloth which half covered the table was a particularly sinister touch. Joseph Bell, tall and gaunt, strode into the room, and a woman patient stumbled in, half supported by nurses. She lay down, and Bell ordered her to be chloroformed. Arthur gazed at the tumor on her neck, large, white, and veined like a marble egg. Seeing the surgeon's knife gleam in the gaslight as it descended, he blacked out. When Dr. Bell asked for questions at a subsequent demonstration, Arthur called from the tiers above the table, "Does that body have a soul in it?"

"Just look at it!" Dr. Bell replied. "Is there *room?*"

Conan Doyle was extremely tight-lipped about the University in his memoirs; but he left a bitter picture in his semiautobiographical and largely forgotten early novel *The Firm of Girdlestone:*

Edinburgh University may call herself, with grim jocoseness, the "alma mater" of her students, but if she be a mother at all, she is one of a very stoic and Spartan cast, who conceals her maternal affection with remarkable success. The only signs of interest she ever deigns to evince towards her alumni are upon those not infrequent occasions when guineas are to be demanded for [from] them.

Conan Doyle described the square, massive, gray buildings, unrelieved by pillars or awnings, lacking all hint of the romance for which he urgently longed: "The University is a great unsympathetic machine, taking in a stream of raw-boned cartilaginous youths at one end, and turning them out at the other as learned divines, astute lawyers, and skilful medical men."

Paradoxically, in view of his dislike of the Spartan mentality, Conan Doyle objected in the same narrative passage to the fact that students were allowed to live freely outside the campus, devoid of moral restraints, and that this led to "drinking, idling and various nameless forms of vice." He made it clear, though, that he had survived the threats to his character, and had learned "self reliance, confidence." Luckily for the biographer, he left a detailed account of the rooms he occupied in Howe Street while he was a student: a tiny bedroom and a larger sitting-dining room, furnished with a dingy sideboard, four dingy chairs, and an "archeological sofa"; a mahogany center table, littered with books and papers; a flyspecked mirror over the mantelpiece, decorated with visitors' cards and flanked with pipes in racks; and along the sideboard, a row of solemn books—"Holden's *Osteology*, Quain's *Anatomy*, Kirke's *Physiology*, and Huxley's *Invertebrata*"—with a skull as a bookend. Two thigh bones stood on one side of the fireplace, and two fencing swords and a pair of boxing gloves on the other.

In these rooms, he read voluminously, with a consuming intensity and remarkable powers of retention, devouring numerous works of science, works on recent discoveries in the new mysteries of spiritualism, or theology, mysticism, and metaphysics, and on the lore of vampires and werewolves. Yet despite this endless reading, combined with his grueling study of medical textbooks, he did not emerge fragile, wraithlike, or addicted to drink and drugs. He grew to be a man with a booming voice which carried a heavy Scots burr; gray eyes piercing and formidable, but often twinkling with good humor; his mouth a stern line which could melt with laughter; his shoulders and chest broad, almost Herculean; his waist and hips lean. He was at once sportsman and mystic-logician: Watson and Holmes.

While Conan Doyle was studying to be a doctor, he wrote two stories, *The American's Tale*, an imitation of Bret Harte told in broad vernacular, and *The Mystery of Sasassa Valley*, a story about three young men in South Africa who explode a local myth about a large red eye which glows in the dark, terrifying the natives. Written with gusto but little art, published in *London Society* and *Chambers's Journal*, these tales reflect the student-author's optimism, good health, and extravagant sense of humor. Indistinguishable from hundreds like them in the magazines of the time, they scarcely suggest the refined genius of the Holmes stories.

Also at Edinburgh, Arthur worked up an undistinguished romance, *J. Habakuk Jephson's Statement*, which appeared in *The Cornhill* in January, 1884. Based on the mystery of the *Marie Celeste*, a ship discovered abandoned off the west coast of Africa, it provided an elaborate Stevensonian explanation of the puzzle. Hundreds of readers of *The Cornhill* wrote in to say that they were convinced Robert Louis Stevenson had written it—*Cornhill* contributions were by tradition anonymous, sparking off national guessing games about their authorship—and Solly Flood, the idiotic British advocate general in Gibraltar, even issued a statement denying that the explanation was accurate; he believed that J. Habakuk Jephson actually existed.

Arthur's final break with Catholicism occurred in Edinburgh. The procession of the sick and dying enhanced a belief that religion was unable to answer the riddle of human misery. He remained silent on the point later, but there can be no doubt that his decision to lapse was a severe blow to his mother. His father, by now, was beyond caring. Alcoholic, subject to fits, Charles Doyle had left his job and entered the asylum, where he existed for all of his remaining years. The older sisters were in service as governesses in Portugal. A younger brother, Innes, had been born; and Arthur, between classes, tried to be a second father to this handsome, well-adjusted, healthy, and outward-looking boy.

Like any character in Captain Marryat or Mayne Reid, Arthur felt his spirit crying out for adventure. The chance came in 1880, when he was twenty. A fellow student visited his rooms one day and asked if he would like a job as ship's surgeon (for which in those days the M.D. degree was not necessary) on a whaling cruise, at ten shillings a month and a share of three shillings per ton of blubber.

"How do you know I'll get the job?"

"Because I have it myself. I find at the last moment I can't go, and I want to get a man to take my place."

"How about an Arctic kit?"

"You can have mine."

"Done!" Arthur exclaimed.

At the port of Peterhead, in March, Arthur went aboard the *Hope*, a 400-ton vessel with a crew of fifty Scots and fifty Shetlanders, which sailed to the fisheries between Greenland and Spitsbergen. He took with him a meager collection of belongings: battered, limp-leather volumes of Scott and Macaulay, books for medical study, a log, a woolen cap and heavy sweaters and trousers, sturdy leather boots, and two pairs of ancient boxing gloves. All his possessions were stowable in a small locker under a bunk. He immediately became popular on board. Even before the *Hope* sailed, he had answered a challenge from the steward, Jack Lamb, to a boxing bout; and Lamb, cheerfully defeated, ran around the ship shouting, "So help me, lads, he's the best surgeon we ever had! He's blackened me eye, he has!"

The voyage lasted seven months. Later, Arthur fondly remembered Jack Lamb singing in his light tenor "Her Bright Smile Haunts Me Still" or "Wait for Me at Heaven's Gate, Sweet Belle Mahone," songs which filled the crew, in Arthur's words, "with a vague, sweet discontent." There were frequent boxing matches, even in choppy seas, seen by almost every man not on watch. Arthur carried out his duties as doctor so successfully that Captain John Gray offered him a chance to become a permanent member of the crew. The extrovert in him rejoiced in the lash of the spray and the singing of the ropes. His muscles swelled as he pulled at the oars of a whaleboat, and the romantic poet vibrated —like Melville before him—to the excitement of the whale chase. He wrote in *The Strand Magazine*, seventeen years later:

The men do not need to be told to be keen. The shout from the crow's nest which tells of the presence of a whale, and the rattle of the falls as the boatswain clears away, blend in one sound. The watch below rush up up from their bunk with their clothes over their arms and spring into their boats in the Arctic air . . . woe betide the harpooner or the boat-steerer who by any clumsiness has missed the fish! He has taken a five pound note out of the pocket of every meanest hand upon the ship. Black is his welcome when he returns to his fellows.

He loved the dazzle of the ice, the clear blue of the Arctic Ocean, and above all the purity of the air. His visionary mind awakened to transcendent longings. Ten years later he told an interviewer in a direct reference to his father and the miseries of Edinburgh:

What a climate it is in those regions! We don't understand it here. I don't mean its coldness—I refer to its sanitary properties. I believe, in years to come, it will be the world's sanatorium. Here, thousands of miles from the smoke, where the air is the finest in the world, the invalid and weakly ones will go when all other places have failed to give them the air they want, and revive and live again under the marvelous invigorating properties of the Arctic atmosphere.

The experience eased the ache of a childhood spent in the damp air of Scotland, the creeping fogs of Lancashire, and supplied an escape from the imprisonment of urban life which was only a step toward release from the body itself. A finer air, the air of Another World, was to attract him soon, when even the Arctic did not seem to offer sufficient freedom.

Arthur needed a sense of transcendence, for despite his robust drive for action and adventure, the bloodiness of the whaler's task struck home to his more sensitive self. Later, the crew had to seek out the sealing grounds, south of Greenland, where thousands of creatures congregated in April on the ice packs. Then, in their boats, Arthur and his companions began their butchery. He wrote, "Those glaring crimson pools upon the dazzling white of the ice-fields, under the peaceful silence of the Arctic sky, did seem a horrible intrusion."

First came the shooting of the mothers and the young; then the journey south to butcher the male seals. Arthur twice fell off both ship and ice blocks; he was almost killed when he slipped between floes while skinning a dead mother seal; and he had many other dangerous adventures when the *Hope* sailed on from the sealing back to the whaling seas. Still, he had a Melvillean sense of excitement in the slow, silent creeping of the harpoon boat toward the legendary beast; the cry of the boat-steerer that signaled the tripping of the harpoon gun's trigger; the dull, greasy squelch of the boat's collision against the whale's side; the striking home of the harpoon; the victim sinking, with the red flag that marked the fatal blow shot firmly into its side.

Despite himself, Arthur took great pleasure in the harpooning. He and his companions had to thrust one harpoon after another into the beast, until it resembled a giant pincushion and the sea was scarlet. Its tail would thrash so violently in its death agony that it would almost upset the boat; and finally the crew themselves would be drenched in blood.

The work continued for seven months. In the weeks after the summer solstice there was perpetual daylight, in which the eyes grew tired and Arthur longed for the cool drizzling darkness of Scotland. These were months of acute loneliness, without word of his sick father, months of exasperation at not being able to follow news of the Empire. The Second Afghan War broke out. There was the defeat of Maiwand, which Dr. Watson later described so vividly; and the field commander, General Frederick Roberts, marched from Kabul to Kandahar. But there were compensations: the cries of innumerable sea birds, each of which Arthur learned to identify; the sight of the grampus, "the most formidable of all monsters of the deep"; the narwhal, with its strange unicorn horn; the white Arctic fox, darting like a spirit across the ice; the mother polar bear, howling over a dead cub, as erect on her hind legs as any human; and above all, the mysterious white whale, glimpsed often, but never caught and killed.

In September, with the cold already acute, the *Hope* headed back to Peterhead, and Arthur looked at the waters off Greenland for the last time. They were to remain in his dreams, and his nightmares, for the rest of his life.

Arthur returned to Edinburgh University filled out to a powerful 195 pounds. A photograph of him on the quarter-deck of the *Hope*, wet with spray, beneath a gray and threatening sky, reveals a man in the prime of condition, hands neatly tucked in his pockets, eyes staring boldly into the ocean mist. In seven months he had become a man. His twenty-first birthday, no doubt celebrated with much heavy drinking and ribbing on board, marked the transition. By the time he returned to his studies, he was financially quite well off. He was able to give his mother fifty pounds from his share of the whaling profits, and still hold back enough to obtain further books for his final year's courses.

He explored his sexuality on his return; he talked of marrying a pretty girl, Elmore Welden. But this romance died, and he was probably not seeing her when, following his graduation, he set forth on another and very different voyage, as surgeon aboard the 4,000-ton *Mayumba*, sailing with cargo and twenty passengers to the Gold Coast, in Africa, on October 22, 1881.

The ship ran into gales in the Bay of Biscay, almost crashing into a lighthouse; malaria and blackwater fever laid the passengers low, along with many of the crew. Arthur himself came down with typhoid fever in Lagos, Nigeria, brushing against death as closely as he had on the ice in Greenland. Off Cape Coast Castle he narrowly missed being taken by a shark while swimming, and a fire swept the *Mayumba* on her journey home. The smoking vessel struggled back into the Liverpool docks on January 14, 1882.

The vision of death and disease on this nightmarish journey again confirmed Arthur's belief that the confident solutions of Roman Catholicism were not acceptable. He went to London and told his horrified aunt and uncles that he was abandoning the Church. The news came as a particularly severe blow to his Uncle Richard, who was still as devout and obsessed as he had been when he resigned from *Punch* in 1850 because of its attacks on the Pope. After a chilly family conference at the late John Doyle's house, in Cambridge Terrace, Richard Doyle tried a last-ditch plea with Arthur over lunch at the Athenaeum Club. It was useless.

Like Charles Doyle before him, Arthur had undoubtedly become the black sheep of the family. He thoroughly enjoyed the role. He took numerous jobs: he dispensed drugs, and he worked in various cities as an assistant to a former fellow student at Edinburgh University, an intriguing young man called Dr. Budd,* who sported a black beard, and possessed a ferocious temper.

Budd fascinated Conan Doyle to the end of his days, and echoes of him appear here and there in characters in the stories. It seems that Budd had started out in great style as a doctor, but had rapidly lost his money. Conan Doyle liked him so much that he decided to help him set up a struggling practice in Plymouth. In almost no time, Budd grew rich as a kind of inspired quack, offering free consultations but charging heavily for medicine, which he brewed in a dark laboratory. He claimed to be able to cure diseases instantly. Crowds of people jammed his consulting room when it was rumored that he had made a case of dropsy vanish with one dose of his powerful potions. He addressed his flock with an extraordinary combination of fury and cajolery— announcing that tea was poison, he made old women swear on a volume of medical jurisprudence that they would abstain from it in the future—and at the end of the day he would throw into a bag the coins he had received as fees, and march off to his house with it, shouting and drunken.

Conan Doyle's mother, whom he called affectionately "the Ma'am," objected to his working for this strange quack, and finally he yielded to her pressure. Budd forestalled his resignation by firing him, and he took off at once by ship for Portsmouth.

Why Portsmouth? Conan Doyle himself never explained; and none of his biographers have been able to give a reason why he chose to settle in this particular port, where he was to remain for the next seven years. Applying Holmesian methods of deduction, we can reach the following conclusion. Some of Lord Macaulay's

* Conan Doyle never disclosed his first name.

finest writing dealt with the history surrounding Portsmouth and that particular area of Hampshire. More important, Portsmouth had been the birthplace of two other of his idols: Dickens had been born at a site which later became 393, Commercial Road, on February 7, 1812; and George Meredith had been born at 73, High Street, on February 12, 1828. Although Conan Doyle never spoke of it, either in his memoirs or anywhere else, one can imagine with what fascination he must have visited those locations, hoping that he would soon be considered fit to join his idols' company. He was fond of *Nicholas Nickleby*, and would know very well that Dickens, even though the great writer had left Portsmouth at two years of age, had set some witty scenes there.

From a cheap lodginghouse near the wharf, where he chivalrously beat up a sailor who was molesting a young girl, the tall, ruddy-faced, and bewhiskered young doctor set out to find a permanent abode. Pacing across the Common away from the waterfront, he discovered in the suburb known as Southsea, a two-story, slate-roofed house, 1, Bush Villas, to rent next to a Baptist church at the extreme end of a street called Elm Grove. Built in 1830, 1, Bush Villas had been empty for some time, and at one stage had been used as a chapter house. Elm Grove was a quiet, pleasant thoroughfare which in 1882 was just beginning to have its view of the hills and the English Channel blocked by new buildings. Elms flung their branches over the street, forming a canopy of leaves. In high summer the green must have made a glorious sight as Conan Doyle walked toward his new home. At night, a Portsmouth guidebook tells us, the gaslight cast a lovely pattern of leafy shadows on the pavements and walls, and the Baptist bell striking the quarter hours just overhead must have been a pleasant if overloud companion for the young doctor in the first lonely months of settling in. He paid the church forty pounds for a year's rental of the house, and began to look it over very carefully.

It was extremely run-down, answering the description given in the first Holmes story, *A Study in Scarlet*, of a house off the Brixton Road ". . . three tiers of vacant melancholy windows, which were blank and dreary, save that here and there a 'To Let' card had developed like a cataract upon the bleared panes." Inside, the house was rather narrow. On the right as Conan Doyle entered the hallway was a large room which would be ideal for consulting purposes. The back room became a dining room, with his large cabin trunk as a dining table and larder combined and a small stool as a chair. Upstairs, he furnished one room with a cheap bed and mattress. The other rooms remained bare, the brown curtains drawn tight so that prying neighbors could not see his poverty. An ironmonger fixed up and polished a brass doctor's plate, brought from Plymouth. Conan Doyle hung his red lamp outside the door. He bought some potted foods, since he could not cook, and began waiting for patients.

It was a pinched life for a young man of adventure. When he walked along the sea front, looking at Nelson's *Victory* riding at anchor, he must have felt an anguish of longing. The great Portsmouth fortress with its bristling artillery suggested war and travel. The only consolations lay in reading and in bringing his nine-year-old brother, Innes, from Edinburgh to stay with him.

A great sadness of those Southsea days was the death of his Uncle Richard. Conan Doyle knew that Richard had had a premonition: not long before his death, he had painted an eerie water color of a hay cart stacked with dead bodies like sheaves in a field; and while in North Devon, Richard had limned the curious and sinister work known as "Lynton Churchyard." This picture showed an old man mowing tall grass among the graves by the sea, while children passed by, scattering flowers on one of the grave sites. On a recent brief visit to London, Conan Doyle had rushed his uncle to St. Bartholomew's Hospital following a heart attack, and had saved him from death by doing so. Now, Richard had been seized by apoplexy at his favorite club, the Athenaeum, and had been brought home to die at his house in the Finborough Road, on December 11, 1883. It was pointed out by the priest who accompanied him that Richard had faced death bravely, and had taken pleasure in the sacrament of Extreme Unction.

Conan Doyle was aware, as few others were, that after the brush with death at St. Bartholomew's Hospital, his uncle had risked criticism within the Catholic Church by becoming interested in spiritualism. Richard Doyle knew the spiritualist author Captain Marryat, creator of some of Conan Doyle's favorite books, and Marryat's daughter Florence, also a believer. Even this early in his life, Conan Doyle was conscious of the fascination spiritualism held for many gifted people. A number of the obituaries of Richard Doyle mentioned his love of fairies and elves, which figured so prominently in his work, not only in the famous cover of *Punch* but in the sylvan scenes he painted on the walls of the Grosvenor Gallery and in the rooms of private houses, and in numerous individual works as well. Conan Doyle himself had studied the research done on spiritualism in Edinburgh by the Dialectical Society.

With few patients, Conan Doyle had a great deal of time on his hands. He wrote sporadically. Later he tended to dismiss these early efforts, perhaps because they were so revealing of the side of his nature he tried to keep secret. They were not what one would expect from the pen of a young, uncomplicated extrovert, earnestly preoccupied with the glories of the British Empire, cricket results, news of the African and Indian campaigns, and the movements of Her Majesty the Queen. They were included in a three-volume anthology, published in 1886 by George Redway of Covent Garden, London, entitled *Dreamland and Ghostland:*

An Original Collection of Tales and Warnings from the Borderland of Substance and Shadow, Embracing Remarkable Dreams, Presentiments, and Coincidences; Records of Singular Personal Experiences by Various Writers; Startling Stories from Individual and Family History; Mysterious Incidents from the Lips of Living Narrators; and some Psychological Studies, Grave and Gay.

Conan Doyle's stories, his first to appear in book form, are the only tales in the anthology of which the author is identified. He is given his first publicity by the introduction, presumably by George Redway himself, which proudly boasts that "the nephew of the late Richard Doyle" has been snared as a contributor. Written in the first person, all of the Conan Doyle stories are presented as though they were true. Certainly, they all contain elements of fact, showing the influence of Poe in their manner of conveying the wildest excesses of fancy in at atmosphere of documentary realism.

From this earliest part of his creative life, Conan Doyle's chief interest emerges—his obsession with the supernatural. Imprisoned as a child in a tiny family house, crammed with his sisters into small rooms, aware always of his epileptic father and his driven, frustrated mother, he had been weighed down from the beginning. Stonyhurst, with its rigid rules and its echoing cold halls, had been just as restricting and oppressive. Edinburgh University and the carving up of dead flesh only served to emphasize the chilly confinements of the human condition. Much as he admired Dr. Joseph Bell, it is easy to see how the long procession of Bell's outpatients, described as though they were specimens, without compassion, must have given Conan Doyle the feeling that life was no more than the memory, the experience, or the promise of suffering. Neither cricket, sailing the Arctic seas, penetrating muddy African rivers, nor the vision of Heaven presented by the Catholic Church provided more than temporary escape. He was faced with the fact that his father was staring blankly at a sanitarium wall, that he himself was trapped inside his big, ill-clad body, with nothing to look forward to but a spectacle of sickness and decay which would end surely in his own sickness and decay, and that he could sometimes not afford to buy even postage stamps.

These early stories reach beyond the boundaries of normal experience into a no man's land between life and death. The best of them are poetic evocations of sexual obsession, stories about men who cannot accept the death of a loved one as final, who try to reach beyond the grave to enjoy sex in eternity. In *The Captain of the "Pole-Star,"* published in *Temple Bar* magazine in 1883, the young author recalls a voyage to the Arctic, writing the tale as a variation of his own log of the *Hope*'s whale-hunting journey. But in this story, the Captain is not the sturdy and unimaginative John Gray of the *Hope*. Instead, he is the neurotic Nicholas Craigie, whose dead mistress haunts him, calling him to join her in the spirit world. She appears, drifting across an ice floe in the light of the waxing moon, keening with a heartbreaking sadness. Several members of the crew notice her hovering in the rigging, with her high call sounding above the wind. At last the Captain answers her cry:

By the sudden intensity of his attitude I felt that he saw something. I crept up behind him. He was staring with an eager questioning gaze at what seemed to be a wreath of mist, blown swiftly in a line with the ship. It was a dim, nebulous body, devoid of shape, sometimes more, sometimes less apparent, as the light fell on it. The moon was dimmed in its brilliancy at the moment by a canopy of thinnest cloud, like the coating of an anemone.

Impelled by a will stronger than his own, the Captain springs onto the pack ice and runs with prodigious speed across the floes until the darkness absorbs him. When he is found, a strange form seemingly made of snowflakes seems to hover over him, and several crew members assert that it is in the shape of a beautiful woman.

The story is written with a marvelous poetic intensity, revealing a romantic genius who refuses to accept the fact of physical death. Like the Captain, he is "psychic," able to see beyond drab reality to the vaporous pleasures of another world. In *The Ring of Thoth*, published in 1890 in *The Cornhill*, a search for a reunion in the Beyond is defeated. An Egyptologist, John Vansittart Smith, visiting the Louvre to look at the papyri which are stored there, observes an attendant with an Egyptian cast of feature. Smith falls asleep at his note taking, unnoticed behind a door, and the museum closes. Waking, he sees the attendant tenderly unraveling a mummy and kissing the dead yet perfectly preserved face of a beautiful woman. It develops that the attendant is a priest of Thuthmoses, who has been kept alive for thousands of years by a mysterious potion, and who has only now discovered the remains of the Governor's daughter who had sexually obsessed him. The priest's necrophilia is dealt with most daringly by the writer. At the end, the priest dies of locomotor ataxia, locked in an embrace with the mummy: "So close was his embrace that it was only with the utmost difficulty that they were separated." The extraordinary perversion of the theme surpasses Poe.

This fascination with love and death appears again and again.

A very powerful example occurs in *The Man from Archangel*, published in *London Society* in 1885, one of Conan Doyle's finest early studies of sexual obsession. John M'Vittie, a lonely misogynist heir to a fortune, settles down in a bleak tract of land on the Scottish coast. A storm blows up, and a two-masted schooner is wrecked on the rocks off shore. The Russian captain, thinking he is going to die, flings his mistress, the beautiful Sophie Ramusine, onto a wave. M'Vittie rescues her, but is embarrassed by her sexual appeal. The Captain returns, determined to take Sophie with him into the sea. He admits he dragged her from the altar before which she was taking her marriage vows to another man. The Captain overpowers her and draws her from her rescuer to the death which will bring them together forever. They are found later in the narrator's boat:

It was only when I turned him over that I discovered that she was beneath him, his dead arm circling her, his mangled body still intervening between her and the fury of the storm.

At last the woman, who had fought the Russian in life, surrenders to him—in death:

Why else should her little head be nestling so lovingly on his broad breast, while her yellow hair entwined itself with his flowing beard? Why too should there be that bright smile of ineffable happiness and triumph, which death itself had not had power to banish from his dusky face? I fancy that death had been brighter to him than life had ever been.

The sexuality of the image, the blending of death with the conquest of love, and the extraordinary significance of the last sentence, clarify Conan Doyle's escapist, romantic, and necrophilic yearnings.

But his most striking story of the period is *John Barrington Cowles*, published in *Cassell's Saturday Journal* in 1886, a neglected masterpiece of terror, which shows his fascination with the supernatural at its most extreme. The narrator, like Conan Doyle himself, is a medical student in Edinburgh. A fellow lodger in a boarding house, John Cowles, is a nervous, reflective young man who has fallen in love with a beautiful and mysterious girl,

Kate Northcott. Her successive lovers have died mysteriously or gone mad. One night, the narrator visits a theater where a mesmerist, named Messinger, is giving a demonstration. Messinger focuses his attention on Cowles, who is in the audience. But Kate Northcott outstares him and compels him to abandon his attempt at hypnotism. She already has Cowles completely under her influence and refuses to yield him up. Cowles discovers on the eve of their wedding that his fiancée is a werewolf, and that werewolves sometimes devour their young. On the edge of insanity, he abandons her, and accompanies the narrator to the Isle of May, off the Scottish coast. She will not be put off. By the light of the moon, she comes to him. Following an irresistible sexual impulse, he breaks from his friend's arms with superhuman strength, and runs headlong, like the Captain of the *Pole-Star*, to embrace his supernatural visitor, plunging over a cliff as he does so.

The yearning for the supernatural and for the sweet death of sex is not the only important element in these stories. They suggest too the Gothic writer's feelings of terror about women, who are portrayed as vampires, luring men to doom. The tales are fantasies filled with both yearning and repulsion, the author's longing for a life beyond the grave balanced by a terror of extinction.

It was inevitable, given his preoccupations, that Conan Doyle should be strongly drawn to spiritualism. He had attended séances as early as 1879, and there is a reference to Henry Slade, the famous medium who claimed to obtain automatic writing on slates, in *The Captain of the "Pole-Star."* Conan Doyle's book *The New Revelation*, published in 1918, when he was a convinced spiritualist, touches on his feelings when he was in his early twenties. He makes it clear that he did not accept the usual concept of God, but believed in an intelligent force in Nature. Much as he longed for it to be otherwise, all the evidence suggested to him that there was no room in Nature for survival of the mind and spirit after death: "When the candle burns out the light disappears. When the electric cell is shattered, the current stops. When the body dissolves there is an end of matter." He maintained that view—reluctantly, as would be expected of a romantic enamored of the supernatural in fiction—for many years; it took more than three decades for his resistance to be worn away and his conversion to be complete.

One of his patients invited him to attend séances in Southsea, but they disappointed him. Sitting in a dark room, the medium in a trance, the table tilting, he became convinced that the entire performance was a fake. He took his problem to a friend, a mathematician and astronomer who had formerly been attached to the Woolwich Naval Observatory, Major-General A. W. Drayson, who told him that he had simply been made the victim of mischievous spirits. ("In a mixed séance, with no definite aim, you have thrust your head into the next world and you have met some naughty boys.") Conan Doyle decisively rejected the explanation, though he remained friendly with Drayson for many years, and dedicated *The Captain of the "Pole-Star," and Other Tales* to him in 1890.

Conan Doyle attended numerous séances at Major-General Drayson's Portsmouth house. In some of these, the medium was a young railway signalman. In others, the medium was a Mrs. Maggs, wife of the editor of two local newspapers, whose popular books on fortunetelling were written under the pseudonym Stella of the Tea-cups.

Conan Doyle was fascinated by the events in Drayson's séance room. These were his first direct experiences of seemingly genuine psychic phenomena. Showers of butterflies came down from the ceiling, followed by flowers in great profusion, eggs, fruit and vegetables, all unharmed, and conveniently solving the problem of paying grocery and greengrocery bills. All foodstuffs, so Mrs. Maggs's control said, came from Brooklyn, New York, as a gift by spirit mail from the spiritualist circle to which Drayson had sent other gifts. Letters arrived by spirit mail from Brooklyn, and so did a large pigeon, which fluttered round the heads of the sitters and left somewhat unspiritual droppings on the Major-General's expensive carpet.

In the midst of these bizarre experiences, young Dr. Conan Doyle managed to attend to more practical matters. He went to an auction and bought a table, three cane-bottomed chairs, a metal umbrella stand, some curtains, three water colors ("Spring," "The

Banjo Player," and "Windsor Castle"), a fireplace fender, a toilet set, and another table. Each day, he swept the house, using a birch broom. In the hall, with its dark pine planks, he put an oakum mat and the umbrella stand. He divided the hall with a red curtain (later replaced by a purple one), draping it in the Turkish fashion, so as to give it a slightly exotic appearance to arriving patients; the idea may have been borrowed from local mediums and fortune tellers. The consulting room was very carefully worked out. He nailed down a small red "drugget," or carpet, in the middle of the floor; in the center of the carpet he put his table, with three medical textbooks on one side of it, and his stethoscope and dresser's case on the other. He arranged the chairs to give an illusion of space being well filled, and he hung his new pictures, along with his father's paintings, "The Haunted House" and "The Ghost-Coach."

Mary Doyle sent her son a large, brown tin box containing a lavish assortment of gifts: two sets of woolen blankets and sheets, a counterpane, a pillow, a campstool, two vases, a tea cosy, pictures and books, antimacassars and tablecloths, and two bear claws for table ornaments. The gifts cheered him, and he was even more delighted when, after days of waiting, it appeared that his first patient had arrived: a condescending, haughty gentleman who cleared his throat as he sat down.

"Bronchial trouble, I believe," Conan Doyle said.

"No, there's a small sum due on the gas meter," the man replied.

But patients did come along at last, ushered in by nine-year-old Innes, since Conan Doyle could not afford a nurse or any servants. A group of gypsies, whom he first mistook for beggars, brought a baby with measles. They could pay him nothing. For three days, there were no patients at all. Tired from writing late at night, Conan Doyle sat in the upstairs room, watching passers-by glance at his name plate and move on. He kept busy, shopping at a market for bread, fish wrapped in newspapers, and Saveloy sausages; brushing the front steps; and reading voraciously in English, German, and French. He worked on his accounts, discovering how to live on twopence a day. And each night between ten and two, with Innes safely tucked into bed, he walked along the ocean front and through the narrow streets of Southsea, breathing deeply, thin as a whip—Dr. Watson to the life.

The patients gradually trickled in, but they trickled out as quickly, and often he was on the edge of starvation. He and Innes frequenlty existed on crusts of bread. A man who collapsed in a fit in the street outside his house at 1, Bush Villas, a row of identical houses, paid for a week's food; when a horse fell on a rich pedestrian, there was enough money for meals for a fortnight. Still, his visits to the pawnbroker were depressingly frequent.

Conan Doyle was appalled by the anonymity of publication in magazines, and the fact that he earned only fifty pounds a year from his efforts. When a tax inspector wrote to him, "This is unsatisfactory," he replied, "I entirely agree." Several years later, he wrote in an article in *The Idler* magazine, "After ten years of such work I was as unknown as if I had never dipped a pen in an ink bottle." Finally, he wrote a full-length book, entitled *The Narrative of John Smith*, which portrayed, perhaps a little too clearly for comfort, a number of literary and political figures in thin disguise. It was never received by the publisher, and the Post Office mailed him forms indicating it knew nothing about this manuscript. He had neglected to retain a copy.

He managed to scrape together some income by subletting rooms to two ugly viragos, the sailor husband of one of them, and their three yapping dogs. Using their rent, he was at last able to afford a housekeeper, a model for Sherlock Holmes's Mrs. Hudson.

3

HOLMES IS BORN

AFTER THREE YEARS in practice, Conan Doyle was ravaged by one of his frequent attacks of depression, following a horrible experience—later described in *The Stark Munro Letters*—which might have come from one of his own tales. He had gone to a woman's house in answer to an emergency call. The woman led him to a cot next to a sitting-room sofa. Holding a candle high, he bent over the little bed,

expecting to see a child. What I really saw was a pair of brown swollen eyes, full of loathing and pain, which looked up in resentment into mine. I could not tell how old the creature was. Long thin limbs were twined and coiled in the tiny cot. "What is it?" I asked in dismay when we were out of hearing. "It's a girl," sobbed the mother. "She's nineteen. Oh! If God would only take her!"

The young doctor was appalled by the experience, beginning to doubt that the force which guided Nature was benign after all. He wrote in his diary later:

Are we mere leaves, fluttered hither and thither by the wind, or are we rather, with every conviction that we are free agents, carried steadily along to a definite and pre-determined end? I confess that as I advance through life, I become more and more confirmed in that fatalism to which I have always had an inclination.

In the summer of 1885, a Gloucester widow, Emily Hawkins, was on holiday in Portsmouth, taking the sea air with her son Jack and daughter Louise, when her son was stricken with a sudden headache, nausea followed by drowsiness, and a feverish shivering. She rushed to Dr. Conan Doyle for help. He diagnosed the sickness as cerebral meningitis, and allowed Jack to be a resident patient for treatment. Unable to tolerate the slightest glimmer of light, the boy had to lie in complete darkness. In those days before penicillin and sulfanilamide, there was no way to save him. One night, Conan Doyle awoke to a loud crash. He ran into Jack's room, and found the boy had knocked over a washstand in his delirium. Doses of chloral hydrate and some arrowroot provided only temporary relief. The boy died; describing his death in *The Stark Munro Letters,* Conan Doyle added a characteristic comment: "There is great promise, I think, in the faces of the dead. They say it is but the *post-mortem* relaxation of the muscles, but it is one of the points on which I would like to see science wrong."

During and after the funeral, Conan Doyle found himself drawn to the dead boy's sister, a sweet, simple, and attractive young woman. His mother came down to meet Louise and nodded her approval. But she angrily pounced on the villa, storming every elusive corner with a broom and dustpan, from the attic to the small beer cellar, where she furiously denounced the housekeeper for ignoring a cobweb. Finally, Conan Doyle told his mother he had decided to propose to the young girl. She hailed his decision forcefully.

Mary Doyle had clearly been delighted by her son's courtly behavior toward the stricken Jack Hawkins, and by his tender wooing of the delicate Louise. He was a poverty-stricken knight to be sure, but still a worthy descendant of the Percys of England. Moreover, Mrs. Doyle observed, Louise resembled her, with her light gold-brown hair, rounded features, gray eyes, and small well-rounded body.

Louise came of Protestant stock, and since Mrs. Doyle had not remained a devout Catholic, it was agreed the couple should be married in the Protestant religion. Arthur was twenty-six, Louise twenty-seven. Mrs. Hawkins most warmly welcomed her daughter's marriage, since she had been impressed by Conan Doyle's consideration in making her son a resident patient. The wedding took place on August 6, 1885, at the parish church near Mary Doyle's cottage, Masongill, at Thornton-in-Lonsdale in the West Riding of Yorkshire, where she had removed after committing her husband to the lunatic asylum near Dumfries. Henry

Doyle, Connie, Arthur's sister, and Mrs. Emily Hawkins were among the witnesses.

Louise was not gifted or well-read, but she made the ideal Victorian housewife, with sewing, mending, and cleaning her chief interests. Her femininity and total lack of complication, her motherliness and warmth, her sheer common sense, appealed to Conan Doyle and his mother.

When he was racked by some complex question of metaphysics, Louise could fix a cup of tea. When he came home from a long walk or from a séance, or sank back pale and exhausted from writing some horrific story, she could ease off his shoes and massage his feet and brow. He loved her with all the passionate adoration of a Victorian man for a little woman who adored him worshipfully. For this tormented genius, as brooding and abstracted as Poe behind the respectable mask of a sports-loving *Times* reader, the relationship worked perfectly.

He became more cheerful, gained weight, sent Innes off to boarding school, and began playing cricket and football with local teams. Louise, whom he called "Touie," augmented their funds with a tiny private income. Conan Doyle's local reputation was enhanced by his marriage. Young ladies now felt safe in coming to him, and parents lost their worries about sending him their sons. His income rose to a still modest but almost sufficient three hundred pounds a year.

Many articles and books indicate that the birth of Sherlock Holmes came about because Conan Doyle, like one of his idols, Sir Walter Scott, was deeply in debt and had to find a way to make money quickly. But in fact by the time he conceived one of the most famous characters in fiction, he was already beginning to prosper. Patients were more numerous; the fulfillment his wife brought him, his mother's joy in his marriage, were giving him his first real happiness since the days of his whaling and sealing voyage. It was in a spirit of enthusiasm that he decided to follow the great masters, Poe, Gaboriau, and Wilkie Collins, in pursuing the art of the detective story. Collins gave him a clear picture of a detective in the famous Sergeant Cuff, tall, cadaverous, beak-nosed, who solved the riddle of *The Moonstone*. Cuff's image was added to those of Dupin, Lecoq, and Dr. Bell already swimming in Conan Doyle's young brain.* Conan Doyle felt a powerful need to create a detective whose deductive powers would be equal to those of his illustrious predecessors, but who would be more fully described, and more amusing.

At first, he called the detective "Sherringford Hope," after his beloved whaling ship, the *Hope*. Then he switched to "Holmes," a name he drew from Oliver Wendell Holmes, whom he admired. Several elements of his hero's character also can be traced to that Boston Brahmin. Oliver Wendell Holmes, distinguished and skillful, was a pioneer in medicine and in criminal psychology, the developer of many of the methods Sherlock Holmes was to adopt. His monographs were numerous, just as Sherlock's were. His wit and neat turns of phrase were also inherited by the detective. He was an expert on tobacco. A whole essay could be written on the parallels between these two men, both of whom had lucid and penetrating minds. Oliver Wendell Holmes was about to embark on a grand tour of Europe, a fact which the newspapers were widely announcing at the time, and which would have made the name "Holmes" ring especially loud in Conan Doyle's head

He changed the Christian name, after he played against a bowler on the Portsmouth cricket team who was called Sherlock. It is noteworthy, too, that a very well-known violinist of Conan Doyle's time was named Alfred Sherlock. He specialized in performing German music (of which Holmes was fond), and was popular, appearing before the crowned heads of Europe. "Sherlock" was also the name of a number of prominent Irish divines, several of whom were noted for their cold superciliousness and aloofness.

Scholars have puzzled for many years over the sources of Sherlock Holmes's famous accoutrements. Speculation could be endless, but some suggestions are put forward here. Conan Doyle himself liked wearing a purple dressing gown and smoking a pipe, and kept various kinds of tobacco in jars. He was often fond of

---

* The beak nose with which Cuff sniffed was appended to many of Conan Doyle's villains later on.

hiding samples of them in his slippers. Holmes's gasogene was a device for making soda water; given Conan Doyle's love of Scotch whisky and soda, and the fact that for many years he was struggling financially, we need not look very far for the probable source of this detail.

As for Watson, the London census shows us that at 18, Cambridge Terrace, the house next to that of Conan Doyle's grandfather, the occupant during the years of Arthur's upbringing was a man called John Watson; and a Dr. James Watson was a warm acquaintance at the Portsmouth Literary and Scientific Society.

There was another Dr. John—John A., not John H.— Watson, with whose work Conan Doyle was almost certainly familiar. He lived in Upper Norwood, which perhaps significantly became an important address in *The Sign of Four*. He was a well-known writer on India, and had served in the First Afghan War, while Conan Doyle's Dr. Watson served in the Second. The real Dr. Watson's accounts and photographs of Indian army life may quite feasibly have sparked Conan Doyle's imagination.

Yet another source was a work by Robert Louis Stevenson. In Stevenson's *New Arabian Nights*, a favorite book of Conan Doyle's, there appeared *The Adventure of the Hansom Cab*. This story supplied not only the matrix for the titles of the Holmes stories* but also some significant elements of the portrait of Dr. Watson. Lieutenant Brackenbury Rich, a veteran of the Indian hill wars, has come home prostrated by a saber wound and by jungle fever, just like the man Conan Doyle was to portray. The description of Rich arriving in London as a kind of foreigner is very similar to Conan Doyle's description of Watson's arrival in the great city.

Discarding "Ormon Sacker," the name he first assigned his narrator, Conan Doyle settled on "John Watson," though it is notorious that Watson's wife slipped up and called him "James" instead of "John" in *The Man with the Twisted Lip*.† The basis

---

* Most of these titles began, *The Adventure of* . . . The shorter versions of the titles, omitting these three words, have been used throughout this book.

† Of course John H. Watson's middle name may have been Hamish, the Scottish "James"!

for Dr. Watson is undoubtedly to be found in one side of Conan Doyle's personality, the side the public knew best; the other side served as the basis for Sherlock Holmes. Arthur Conan Doyle graduated from Edinburgh University in 1881; the fictitious Dr. Watson from London University in 1878. Conan Doyle, while on his voyage to Greenland and the Arctic Circle on board the *Hope,* had ached for news of life on the Frontier; Watson nobly did what Conan Doyle would have liked to have done: he served at the battle of Maiwand, which took place during the voyage. Like Conan Doyle in Africa, Watson was stricken with enteric, or typhoid, fever and was glad to return to England. Like Conan Doyle, he subsisted on eleven shillings and sixpence a day when he was released into private life. Watson had been to London just twice, and the date of the second visit was almost identical to that of Conan Doyle's first stay in the Great Wen, "that great cesspool into which all the loungers and idlers of the Empire are irresistibly drained." Watson, as we know, looked like Conan Doyle—"as thin as a lathe and as brown as a nut."

The details used by Dr. Watson in describing his visit to Holmes's laboratory at Barts would have been equally applicable to Dr. Bell's laboratory in Edinburgh. During this visit, in an instant, Holmes—as Conan Doyle might have done—has grasped the fact that Watson served in Afghanistan, and further biographical details inevitably follow. They discuss sharing rooms. Each confesses to the other the drawbacks of his own personality (that is, of the side of Conan Doyle's personality that each embodies). Sherlock says he is prone to deep silences—a confession Conan Doyle must certainly have made to his new bride—and is apt to rise at all kinds of odd hours. We know that Conan Doyle liked to walk and work late at night, and one imagines that Louise often had difficulty in rousing him to attend patients in the morning. The unusual pair moves into lodging at 221B, Baker Street.

Holmes and Watson live side by side, like a married couple— or the two opposing sides of Conan Doyle's own personality. Each also exhibits characteristics of Conan Doyle's father, Charles. Like Conan Doyle, Holmes enjoys long walks, which "take him into the lowest portions of the city." Like Charles Doyle, he is remote and puzzling, alternating bursts of manic creative energy with long periods of exhaustion and isolation. He reflects Conan Doyle's early friendlessness and misery in Southsea. Both men are melancholy, as Conan Doyle must have been. Watson is stimulated only by Holmes and his activities, Holmes only by crime itself, and both reflect the fact that Conan Doyle, poor and struggling, was able to gain a quickening of pleasure only from some of the more peculiar cases he handled, the strangeness of his readings, and the stimulus of writing his fantastic tales, which resemble the hallucinations induced by certain drugs.

As for Holmes's actual use of drugs, it is easy to understand why Conan Doyle made him a drug addict. Charles Doyle's *grand mal* epileptic seizures would have necessitated, at that time, the use of sedative drugs, including hyascin and morphine. Significantly, Holmes's drug taking would cease in 1896, three years after Charles Doyle's death.

It is also important to note what was at Conan Doyle's elbow when he was preparing *A Study in Scarlet*. The leading article in one of his favorite publications, *Chambers's Journal*, for March 8, 1886, was about cocaine. Giving a meticulous and on the whole accurate history of the drug, the article summarized the recent findings about it: cocaine was now coming into use as a more satisfactory local anesthetic for patients with diseases of the mucous membranes. Since Conan Doyle began preparing the story on March 8, it is safe to deduce that the article supplied him with the idea for Sherlock Holmes's most celebrated addiction. In addition to the significant fact of its use by Charles Doyle, morphine had been the extract of opium used by Wilkie Collins, whose novel *The Moonstone* supplied the inspiration for Conan Doyle's second Holmes story, *The Sign of Four*.

Some further ways in which Holmes and Watson resemble their creator—and a few in which they differ from him—may be noted. Watson is widely read, like Conan Doyle, but does not share his skill in deduction. Holmes, like Conan Doyle, is a capital boxer and fencer, and can bend a poker. Unlike Conan Doyle, however, he is described as being so ignorant of astronomy that he does not know that the earth revolves around the sun, and does not care because the fact is irrelevant to the art of detection. This is a rare departure from the dual self-portrait we can observe in the characters, and Holmes's ignorance seems quite absurdly improbable. Could he have been pulling Watson's leg?

The procession of visitors to the world's "only unofficial consulting detective" is reminiscent of the stream of visitors to Bell in Edinburgh, and to Conan Doyle in Southsea. The sitting room becomes a consulting room. Just as Innes Doyle was sent from the room when particularly gruesome cases were being discussed, Dr. Watson is banished when Holmes's clients are relating in confidence their various *outré* stories. Watson soon discovers that Holmes is a philosopher. So was Conan Doyle; their theories, drawn from a variety of sources, are remarkably similar. Agnostics, they see a force of Nature which links all events in an inevitable chain; Holmes has written an essay on the subject called *The Book of Life,* and Conan Doyle was to publish many such essays in future years, inspired by Winwood Reade's *The Martyrdom of Man.*

Conan Doyle devised a method of work he never abandoned in the composition of detective stories. He thought of the solution to the crime first; then he developed the remainder of the story, working with as much artistry as possible to conceal the solution from his readers until the last pages. He spent three weeks writing the short novel (originally called *A Tangled Skein*), conjuring it up while walking and playing sports, or sitting indoors with a snowstorm raging in March. He wrote early in the morning and late at night, before, during, and after consulting hours. He wrote with extraordinary rapidity, in his neat, elegant hand, more legible than most physicians'; and the manuscript pages were marked with surprisingly few alterations.

A Study in Scarlet begins with a message for Holmes summoning him to 3, Lauriston Gardens, off the Brixton Road. Holmes and Watson find the house dark and apparently untenanted. In the dining room there is a dead man, his face fixed in an expression of terror. On the wall in blood-red letters is a single word—RACHE. This, Holmes announces, is the German word for "revenge." The dead man turns out to be an American,

Enoch Drebber, who has been accompanied by his secretary, Joseph Stangerson. Aided by a group of street urchins known as the Baker Street irregulars and reminiscent of the more malign group which surrounds Fagin in *Oliver Twist*, Holmes unravels the puzzle. Joseph Stangerson is found murdered shortly afterward; Holmes produces the murderer; and the author breaks off to give us a rather clumsy account of the activities of the Mormon community of Utah, which leads in turn to the revelation that the deaths are the result of a revenge connected with Mormonism.

Conan Doyle clearly plucked the address 3, Lauriston Gardens out of the air, since it did not exist, but the journey there by hansom cab is very much like the one he took with his uncle in the fog when he first came to London ("a dun-coloured veil hung over the house-tops, looking like the reflection of the mud-coloured streets beneath"). The appearance of the sad and grimy interior of the house, almost to the exact positioning of the rooms, is that of 1, Bush Villas. Above all, Conan Doyle remembers the dust which he had allowed to accumulate. "The solitary window" (his consulting room had only one) "was so dirty that the light was hazy and uncertain, giving a dull gray tinge to everything, which was intensified by the thick layer of dust. . . ."

The description of the dead man lying in the room would have applied perfectly to that strange quack called Dr. Budd, whom during many quarrels Conan Doyle would probably have liked to see dead, and who, oddly enough, did die at an age, forty-five, only one or two years in advance of that of the unhappy victim.

We are plunged into the mystery of Drebber's murder. As it is unraveled, the parallels with Conan Doyle's experience and reading both surprise and fascinate. The background of vengeance which is explored in the story, and the evocation of the wilderness world in the flashback which it includes, owe their origin to his devoted early interest in the work of Mayne Reid. In his opening description of the American wilderness, his attitude is the opposite of Reid's, with distaste substituted for rapture; but the actual flow of descriptive language is very similar indeed. The idea of the Mormons as evil conspirators can be attributed to his awareness of the Fenians and other terrorist groups which were active in London at the time.

There are other sources as well. Why did he select the Mormons as his villains? And why was he so conscious of them during the writing? The reason lay close to his elbow. As we know, he wrote the story in March, 1886, finishing it in the middle of April. On March 30, an item appeared in the London *Times* entitled "The Last Struggles of the Mormons." The writer discussed the desperate efforts being made by the United States government to drive the Mormons from Utah, and their leaders' announcements that they would make a final stand in Nevada for their right to be polygamous. They threatened to take up their cause with Congress if necessary. Given his rigid Victorian morality, drilled into him by his mother and his Jesuit teachers, and not shaken even by the freer life of the medical student, Conan Doyle must have been very much against the Mormons in their search for moral freedom. Later he was to take an equally strong stand against suffragism. Above all, though, the news item must have aroused fascination with a subject he had barely thought about.

Evidently, too, an article which had appeared in *The International Review* of February, 1882, had stuck very firmly in the back of his mind. Entitled "Utah and Mormonism," it begins as follows:

On the map of the Continent of North America, forty years ago, between what was then laid down as the great chain of the Rocky Mountains in the East, and the Sierra Nevada range near the Pacific Ocean, and reaching from the headwaters of the Columbia on the North to the Rio Grande on the south, was a vast region marked the Great American Desert.

Conan Doyle's flashback in *A Study in Scarlet* begins:

In the central portion of the great North American Continent there lies an arid and repulsive desert, which for many a long year served as a barrier against the advance of civilization. From the Sierra Nevada to Nebraska, and from the Yellowstone River in the north to the Colorado upon the south, is a region of desolation and silence.

The rest of the article, by John H. McBride, is steeped in a fanatical hatred of Mormons, condemning them for murder and pillage, which unhappily Conan Doyle simply echoed without much evidence of further research.

Another source was Robert Louis Stevenson's equally ill-informed novel *The Dynamiter*, which had appeared in 1885. Here, again, the parallel is remarkably close, since one of the several narrators of the tale, written during the Fenian terrorist explosions which were shocking mid-Victorian London, talked of his life in the Mormon settlements. Conan Doyle, like Stevenson, named his leading female character Lucy, and he also adopted from him several other touches of detail and elements of plot.

The theme of vengeance, in which one man returns from the past to destroy another, may have been suggested by an item appearing in the London *Times* on February 27, 1886. John Brown Tower, who had provoked a former acquaintance, was strangled and flung into the Thames when the man he had once known returned to avenge himself.

A Study in Scarlet completed, Conan Doyle rolled it up and mailed it in a cardboard cylinder to the esteemed editor James Payn, who had already published some of his work in *The Cornhill*. Payn kept the story for a month, found it "capital," but returned it because it seemed to be in direct competition with the "shilling shockers" which were flooding the market. Also, because of its length *The Cornhill* would have had to devote an entire issue to it. Conan Doyle then sent the story to Arrowsmith, in Bristol, and began working on a historical novel, *Micah Clarke*.

Arrowsmith returned *A Study in Scarlet* after two months. It was evident that the rolled-up pages had not been flattened out on an editorial table; the manuscript had not been read. Now the story went off to Ward, Lock, which Conan Doyle admired for its publication of his idols Sir Walter Scott, Jules Verne, and Bret Hart. The editor, Professor Bettany, showed it to his wife, who felt it was good. Like James Payn, the publishers were hesitant because "shilling shockers," including several they themselves had brought out, were a glut on the market. But they accepted it, bought all the rights for twenty-four pounds, and said the story would appear about a year after its acceptance.

The tale was published in *Beeton's Christmas Annual* in December, 1887. The *Annual*, a small paperback, was priced at exactly a shilling: "a shilling shocker," indeed. On the white-and-red cover, the story was announced in scarlet letters, together with the picture of a man reaching up from his desk to light an oil lamp. Advertisements for numerous drugs, potions, and stimulants in the opening pages were amusingly appropriate. The illustrations by D. H. Friston portrayed Holmes quite wrongly as effete, plump, and foppish; and Watson seemed far too robust a figure. Both men, it must be remembered, were extremely thin, and—though the bronzed complexion of one contrasted with the pallor of the other—neither was very healthy.

Every book on Holmes or Conan Doyle indicates that when this "shilling shocker" appeared it was ignored or abused. This is emphatically not the case. In fact, when Ward, Lock brought out *A Study in Scarlet* in book form in 1888, again as a "shilling shocker," they reprinted on the flyleaf some of the warm reviews it had received after publication in the *Annual. The Scotsman* wrote, "This is as entrancing a tale of ingenuity in tracing out crime, as has been written since the time of Edgar Allan Poe. The author shows genius. He has not trodden in the well-worn paths, but has shown the true detective should work by observation and deduction." *The Bristol Mercury* said, "The story is very exciting and well-told," and *The Hampshire Post*, evidently proud that the author was living in that county, wrote that he "is to be congratulated on the character of the murder, and also upon its originality." Several critics pointed out the parallels with Poe, some saying that Conan Doyle had not markedly improved on the original, and that Holmes was "merely" another Dupin. But by and large the reviews were encouraging, and if the author felt a sense of depression at the reception of his tale, that can only be attributed to his moods of Holmesian despondency.

The 1888 edition, the first in book form, was illustrated by Conan Doyle's father, Charles Doyle, a device which the editors at Ward, Lock used to secure more attention for the work. Announcing his contribution, an editorial encomium read: "Charles Doyle is a younger brother of Richard Doyle, the eminent colleague of John Leech in the pages of *Punch*, and son of the eminent caricaturist whose political sketches, signed H.B., were a feature in London half a century ago."

Charles Doyle's illustrations, drawn in an asylum while he was experiencing great physical distress, were pallid and watery, much inferior to his earlier illustrations of children's books. But they have one great fascination. The likeness of Holmes is a self-portrait of Charles himself. The tall, attenuated figure, the pale beard, the fair hair, all represent a younger Charles Doyle; and this is certainly the only bearded Holmes in the history of illustration.

The timing of the first book publication of *A Study in Scarlet* was perfect. In 1888, the citizens of England were aware of the horror of murder as they had never been before. Prostitutes had been found hideously butchered in Whitechapel; Jack the Ripper was abroad; and many believed he was the agent of a secret society. Conan Doyle's story of mystery and terror, the blood-red word RACHE on the wall, the staring face on the floor, the pursuit of a mysterious killer, was ideally calculated to appeal to public taste. The first appearance of Sherlock Holmes was perfect in a period when the public clamored for good detection at Scotland Yard. Magazine after magazine, newspaper after newspaper, cried out for just the kind of deductive genius which Holmes, in fiction, embodied. The failure of the police to solve the puzzle of the Ripper murders only accentuated a psychological need for a Holmesian hero. If the public could not find him in life, they would find him in books, and find him they did. Yet Holmes's huge popularity was still three years off.

During the year he waited for *A Study in Scarlet* to be published, Conan Doyle worked on *Micah Clarke*, a historical novel set partly in the country around Portsmouth during the Western Rebellion, when James, Duke of Monmouth tried to obtain the throne, thus dividing the loyalties of the people. Micah Clarke, strongly reminiscent of Conan Doyle himself, is a dashing young man with a rebellious streak who becomes a supporter of Monmouth. He wins the spurs of gallantry in a lost cause when the King defeats Monmouth and arraigns many Protestants for treason. The character of the sweet-natured Puritan girl, Ruth Timewell, is clearly based on Louise Doyle ("Touie"), and her lack of knowledge of literature, her preference for such books as *Bull's Spirit Cordial*, is commented on with amusement and tenderness by the author. The book suffers from deliberately anti-quated "period" diction in the dialogue and some of the descriptive material. The final battle set piece is admirably done, however, and there are some effective moments in the last chapters, when the evil Judge Jeffreys appears, not as the typical grotesque Hanging Judge of legend, but as a figure of poisonous beauty, a handsome man fallen down—a typical Conan Doyle touch. The descriptions of war have a remarkable intensity, being alive with the author's love of battle; the setting of Havant, a town near Portsmouth he visited often, and from which the Southsea water supply was drawn, is carefully evoked; but the novel lacks the graveyard charm of the ghost stories, and the honed-down edge of the Holmes adventures. (Another book he wrote at the time, *The Firm of Girdlestone*, is today of interest only for its portrait of medical life.)

Micah Clarke was turned down by Blackwoods, whose editor pronounced the mode of speech "incorrect" for the seventeenth century. The comment from the publishing house of Bentley Ltd. was, "The novel's principal defect is that there is a complete absence of interest." Cassell's publishing company declared that historical novels could not be commercial successes. Conan Doyle wrote in *The Idler:*

I remember smoking over my dog-eared manuscript when it returned for a whiff of country air after one of its descents upon town, and wondering what I should do if some sporting, reckless kind of publisher were suddenly to stride in and make me a bid of forty shillings or so for the lot.

As a last-ditch effort, he sent the manuscript to the author and collector of fairy lore Andrew Lang, at Longmans, Green. Lang accepted it at once. Conan Doyle wrote in his diary, "A door has opened for me into the temple of the Muses."

He was greatly cheered by the critical reception of the book when Longmans published it in February, 1889. By a pleasant coincidence, there had occurred only a few weeks earlier the birth of his first child—Mary Louise Conan Doyle, named after his beloved mother and his wife.

Stimulated by the response to *Micah Clarke*, Conan Doyle

plunged immediately into another historical novel, *The White Company*. He spent every free moment in the Portsmouth Library, ransacking the shelves for details of the lives of the Plantagenets, his ancestors. His mind was crowded with scenes of chivalry and of the pursuit of evil. Rejoicing in his daughter's development, and receiving encouraging letters from his mother almost every day, Conan Doyle was filled with enthusiasm as he composed this new adventure story.

The White Company is set in the fourteenth century, partly in the New Forest, which he had explored from end to end with Major-General Drayson, obtaining atmosphere and background. Somewhat dated today, it is the vigorously told and scrupulously accurate story of a handsome and good-natured young man, Alleyne Edricson, who has been raised in a Cistercian monastery. Released with the blessing of the holy father of the order, he sets out on a life of heroic adventure, in the company of his two friends, reminiscent of the companions of Robin Hood. The three men join the banner of the chivalrous knight Sir Nigel Loring, who is seeking to do battle for his lady fair. Sir Nigel is the leader of the White Company, a magnificent group of Saxon bowmen, who are free companions of his quest. In Spain, Alleyne Edricson wins the spurs of gallantry. At the end of the story, in traditional fashion, he weds Lady Maude, daughter of Sir Nigel, and obtains his own knighthood.

The one quality shared by all of Conan Doyle's work of this period, including *The White Company*, is a sweeping energy and vitality—the energy which people sensed in the man himself when they encountered him striding through the New Forest with Major-General Drayson identifying plants and trees (he had been well trained in botany at Stonyhurst and Edinburgh). He was equally eager in attending séances with Drayson, and, of course, in writing new works into the small hours of the morning and during the day between patients.

His marriage, happy and secure, was itself a great source of energy. Louise picked up the slack in his life. Simple and unintellectual, she did not threaten an invasion of the private world of his imagination as a more cerebral woman might have done; and if their conversation verged on the banal at the end of the day, then that was a pleasant relaxation from wrestling with some complex problem of plotting. He could fondle the baby, and put his feet up; he could relish pipe smoking as much as Holmes did.

When he provided Watson with a wife, Mary Morstan in *The Sign of Four*, he not only gave her the name shared by his mother and his daughter but portrayed her in terms almost identical with those in which, in *The Stark Munro Letters*, he described the first appearance of the character representing Louise. Speaking of Miss Morstan, who has just come to consult Holmes, Dr. Watson recalls:

There was . . . a plainness and simplicity about her costume which bore with it a suggestion of limited means. The dress was a sombre grayish beige, untrimmed and unbraided, and she wore a small turban of the same dull hue, relieved only by a suspicion of white feather in the side. Her face had neither regularity of feature nor beauty of complexion, but her expression was sweet and amiable, and her large blue eyes were singularly spiritual and sympathetic. In an experience of women which extends over many nations and three separate continents, I have never looked upon a face which gave a clearer promise of a refined and sensitive nature.

The Sign of Four was just beginning to bubble in his brain like Dr. Jekyll's potion in the alembic when a gentleman from America arrived with an interesting offer. The accomplished Joseph Marshall Stoddart was a Philadelphian, for many years the editor of the *Encyclopedia Americana*. He had been the American representative and publisher of Gilbert and Sullivan, and had brought Oscar Wilde to lecture across the States—sometimes, shrewdly if tactlessly, in cities where *Patience*, the Gilbert and Sullivan opertta which parodied Wilde, was being presented. After starting his own publishing company, he had returned to his alma mater, *Lippincott's Monthly Magazine*, to become managing editor in January, 1889. Anxious to obtain distinguished contributors, he sailed to London, contacted Conan Doyle and Oscar Wilde, and invited them to supper at the Langham Hotel, with an Irish M.P. for South Louth, Thomas Patrick Gill.

Stoddart was a genial host, and Wilde, in good form, told

witty stories, and confessed a rather surprising admiration for
Micah Clarke. The result of the supper was that Conan Doyle was
commissioned by Stoddart to write another Holmes story—*The
Sign of Four*—while Wilde was commissioned to supply a novella,
and in due course provided *Lippincott's* with the immortal *Picture of Dorian Gray*.

Conan Doyle honored the Langham Hotel, where the meeting had taken place, by giving it an important dramatic position
in several Sherlock Holmes stories. It is mentioned in *The Sign
of Four* itself; the legendary King of Bohemia in *A Scandal in
Bohemia* will stay there; and so will the Honorable Philip Green,
the hero of the Holmes story *The Disappearance of Lady Frances
Carfax*. Conan Doyle liked to use hotels in his stories, and also
clubs; the silent and stuffy Diogenes Club, which emerges in two
stories, *The Greek Interpreter* and *The Bruce-Partington Plans*, is
clearly modeled on the Athenaeum; since Diogenes lived in a barrel and grew fat, the name is clearly a reference to the fact that
the club is frequented by Holmes's fat brother, Mycroft, a man
of sedentary habits.

Conan Doyle returned to Southsea in a rare good humor. He
worked hard on this second Holmes story, as well as on *The
White Company*, and still managed to find time to play cricket
and football. He also answered numerous letters from his admirers, the first trickle of what was to become a deluge, relaxed
with his wife and baby, and devoured books about the Middle
Ages.

The Sign of Four was sent off to Joseph Marshall Stoddart
in October, 1889. The opening, in which Holmes injects himself
with cocaine before the shocked gaze of Dr. Watson, is riveting.
Holmes talks with all the lofty confidence of Dupin and Lecoq
as he revels in his state of heightened drug-induced consciousness.
Like Lecoq, he is a specialist in footprints and tobaccos, and like
Joseph Bell, he is fond of analyzing the bits of substance found
adhering to shoes. Like Dupin, he can read his friend's past history from simple observations. And his client is Mary Morstan,
Conan Doyle's composite perfect woman.

Holmes's eyes glisten as he leans forward to listen to Mary Morstan's story. Nervous, she has arrived at Baker Street to tell Holmes a disturbing tale. About ten years earlier, she received a summons from her father, an officer in the Indian army, to meet him at the Langham, but he failed to keep the appointment. Six years before her visit to Holmes, the *Times* personal column ran an advertisement seeking her address, which she supplied. She then received a box containing a pearl, and each year thereafter on the same day a similar box and pearl arrived by mail. Now Mary has been sent an unsigned letter asking her to appear at the Lyceum Theatre,* with two friends if she feels mistrustful, at seven o'clock that night. Holmes, Watson, and Mary go to the Lyceum as arranged, and are taken by a coachman to a terrace house where they meet a strange little man, Thaddeus Sholto. He reveals that he is the son of a former army major who told him, just before dying, that Mary had been deprived of her rightful inheritance of an Indian treasure.

The treasure is to be found at Pondicherry Lodge. But on arrival there, the visitors discover that Thaddeus† Sholto's twin brother is dead and the treasure is gone. Holmes deduces that a man with a wooden leg and a creature the size of a child have been responsible. He and Watson relentlessly track down the killers in a chase that culminates on the Thames.

The story is charged with Conan Doyle's vivid memories. It is agreeable to note that Holmes and Watson rendezvous with Mary Morstan at the Lyceum, where young Arthur first saw Irving's *Hamlet*, and that the dense, drizzly fog on this occasion is of the kind which greeted the fifteen-year-old boy on his first trip to London.

Blending elements of Wilkie Collins' *The Moonstone* with Gaboriau and Poe and details drawn from his own experience, Conan Doyle here presents some of his most impressive writing. The story has the hectic lividness of a nightmare—the amber and black carpet and tiger skins of a room in a squalid house; Thad-

---

* Known more accurately as the Royal Lyceum Theatre but never referred to as such by Conan Doyle.

† "Thaddeus" actually means "Judas," a subtle Doylean red herring, since Thaddeus is falsely arrested for his brother's murder.

deus Sholto, resembling Wilkie Collins in appearance, fragile, puffing at a hookah, and swathed in astrakhan against the chill of the London night; the grounds of Pondicherry Lodge dug up in a frantic search for treasure; the dead body of Thaddeus' twin brother Bartholomew in an upstairs room, a poisoned thorn shot into his scalp, the corpse described with a morbid eeriness which equals even Conan Doyle's great models:

Moonlight was streaming into the room, and it was bright with a vague and shifty radiance. Looking straight at me and suspended, as it were, in the air, for all beneath was in shadow, there hung a face—the very face of our companion Thaddeus. There was the same high, shining head, the same circular bristle of red hair, the same bloodless countenance.

Holmes reincarnates Dupin as he examines the contents of the locked room; we are back in the bloodstained world of *The Murders in the Rue Morgue* as he deduces that a man has entered the window without the aid of roof, water pipe, or, in this case, even lightning rod. But Holmes is more fortunate than Dupin; he has boot marks and the imprint of a wooden stump to go on. Holmes's discovery of tiny footprints, like those of a child, leads him to determine the existence of a subhuman creature, just as a tuft of tawny hair clutched in an old woman's hand led Dupin to infer the presence of an orangutan. It emerges that the dwarfish intruder is Tonga, an aborigine of the Andaman Islands, cruel and hideous in his habits. There is the terrifying pursuit of the villains along the Thames—one of Conan Doyle's most inspired passages. The aborigine is first glimpsed lying in the villain's boat like a large black dog. His emergence supplies a moment of transcendent horror, perhaps the most chilling single moment in any of Conan Doyle's stories:

Holmes had already drawn his revolver, and I whipped out mine at the sight of this savage, distorted creature. He was wrapped in some sort of dark ulster or blanket, which left only his face exposed, but that face was enough to give a man a sleepless night. Never have I seen features so deeply marked with all bestiality and cruelty. His small eyes glowed and burned with a sombre light, and his thick lips were writhed back from his teeth, which grinned and chattered at us with half animal fury.

What were the sources for this blood-curdling creation? His peg-legged keeper was probably modeled on Long John Silver, in Stevenson's *Treasure Island*, a book Conan Doyle admired. It will be recalled that the opening of the flashback about the Mormons in *A Study in Scarlet* was drawn from an article in *The International Review* for February, 1882. A piece in the March issue of the same year gives an equally harrowing and xenophobic account of the aborigines of the Andaman Islands.

Simultaneously with the appearance of *The Sign of Four* in *Lippincott's Monthly Magazine* as *The Sign of the Four*, *A Study in Scarlet* was starting to appear as a dime novel in pirated editions in the United States. It was widely and well reviewed when Lippincott published the authorized edition in 1890. The American response to *The Sign of Four* was also very warm. The British response, when the story was published by Spencer Blackett in London, was favorable too, though not quite favorable enough for the impatient and high-strung young man who had written it. He was more emphatically buoyed up by James Payn's acceptance of *The White Company* for a year's serialization in *The Cornhill*, to begin in January, 1891, and end in December; and by that editor's glowing statement that this was "the greatest historical novel since *Ivanhoe*."[*] He did not know that Payn had taken the book as an act of desperation. Payn's continued attempt to turn *The Cornhill* into a popular magazine had failed to win readers. Circulation had fallen alarmingly during each successive month of his editorship, and it fell more steeply than ever in 1891. Finally, yielding to pressure, the publishers replaced him with a *littérateur*, and returned to the magazine's old tradition of publishing belles-lettres.

Meanwhile, *Micah Clarke* had gone into second and third printings by Longmans, Green, and Conan Doyle, his moods alternating between buoyancy and depression, decided to make his

---

[*] Some critics agreed, though the more intellectual periodicals made little of the book; it became a great commercial success, and still sells today.

first trip to Europe in over thirteen years. He had long hoped to visit his sister Annette in Portugal, but she had died in 1879 in an influenza epidemic. Instead, he traveled to Berlin. In 1883, he had written a remarkable article for *Good Words*, entitled "Life and Death in the Blood," which had shown a fascination with the pioneer research work done in the field of bacteriology by Dr. Robert Koch, of Berlin.

In his memoirs, published almost thirty-five years later, he indicated that he had had little or no interest in Dr. Koch's work, but this was a lapse of memory, forgivable in a man of advanced years. In fact, he obviously caught "Koch fever," which swept Europe and America in the wake of Koch's announcements at the International Medical Congress of Berlin in August, 1890, indicating the existence of tuberculin, a possible cure for tuberculosis. Every doctor on both sides of the Atlantic clamored for more information. Conan Doyle set off at once. Enthusiastic as ever, he took the next available train to London.

He traveled to Berlin by boat train and transcontinental express. The city was overflowing with thousands of doctors who, in many instances, had brought their patients with them in the irrational hope of obtaining an immediate cure. Each day, demonstrations were being given either in the special hall arranged at the German Health Office, at the Polyclinic under Professor Brieger, at the private clinic of Dr. Levy, or at the Charity Hospital under Dr. Franzel. During early November, newspapers in Berlin, Paris, London, and New York published more and more hysterical reports on Koch's discoveries, although the doctor himself expressed the gravest doubts about their value.

On the date of Conan Doyle's arrival, which can be placed at about November 10, there was to be a special demonstration at the large Surgical Clinic theater of the Berlin University Medical School under the University's distinguished Professor of Surgery, Geheimrath von Bergmann. Conan Doyle arrived at the building to find that it was completely filled. He bribed an attendant to admit him to the outer hall, but it was impossible to obtain entry to the lecture theater itself. In desperation he flung himself in the path of Professor von Bergmann when that im-

posing personage arrived. The young man shouted above the hubbub, "I've come a thousand miles and I've got to see your experiment!"

Von Bergmann looked at him as though he were a cock-
roach. "*Perhaps, mein Herr, you vould like to take my place!*" he
snarled, leaving the supplicant thoroughly deflated as he swept off.

Conan Doyle was compelled to rely on notes supplied by
a friendly American doctor who had noticed Von Bergmann's
public humiliation of him. Subjecting these notes to a Holmesian
analysis, he decided that tuberculin was not a certain cure, a point
which Koch had constantly reiterated, but which mass opinion
had refused to accept. He sent letters to the editor of the *Daily
Telegraph* in London, cautioning readers not to take the experiments as final. It was the shot before an avalanche. Only a few
weeks later, tuberculin was being condemned, and Koch was
forced to suffer for the excessive enthusiasm of the yellow press.

While on the train to Berlin, Conan Doyle had met a Harley
Street dermatologist named Malcolm Morris, who advised him to
abandon the struggle of general practice and enter a specialized
branch of medicine. He welcomed the advice, but made a serious
mistake in his way of following it. The rash, impressionable Watson in him evidently overruled the cool, collected Holmes. Thinking of some work he had done in Southsea testing eyes and fitting
spectacle lenses, he decided to become an ophthalmologist. Without prospects, he handed his daughter over to her maternal grandmother, paid up his annual lease—which still had eight months to
run—had all his furniture packed up and stored, and whisked the
obliging Louise off with him to Vienna so that he could study
the human eye at the Krankenhaus. This impulsiveness led him
headlong into a cul-de-sac. Unable to grasp detailed medical ter-
minology in German, he failed to understand the content of the
lectures, and spent most of his time figure skating with Louise at
the Prater, drinking with a robust representative of the London
Times, Brinsley Richards, and writing a quite unremarkable fic-
tionalized tract about an alchemist and the evils of riches, *The
Doings of Raffles Haw.*

Back in London after his futile six months in Austria, he insisted on becoming an eye specialist even without the supporting diplomas. He found rooms at 23, Montague Place, directly facing an entrance to the British Museum, and opened a small office and consulting room at 2, Devonshire Place. He was unable to attract a single patient.

4

PHANTOMS AND DETECTIONS

WHILE AT Devonshire Place that summer, Conan Doyle, in common with every other civilized person in London, became aware of a new presence on sitting-room tables—*The Strand Magazine*. Britain had never before seen a publication like this, offering photographs on almost every page. The previous year, when the young literary editor H. Greenhough Smith had suggested such a periodical to his publisher, George Newnes, the idea had been instantly accepted. For four months, the Newnes offices in Southampton Street had been the scene of thunderous activity, as plans for the first issue were drawn up. The moment the magazine appeared, with its cover picture of a view of the Strand, including a large gas globe in the foreground, it became an instantaneous success.

More than 300,000 copies were sold in the first month, an unprecedented event in the history of British magazine publishing. Filled with adventure stories, portraits of the homes of celebrities, interviews with famous actors and opera stars, *The Strand* was unabashedly popular in tone, in direct contrast with the ailing *Cornhill* and the flourishing but snobbish *Yellow Book*. Each issue of *The Strand* enclosed a Royal Academy print, free of charge, and in April, 1891, that print was of "Lancelot and Elaine," by an up-and-coming young artist of thirty-one, Sidney Paget.

The strong feeling at *The Strand* was that a new form of literary art should be encouraged. Instead of the serial novel which was then popular, the magazine would present a series of short stories with a recurring central character or characters. Conan Doyle decided to test his chances by submitting a humorous story about a phonograph, *The Voice of Science*. When this was accepted for the March issue, he took a very bold step indeed. Sherlock Holmes, he decided, would ideally satisfy the magazine's demands for a continuing character.

At Devonshire Place, writing at his old desk from Southsea, with Louise waiting at home and taking care of two-year-old Mary, he finished two Holmes stories in two weeks: *A Scandal in Bohemia*, suggested by his sojourn in Vienna, and *The Red-headed League*, about a gold robbery. In *A Scandal in Bohemia*, Wilhelm Gottsreich Sigismond von Ormstein, Grand Duke of Cassel-Felstein, and hereditary King of Bohemia, materializes at 221B, Baker Street in a mask. The plot thickens as the author introduces us to Irene Adler, an opera singer who intends to blackmail the monarch by producing an incriminating photograph. In attempting to outwit her, Holmes disguises himself as a clergyman and a groom.

One of his favorite publications, *Chambers's Journal*, supplies a most likely origin for Conan Doyle's fascination with the theme of disguise. In its issue for April 4, 1886, published when Conan Doyle was completing *A Study in Scarlet*, appeared a piece called "My Detective Experiences." The narrator describes how he discovers the loss of a hat, two umbrellas, and a sealskin coat from the entrance hall of his house, and calls the police. Shortly afterward, he finds on his doorstep (italics mine):

an *herculean* individual in the garb of a navvy, with large sandy whiskers and *red hair*, who informed me that he was a detective. I ushered him into the dining-room. . . .

The doorbell rings again; another detective arrives in disguise (italics mine again):

I beheld a somewhat diminutive individual, attired as a *clergyman*. He was an elderly man, with silver hair, a clear, pink-and-white complexion, and wore a superfine coat, with a broad cravat. His "get-up" to the last detail was faultless, *even to the gold eye glasses*.

It cannot be mere coincidence that in *A Scandal in Bohemia* Conan Doyle disguises Holmes as a humble groom and a clergyman, that the King of Bohemia is described as resembling a "Hercules," that Conan Doyle later wrote a story entitled *The*

Golden Pince-Nez, or that his next tale was *The Red-headed League*.

Irene Adler outwits Holmes, thus becoming the only woman to do so, and perhaps the only woman who ever fascinated him. In later years, he always thinks of her with intellectual relish. Her beauty, her brilliant use of male disguise, and her maneuver in switching photographs haunt him until the day he dies.

Both the title and the subject matter of *A Scandal in Bohemia* reflect Conan Doyle's recent experiences in Austria-Hungary under Emperor Francis Joseph. During that severe winter, when the Danube froze over and the temperature fell to 28 degrees below zero, when parts of the country were shaken by earthquake and ravaged by a typhoid epidemic, there were indeed several scandals in Bohemia. Count Wimpffen, Austro-Hungarian ambassador to Paris, had committed suicide after a financial reverse. The apparent suicide at Mayerling of Crown Prince Rudolf, the heir to the throne, and his mistress Marie Vetsera had rocked the country. Who formed the basis for Irene Adler? And for the King of Bohemia who called at Baker Street?

To answer the first of these questions we have to consider the two most-talked-about people in Vienna in the winter of Conan Doyle's sojourn there. Ludmilla Hubel was a gifted singer and actress. She had become involved with the Emperor's nephew Archduke John Salvator of Tuscany, who had become a possible heir to the throne after the death of Crown Prince Rudolf. Ludmilla Hubel's involvement with him had caused a major scandal; extremely comprising photographs showing her with the Archduke had been used against her by the press.

Archduke John defied his family, refused to abandon Fräulein Hubel, and finally married her. In view of his royal uncle's attitude, he renounced all his rights, privileges, and rank, and assumed the name John Orth. Three weeks after the Conan Doyles arrival in Vienna, "Orth" had bought a ship, which he renamed the *Santa Margarita;* he had all photographs of it burned, so that it would not be recognized. He then spent a fortune trying to buy back every photograph in existence of himself and his wife, and burned them also. He set sail with his wife for South America. He

BUSINESS REPLY MAIL

FIRST-CLASS MAIL   PERMIT NO 42   HIGHTSTOWN NJ

POSTAGE WILL BE PAID BY ADDRESSEE

BusinessWeek

PO BOX 676
HIGHTSTOWN NJ 08520-9395

Analyze the offer

CSA8930
CSA9029

BusinessWeek

Yes, please enter my subscription to Business Week:

☐ 51 issues for $42.95 – Save 79%
☐ 30 issues for $29.95 – Save 75%.

With my paid subscription, I will gain FREE access to the Business Week Web site.

☐ Mr. ☐ Ms.
Name _____

Company _____

Street _____

City _____ State & Zip _____

☐ Home address ☐ Business address
☐ Payment enclosed (Please use separate envelope) ☐ Bill me later

Offer good in U.S. and possessions. In Canada, 51 issues C$61.95, 30 issues C$45.95. Prices and Terms are subject to change. Local taxes, if applicable, will be added to your order. Please allow 4-6 weeks for shipment of first issue.

Access to our Web site, www.businessweek.com is included with paid subscription of either offer.

NEWSSTAND $201.45

YOU PAY $42.95

Realize the savings!

had with him over a quarter of a million pounds in gold; he had bought through his agents in South America an enormous estate in Chile. From the moment his vessel left for Montevideo, neither she nor her captain, crew, and distinguished passengers were ever heard of again. There were rumors that the *Santa Margarita* had sunk in a storm. There were also stories that the Prince had appeared as a Chilean revolutionary, and that he had been seen in New York and in Tahiti. None of these stories had the slightest foundation in fact, and the mystery remains unsolved.

There can be little question that Irene Adler was based on Ludmilla Hubel. If Ludmilla had acted as unselfishly as Irene Adler, Conan Doyle is telling us, and had disappeared from her lover's life, a tragedy might have been averted. It is noteworthy that the ending of the story *The Five Orange Pips* (1891) contains yet another echo of this Austrian affair. The Ku Klux Klan killers in that tale disappear at sea on board the vessel *Lone Star*, of Savannah, and are never heard of again.

Why did Conan Doyle choose the name Irene Adler? Would it be too farfetched to suggest that the "Irene" was suggested by the name of the great beauty and star of the London stage Irene Vanbrugh? As for Adler, the second most talked about person in Vienna that winter was *Viktor* Adler. The vigorous leader of the Social Democrats, considered a threat to the throne, had recently been jailed for his views. There was a general hysterical fear that he might escape and succeed in toppling the throne. It seems only appropriate that Conan Doyle would give the name to another threat to a mid-European monarch. In making his character the King of Bohemia, Conan Doyle is at his most amusing.

Quite clearly, Sidney Paget, who illustrated the story, also knew a thing or two. His portrayal of the King of Bohemia is modeled after none other than Wilhelm II, nephew of the notorious Edward, Prince of Wales; Wilhelm only three years earlier had succeeded to the throne of Germany following the death of his father, Frederick III. Wilhelm had been very much in the news because of his famous collision with Bismarck over the anti-Socialist law, which seriously affected left-wing figures— that is, persons of Viktor Adler's type—in Berlin. And Conan

Doyle introduced elements of Edward, Prince of Wales, into the character.

In his timing of *A Scandal in Bohemia* for publication in England's most popular magazine, Conan Doyle carried off an impressive *coup de théâtre*. When he started work on the story in late April, the scandal of the decade was about to break; he was clearly aware of this fact, for his earlier *Strand* story, *The Voice of Science*, wittily refers to it. When he finished *A Scandal in Bohemia*, in early June, 1891, the affair was already in full swing. All London, from the denizen of high society to the common street drudge, was buzzing about the Tranby Croft affair, in which Sir William Gordon-Cumming, a military man, had brought an action for slander against five men who had accused him of cheating at baccarat at Tranby Croft. The subsequent to-do sent a wave of lurid gossip crashing all the way up to the prim iron gates of Buckingham Palace itself. The scandal reached its height when the Prince of Wales appeared in the witness box and disclosed that he had been a frequent gambler himself, and had been present at the game in question. When it was revealed that Gordon-Cumming had in fact cheated (so that he subsequently lost the case and was cashiered out of the army), the Prince was disgraced, and had to be reprimanded sternly by his mother, Queen Victoria. *A Scandal in Bohemia*, with its echoes of scandal involving a German-speaking prince, as well as of recent events in Vienna, was aimed directly at the public taste.

Conan Doyle's second story of that season, *The Red-headed League*, begins very much as does the article "My Detective Experiences," with a meeting with a man with red hair. He is a pawnbroker called Jabez Wilson. Holmes sums up his background instantaneously, and with a typical touch of Bell-like irony:

Beyond the obvious facts that he has at some time done manual labor, that he takes snuff, that he is a Freemason, that he has been in China, and that he has done a considerable amount of writing lately, I can deduce nothing else.

Wilson tells Holmes and Watson that he has answered an advertisement for a man with red hair. Despite severe competition he wins the prized job of copying out the *Encyclopaedia Britannica*.

Here Conan Doyle's humor is at its best; the description of the unhappy pawnbroker, laboriously working his way from "Abbots" to "Attica" and seeing the B's loom up alarmingly ahead, is one of the wittiest passages in the Holmes stories. Faced with what he calls "a three pipe problem," Holmes discovers that the whole thing has been an elaborate hoax to lure Wilson out of his pawnshop while thieves tunnel from his cellar to an adjoining bank vault filled with gold bullion.

Neither *A Scandal in Bohemia* nor *The Red-headed League* has the flawless logic which Conan Doyle brought to his longer stories, or to most of his later ones. It is inconceivable, for example, that the King of Bohemia would arrive at Holmes's rooms dressed so sumptuously that after alighting from his brougham he would stand out at once from the hordes of gray- or black-suited men in the street outside. And it is hard to believe that a pawnbroker, however inept, would fail to smell a rat, and would show only temporary misgivings, when he was set to work copying out the *Encyclopaedia,* which he must have known was available in type. Moreover, it is too much to ask us to believe that the constant chipping and digging and tunneling that took place in the cellar while he was away performing his futile task would not attract attention from visitors to the adjoining bank vault during daylight hours.

Nevertheless, despite their fantastic lack of logic, the stories have a magical charm and humor which sweep away resistance. It was without much confidence that Conan Doyle mailed them off to Greenhough Smith at *The Strand.* The literary editor was a cold fish, not easily impressed. With his rimless spectacles, pale blue eyes, wing collar, and slicked-down hair, he looked more like a pharmacist than a man of letters. But he was shrewd, with a surprising flair. He and the art editor, W. H. J. Boot, had even managed the *coup* of persuading Queen Victoria herself to contribute to the magazine—a picture of her first baby, drawn by herself, and annotations to an article on her dolls, in which she meticulously supplied marginal corrections of the author's rasher misstatements.

Conan Doyle's manuscripts arrived on a day when Smith had

been combing through a more than usually depressing collection of unsolicited writings. Myopic, he read at a stand which slanted up from his desk, directly under a gaslight which dangled in a bell-shaped glass from the ceiling. Spreading out Conan Doyle's stories with his long fingers, he felt his pulse quicken. In an unprecedented long rushing movement, he flung himself toward the door, then downstairs to the office of William Plank, George Newnes' private secretary, and through it without further ado to the thirty-foot-long, ground-floor sanctum sanctorum of Newnes himself, with its tall windows overlooking Southampton Street. Newnes, bearded and stocky, looked up astonished as his normally level-headed employee confronted him, shaking with excitement, and holding a sheaf of papers in his trembling hand. "They're two stories by Dr. Conan Doyle!" Smith cried out. "This is the greatest short-story writer since Edgar Allan Poe!"

Newnes was compelled to agree; but this being England, Conan Doyle was coolly informed of the momentous acceptance not by telegram, but by letter. He arrived the day after he received the acceptance, formidable in a tall top hat, with two more stories tucked under his arm.

He did not share Greenhough Smith's and George Newnes' view of his tales, regarding their writing as mere hack work, to keep the home fire burning while he did research for another solidly academic historical novel, *The Refugees.* He thought so little of his stories that he did not record in his letters, diaries, or memoirs a single word about the choice of illustrator made by W. H. J. Boot.

Boot summoned the painter Sidney Paget* from his studio at 11, Holland Park Road to illustrate the stories, which would be run in a sequence of six, the last two to be supplied right away. Conan Doyle would be paid thirty guineas for the six, and young Paget would receive twenty guineas. The artist bustled back to his studio with copies of *A Scandal in Bohemia* and *The Red-headed League;* his work would have to be completed in a week to be in time for the July issue. He did not have to look far for a model for Holmes. Walter Paget was tall, elegant, dark-haired, and

---

* He should have summoned Sidney's brother Walter, but asked for Sidney by mistake.

handsome; he would present an ideal image to the reader. As for Watson—there could be no better model than Conan Doyle himself.

From oblique references in several places, we can infer that Conan Doyle thought little of Paget's work. Conan Doyle saw Holmes as tall, cadaverous, ugly, like Wilkie Collins' Sergeant Cuff; Paget saw him as a fine figure of a man, rather like one of the Mayfair dandies, those "greenery-yallery, Grosvenor Galley/ Foot-in-the-grave" young men of the *Yellow Book* clique. But Paget's use of a sexually attractive, well-fleshed nineties face and figure paid off handsomely. His image of Sherlock Holmes had hundreds of thousands of young women yearn for this fictional character as they might yearn for a stage actor, and a similar number of men wanted to emulate his flawless tailoring and various forms of headgear. Sherlock Holmes became a star before movies were born, and through no wish of his creator.

A Scandal in Bohemia, published in the July issue of *The Strand*, made Conan Doyle famous overnight. The story appeared at the height of the London season, when gossips proliferated like hothouse orchids and the drop of a name could cause the destruction of a reputation or the start of another. The members of fashionable society, whether meeting for elaborate eight-course luncheons and dinners, or jostling stirrup-to-stirrup on Rotten Row, loved to discuss the latest scandals of royalty or near royalty, and they were of course mad about the Tranby Croft affair. To these urgent topics of conversation, which were to be discussed lightly, amusingly, superficially, never too earnestly or long-windedly, could now be added some amusing speculation about the real identity of the King of Bohemia— could he be a thinly disguised relation of the Queen's? And who in truth, was the wicked and ingenious opera singer Irene Adler? The theme of blackmailing a royal personage was exactly, uncannily right for the period.

The Red-headed League, with its fantastic comedy surrounding an attempted bank robbery, was again a perfect subject for conversation. The picture of a humble pawnbroker laboriously copying out the *Encyclopaedia Britannica* confirmed the view of the upper middle class that the working orders were simply dolts. Sherlock Holmes could be seen as a representative of aristocratic thinking, if not of lineage. He was the man who could set Scotland Yard to rights on virtually everything.

Holmes! Within two months he was one of the most famous figures in London, as famous as the Prince of Wales, Sir William Gordon-Cumming, or Mr. Gladstone himself. When Walter Paget, the illustrator's brother, went to the Covent Garden Opera House, a woman cried out, "There goes Sherlock Holmes!" and from that moment on, very few people watched the stage. Surrounded by a stockade of gossips, Walter Paget cringed like a captive. For years after, he had as much cause to regret sitting as his brother's model as he had to regret losing the job of illustrating the Sherlock Holmes stories.

Overexcited by his success, all nerves and unable to sleep, exhausted by the effort of rushing out his stories so rapidly, Conan Doyle was stricken with influenza, and almost died at exactly the moment when he became nationally famous. Barely able to move, he lay sick and weak on his bed for weeks, tenderly nursed by Louise. When he finally came round and was able to sit up, he resolved that his destiny was to be a writer. At last he was sure. He flung a handkerchief up to the ceiling; he could find just enough strength for that. Pale and hollow-eyed, hobbling on a crutch like an old man, the thirty-two-year-old genius at last had found himself.

He decided to move at once from the Montague Place rooms into a house. Abandoning his negligible practice, he began to haunt real estate agent's offices. It is strange to note that he chose to move into an area he had already made famous in *The Sign of Four*. The sinister Pondicherry Lodge was situated in Upper Norwood; the house at 12, Tennison Road, where he was about to establish himself, was only a short hansom cab ride away, in South Norwood. Just before he moved in, Dr. John A. Watson of India died in Upper Norwood.

In appearance, the sixteen-room villa, Swiss in style, with its electric bells, hot and cold running water, and small garden, was not much like the grandiose Pondicherry Lodge, but rather like Briony Lodge in *A Scandal in Bohemia,* except that it had three stories, not two. Made of red brick, one of a row, it stood a little back from the road, with trees shading the front garden. The roof had two eaves, and there was a wide balcony over the porch. The window frames were freshly painted white. There was a tennis lawn at the back, shared with the neighbors on each side.

The furniture arrived from storage, carefully labeled for placement in the rooms. In the hall, a large bust of John Doyle stood on a pedestal next to the Southsea umbrella stand. The study was on the ground floor to the left of the front door; the desk was to the left of the study door, and faced a fireplace, next to which stood four rows of shelves crowded with Conan Doyle's favorite books. Over the mantelpiece hung Charles Doyle's two paintings from Southsea. On the mantelpiece itself was a sketch, attributed to John Doyle, of Queen Victoria riding in Hyde Park at the age of six. Conan Doyle also put up a green-baize notice board for his notes, reminders, and unanswered correspondence. The room was snug and cozy, ideal for his purposes.

The dining room was decorated with oil paintings by a brother of Louise's; and on top of the dining-room bookcase, Conan Doyle put a stuffed white falcon, the skull of a white seal, harpoons, guns, and a length of tackle, all souvenirs of the whaler's voyage to the Arctic. The drawing room reflected Louise's feminine taste. The mantel was crowded with vases, and was flanked on each side by tall tufts of broom; the standard lamp beside it had a white, frilly shade; and the wallpaper was richly flowered, with poppies and roses. In the corner of the room on a special stand was a blue-and-white plate which had been given to Conan Doyle as a farewell present by one of his elderly female patients, whose son had stolen it from the Khedive's palace during the British bombardment of Alexandria in 1882.

By the end of August, Arthur, Louise and their little daughter Mary were firmly settled in. Conan Doyle's delightful and forgotten little novel *Beyond the City* gives a full picture of his new suburban life. We are shown two old ladies watching while the characters resembling him and Louise arrive in a four-wheeler with the last of the things—boxing gloves, Indian clubs, dumb-bells, a purple cricket bag, a set of golf clubs, and a tennis racket. He is seen carrying a pink sporting paper in one hand, and a bull pup in other. The local characters appear: the militant suffragette, whom he satirizes with all the cruelty of a staunchly antifeminist late Victorian gentleman (he even makes a fuss over the fact that she smokes); the two characters Clara and Ida Walker, whom he models on his sisters Connie and Lottie, soon to return from their long sojourn in Portugal; the naval man who is facing insolvency; the infatuated Charles Westmacott, whose ecstatic state is due to Ida Walker's acceptance of his invitation to take a ride on a tandem tricycle.

South Norwood—its air clean and fresh after the brown smoke of the city, and only a brief tricycle spin from the Crystal Palace, with its exhibitions and gardens—proved to be ideal for the Conan Doyles. And in many subsequent Sherlock Holmes stories the setting was not London, but the countryside, which was only a half hour or less by train from their new home; it is clear from internal evidence that Conan Doyle explored the area most thoroughly to obtain backgrounds for his tales.

While writing Holmes stories at the rate of one a month and doing research for his new novel, *The Refugees,* three weeks out of four, he managed to fit in a great deal of physical activity. He even went to Holland to bat with the British cricket team. He found time for tennis, for soccer with a Norwood team, and for bowls. He fixed up a darkroom in the cellar and indulged in the hobby of amateur photography, a reference to which he had woven into the complex plot of *The Red-headed League.* And he became fascinated with a new diversion, tricycling. A picture in *The Strand* for August, 1892, shows him, eyes characteristically narrowed, cheeks plump, mouth genial but firm under the walrus mustache, dressed in checked motoring cap, gray-tweed Norfolk jacket, and riding boots, setting out on a thirty-mile spin through Norwood and its neighboring suburbs, with Mary, bonneted and buttoned, looking quite plain, rather apprehensive, and not very well, on the tandem before him.

Conan Doyle described his cycling expeditions perfectly in *Beyond the City:*

The great limbs of the athlete made the heavy machinery spring and quiver with every stroke; while the mignon grey figure with the laughing face . . . held firmly to her perch . . . mile after mile they flew, the wind beating in her face, the trees dashing past in two long ranks on either side until they had passed round Croydon and were approaching Norwood once more from the further side.

The tricyclist-author never stopped working for a day. Often, he would have friends in to chat and enjoy a drink, while he continued writing in their presence. He followed every word of the conversation, occasionally interrupting to correct a point about Home Rule in Ireland or the Indian situation or the goings on of Mr. Gladstone. Working in this way, he managed to finish a Holmes adventure every fourth week for three more months. In October, he was still rushing out these stories, for which he continued to pluck details from his experience and his reading.

The Man with the Twisted Lip, one of the most powerful of these tales, can be traced directly to two episodes described in the reports on the provincial assizes which had appeared in *The Cornhill* for January, 1890. A young man, caught in a potential scandal, forms the subject of one part of a report; a hideously scarred and filthy street beggar forms that of another. With great ingenuity, Conan Doyle simply combined the two stories, making the young man assume a disguise as the mendicant.

The Five Orange Pips is based on an assortment of reports on the British activities of an itinerant branch of the Ku Klux Klan; and it opens with an exact description of the gale which, the London *Times* tells us, was sweeping through Norwood during the week in which it was written. ". . . the wind cried and sobbed like a child in the chimney," Watson remembers, and Arthur and Louise may have worried that it was little Mary crying.

The Blue Carbuncle, about the theft of a precious jewel, is another chip off *The Moonstone*, and the idea for the marvelous tale *The Speckled Band* is based on a magician's clockwork snake, kept in a basket by the fire, with which Conan Doyle used to alarm susceptible visitors. In story after story, Holmes, always the bold Victorian knight helping terrified ladies or nervous young men in distress, continues to echo his creator's personality. The procession of hapless female visitors is typified by Helen Stoner in *The Speckled Band:*

"It is not the cold which makes me shiver," said the woman in a low voice, changing her seat as requested.
"What, then?"
"It is fear, Mr. Holmes. It is terror."

In a time of violence, less than four years after the murders by Jack the Ripper, words like these echoed the feelings of thousands of women and Conan Doyle's lines sent a thrill of delight and alarm through staid and strait-laced Victorian homes. The circulation of *The Strand* rose to half a million, and a deluge of letters disclosed the reason: neither the interviews with the famous, the distinguished stories of Grant Allen, nor the pages describing the scientific and historical curiosities for which Victorians had a mania, could compare with the ineffable glamor of the Holmes stories. Their author was still rushing them through, but was increasingly eager to yield to his exasperation with plot-making, kill Holmes off, and stop the series.

In November, 1891, his mother, the heroic Ma'am, forbade him to do so. From Masongill Cottage in Yorkshire she wrote, "You won't! You can't! You mustn't!" She was a passionate follower of the Holmes adventures, and, unaware of the irony, the vigorously antifeminist author meekly obeyed. He even let her give him, when inspiration really threatened to run dry, the theme of *The Copper Beeches,* a marvelous Holmes story about a girl's act of impersonation.

By December, even the cautious Greenhough Smith and the tight-fisted George Newnes could deny their author nothing. They offered him the unheard-of sum of a thousand pounds for a new Holmes series, to run well into 1892. He was reluctant to proceed. By Christmas he was immersed in writing *The Refugees,* which combined the worst of French historical fiction with a lame imitation of Mayne Reid. But the offer was tempting. He had to consider his responsibilities as head of the family, and the imminent arrival of his sisters Connie and Lottie from their years as governesses in Portugal. For a time they would depend on their famous brother for support.

The stories continued to be full of echoes of his readings. Both before and after his reluctant acceptance of George Newnes' offer, his talent was at full stretch. *The Speckled Band* immediately became famous as one of the most skillful of all the Holmes adventures. In this story, a terrified girl, who had found her sister mysteriously murdered on a night when, once again, a gale whistled, calls on Holmes because she now feels herself threatened. The unnerving villain, Dr. Grimesby Roylott, follows her to Baker Street. Dr. Roylott is reminiscent in appearance and behavior of the George Moriarty whom Conan Doyle had evidently read about as a schoolboy. The locked-room puzzle harks back to Poe; the regular striking of a steeple clock, chiming out the hours as Holmes and Watson wait in the sinister mansion to identify a killer, is clearly reminiscent of the bell of the Baptist Church at Southsea; and the speckled band itself, an Indian swamp adder which wraps Roylott's head in a deadly embrace, can be traced not only to the parlor trick at South Norwood but apparently to the contents of an article by Sir Joseph Fayrer in the December, 1889, issue of one of Conan Doyle's favorite magazines, *Nineteenth Century*, which discussed that very creature. ("In our islands, the common adder is the only venomous snake, and its power is feeble compared with that of the snakes of India.")

Another classic story of the series is *The Engineer's Thumb*, in which the hapless victim of a conspiracy is called to check a counterfeiters' hydraulic press, ostensibly being used to process fuller's earth. The hydraulic press was the subject of numerous articles published in scientific journals between 1888 and 1892. The idea of the press ceiling descending on the victim's head was adapted from Wilkie Collins' paranoid horror story *A Terribly Strange Bed*, in which a canopy descends and almost smothers the central figure.

Perhaps the best story of the group is *The Beryl Coronet*, in which, amusingly enough, the names of the chief characters are Arthur and Mary. In this adventure, a banker is visited by a mysterious royal personage, almost certainly the Prince of Wales, who has immediate access to the crown jewels, those glittering ornaments which Conan Doyle so vividly remembered from his early visit to London. The Royal Person borrows fifty thousand pounds to cover some outstanding debts, an action which would suggest the Prince. An unscrupulous rogue, Sir George Burnwell, makes off with some of the jewels in the coronet which the banker takes as collateral. Again, the parallel with the Tranby Croft affair scarcely needs stressing.

In interviews for magazines, Conan Doyle said that his favorite authors were James M. Barrie, Rudyard Kipling, Gilbert Parker, Hall Caine, Robert Louis Stevenson, Rider Haggard, George Moore, and Israel Zangwill. Among American writers, he was familiar with Eugene Field, Henry James, Hamlin Garland, and Richard Harding Davis. His favorite historical romance was *In the Valley*, by Harold Frederic. He was especially devoted to Henry James, telling the essayist-editor Robert Barr, in a conversation recorded in both *The Idler* and *McClure's Magazine*, that James's beautiful clear-cut style and artistic restraint had profoundly affected him. He told Barr, "I'm sure his *Portrait of a Lady* was an education to me, though one has not always the wit to profit by one's education." He liked William Dean Howells for his "honest, earnest" work, but not for his cold attitude toward writers and critics who differed from him.

Conan Doyle felt very strongly that art was intended to amuse mankind, "to help the sick and the dull and the weary," as he told Barr. He did not believe that fiction need be strictly realistic, and referred to Swift's *Gulliver's Travels*, Cervantes' *Don Quixote*, Dante, and Goethe as support for his argument. He declared that he very much believed that the age of fiction was coming, that religious, social, and political changes would be affected by novelists. Just as he made this observation, the interview with Barr was interrupted by a violent clap of thunder over the Crystal Palace, and he and Barr went in to take shelter from the rain.

In the early months of 1892, Conan Doyle completed four more stories, part of a series of ten which was to appear the following year in *The Strand*. The first of the series, *Silver Blaze*, is a virtual silver mine of Doylean humorous references. It concerns the theft of the "favorite" for the Wessex Cup race. In *Harper's Weekly* (New York) the horse was described as being of the "Somomy" stock. (In *The Strand*, the word "Isonomy"* was used.) This is a very subtle reference to Oscar Wilde, not forgotten from the meeting at the Langham Hotel. In his famous stab at Wilde, which was to result in the libel suit which destroyed poor Oscar, the Marquess of Queensberry† forgetting the Queensberry rules and hitting firmly below the belt, would soon dub him a "somdomite" (*sic*). It is outside the Café Royal, Wilde's favorite haunt, that Holmes is attacked by ruffians in a later story *The Illustrious Client*, in an incident which is a special reference to Queensberry and his thugs chasing after Wilde.

Silver Blaze is also prophetic in that the stolen race horse is owned by a Colonel Ross; Wilde's closest friend and chief supporter was Robert Ross. A stable boy is given opium-laced curry in the course of the kidnaping of the horse; Wilde's sexual relationships with stable boys, so infamous, were gossiped about in 1892–93 and later helped to bring about his ruin. It was typical of Conan Doyle that he should weave these elements into a seemingly innocuous tale. There are subtle references to Wilde in several of the other stories—in the language used by the fragile Thaddeus Sholto in *The Sign of Four*, for example, and in the presentation of a team of burglars named Ross and Clay (based on Robert Ross and his friend the homosexual John Gray) in *The Red-headed League*. The hint of homosexuality in the relationship between Ross and Clay in the story is a foreshadowing of the events, years later, of the Irish crown-jewel robbery, also involving a homosexual liaison. It is odd, too, that the name of the second favorite for the Wessex Cup should be Desborough. Lord Desborough became a great friend of Conan Doyle's—indeed, one of his favorite people—during World War I, when the author

---

* "Isonomy" is scarcely less suggestive than "Somomy," however. This new-fangled word, not to be found in *The Oxford English Dictionary*, also refers to sodomy; it was most subtle of Conan Doyle to use a "Greek" neologism: it literally would mean, "division equally, down the middle."

† Conan Doyle borrowed the Marquess of Queensberry's name—John Sholto Douglas—for the Sholto twins in *The Sign of Four* and John Douglas in the later narrative *The Valley of Fear*.

was to sit on Desborough's committee for the formation of the first volunteer battalions.

In *The Cardboard Box*, the alarming contents of the box—one male and one female ear—recalls Jack the Ripper's threat to send the ears of his victims to Scotland Yard. *The Stock-broker's Clerk* is reminiscent of *The Red-headed League* in that a man is decoyed from his regular employment so that criminals can do their work, and its business setting recalls *The Firm of Girdlestone*.

While writing these stories, Conan Doyle found time to rework his historical tale about an old soldier who had served Wellington, *A Straggler of '15* (*Harper's Weekly*, March 21, 1891), as a vehicle for Henry Irving, who had affected him in *Hamlet* eighteen years earlier. Sentimental and warmhearted, the one-acter delighted Irving, who retitled it *A Story of Waterloo*, and asked only for a few minor changes at the beginning. With the enthusiastic approval of his secretary, Bram Stoker, who later wrote *Dracula*, he included it as part of a bill of three playlets, first in the provinces, starting with Bristol on September 21, 1894, and then two years later at the Lyceum in London, where it was a great success, despite a characteristically acid review by George Bernard Shaw.

In that winter and spring of 1892, Conan Doyle began, for the first time, to move in literary society. Not, of course, in the elevated circles which eddied out from the aesthetic magazine *The Yellow Book*, not among the poets and poetasters, the silken young men, most of whom were far too effeminate and weedy for his robust taste, and most of whom would have found his large figure and military manner hopelessly provincial and alienating. Instead he swam powerfully in the mainstream of English middlebrow culture. He attended the famous afternoon teas at *The Idler*, where he met the two editors—Jerome K. Jerome, genial author of the recently successful, humorous *Three Men in a Boat*, and again Robert Barr, whom he portrayed in fictional guise in several later stories. He also met some of the magazine's contributors, including Israel Zangwill, Barry Pain, Anthony

Hope, Gilbert Parker, and Eden Phillpotts. The teas often stretched into dinners, with singsongs and heavy drafts of beer and wine.

Another jolly companion of those *Idler* days was James M. Barrie, not yet author of *Peter Pan*, whose health was fragile but who was in every way a man after Conan Doyle's own heart. He was a cricketer; his private team, the Allahakbarries, made up very largely of literary and theatrical figures, was in full bloom, and Conan Doyle applied for membership and was instantly accepted. In later years, he played for the Allahakbarries against the team of the actress Mary Anderson. Like Conan Doyle, Barrie had been to Edinburgh University, and he knew Scotland inside out; his recent portrait of a small Scottish town, *A Window in Thrums*, was exactly to Conan Doyle's taste.

Their friendship deepened rapidly. Sentimental and kind-hearted, Barrie shared with Conan Doyle a fascination with ghosts, fairies, and elves, and the two had much to talk about. While on a lecture tour in Scotland in the early summer of 1892, Conan Doyle stayed with Barrie at his house at Glen Cova, fifteen miles from Kirriemuir, on the banks of the river Esk. The two men fished happily and talked. When Barrie grew weak from bronchial attacks and had to take to his bed, Conan Doyle proved an excellent physician. He next went on to Alford, in Aberdeenshire, for the fly-fishing, and then to Edinburgh to lunch with W. E. Henley, the crippled editor of *The National Observer*, poet, critic, and model for Long John Silver in *Treasure Island*.

Conan Doyle also paid visits that summer to Box Hill, to see one of his childhood idols, George Meredith. On his second trip there, he was accompanied by Barrie and by the celebrated "Q" —Arthur Quiller-Couch. Meredith, talking in a quirky complicated style like that of his own novels, was so unsteady on his feet that he kept falling over and had to be supported by his distinguished visitors. His eccentricity, borne like a banner, became an aggravation to Conan Doyle, who returned disappointed to the Meredith novels he loved, and did not revisit Box Hill.

The Great Shadow, another tedious historical novel boasting the authorship of Conan Doyle, appeared that year. With its echoes of his visit to the Napoleon Room at Madame Tussaud's, it was in itself somewhat of a waxworks display. It was, of course, well received—by now, Conan Doyle could do no wrong—and *The White Company, Micah Clarke,* and the collected edition of the first group of stories, *The Adventures of Sherlock Holmes,* were all selling capitally. Moreover, he would no longer be pirated in the United States; Congress had finally approved the new International Copyright Act. He was delighted, too, that his sisters Connie and Lottie were greatly enjoying life at the villa in South Norwood, and their dashing tricycle spins to Croydon.

Conan Doyle's chief worry, apart from the looming deadline for more Holmes stories and the problem of finding more ingenious puzzles to strike sparks from the iron heat of Greenhough Smith, was the mysterious decline in Louise's health. She seemed pale and fretful all spring and summer, breaking out into night sweats and not responding enthusiastically to the suggestions for tricycle excursions. When she became pregnant with their second child, she seemed more than naturally weakened. It is disagreeably ironical that the well-trained doctor-author did not recognize the early symptoms of tuberculosis; but he did sense the urgency in her pleas for a holiday with him in August.

They made the bookings through Thomas Cook & Son and set off on a cruise ship to the Norwegian fjords, with Jerome K. Jerome and sister Connie, whom Jerome was earnestly wooing. It was a rough voyage, with storms almost the whole way. Connie, tall and hearty as Brünnhilde, invaded the cabins of seasick passengers with bouncing jollity and numerous nostrums, only to be told rather faintly to go away. Louise lay hopelessly ill in her cabin; Jerome was scarcely heard from. Conan Doyle insisted on spending his time studying Norwegian. When the party arrived, they met a Norwegian officer who said something in his native language. Thinking the officer was requesting the time of day, Conan Doyle searched out his pocket watch, but while he was doing so, the man climbed aboard the writer's small tourist's pony and trap and galloped cheerfully off, leaving the Conan Doyles without their own vehicle. Later, sharing Connie's cart, Arthur and Louise and Jerome made a visit to the famous Norwegian white leper colony, talking to the inmates and observing their symptoms with interest.

Back in London in September, Conan Doyle found a telegram summoning him to Barrie's house at Aldeburgh, in Suffolk. Barrie's bronchitis had worsened, and he was heading for a nervous breakdown. He most urgently needed Conan Doyle's professional help. The D'Oyly Cartes had recently quarreled with Gilbert and Sullivan over money, and in desperation had begun commissioning comic operas from all and sundry to fill the hiatus at the Savoy Theatre. Barrie was to supply a comic opera entitled *Jane Annie; or the Good Conduct Prize,* named after his favorite sister, which would deal with the adventures of two youths who invade a girl's school and are chased out by the provost. Barrie was simply not up to finishing it, and Conan Doyle found himself saddled with the job of rewriting the first act, reconstructing the second, polishing the third, and working closely with the composer of the score, Ernest Ford.

The D'Oyly Cartes were not entirely pleased with the result, which combined the boisterous and the sentimental in equal parts, but they had no alternative to opening the show. At the first night at the Savoy Theatre, on May 13, 1893, the collaborators shared a box. They were enthusiastically greeted by the crowd as they arrived, but the audience's enthusiasm drained away well before the end, and there were no calls for "Author!" when the closing curtain fell. Conan Doyle and Barrie crept off quietly to console each other over a very bad dinner at the Athenaeum. The D'Oyly Cartes, with nothing to put in its place, kept *Jane Annie* artificially alive for seven lamentable weeks before according it a quiet and well-deserved burial.

In November, 1892, Conan Doyle's second child and first son was born—Alleyne Kingsley. His first name was that of the hero of *The White Company;* his second, that of one of his father's favorite authors, Charles Kingsley, creator of *The Heroes* and *The Water Babies.* The infant was very handsome, with clear, blue-gray eyes and blond hair. He grew into a strong and athletic youth. The children underwent a traumatic experience at Christmas. Instead of dressing up in his customary seasonal scarlet robes and flowing cotton-wool beard, Conan Doyle made an unexpected appearance in the sitting room as a prehistoric dragon. Covered in phosphorescent paint, with flaring false eyes, giant claws, and a green-scaled body, he rushed in, causing consternation among wife, children, sisters, and friends that took him months to live down.

During 1893, he corresponded with Robert Louis Stevenson, now living in Samoa, whom he had never met, but whom he had admired for many years. (In one letter, Stevenson addressed him, "O! Frolic fellow Spookist!" in reference to their mutual interest in spiritualism.) Stevenson wrote in July, 1893 that he was delighted to hear that the Conan Doyles might be visiting Samoa (". . . our rations are often spare. Are you Great Eaters? Please reply"). Stevenson gave them the instructions for getting there: the Conan Doyles were to come from San Francisco by the down mail, disembark in Samoa, and remain for twelve to fourteen days; they could then proceed "to Auckland via Tonga and possibly Fiji." Unhappily, pressure of work on the Holmes stories prevented the trip.

In further letters, Stevenson expressed pleasure in Conan Doyle's book *The Refugees*, and revealed that he had held his native overseer Simale enthralled with *The Engineer's Thumb*, which, he prayed God forgive him, he had narrated as though it were a true story. He wrote ". . . if you could have seen the drawn, anxious features and the bright, feverish eyes of Simale, you would have (for the moment at least) tasted glory." But he added that if Conan Doyle were to come to Samoa, he could not be introduced as the author of *The Engineer's Thumb*, since the local inhabitants did not know what it meant to make up a story. Unfortunately, Stevenson was in declining health, and this agreeable flow of letters soon ended.

In late January, 1893, depressed by the severe winter weather, and concerned for Louise's health, Arthur set off with her for their second holiday in six months. They left the children to be cared for by her mother. During the Channel crossing from Folkestone to Boulogne, and on a series of train rides, with an extra change of trains at the French border because of a cholera epidemic, he never stopped writing Holmes stories. One of these, *The Musgrave Ritual*, was as stuffed with personal references as an old attic trunk. Arthur's untidiness—Louise complained about it constantly—is transferred to Sherlock Holmes, with Watson describing it in words that might easily have been hers:

. . . when I find a man who keeps his cigars in the coal-scuttle, his tobacco in the toe end of a Persian slipper, and his unanswered correspondence transfixed by a jack-knife into the very center of his wooden mantelpiece, then I begin to give myself virtuous airs.

The last eight words of this statement contain an extremely sly little dig at Louise. Holmes's accumulation of papers ("he had a horror of destroying documents"), his stacks of manuscripts everywhere, his bursts of energy and sudden relapses into silent reading or contemplation, his clipping out and filing of articles on every subject which might be of value to him—no story has more in it of Conan Doyle-as-Holmes. The detective even tells Watson that when he first came to live in London, he took rooms in Montague Street. Conan Doyle, of course, took rooms only a step away, in Montague Place. The portrayal of the Musgrave family, with its passion for ancestral ritual and heraldry, is clearly drawn from recollections of his mother's discussions with him.

The story is not only reminiscent but premonitory. Just as Conan Doyle moved to Norwood after describing it in *The Sign of Four*, so he was to move into a house almost as large and imposing as the Musgrave residence, not far away from it in Sussex. Like *The Beryl Coronet*, the ending of the story, in which the lost crown of England is discovered, recalls its author's inspection of the crown jewels at the age of fifteen. The crown referred to is that of Charles I—St. Edward's Crown—and was originally worn by the ancient sovereigns of England. After Charles I's execution, the real crown was defaced, indeed, the impudent poet George Wither was caught dressing up in the robes and crown and darting apishly about the treasure room in Westminister Abbey, mocking the sacred gems.

The Musgrave Ritual also contains a reference to another episode, doubtless mentioned in the tour of the Tower of London which Conan Doyle took in 1874. In 1671, the Irish adventurer Thomas Blood arrived at the Tower of London dressed as a clergyman—Holmes's disguise in another story—with a woman friend posing as his wife. She distracted the keeper, Edwards, by becoming "indisposed," and while he and his wife attended to her needs, Blood made a rapid survey of the design of the room. Subsequently, a ruffian pretending to be Blood's nephew gained the favor of Mr. and Mrs. Edwards and proposed to marry their daughter. At the engagement party, Blood, his "wife," his "nephew," and others overpowered the Edwardses and the guards, and made off to St. Catherine's Gate with Charles I's State Crown (this is not to be confused with St. Edward's Crown, which had been broken up). The gang was intercepted and the crown, minus some gems, retrieved; Charles II was so amused by the whole incident that he gave Blood a free pardon and installed him in his personal bodyguard at a salary of five hundred pounds a year. This crown had been on exhibit at the time of Conan Doyle's visit to the Tower in 1874.

The story of *The Naval Treaty*, written after the Conan Doyles' return to London, is drawn in its entirety from a case which occurred just a year after the author's first visit to London. A clerk named Charles Marvin had been accused of using his position at the Foreign Office improperly to sell the secret details of a treaty to the yellow press. Once again, Conan Doyle's detailed adolescent reading of the sacred pages of the London *Times* can only be marveled at.

Like *The Musgrave Ritual* and *The Beryl Coronet*, this story anticipates the events of the theft of the Irish crown jewels in 1907. Percy Phelps, a schoolmate of Watson's, now working in the Foreign Office, seeks the help of the great detective after he has lost the original of a secret treaty. Conan Doyle's cousin, Sir Arthur Vicars, who was responsible for the jewels in Dublin Castle, was to contact him in much the same manner. Lord Holdhurst in the story, with his prematurely gray hair and dignified manner, is modeled with great skill on Arthur J. Balfour, the second most powerful figure in the Conservative party (after the Prime Minister, Lord Salisbury), soon to be leader of the Opposition. Knowingly, Conan Doyle places Lord Holdhurst's chambers in Downing Street, and his nephew's country place at Woking, in Surrey, the home of Balfour's brother and nephews. Soon after, Conan Doyle and Balfour were to become very close friends. It is significant that the treaty is rolled into a cylinder, just as Conan Doyle's manuscripts always were; and the narrative also clearly refers to the disappearance of his politically controversial early manuscript, *The Narrative of John Smith*, which was lost by the Post Office. As if all these crowded references to the author's past and future were not enough, the tale yields a further treasure: twice—in London and in Woking—the protagonists hear church bells chiming the quarters, just as the church bell chimed in Southsea, and in *The Speckled Band*.

On their way to Switzerland, the Conan Doyles ran into severe snowstorms; but they battled on, going all the way to Berne and up into the Oberland, where they gazed astonished at the three-hundred-foot Reichenbach Falls, and the boiling waters below. Chunks of ice drifted in the race, which resembled a maelström described by Edgar Allan Poe. Louise's incipient disease worsened at the Falls, and back in London, she complained of pains in her side, and a severe cough. When Arthur discovered blood in her sputum, he brought in a South Norwood practitioner for a second opinion, and the Harley Street lung specialist Sir Douglas Powell for a third. The news was desolating; in 1893, the diagnosis of consumption was a death sentence. If only Dr. Koch's tuberculin, which Conan Doyle had condemned in the pages of the London *Daily Telegraph*, had worked, this would no longer have been true. It had not worked. Conan Doyle must have been tormented with the feeling that by not correctly observing Louise's early symptoms, despite the fact that he was a doctor, by insisting on taking her tricycling in wet weather without protective covering, by allowing her to make the stormy crossing to Norway while pregnant, and to take the freezing train journey to Switzerland, he himself had unwittingly undermined her health.

Certainly, friends noticed that he was very distracted that

late winter and early spring. Moreover, he made it plain to everyone that Greenhough Smith's deadlines had become unendurable, forcing him to neglect Louise. Though he never actually hated Holmes, as so many historians insist, he had become wearier than ever of dredging up puzzles out of the confluent streams of his reading and experience. The last story of the series, *The Final Problem,* appearing in *The Strand* in December, 1893, firmly disposed of Holmes, to Greenhough Smith's abiding honor. Impatiently written, it is not one of the better tales. But it is notable for its evocation of a crime-ridden London, mirroring Conan Doyle's first experience of the city and bringing back from those early days the name of Moriarty, now assigned to the diabolical Napoleon of crime who controls a spider's web of gangs in the dark underground below the red and slate-gray roofs of the city.

The climax, unhappily off stage, in which Moriarty and Holmes plunge over the Reichenbach Falls, clearly reveals Conan Doyle's impatience to dispose of his hero, but the evocation of the Falls has all the immediacy of recent memory as well as a poetic quality worthy of a student of Mayne Reid's. The scene was wonderfully illustrated by Sidney Paget: horrendous cliffs, reminiscent of Gustave Doré's chasms in his illustrations for Dante's *Inferno,* a suggestion of spray and black depths, and two figures poised on the brink against a Gothic crag, hearing the thunderclap of doom.

There is a very curious fact here. The reason Watson is not present at the Reichenbach Falls to assist Holmes is that he has received a message asking that he come at once to the aid of a lady who has been wintering at Davos, and who is hemorrhaging as a result of consumption. It emerges that the lady never existed; the message is simply a device to distract Watson, and bring about Holmes's death. Quite subtly, Conan Doyle is giving us the important reason why Holmes had to be killed off: the consumptive Louise brought about the death of Holmes, simply because she required Conan Doyle's attention. By hitherto neglecting her for Holmes, he had, in the light of his own guilt feelings, helped to bring upon her a death sentence. The choice of the Reichenbach Falls as the setting for Holmes's "death" is, of course, quite deliberate, since the severe cold of the area above it had aggravated Louise's illness. Soon after, he took her to Davos; once more, in his life, reality fulfilled the presentiments of art.

There has been much speculation about the identity of Moriarty. We have already seen the source of his surname in the reports about the criminal George Moriarty in the London papers in 1874. The professor is described as a remarkable mathematician and author of a brilliantly abstruse work on asteroids; these elements of the character are drawn from Conan Doyle's mathematician-astronomer friend of Southsea, Major-General Drayson, a specialist in asteroids. Physically, Moriarty's spidery figure, deathly complexion, and pallid brow suggest the editor of *The Cornhill*, James Payn. It is significant, therefore, that Conan Doyle gave him Payn's Christian name.

The model for his character and activities is the famous nineteenteenth-century criminal Adam Worth, as a study of Worth's career clearly indicates. First, Worth was known in his time as "the Napoleon of crime," and this is the exact appellation which Holmes gives to Moriarty. Worth's pseudonym, or alias, was Harry Raymond. Consider the following:

H A R (R Y R A Y M O) N D
(M O R I A R T Y)

One is close to being the anagram of the other. Now consider the parallels in their activities. Adam Worth was rich and ran a vast network of crime. One of his most famous *coups* provided the basis for the plot of *The Red-headed League*. In 1869, he rented from a well-known *pawnbroker* a house next to the Boylestone Bank in Boston. He tunneled through the cellars adjoining, to rob the Bank of $450,000 in cash and securities, including *gold coins*. Later, he similarly robbed the vault of the Ocean Bank of New York. In *The Resident Patient*, the Worthingdon bank gang is mentioned.

But the final, delightful clue to the correct identity of Professor Moriarty occurs in a later adventure of Sherlock Holmes, *The Valley of Fear*. We are told in that novella of Moriarty's apparently illegal acquisition of a painting by Greuze entitled "La

Jeune Fille à l'Agneau." No such painting exists, although since Greuze frequently had his lovely young female models appear with animals or birds, the title is wittily plausible. Now consider: on May 25, 1876, Adam Worth brought off his most celebrated feat, the talk of England when Conan Doyle was a boy—the theft of Gainsborough's painting "The Duchess of Devonshire." And from whom did he steal it? Messrs. *Agnew*, in Bond Street:

A G N E A U

A G N E W

"La Jeune Fille à l'Agneau" literally means "The Young Woman with the Lamb." But a person uninformed in French might translate the title as "The Young Woman at Agnew's." *Voilà!* We have our man.

It is not hard to imagine Conan Doyle's sigh of relief as he tossed away his pen at the end of this last story in the cycle. Greenhough Smith condescended to plead for Holmes's life. A bristling and red-faced George Newnes tried similarly to reason with his obdurate author. It was useless. In great fear and trembling, Newnes published the story. Not until the death of Queen Victoria seven years later was there such widespread mourning. Over twenty thousand people canceled their subscriptions immediately. They, and tens of thousands more, wrote angrily to *The Strand*, protesting this bloody act of murder. "You beast!" one woman's letter began.

Young men in the city wore black silk bands around their hats, or upon their coat sleeves, and women appeared in mourning. The Prince of Wales was especially dashed by the great detective's demise, and it was rumored that Queen Victoria was Not Amused. Why was there such a heartbroken response? Partly because the stories were so intensely imagined that people believed that Sherlock Holmes really existed, and that a Dr. Watson (some said, Dr. Watson of Upper Norwood) had written the accounts of his exploits. That legend even perists to this day, with Conan Doyle relegated to the role of Dr. Watson's literary agent.

More important, people felt that a representative of pure

disinterested goodness in a wicked world had been swallowed up at the Reichenbach Falls; that an embodiment of reason had been killed by an embodiment of madness. The symbolism was, many felt, all too clear: the sturdy, reasonable security of the Victorian age was crumbling rapidly before the forces of moral and intellectual disorder. With Sherlock Holmes, another stabilizing element had been removed; the thousands of dark presences that lurked beyond the light thrown by gas lamps and oil lamps of London could move as freely as they wished. Scotland Yard's efforts continued to disappoint; now all hope for a fictional corrective had been expunged. On a more mundane level, there was the sheer displeasure of being deprived of new and exotic Sherlockian adventures amidst the unexotic purlieus of London suburbs and quiet country towns. It would no longer be possible to walk down Baker Street or Tottenham Court Road, or to visit Norbury or Stoke Poges, and imagine what horrifying Conan Doyle detective drama might occur just around a corner. England would no longer be alive with fantastic Holmesian delights and terrors, its hedgerows and primroses and gray streets and church towers would no longer vibrate with the magic exchanges between detective and doctor and villain.

For after only a few years, the Sherlock Holmes stories had assumed the status of fairy tales—magical, improbable, buoyed up by an imagination as inexhaustible as that of Hans Christian Andersen or the brothers Grimm. When the Countess of Morcar's blue curbuncle materializes in the crop of a Christmas goose and John Doyle's famous colophon "H.B." is found in the lining of the goose owner's hat, when a King of Bohemia emerges from the fog in a mask, when a black baby's face is hidden in an androgynous yellow mask, we are in a world no less fantastic than that occupied by the ugly duckling, the flying trunk, the marsh king's daughter, Rumpelstiltskin, or Hansel and Gretel. The people of an increasingly scientific age yearned for fantasy, for magic, and for wild adventure; and now they were, it seemed, to be deprived of the most delectable fantasies yet obtainable.

Luckily, the Conan Doyles were not in England when the outbreak of protest and grief swept across London in December,

1893. They had returned to Switzerland in October with the promise of better weather, and had taken rooms at the Kurhaus Hotel, in Davos. It was a beautiful place. The two parishes of Davos-Platz and Davos-Dorf (or Dörfli) stood in a handsome valley five thousand feet above sea level, surrounded by white peaks sparkling in the winter sunshine, and shivered by the constant ringing of bells—from carts, carriages, omnibuses, sleighs, toboggans, and numerous other vehicles for hire; from churches, chapels, cows, goats, and sheep.

November was a month of profound, almost Italian azure skies; December, too, was perfect; and Conan Doyle was a frequent speaker at the Davos Literary Society. He reveled in amateur photography, capturing the brilliance of rocks and snow. He made frequent sleigh rides to St. Moritz, which was only a short distance away; and while Louise rested flat on her back heaped with fur rugs on the hotel balcony—the required treatment of the time—Conan Doyle went tobogganing or watched toboggan races, helped to introduce the Norwegian sport of skiing and ski-running, skated on the large Davos rink, and climbed in various expeditions through the foothills of the Alps.

In this setting of transcendent beauty, he was as nostalgic as ever. He wrote *The Stark Munro Letters* at Davos that winter of 1893. Justly praised when it appeared the following year, the *roman à clef* remains one of his most attractive and good-natured works, alive with sympathetic detail and spoiled only by the ending, in which the characters representing himself and Louise are arbitrarily killed off in a train wreck.

Conan Doyle must often have fretted for England in those months. But he was shocked by the public's grief over Holmes, who he refused to accept as a real person; and, perhaps, by the same public's heartless ignoring of his father's death, from swallowing his tongue in an epileptic seizure at the lunatic asylum near Dumfries, which had preceded Holmes's by just over two months, and had not even been acknowledged by an obituary in the *Times*. Although his portrait of his father in *The Stark Munro Letters* is not warm, he did soften toward Charles Doyle in later years. He wrote most considerately of him in his memoirs, organized an exhibition of his work in London in 1924, and always regretted that his presence in Switzerland on October 12 made it impossible for him to attend his father's funeral on that day.

In England, Conan Doyle's literary affairs were handled that winter and from then on by a literary agent, A. P. Watt, who might be called his ten-percent solution. His sister Connie wrote particularly happy letters from London. She was no longer flirting with Jerome K. Jerome, but instead was seriously enjoying the company of a young writer, E. W. Hornung, who was to marry her later, and who created the famous fictional amateur thief Raffles, the name borrowed from Conan Doyle's alchemist, Raffles Haw.

It is significant that at this time, following his father's death and his wife's death sentence, and given the fact that the husband of a tubercular woman was then condemned to sexual abstinence, Conan Doyle reverted to an interest in other worlds. He began to make a new study of psychic phenomena, re-examining at Davos the findings reported by the Scottish Dialectical Society during the period of his childhood. He had largely given up this preoccupation after his marriage. Louise had evinced little or no interest in séances, and the Ma'am had always rigidly refused to have anything to do with such stuff and nonsense. Conan Doyle's marriage had until now fulfilled him, and when he had given up medicine, he had stopped being so morbidly preoccupied with death, dealing with the subject of personal extinction more or less in a spirit of ironical melodrama in the Holmes stories. But now, in Switzerland, surrounded by dying consumptives and aware of Louise's own peril, he began to brood once more on the possibility of survival of the human spirit.

The records of the British Society for Psychical Research show that Conan Doyle joined by mail in November, 1893, significantly just three weeks after the death of Charles Doyle. He was impressed by the journal and the reports of the Society, and in particular by the presence on its Board of many distinguished political and scientific figures who supported psychical investigation. Foremost among the politicians was Arthur Balfour, Conan

Doyle's Lord Holdhurst in *The Naval Treaty*. This glittering intellectual, always talking in a quick, nervous rush, casual and debonair, who was to become Lord Salisbury's successor less than a decade later, had a very good reason for being a mainstay of psychical research.

At the age of twenty-seven, in 1875, Balfour had fallen in love with the tall and beautiful May Lyttelton, a favorite niece of Gladstone's. One month after they had unofficially announced their engagement, she had died suddenly of typhoid fever. From that traumatic moment on, Balfour's sexual feelings had apparently become sublimated. His energies were channeled instead into the service of his ambition and of his obsession with wrecking Gladstone's plans for Home Rule. His furious treatment of the Irish when he was Chief Secretary for Ireland had earned him the name "Bloody Balfour." No sooner had May Lyttelton died than he plunged into psychical research, and made several attempts to contact her through mediums. A cool logician, he realized almost at once that he was being fooled, that the figure of the beautiful girl in white who came through the séance curtains was simply the medium in disguise. But to the end of his life in 1930, he continued futilely to hope.

His brother-in-law Henry Sidgwick, the distinguished moral philosopher of Trinity College, Cambridge, had preceded Balfour as president of the Society for Psychical Research. Among the vice-presidents were such important figures as the philosopher William James, who had been intrigued by the mediumship of his fellow American Leonora Piper; the physicist Oliver Lodge, who believed among other things that Mrs. Piper had brought back his beloved Aunt Anne; the poet and essayist F. W. H. Myers; and the naturalist Alfred Russel Wallace, an important figure in the development of the theory of evolution. Conan Doyle was greatly affected by the involvement of these distinguished men, but he was impressed most of all by the inclusion among their number of the remarkable scientist William Crookes, whose important accomplishments included the discovery and isolation of the chemical element thallium. Crooks had become the most celebrated supporter of spiritualism of his day, as a result of his widely reported interest in the mediums Daniel Dunglas Home and Florrie Cook.

The story of the Cook mediumship fascinated Conan Doyle. More than any other episode in the then existing history of spiritualism, it had the effect of drawing him toward the brink of conviction. Florrie Cook had been born in London about 1854. She had emerged as a medium as a child, and with her younger sister and near twin, Kate, had apparently levitated tables and floated up to the living-room ceiling of her parents' cramped and gloomy house in Hackney. The two Cook girls were often found insensible on the floor after "materializing" a variety of female figures. Their mother briskly rejected impolite suggestions that the children were simply enjoying a fancy-dress party with the aid of cheesecloth and phosphorescent paint. Even when Florrie was caught buying some paint, her mother remained obdurate.

In 1870, Henry Cook, the girl's father, placed them in the charge of the mediums Frank Herne and Charles Williams. That year, they emerged to give séances of their own. At her first individual séance, when she was sixteen, Florrie Cook appeared with a spirit which announced itself as John King. Tall and bearded, King had already been the spirit control, or contact, of numerous mediums, including the well-known Davenport brothers. On April 20, 1872, John King's daughter, Katie, appeared for the first time, while Florrie Cook apparently remained behind the curtain of a corner cabinet constructed rather like a Punch-and-Judy theater. The sitters were fascinated to see the slim, well-rounded figure of a girl, naked under phosphorescent white drapery, gliding about as she sang sweet songs and spiritualist hymns, her face glowing with the soft silver light of the moon.

Katie King's appearances increased in frequency. John King often materialized with her, shaking the sitters' hands and leading them out of the room, along a corridor, and up and down stairs. A few spoilsports rudely noted that John and Katie King showed suspicious resemblances to Florrie Cook's mentor Frank Herne and to Florrie herself. But the Hackney circle brushed the complaints aside, and by 1873, Florrie Cook was the most famous medium in London. Night after night, the luminous, moonlike face glimmered at the top of the cabinet, and the figure of Katie King drifted through the audience, embracing the men in a somewhat unspiritual manner; they could feel a stirringly earthly reality under the drifting veils.

Sometimes, in a high-pitched, unnatural voice, the ghost would describe her earthly career as a murderess; the reason for her materialization was that she was returning to earth to expiate her sins.

Occasionally, a black face instead of a white one would appear at the top of the cabinet, nod twice, and disappear. This was supposed to be Katie's "other self," the evil half which had dominated her while she was alive, an odd comment on contemporary prejudice.

On December 9, 1873, the spiritualist William Volckman, engaged by the London Dialectical Society to analyze the facts of psychic phenomena, appeared at a Hackney séance with the Earl and Countess of Caithness and Count de Medina Pomar. Volckman watched Katie King emerge from the cabinet, her draperies shining in the thin moonlight that filtered through the living-room curtains. She moved around the silent semicircle of figures, squeezing the men's hands in turn. Suddenly, Volckman gripped her firmly around the waist, and triumphantly announced, "This beauty is Miss Florence Cook!" Katie uttered a somewhat unspiritual remark, a struggle ensued, and the gaslight went out. Florrie Cook's lover, Edward Corner, plucked the spirit from Volckman's busy hands. Smarting from the loss of a few tufts from his mustache and beard, Volckman lashed out at Corner, who whisked the fainting figure of Katie into the cabinet. Five minutes later the gas went up, and Volckman and the others examined the cabinet. Florrie was disheveled and in a fainting condition, but she was still tied by tape, as at the beginning of the séance, the knot sealed by the signet ring of the Earl of Caithness.

William Crookes attended one or two of the Hackney séances, and became fascinated. He had been going to séances in an attempt—hitherto unsuccessful—to contact his beloved younger brother Philip, who had died on a cable-laying expedition in Cuba. He had seen the mediums Henry Slade, Mrs. Marshall, Daniel Dunglas Home, and other famous figures, but Florrie Cook impressed him most deeply, and in order to examine her mediumship, he installed her in his house. His critics said that his examination could not be described as scientific, and that he had very poor eyesight; the presence of this attractive young woman in the home of a man with ten children and a wife was furiously gossiped about in every salon in London.

On March 20, 1874, at the handsome house of J. C. Luxmoore, J.P., at 16, Gloucester Square, Florrie was placed in an electrical circuit, with a galvanometer to record her movements. The galvanometer fluctuated somewhat, but Crookes attributed this to the drying of the blotting paper under the electrodes on Florrie's wrists. Since at no stage did the galvanometer fall 200 divisions, Crookes concluded that Florrie had not moved from the cabinet in the darkness. Critics pointed out that he had quite deliberately misinformed the sitters. In the first place, he well knew that the wires to which she was attached were very long, and that she could move about the circle quite easily without detaching them. As a scientist, he was aware that alternatively to slip out of the circuit without distributing the galvanometer unduly, all she had to do was replace herself with, say, a damp handkerchief in the circuit, or connect the terminals by bringing the blotting pads together.

Crookes came under severe censure in the matter. Later, he insisted that he had established the separate realities of Florrie and Katie, saying, "I asked her permission to clasp her in my arms, so as to be able to verify the interesting observations . . . permission was graciously given, and I accordingly did—well, as any gentleman would do under the circumstances."

In May, 1874, Katie King returned forever to the spirit world, giving each of her friends, led by Crookes, a small farewell bouquet of violets tied with a pink silk ribbon, a portion of her dress and veil, and a lock of hair. She invited the authoress Florence Marryat into the cabinet, threw off her white garment, and asked Miss Marryat to touch her naked body from head to foot. "Now," said the figure, "you can see that I am a woman." Miss Marryat commented, "Which indeed she was."

Miss Marryat reported that Katie dissolved like wax before

the sitters, leaving nothing except the light of gas burners where she had stood. Crookes quarreled with Miss Marryat, denying the veracity of this particular part of her report, and withdrew from his involvement with the mediumship. Later, on January 9, 1880, Sir George Sitwell seized Florrie's new control, Marie, when he observed that she wore stays. She screamed and ran from the room, and it was discovered that the cabinet was empty, with Florrie's clothes lying on the floor.

There can be question that Conan Doyle was captivated by the story of Cook and King. Despite the fact that both Arthur Balfour and his brother-in-law Henry Sidgwick gravely doubted Crookes's conclusions in the matter, believing that he had either been duped by Florrie because of his extremely poor eyesight, or aided and abetted her because of a romantic involvement, Conan Doyle unhesitatingly accepted the genuineness of the mediumship. The story resembled one of his own accounts of the survival of sexuality in death; talking to her sitters, Katie King had frequently referred in a somewhat suggestive manner to her love affairs in the Other World.

Very oddly, at the same time that Katie King was making her famous appearances in London, she was also being seen in Philadelphia. It is agreeable to learn from the pages of *Galaxy* magazine that she was a visitor at the house of a Mr. Holmes, and that another spirit visitor to the séance room was named Watson. This Katie King did not resemble the London one. She announced at one séance that "they are killing my medium in London . . . send her here. They'll kill her if she stays there. They are not so skeptical here as they are there." She added, "Professor Crookes is a humbug. He will kill my medium if she don't come away. . . ."

A gentleman asked, "Is it true that you allowed Professor Crookes to embrace you?"

"Yes," she replied, "he squeezed me."

"Will you not one day allow me to do the same?"

"If you do," Katie said firmly, "I'll thump you." Taking a pair of opera glasses "to travel to London with, and inspect Professor Crookes," she disappeared. In December, 1874, Eliza White, the Holmes's landlady, disclosed that she had been Katie slipping through a false panel in the cabinet and dressing in white robes.

The seeming apparition of Katie King appealed to the romantic and visionary side of Conan Doyle's nature. In his history of spiritualism, published in the mid-1920's, he wrote with scarcely controlled emotion about the image of Crookes, virile and bearded in his prime, walking with the voluptuous Katie through the rooms of his house in Mornington Road or sitting transfixed while the children played at her feet and she told them pirate tales of the Spanish Main. Indeed, Conan Doyle's acquaintance with this episode may have sparked off his own writing of many pirate tales in the years that followed, tales which he liked to relate to his own children.

The Watson in him, rather than the Holmes, responded to Crookes's experience. It is unfortunate that he did not apply the rules of logic to an examination of the reports written by Crookes in a series of letters to *The Spiritualist* in 1874. Conan Doyle's weakness was that he assumed that major scientists were incapable of unscientific observation, even in matters which affected them emotionally. A careful re-examination of the Crookes reports shows them to be entirely unscientific, and one can well understand why the Royal Society took a dim view of them at the time. Crookes makes no mention of securing the windows during the apparitions of Katie King, of tying or binding Florrie Cook, or of examining the library in his house which was used as a séance cabinet. Moreover, he neglects to mention that the last two séances (the only ones in which, he claimed, the faces of Florrie Cook and Katie King were seen simultaneously) took place not at his home, as he implies, but in the house in Hackney, with Kate and Florrie Cook's bedroom serving as the cabinet.

In later years, Crookes, first in his inaugural address as President of the British Association of Science, in Bristol in 1898, and afterward in various magazines, was to assert his continued belief in the genuineness of the Florrie Cook phenomena. This conviction is taken by spiritualists to indicate the value of the phenomena, or at least the value of his scientific observation of them. After his wife's death in 1916, he was convinced that he saw her materialize at a séance conducted by a Mrs. Harris, and in a photograph taken by the psychic photographer William Hope.

It is extraordinary to reflect that the séances in Mornington Road took place in the crucial year of 1874, when Conan Doyle first came to London. Indeed, when he arrived late in November, the magazines were still full of the controversy surrounding the events. Captivated by Crookes's support of Miss Cook, ravished by the romantic image of man and spirit in a platonic friendship, Conan Doyle came, in Switzerland in 1893, to the very edge of a belief in the hereafter.

In January, 1894, he received from London the *Proceedings* of the Society for Psychical Research, which contained as an introduction a lengthy and important inaugural address by Balfour, its newly elected President. Balfour examined with intensity and skill the subject of mesmerism; and only a week after receiving the *Proceedings*, Conan Doyle began work on one of his most remarkable inventions, a macabre novella about mesmerism entitled *The Parasite*, which incorporated some of Balfour's illuminations on the subject. Later disowned by him, and virtually ignored by his biographers, the work remains a strikingly personal revelation of neurotic sexual obsession, reminiscent of Poe but nevertheless expressive of Conan Doyle's mysterious and highly individual character as an artist.

The novella is in diary form. Professor Gilroy is a neurasthenic physiologist who, unable to endure experience, has retreated into a world of pure reason. He is reminiscent not only of Sherlock Holmes but of Frederick Fairlie, the hypochondriac uncle in Wilkie Collins' *Woman in White*, and, of course, of the unhappy Charles Doyle. Gilroy meets a clairvoyant, Helen Penclosa, a pale woman from the West Indies with strange, furtive eyes, the eyes of a cat; she brings to mind Bertha Mason Rochester, the deranged West Indian wife of Edward Rochester in *Jane Eyre*. Gilroy is disgusted by her séances. He reflects, "Are you to turn on a light suddenly and expose her slapping a surreptitious banjo? Are you to hurl cochineal on her evening frock when she steals around with her phosphorus bottle and her supernatural platitudes?"

The narrator describes a typical séance as "something between a religious ceremony and a conjuror's entertainment." But he is partially convinced of the clairvoyant's power when she successfully mesmerizes his fianceé; and he is gradually drawn into the spider's web in spite of himself. He begins to feel an irresistible sexual attraction for Miss Penclosa. A Celt, like his creator, his nerves quiver when he is in touch with the inexplicable. He fights against her sexual allure; he even locks his door against the transcendent sexual experience he secretly longs for. Nothing could be closer to Conan Doyle's own feelings as he locked himself in against desire for Louise's sake.

Then, in an extraordinary passage, rivaling parts of *The Monk*, by Matthew Lewis, in its expression of sexual frustration, Gilroy manages to release himself from his self-created prison by working the key under the door. Compelled by a force as powerful as electricity, he rushes to Miss Penclosa's apartment. In the scene with her, alive with conflicting expressions of hatred and desire, which impel Gilroy simultaneously to make love to her and to flee into the night, he becomes the vehicle of his author's combined need for and fear of sexual infidelity. Guilt follows rapture. In one of the finest narrative passages in Doyle's work, Gilroy, temporarily fulfilled, learns of a bank robbery. The bank has been recently repainted green. He is unable to remember what happened after he left Helen Penclosa's bedroom, but finding green paint on his sleeve, he realizes that she has driven him to robbery by her mesmeric powers. The equating of crime and sex is representative of the author's guilt feelings.

Although Gilroy escapes discovery, his erratic behavior causes his dismissal from the university. Helen Penclosa mysteriously falls ill, her power coursing through Gilroy like a faltering electrical current. Deranged, sleepless, under the influence of the mesmerist, he attempts to murder his fiancée or at least disfigure her with sulphuric acid. At the last minute, he can't go through with it, and decides to kill Helen Penclosa instead. But by the time he arrives at her apartment, she is dead.

The powerful force of the story, carried forward in the headlong rushing movement of a nightmare, springs from the same psychological compulsion that animated Conan Doyle's earlier tales of psychopathology. Helen Penclosa, the temptress, is as much a symbol of primitive sexuality as is the little monkey which haunts the clergyman in Sheridan Le Fanu's masterpiece, *Green Tea*. Like the Andaman Islander Tonga, in *The Sign of Four*, like Dr. Grimesby Roylott, back from India with his swamp adder, and like the various blacks who crop up in Conan Doyle's stories, she represents the threat of the dark beasts who prowl in the jungle of the blood.

After cleansing himself with this curious self-revelation, Conan Doyle turned yet again to the writing of historical romance. In 1892, he had read with great interest the picaresque memoirs of the Baron de Marbot, a former lieutenant general in Napoleon's army, which had been adroitly translated with some additional glosses by Arthur Butler for Longmans, Green, almost fifty years after their original publication in Paris. With a number of critics, Conan Doyle was delighted by the quixotic, highly improbable adventures of Marbot, a sly, sharp-witted yet paradoxically inept figure of fun. Vain, innocent, and chivalrous, he shows himself in these memoirs to possess a head as thick as his heart is strong. He combines an exaggerated estimate of his own worth ("I am an excellent soldier, I do not say so because I am prejudiced in my own favor, but because I really am so") with a Watsonian clumsiness of performance.

Conan Doyle began in Switzerland the first of a series of stories based on Marbot's antic character. The stories, which were written over several years, are uneven, but the best of them convey the author's impish humor and strong sense of irony. In *How the Brigadier Held the King* he shows his hero, Gerard, playing a game of *écarté* with the British guards for his freedom. He wins, and is about to leave the prison when he runs smack into the daunting figure of the Duke of Wellington.

In another quixotic tale, Gerard contrives a complicated escape from Dartmoor prison, later to be echoed more darkly in the Princetown convict prison of *The Hound of the Baskervilles.*

After a series of misadventures, he executes a complete circle and bumbles his way all the way back inside the walls.

The Brigadier Gerard stories—the name Gerard was evidently taken from the central figure of one of Conan Doyle's favorite novels, Charles Reade's *The Cloister and the Hearth*, which had greatly influenced *The White Company*—are attractive and youthful *jeux d'esprit*, and they contain an affectionate, if not entirely flattering portrait of Napoleon Bonaparte. Gerard's first meeting with Napoleon, whom he both despises and adores, is vividly amusing. Conan Doyle had not forgotten the visit to the Napoleon Room at Madame Tussaud's in 1874. Indeed, he was fascinated throughout his life by the mystery of this unheroic, potbellied figure, who looked like a French schoolmaster and controlled the destiny of empires.

The Gerard stories, like the Sherlock Holmes stories before them, were written in two groups. In April, with *How the Brigadier Won His Medal** finished at Davos, Arthur kept a promise to take Louise, who was feeling much stronger, to visit their children and her mother, Mrs. Hawkins, at South Norwood. He arrived home to find a letter from America, written by that formidably Lincolnian and whimsical veteran of the Civil War, the impresario Major J. B. Pond, inviting him to come to New York and several other cities for a lecture tour. The choice of subjects was to be his own. Conan Doyle's letters show that he was delighted. He had a warm fellow feeling for Americans. His first letter to the London *Times*, written from the Reform Club and published on December 24, 1892, had suggested sending crack British regimental bands to the World's Columbian Exposition in Chicago, and contained the comment, "If there are any two races upon earth between which such courtesies would prevail, they are our own and our kin of the United States."

He accepted Major Pond's offer at once. This was, perhaps, unfortunate, for with characteristic impulsiveness, he did not stipulate that a full itinerary should be sent to him in advance, and in consequence Major Pond was able to exploit him unmercifully.

* Originally entitled *The Medal of Brigadier Gerard*.

5

AMERICA, EGYPT,
AND FALLING IN LOVE

CONAN DOYLE was not scheduled to leave for New York until September. He booked passage on the North German Lloyd steamer *Elbe*, and began, during that summer of 1894, to study at the library of the Society for Psychical Research, exploring the subjects of dreams, mesmerism, and telepathy, talking frequently to Arthur Balfour, Oliver Lodge, and F. W. H. Myers in detail about the problem of communicating with the dead. He moved from dark séances, with their silver trumpets,* cabinets, and luminous flying tambourines to the dazzling excitements of the cricket ground at Lord's, where he watched the great W. G. Grace perform superbly, and where he himself was a more modest success, batting or bowling with furious energy for the Marylebone Cricket Club. He was excellent at billiards and backgammon, fished with J. M. Barrie, and was frequently seen over lunch at Simpson's, the Gaiety, and Adelphi and the Café de Globe.

Genial, his eyes crinkling at a good joke, his voice with its rich Scots burr relishing an adept quotation, his mind endlessly inquiring, alive, and humorous, he was one of the most popular figures in London literary circles. He worked diligently in the somber twilight of the Reading Room of the British Museum, and in the splendor of the London Institution Library in Finborough Circus, not far from his Uncle Richard's old house in the Finborough Road. He read the scores of newspapers published in London, the numerous journals of science, as well as the more

---

* The spiritualist term for an aluminum megaphone through which the dead could speak.

popular magazines. He planned and wrote more Gerard stories. He prepared his lectures for America, on Stevenson, Olive Schreiner, Barrie, Kipling, Meredith, Walter Bagehot, and of course, the late Sherlock Holmes.

Louise returned to Davos in June, with her sister-in-law Lottie Doyle to keep her company. Arthur stayed on in London, doing research on the Napoleonic period, and visited Louise in Switzerland only twice before his departure for the United States. London had not changed much since he was a boy. The slush and mud of winter were as appalling as ever; ten thousand four-wheelers and hansom cabs now rolled through the streets, their number growing steadily. Electricity was a novelty, and the privilege of the prosperous; William Crookes's house was the first in London to be lit by it. On the horse-buses, men did ride inside now with the ladies, and the ladies, well covered with larger hats, veils, and parasols, sometimes braved the changeable weather on top. The great men's clubs were still silent except for the sound of gentlemen slowly rustling the pages of the newspapers, and down by the Thames the human refuse still swarmed, dressed in its tatterdemalion finery in imitation of the aristocracy.

But the overriding impression in London, to be conveyed by Conan Doyle in more than one passage, was of the crush of businessmen with pallid, intent faces, concerned only with getting rich, dressed in black as though in attendance at a funeral, their eyes staring ahead as they walked along the streets. Over everyone ruled Queen Victoria, flattering Lord Salisbury or grumbling at Gladstone, with her black-and-silver teapot figure and her tired eyes, administering the greatest empire the world had seen since Rome.

In his thirty-fifth year that summer of 1894, Conan Doyle looked remarkably like the Queen's grandson Kaiser Wilhelm, of Germany, after whom Sidney Paget had modeled his portrayal of the King of Bohemia. The young author had a more powerful physique. He frequently provided indirect self-portraits in his writings, as he described men with the shoulders and limbs of Hercules. His figure had filled out after the Portsmouth days.

Still a fine boxer, he was 6 feet 4 inches tall, and weighed in at a vigorous 235 pounds. His back was as straight as a general's, his hair close-cut; his face glowed with robust affability and good cheer. Energy seemed to flow from his broad forehead and his fingertips, and from his sharp eyes, alternatively inquisitive, alive with humor, somber, angry, or veiled in dreamy reflection.

He continued to assemble masses of data for his Holmesian files, filled with clippings and annotations on historical events, murder cases, the latest developments in science, discoveries made during explorations of the heavens, adventures into the dark places of the human mind. These files were as extensive, as meticulously docketed and indexed, as the late Sherlock Holmes's own.

His moods shifted as unpredictably as shadows in the moon. One moment he was plunged in gloom, feeling that Nature was blind and stupid, driving life forward without any significant purpose, unthinkingly causing his wife's twilight existence and his father's pathetic death in the grip of delirium tremens; the next, he felt that Nature was benign, creating the beauty of a snow crystal and compelling men to be aware of themselves, the ultimate purpose of creation. Paradoxically, he could obtain as much pleasure from observing the innocent face of a child as he could from reading about the trial of Madeleine Smith, which had taken place before he was born and which his father had most expertly etched; or about the brutal slaying of her infant brother by Constance Kent; or about the horror of the Jessie McLachlan case.

His mind ranged to South Africa, to India, Egypt, the West Indies, and South America, pursuing the details of Imperial administration. He followed the news of exhibitions, whether artistic or scientific. He was aware of discoveries in physics, physiology, and astronomy, of the searching of the ocean depths and the probing toward the poles. He was fascinated by every movement of the Queen, and like everyone else in England, he waited most eagerly for Her Majesty's Diamond Jubilee, which lay only three years in the future.

Yet, despite his boundless curiosity, his physical massiveness, and brass-band optimism, he was acutely unhappy, confused, and uncomfortable most of the time. He suffered from insomnia and from nightmares, which were to supply elements of his horror stories and were to become extremely severe by 1906; he was "all nerves," like Sherlock Holmes. He fretted excessively over a bad review; he was rigid and unyielding toward his critics and his enemies; and he was very much preoccupied with the problem in the Sudan, where border raids suggested a new and bloody insurrection against the British in Egypt.

In the late summer of 1894, Conan Doyle undertook the role of special investigator for the Society for Psychical Research. With two other prominent members, Frank Podmore and Dr. Sydney Scott, he went by railway to Dorset to investigate a haunting at the home of a Colonel Elmore, an odd man with a scarred face, who, like Dr. Watson, had done service in the Second Afghan War. The Colonel lived with his wife and his only daughter, a moody woman of thirty-five, in a large and sprawling house. They had complained in a letter to the Society of hearing eerie sounds, the moaning of someone in pain, the dragging of chains across the bare floor, and pitiful weeping in the small hours. The servants had fled and the dogs refused to go near certain rooms. In inviting Conan Doyle, Podmore, and Scott, the Colonel made it clear that they must not disclose their identity or purpose to his wife and daughter. They were to pretend they were old army friends of the Colonel's, recently returned from India.

That evening, Conan Doyle, Podmore, and Scott joined the Elmores for dinner, and talked obediently about the Afghan war. After dinner, the three men settled down with the Colonel for a rubber of whist in the card room, while the ladies retired to the drawing room. The three investigators retired at about 10 P.M. They heard nothing all night, and reported this to Colonel Elmore in the morning. The reply was that the disturbances were "not continuous." The next night, Conan Doyle, half-asleep in his four-poster bed, sat up suddenly, his senses acutely sharpened. He heard a sad, even a heart-breaking sound—a woman was helplessly weeping, moaning words he could not quite make out. A few seconds later, he heards chains being dragged along the flags outside his room. There was a pause. He dashed out to the minstrel's gallery carrying a gas lamp high in his hand. Podmore and Scott, who were posted on camp beds in the gallery, ran toward him saying that they had seen a white-garbed figure moving by, with blank, staring eyes.

The next morning, Conan Doyle discussed an idea with his companions. All three would arrange pillows in their beds to give the appearance of sleeping figures, and then, very carefully, would steal out and intercept the ghost. After waiting several hours that night, at last they heard the dragging of chains, and a faint crying. But when they came out of the shadows, no figure was visible.

The next morning, the daughter, who had been absent the whole of the previous day, appeared at breakfast. Observing that her eyes were red from weeping, Conan Doyle concluded that she herself was the ghost. He and his colleagues conferred with her privately and discovered that they were right. She promised not to continue her impersonation if they would keep the truth from her father, and they agreed. Conan Doyle released the story to Jerome K. Jerome, who recorded it in his memoirs, but it is not included in the reports of the Society.

At this time, like so many writers, although he was kind and considerate, Conan Doyle often seemed isolated from others in the deepest part of his being. While he was jolly company, the "life" of the golf or cricket club, surrounded by famous and talented friends, he was never more at home than when he was traveling in a world of pure imagination. In his early days, his social position had prevented him from forming very many close associations. Now that these were eminently available, they still did not affect him very much. In spite of everything he felt alone.

Conan Doyle's life with his children and his wife was always necessarily restricted by two things: the natural reserve and aloofness of a Victorian paterfamilias, and his constant obsessive involvement in work. Indeed, in later years, what the children chiefly remembered of him was the securely fastened door of his study, with meals placed in front of it, and his habit of writing even when standing in line for tickets at a railway station, sitting on luggage, or walking up and down the deck of a ship. The result of this enormous absorption in work was that the children felt somewhat remote from him, admiring, loving, but seldom really feeling that they knew him.

Conan Doyle sailed for America on the *Elbe* in September. He was accompanied by his brother Innes, now a younger, more slender, and more handsome version of himself, who at nineteen had become a subaltern in the Royal Artillery Regiment at Aldershot, and whose military billet had been referred to in the Holmes adventure *The Crooked Man*. The *Elbe*, shortly to be sunk in a collision in the North Sea, proved to be an unfortunate choice. The crew was arrogantly anti-British, and not a single Union Jack hung with the German and American flags dangling from the walls of the dining saloon. Noticing the omission, Conan Doyle and Innes obtained a tablecloth from a steward, painted the Union Jack on it, and on their second night marched into the saloon and hung it up, to the astonishment of their fellow passengers.

When the *Elbe* docked in New York, Major J. B. Pond, loud and daunting, strode into Conan Doyle's stateroom and said, "Dr. Doyle, I presume." It is perhaps fortunate that the response of Conan Doyle to this laborious joke did not go on record. He and Innes sat through a grueling press conference in the first-class lounge, during which a woman reporter from the New York *Herald* insisted on asking him, "Are you influenced by Edgar Allan Poe?"

The silence was like a snapped bowstring. Conan Doyle somehow regained his composure and said, "Oh, immensely. His detective is the best in literature."

The lady was not to be silenced. "You mean," she asked, "except for Sherlock Holmes?"

Conan Doyle froze and got to his feet, towering over her as she looked coldly up at him. "I MAKE NO EXCEPTION!" he roared.

He strode off from the conference, down the gangway, and over to the nearest hansom cab, to attend a performance of Charles Frohman's production of the military play *Shenandoah* at the Academy of Music, on the corner of Fourteenth Street and Irving Place, while Innes was left to make sure the luggage got across by four-wheeler to the annex of the Aldine Club, where they had been offered rooms. The Aldine Club, in a three-story building at 20 Lafayette Place, had been established four years earlier for printers, publishers, authors, and artists. Conan Doyle lectured there on October 3; and at another literary club, the Lotos, at 556 Fifth Avenue, on October 4.

His first public appearance was at the Calvary Baptist Church, which must have brought back memories of the church adjoining his residence in Southsea, on Fifty-seventh Street between Sixth and Seventh Avenues. He made an undistinguished entrance for such a famous writer. He had lost his collar stud and had to borrow one from Major Pond. His clothes awry, he stumbled on his way up to the stage and dropped his notes. Retrieving the scattered pages with some difficulty, his face flushed with embarrassment, he plunged headlong into a speech for which all of his carefully prepared material was now in hopeless disorder. The audience nevertheless found his talk very enjoyable, feeling that he made up in charm for what he lacked in organization and polish, and he received a vigorous round of applause at the end.

A welcome visitor at the Aldine Club was S. S. McClure, publisher and editor of *McClure's Magazine*. McClure, a dynamic man with a flair for spotting talent, had first read *A Study in Scarlet* while on a train from Scotland to London, and although he had not acquired the right to that work, he did later decide to buy the two early series of Holmes stories for publication in the United States. He had paid A. P. Watt twelve pounds a story. Judging the tales, to quote his own remark, "by the solar plexus rather than the brain" he began to syndicate them in American newspapers; but since the usual syndicate story ran five thousand words rather than the eight or ten thousand of the Holmes tales, he had many complaints from editors. Later, in London again, he had bought the American serial rights to *The White Company* for $375; the book had been turned down by every publication except the New York *Sun*.

McClure was without funds when he came to see Conan

Doyle. He had become swamped with business problems while starting his new magazine, and could not pay his English authors. Conan Doyle said cheerily that there was no need to worry; he would invest immediately in the magazine. After lunch at the club the two men strolled over to McClure's office, where Conan Doyle at once wrote out a check for five thousand dollars. McClure wrote in *My Autobiography*, "[It was] exactly the sum we were owing to English authors. When that check was written, it put new life into the office staff. Everyone in the office felt a new vigor and a new hope."

Although Conan Doyle was too discreet to mention it later, there can be no doubt that he was thoroughly ill-treated by Major Pond. Agreeable though the rooms next to the Aldine Club may have been, there can have been no excuse for Pond's not housing his famous author at the Savoy, the Netherland, or another of the grand hotels of the era. Moreover, Pond rushed him into so many speaking engagements that Conan Doyle had no time to ride in the park or otherwise enjoy the city. The tour was no better. He hated the overheated hotels, houses, and railway cars; he lectured in a frock coat buttoned up to the neck so that he could dispense with a waistcoat; and he was appalled by the enthusiastic celebrity hunters in his audiences. The moment a lecture ended, he fled to the wings, and then to a cab he had arranged for with Major Pond. According to an article in *The Bookman*, when the Major told him a society lady wanted him to come to her latest soirée he became hopelessly flustered, saying, "I cannot, I cannot! What do they want of me? Let me go away! I haven't the courage to look all those people in the face."

Conan Doyle was convinced he was a failure as a public entertainer, and long before the end of the tour, which extended no farther west than Chicago, and southeast to Washington, D.C., he had become thoroughly weary of it. But he did like the ordinary people he met, admiring their good health, good manners, and naïve eagerness. At the Palmer House in Chicago, he dined with Eugene Field, and they enjoyed each other's company; he admired the newspaperman and poet, and Field admired him. Innes proved a pleasant companion throughout.

Conan Doyle was greatly pleased, too, with some excellent news from England. Henry Irving had opened in *A Story of Waterloo* at the Princess Theatre, Bristol, on September 21; the audience followed the play, according to Bram Stoker, "with rapt attention and manifest emotion," and accorded this admirable study of pathetic senility a standing ovation. Friends cabled him to this effect, but he was nevertheless astonished when, at a Chicago *Times-Herald* luncheon in his honor, the newspaper's owner and editor, H. H. Kohlsaat, arrived late, extremely flustered, sat down next to him, and told him that he was delighted by the success of the play. "The cables are excellent," Conan Doyle said.

"They are right," Kohlsaat replied. "I was there!"

"You must have arrived on a magic carpet."

"Alas, no," Kohlsaat said. "Only on the S.S. *City of Rome*."

Toward the end of the journey, leaving Innes in New York, he made a Thanksgiving visit to Rudyard and Caroline Kipling at their wooden house, Naulakha, near Brattleboro, Vermont. There must have been a great deal to discuss: cricket, one imagines, for which Kipling also had a passion; and the state of the Empire, which obsessed them both. And one likes to think that they talked about Southsea, where Kipling had spent part of an unhappy childhood. Unfortunately, there was no opportunity to play cricket; but Conan Doyle did demonstrate his skill at golf on a nearby field, watched by interested neighbors who were unfamiliar with the sport. They were an oddly assorted pair as Kipling tried out Conan Doyle's spare club, brought in the old purple golf bag—Kipling with his thin, hairy figure, his myopic, liquid dreamer's eyes peering through spectacles, and Conan Doyle like an amiable sea lion, paddling across the damp turf to shoot a hole in one. Caroline was a delight. Her family, which lived nearby, dropped in to roast chestnuts. And the cook at Naulakha was a New England treasure. "Capital," or some word like it, must have been on Conan Doyle's lips as he took the train to Boston for more appearances.

When he arrived in Boston, the cabbie refused to accept a fare, and instead asked for a ticket to the evening's lecture. "How on earth did you recognize me?" Conan Doyle asked.

The cabman took a deep breath and said, "If you will excuse me, your coat lapels are badly twisted downward, where they have been grasped by the pertinacious New York reporters. Your hair has the Quakerish cut of a Philadelphia barber, and your hat, battered at the brim in front, shows where you have tightly grasped it, in the struggle to stand your ground at a Chicago literary luncheon. Your right shoe has a large block of Buffalo mud just under the instep; the odor of a Utica cigar hangs about your clothing and the overcoat itself shows the slovenly brushing of the porters of the through sleepers from Albany. The crumbs of the doughnut on the top of your waistcoat could only have come there in Springfield."

Conan Doyle looked at him in blank astonishment. The cabman let out a roar of laughter that must have echoed all over Back Bay. He added, "And stenciled on the very end of your walking stick in perfectly plain lettering is the name Conan Doyle."

Arthur liked Boston best of all the places on his trip. The gilded dome of the State House gave him a sense of security and dignity, and the "dear old crooked streets of faded brick," as he described them, reminded him agreeably of London. Depressed by the flat gridiron aridity and harsh clangor of Chicago, disappointed by New York, he at last felt he had reached a haven of civilization. Boston literary society paid little attention to his arrival; but the snobbery did not hurt him. His chief disappointment was that Oliver Wendell Holmes was no longer alive.

By now, he was thinking of getting home to London, and eager to join Louise and the children, as he had promised, for Christmas at the Grand Hotel Belvedere in Davos. Just before they sailed, Arthur and Innes were guests of honor at a farewell dinner at the Lotos Club. Arthur was now considerably more polished as a speaker than he had been at the beginning of the tour. He brought the house down with his story of the Holmesian cabman in Boston. Sir Henry Cunningham, David Christie Murray, Dr. Henry van Dyke, and other prominent figures toasted him heartily, and applauded his description of Chicago as "a half-formed boy always growing out of his clothes." He caused an-

other great burst of laughter when he looked around the whisk-
ered assembly and said, "I feel like Daniel, who, when seeing the
lions approaching him, said, 'There will be no after-dinner speaking for me.'"

As he was packing, Conan Doyle received a telegram from
A. P. Watt advising him that Robert Louis Stevenson had died
in Samoa. He very much regretted that they had never met. He
sailed with Innes on December 8 with a heavy heart, exhausted
and depressed, having been thoroughly irritated by Major Pond's
relentless booming effusiveness. He spent the first few days flat
on his back in his cabin. Luckily, the service and cuisine of one
of the finest ships of the Cunard Line improved his spirits a little,
and gave him a lifelong love of that company's vessels. Innes
braced him up with walks around the decks, and the *Etruria*'s
notorious reputation for being a Jonah—she was extremely accident prone—was not confirmed on this particular voyage. Pipe
organs reverberated through the public rooms; and with his love
of science, Conan Doyle must have been fascinated by the fact
that she was the first transatlantic vessel with refrigeration machinery and electric power. His cabin was fitted up with an unprecedented electric hot-water heater, electric lights, and a special
electric fire in the bulkhead.

While Conan Doyle was in America, a collection of his stories, *Round the Red Lamp*, was published to good reviews in London. The volume included, along with his tales of medical life,
two horror tales written in 1892. In these, the overtly sexual element that is found in the earlier stories has undergone some
changes. There is a hint of more specialized perversion, for example, in the story of *Lot No. 249*. A reptilian specialist in Oriental languages, Edward Bellingham, keeps an Egyptian mummy
in his rooms at Oxford. The mummy is male, and like the priest-
turned-attendant in *The Ring of Thoth*, Bellingham is entangled
with it emotionally. The story shares with so many of Conan
Doyle's horror tales a compulsive, nightmarish quality. Disgusted
by Bellingham's association with the mummy, his healthily mas-
culine associates insist that he burn it, but he does not comply.

The mummy, propelled by Bellingham's will and its own mysterious purposes, achieves the unusual feat of terrorizing Oxford. The climax is representative of Victorian repressiveness: the academic colleagues of the necrophilic professor force themselves into his rooms and destroy the mummy.

Another story, *De Profundis* (the title was later employed by Oscar Wilde for a very different purpose), recalls *The Captain of the "Pole-Star"* as clearly as *Lot No. 249* recalls *The Ring of Thoth*, and once again there is a revision of the sexual theme. A woman loses her husband during a smallpox epidemic, and he is buried at sea. As she travels by ship across a moonlit ocean, he rises from the waves and, his face hideously scarred, stretches out and begs for her to join him. What these stories lack is the clinching logic of the earlier tales. Bellingham, instead of locking himself in the mummy's arms as it is hacked to pieces by his visitors, survives its destruction and that of the precious papyrus which connects him with it, and disappears into the Sudan. The woman whose husband rises, crimson with sores, from the sea, does not correctly follow an obsession and leap from the rails into the moonlit ocean to join him in death.

While Innes went on to Aldershot, Conan Doyle returned to Davos with gifts for all the members of his family, who had assembled there for the Christmas festivities. He had now become locally famous, not just for his writing but for his activities in pioneering ski-running and for having undertaken a dangerous mountain expedition on skis the previous March, between Davos and Arosa. This winter, he was busy helping Norwegian friends to market skis, not generally used in that part of Switzerland at the time, and to devise new and invigorating mountain journeys for tourists.

The Watson in him inspired him to write a new book, *Rodney Stone*, a bouncing romantic novel about boxing in the time of the Prince Regent. The historical detail is rich, but Conan Doyle made a mistake in using a dandy, based on Beau Brummel, as his central figure. He knew nothing of men like this, and was unable to bring to life this affected, slightly absurd creature who becomes "a man" at the end.

The Conan Doyles remained in Switzerland during the summer of 1895, not in Davos, where the weather had become unpredictable, but in Maloja and Caux. Even there, they experienced an unnatural cold spell, and they decided to winter that year in Egypt, which in those days was considered to be, next to Switzerland, the best place for a consumptive. Louise, delighted at the prospect of a change of scene, was permitted by her doctors to travel.

While Louise began packing, aided by two maids, Conan Doyle made a brief trip to England to see George Newnes and Greenhough Smith at *The Strand*. After lunch with them at Simpson's, he had an opportunity to talk at the Newnes offices to *Strand* author Grant Allen, who had suffered from tuberculosis. Allen told him that he need never have gone to Switzerland in the first place. There was a town called Hindhead, in Surrey, which was an ideal retreat for consumptives: the elevation was excellent, the climate mild, and the air crisp and clean. With his usual swiftness of decision, Conan Doyle determined at once to make arrangements to live there. He took a train to Hindhead, made exhaustive inquiries, and bought some acreage with a wonderful view across purple heather and gorse. He rushed across to Southsea to hire an architect—a spiritualist, William Ball, whom he had known during his struggling days there—took him back to Hindhead, enthusiastically drew up a complete set of sketches and plans on the spot, and then, after scarcely drawing breath, went off by train and steamer to Caux to pick up Louise and Lottie for the trip to Egypt.

As if all this activity were not enough, he worked throughout the entire journey on stories of Brigadier Gerard, bombarding Greenhough Smith with notes about their publication, and rummaging through suitcases bulging with works on Napoleon, mostly bought at an auction at Bernard Quaritch of London. Every moment of the journey by ship to Alexandria was occupied with reading and note taking, as he embellished and re-embellished the accounts of Marbot's actual misadventures.

It was an uncomfortable time to arrive in Egypt. There was considerable tension between Abbas Hilmi, the hot-headed and swarthy young Khedive, and the imperious and bristling consul general, Evelyn Baring, Baron Cromer. In several recent head-on collisions, the two men had differed radically on the deployment and personal conduct of British occupation forces along the Nile. Sir Horatio Herbert Kitchener, in command of the forces, was also involved in frequent arguments with the Khedive. Commanding, frosty and aloof, Kitchener bullied his subordinates unmercifully. He was still, after many years, smarting at the shock of Gordon's assassination in Khartoum. His one consuming ambition was to crush the Khalifa, Abdullah el Taashi (or Taaisha), the successor of the Mahdi, whose black-clad dervishes were riding menacingly along the Egyptian border.

Popular feeling in London, and even in the British colony in Cairo, was strongly in favor of a reconquest of the Sudan. By the time the Conan Doyles arrived, Kitchener was becoming something of a popular hero. His carved basalt face and fleshless figure reminded people of Wellington, and his word, in some quarters, was almost law. Both Cromer and the Khedive were most reluctant to plunge Egypt into war at this time. The very question of British sovereignty was being challenged by the French and the Italians. Yet the tide toward war was already beginning to swell. When Gladstone's Liberals were replaced by Lord Salisbury's Conservatives in London, the course of history was inevitable.

Conan Doyle, despite his political position as a Liberal Unionist, agreed with Lord Salisbury and Kitchener that the Sudan should be reconquered. Moreover, it is easy to see that he did not visit Egypt exclusively for the sake of Louise's health. He wanted to show the dervishes a bit of a fight himself.

As an assiduous reader of newspapers and magazines, Conan Doyle was well aware that the Sudan was weakened and ripe for invasion. That country of plains and deserts had recently been visited by plagues suggesting the wrath of a vengeful Allah. Locusts had swept down in rustling gray-green clouds, eclipsing the sun and consuming almost every ear of wheat and blade of grass. Whatever small shoots of grain escaped them had been consumed by millions of mice which rippled across the land like a dirty brown river. By October, 1895, shortly before the Conan Doyles arrival, the Sudan was a wilderness, a shriveled fruit ready for the plucking.

Determined to play his part in the anti-Sudanese movement, Arthur settled with Louise into the Mena House Hotel, almost under the shadow of the pyramids. The building was a microcosm of the Empire. The large hall and the lounges with their potted palms were filled with an ever-changing spectacle of turbaned waiters, khaki-clad officers lounging in their puttees and gun-straps, their faces almost black with the sun and their mustaches waxed at the ends, ladies in rich pink or blue tulle hats and flow-ing silks, and hurrying pages calling out messages. While four women in a musical quartet played popular tunes, flies buzzed about, despite the efforts of whisk-wielding servants. Military faces grew damper by the minute, and ladies were increasingly pale and enervated.

Louise and Lottie, affected by the change of climate, spent most of the time resting; but Arthur reveled in the scene. He sat up late every night to work on his adaptation for the stage of a novel by James Payn—*Halves*, a story of two brothers. He fre-quently visited Cairo, staying overnight at the Gezirah Palace Hotel, built by the late Khedive to accommodate the crowned heads who had arrived to see the opening of the Suez Canal. In front of the hotel, he sat and watched the extraordinary proces-sion of people of many races and creeds walking by. The native men passed in a flock of white-sheeted figures, the women were veiled in deep black.

To travel through the streets, he used a carriage with two *sais*, or runners, always in front of it to clear the way. Gorgeously costumed, they carried gold-tipped staffs which could knock over anyone who blocked the wheels. The bazaars were a wonder: labyrinths of shops under a tracery of ropes which cast a compli-cated network of shadows, the owners sitting cross-legged in front, with their wares piled up on shelves. Craftsmen making jewels, tinware, slippers, and clothes, constantly haggled with every passer-by. There were five hundred mosques in Cairo; at six in the morning the visitor was wakened by five hundred muezzins calling the faithful to prayer. The Fish Market was an astonishment—a puzzle of lanes, opium dens, abject dives, and seedy shops.

Conan Doyle was a frequent visitor to the Turf Club, where he enjoyed the port and chatted with Cromer. He also went to the race track, where he met Kitchener, observing the slash across his face made by a dervish's blade, a detail he later employed in descriptions of certain faces in his stories. He especially relished the Turf Club. Looking across the white-robed waiters and feather whisks, he could sit over a drink and see them all: Rogers, who stamped out cholera; Scott, who reformed the Egyptian laws; Hooker, who ended the locust plague; Wingate, the conqueror; and that already legendary enemy of the Khalifa, Slatin Pasha himself.

Perhaps the most bizarre feature of Cairo at the time was the adoption by the police of the Sherlock Holmes stories as a textbook in detection for their younger recruits. Conan Doyle was not particularly amused by this practice, especially when a young police officer came up to him, examined his face minutely, and said that according to the book, he "showed criminal tendencies."

Christmas in Cairo was agreeably unconventional, with Christmas trees among the fans, and Coptic children singing carols. On January 3, 1896, Arthur, Louise, and Lottie set out for a trip along the Nile. They traveled in a Cook's Tours steamer, the *Nitocris*. Chugging and shuddering, the little paddle boat was surprisingly comfortable, with berths for eight passengers, a crew of sixteen, and delicious food served in the spacious saloon. It was a dangerous journey. Rebellious tribesmen kept riding up to the edge of the Nile and frowning at them menacingly from beneath the shadows of the palm trees.

A long and exhausting trip, which included visits to the tombs of Memphis and Sakkara, the house of the French Egyptologist A. E. Mariette, and the tombs of Beni Hasan, made the voyagers irritable and fretful. Conan Doyle was fascinated by the evidence of animal worship—the carved figures of the sacred hawk, the ibis, the dog, the owl, the goose, the plover, and above all the cat. The cool and somber beauty of the funerary chambers astounded him, but he and Louise and Lottie were horrified by a religion which worshiped death itself. Conan Doyle later wrote, "the idea that the body, the old worn greatcoat that was once wrapped around the soul, should at any cost be preserved is the last word in materialism."

These words were written after a quarter of a century had elapsed; but from remarks made by Conan Doyle closer to the event one can see that he had already warmed even more toward the idea of personal survival after death. However, the question of communication with the dead was still unresolved for him.

The Nile journey continued. The pale scrubby palms, the flat sterile sunlight of Egypt, the steady ripple of the brown water, began to get on Conan Doyle's nerves. After passing the Cataracts, the little party arrived at the last outpost of British and Egyptian power—Wadi Halfa, a dusty, umber little town of winding streets and mud-built houses, where the heat threatened to dry up the eyes like grapes, and the palm fronds hung down the trees like dying birds. Conan Doyle borrowed a pair of field glasses from the local garrison commander, and stared out into the blinding light of the desert. It was the Sudan.

Back in Cairo, Conan Doyle decided to visit the famous Coptic monastery with a great friend, Colonel Henry Lewis, and was dismayed to find that with war just round the corner, he would not be able to obtain the use of a carriage; they had all been commandeered. He appealed to Thomas Cook & Son, which supplied an incredible vehicle. It was a massive, gilded coach, lined with scarlet plush and drawn by two handsome bay horses with crimson plumes, which had been used as a special convey-ance for the Empress Eugénie at the time of the opening of the Suez Canal.* Jolting and swaying on the rough roads and across the rolling sands, this baroque monstrosity with its turbaned coachman was a serious embarrassment to the passengers. Con-vinced he would be a sitting duck for any rebel tribesman who might mistake him for a British sirdar, armed only with a single

---

* It had also been prepared for Napoleon III, but he did not attend the opening.

revolver, Conan Doyle grew angrier and more self-conscious by the hour. The water supply started to run low, and by nightfall the leather bags were empty.

At the end of the day, the golden coach ground to a halt in a sand dune. The Nubian driver jumped down from the seat and looked about in bewilderment, scratching his head. He had no idea where he was. Night fell like a guillotine blade. There was a strange sprinkling of rain. Conan Doyle imagined an unpleasant death in the desert, but luckily he had retained his old seaman's knowledge. The rain cleared, two large cirrus clouds parted, the moon shone clear on the desert, and he looked up instinctively at the stars. The position of the Great Bear told him that they were heading in the wrong direction; carrying a lantern ahead of the coach, he led the driver back on the correct path.

At last the party sighted in the desert the gleam of a friendly lamp, from the tent of a German land surveyor. Seemingly unsurprised by the sight of the famous author of the Sherlock Holmes stories descending from Napoleon III's coach, the German told them where to find the halfway house in which they were supposed to rest for the night. Two hours later, a glow in the dark suggested that they had arrived at their destination; they were shocked to find instead that the driver had made a complete circle, and brought them back to the surveyor's camp. At last, however, they did reach the wooden hut where food and drink awaited them. After a fitful sleep, they recommenced their journey at dawn.

At noon on the second day, the travelers arrived at the Natron Lakes and saw the Coptic monastery looming up ahead of them. It was a disappointment. The building was filthy, the world-famous library scattered all over the unswept floors, and the abbot was too ill to show them around. Conan Doyle, drawing on his medical training, palpated the abbot's chest, and prescribed medicine, which he later sent from Cairo.

Back in the Egyptian capital, he learned that war had been declared on the Sudan. Troops in sun helmets and gun holsters were marching through the streets of Cairo as his golden coach rolled by, bugles were sounding, and Union Jacks waved from the rooftops. Turned down for military service by Kitchener and Cromer, he would have offered to write about the crisis for *The Strand*, but his correspondence with Greenhough Smith shows that he was fighting one of his frequent battles with the magazine. He had been infuriated by Smith's questioning of some details of *Rodney Stone*, brushing aside charges of inaccuracy which were later reasserted by Max Beerbohm; and when Smith let slip some typographical errors in the first number of the serialization, he was so angry that he temporarily refused to respond to any further requests for work. ". . . surely the *Strand* has had enough of me by now?" he asked in one letter.

Instead, Conan Doyle cabled *The Westminster Gazette*, in London, asking for a job as war correspondent. His request was granted by return cable. He and Colonel Lewis went by camel to the Sudanese border, since all the Cook's river boats had been commandeered. They found that their arrival was premature. At dinner at headquarters Kitchener explained that it would be several weeks before the reconquest of the Sudan would be possible. He told them that the chief reason for the campaign was not simply to crush the Khalifa but to make sure that the water supply of the Nile basin was protected from the rapid incursion of the Belgian Congolese and French forces.

Conan Doyle would dearly have loved to stay on at Wadi Halfa until Kitchener was ready to begin his onslaught on Dongola. But he knew that Louise could not survive the approaching spring heat of Egypt. He must have felt more circumscribed than he had ever been. To his sexual frustration could now be added the frustration of another expression of his manhood—tangling with the dervishes in a war. In addition, he would have some highly embarrassing explanations to make to the editor of *The Westminster Gazette*, for which he had written little. He probably felt more like Brigadier Gerard than anybody else as he took his uncomfortable camel ride back to Cairo.

He returned with Louise and Lottie to England in May, 1896, only to find to his increased disgust that the Hindhead house was still not ready. Since the house at South Norwood had been sold through friends in his absence, he and his family would have to put up at a guesthouse. His chief consolation at this difficult time was his reunion with his children, Mary and Kingsley, both of whom were growing up healthily under the care of their maternal grandmother and their paternal aunts; and he was pleased by the good reviews of *The Exploits of Brigadier Gerard*, a publication in book form of the first series of the stories. He wrote, rather desultorily, another book with a Napoleonic theme, *Uncle Bernac*, which turned out to be an artistic failure, reflecting his mood of depression and impatience at the time.

He was altogether more at ease in a handsome and lively adventure story, *The Tragedy of the "Korosko,"* based on the Nile paddle-boat journey, in which he imagined a party similar to his own being captured by dervishes. The observation of the characters is shrewd but affectionate, the evocation of Egypt is impeccable, and the final scenes are stirring. He matched the best colonial adventure writing in this small epic of courage and survival. It was a great success both in its serialization in *The Strand* (it encouraged George Newnes to make a similar, and happily less dangerous, journey up the Nile on the *Nitocris* in 1898), and in book form.

During several quiet months with his family at Moorlands, a pleasant guesthouse in Hindhead, Conan Doyle was depressed and run-down. He was short-tempered and often terrified his children. Even cricket and golf and billiards seemed to have lost their savor. It was a dark period; and the frustration of his misadventures in Egypt still prominent in his thoughts, must have rankled him fiercely.

But in the midst of his despair, a surprising event took place. In March, he wrote to his mother* to say that something extraordinary had happened. He had fallen in love with an exquisite young woman in her twenties. Jean Leckie lived in Glebe House, Blackheath,† in London, with her parents. Scottish, she was a direct descendant of Sir Walter Scott's immortal Rob Roy.

---

* He continued throughout his life to seek his mother's advice on every matter, writing over 1,500 letters to her home, Masongill Cottage.

† Blackheath is the location of Torrington Lodge in *The Norwood Builder*; also Watson played Rugby for Blackheath, as is indicated in *The Sussex Vampire*.

This fact, as well as her beauty, appealed deeply to Conan Doyle's romantic sensibility. But another detail cannot be overlooked. For Sherlock Holmes, Irene Adler had been "the" woman. She had combined cleverness with great skill as an opera singer. It is pleasant to note that Jean Leckie was a well-trained opera singer. She had not sung professionally, but she had been taught expertly in Germany, and was a skilled mezzo-soprano.

She had soft brown hair, an exquisite forehead, a long, grave, delicately chiseled face, with sadly reflective, tender eyes that often seemed to be looking at something far away. Her nose was straight, her mouth soft, her jaw line firm and rounded. Her neck was one of her loveliest features; it was long and slender, and her shoulders sloped beautifully. She had a delightful speaking voice, and a strange, magnetic attraction for animals and birds.

In character, she was warm, dedicated to her work, quiet, and reserved. She was discreet and hated gossip. She was practical and sensible, and lacked, at that time, Conan Doyle's mystical bent and leaning toward spiritualism. Unlike Louise, she had an exceptionally fine intellect, read extensively, and was a skilled conversationalist. At the same time, she was emphatically feminine, and despite the fact that she was a quintessential Victorian woman in believing that men should be worshiped, she was not uncritical or entirely bland. Conan Doyle fell in love with her at first sight, and she with him. From that moment on, she was the center of his life, and he was the center of hers; no power on earth could ever drive them apart. Their relationship was one of the most extraordinary in the history of literature. They almost never quarreled. Their differences were slight and easily settled, and at first involved only the question of spiritualism, of which she was initially afraid, although subsequently she was converted to his point of view.

Jean trusted and believed in Conan Doyle completely. She brought him a happiness he had never known before, and would know with no one else. But their relationship had to survive great suffering. From the very first moment, he told her that he would not divorce his wife. He would never hurt the sweet, simple, and devoted Louise, and emphatically would never betray her sexually.

For the rest of Louise's life he would neither marry nor sleep with Jean. Jean accepted this situation; indeed, she had no wish to change his views. Despite later pressure to consummate the relationship from his sister Connie and her husband, E. W. Hornung, he and Jean staunchly maintained their code of honor. His mother, with her romantic ideal of the pure and glittering knights of yore, supported him wholeheartedly in this position. The family agreed that Louise must never know. As far as we can tell, she never did.

The effect on his health, the sheer pressure on a man in his prime, with normal desires, was crushing. He began to head toward a nervous breakdown. Denied sexual fulfillment with the two women he loved, he suffered from racking insomnia. His nightmares took him into landscapes more terrifying than any he had conceived in his tales. He tried to wear himself out by playing golf and cricket, but was unsuccessful. He attended more séances, at one of them contacting a cricketer who had been killed in one of Kitchener's skirmishes, and again visited a "haunted" house with Scott and Podmore, hearing deafening rattles in the night, which he later believed to have been caused by the spirit of a child who had been buried in the garden.

6

TYPHOID IN BLOEMFONTEIN

IN OCTOBER, 1897, the house at Hindhead was at long last finished, and the Conan Doyles and their two young children could move in. The house was named Undershaw, not in whimsical reference to George Bernard Shaw, but because it stood under a rich interlacing of branches at the back, and "shaw" was an old word for "forest." Undershaw was set near the top of a ridge, well away from the road and considerably below the road level. Carriages had to roll down a 150-foot winding drive, densely lined with bushes and trees, which led to a forecourt at the western end of the house, and thence to the front door. The main façade faced south, and looked over a specially laid lawn tennis court; the garden sloped steeply down an incline, with croquet hoops on the flat portion, and three acres of forested ground below. Beyond lay the beautiful Nutcombe Valley. The view was, as it remains today, one of the loveliest in that part of England.

The house was in two stories of red brick and tile, with gables, the servants' rooms in effect taking it up to three stories at the western end. On the Conan Doyles' specific instructions, the upper stories had been faced with red tiles, nostalgically matching those at South Norwood. Lightly timbered alcoves enclosed both the front door and another door in the southern façade; the struts and boards were painted pure white. There were large bay windows under the easternmost gable; the one on the ground floor looked out on the valley from the large hall, while the one above it looked out from the master bedroom.

The drawing room was in the southeast corner of the ground floor. It was handsomely wood-paneled, spacious and light-filled; a high, fitted shelf running all around the room held souvenirs of the Arctic, Switzerland, America, and Egypt. The fireplace, flanked by wing chairs, was so deep-set that it formed a cozy alcove. The billiard room was enormous, just as Conan Doyle had asked the architect-designer to make it, and filled the northeast corner of the house. It was very dark, and even by daylight had to be illuminated by electric lamps, which sent fans of light over the green baize. The front hall was magnificent. It stretched up to the full height of the house on the southern front, diminishing to one story on the northern. The stained-glass windows, containing many heraldic shields of the Doyle family (his mother was horrified to discover that by an oversight hers was not among them) were finely wrought, and are still intact today. On the doors, beaten-brass fingerboards still carry Conan Doyle's monogram. Since Louise now suffered from extremely poor health, and her hands were arthritic, all the door handles in the house were designed on the push-pull principle, so that they did not have to be turned.

Conan Doyle was fascinated endlessly by the view—a Gothic valley reminiscent of Feldkirch's setting without the grim mountains, with gorse and bracken, mown and unmown grass, and rolling lines of hills far away. The library was in chaos within a week. It was filled not only with the owners' vast accumulation of books, including one of the finest collections of philosophical works in private hands, but also with cricket bats and tennis rakuets, purple golf bags and a random assortment of cricket and tennis balls, guns leaning against the walls, trout-fishing rods and hooks and bait jumbled together higgledy piggledy everywhere. The grounds were equally untidy. They were strewn with the shattered fragments of clay pigeons left from sporting afternoons; and rather threateningly, on the lawn to welcome visitors, lay five large, rusty old bird traps with iron teeth.

The Conan Doyles stocked the stables with four stallions and two saddle mares, one of which they frequently entered for gymkhanas at Hindhead. The lawn tennis court was tramped almost to rubble and very clumsily rolled most of the time. When it rained, mud slides were frequent.

After all the furniture had been moved in from storage, including some heirlooms from his grandfather's house in Cambridge Terrace and from his uncle's house in the Finborough Road, Conan Doyle settled down to complete a final draft of his play based on James Payn's *Halves*, and in an attempt to pacify a still-furious public, decided at last to give them a play built around Sherlock Holmes.

When people asked if he was "resurrecting" Holmes, he angrily rejected the idea. He made it clear that the new work dealt with an early and previously unrecorded episode in the great detective's life, and that he would also revive Moriarty for the occasion. He would prove that he did not "hate" Holmes, as people kept saying. Actually, he was at once fascinated and repelled by Holmes; he saw too much of himself in the character to be quite at ease with it.

Conan Doyle wanted the great Herbert Beerbohm Tree to play Moriarty, and went to Tree's house to read him the entire work. Tree said, "Capital! I will play Moriarty *and* Holmes!"

"Wouldn't that be a trifle difficult?" Conan Doyle asked him. "After all, they appear on the stage at the same time."

Tree brushed off the problem like a wasp from his jacket. "I could play Holmes *in a beard*," he said. It is needless to add that Conan Doyle decided not to cast him for any part in the play.

A. P. Watt felt that the script needed more work; eventually, a revised draft was mailed to Charles Frohman, the leading theatrical producer in New York. Conan Doyle was pleased. He recalled very clearly his pleasure in Frohman's *Shenandoah* at the Academy of Music in New York. Frohman left for England immediately to discuss the production of the play. Small and frog-like in a big astrakhan coat, Frohman impressed Conan Doyle with the extraordinary power of his personality, the energy that pulsed out of his bulging eyes, the swift movements of his body on its stocky bowlegs. They got along famously. Finally, Conan Doyle said, "It will be perfectly all right, Mr. Frohman. But I make one stipulation. You are a genius of the romantic production. There must be no love business in *Sherlock Holmes*."

Both men agreed that the perfect choice for the part would be William Gillette, the great American actor whom Conan Doyle had seen that summer in London in his own very distinguished play, *Secret Service*. Tall, strikingly handsome, with aquiline features and a well-knit figure, Gillette could easily convert himself, not into the cadaverous detective that Conan Doyle had envisaged, but into the image of Holmes which the world knew from Sidney Paget's drawings.* Back in New York, Frohman sent the play to Gillette, who was on tour. Gillette reconstructed it, providing a plot which was essentially a cunning version of *A Scandal in Bohemia*, but contained also elements of several other stories, among them *The Copper Beeches* and *The Final Problem*. He also included aspects of the great Staunton case, which apparently had given the Ma'am the idea for *The Copper Beeches;* the Stauntons had been accused of kidnaping a pathetic young girl and starving her to death.

In Gillette's version, a mysterious Highly Placed Person engages Holmes to secure some highly embarrassing love letters which, in the wrong hands, would imperil his forthcoming marriage. They have been in the possession of a young girl who has died, leaving them to her sister, Alice Faulkner. An evil man and wife, determined to obtain the letters, are keeping the girl locked up in a secret room. Professor Moriarty would like to have the letters in order to destroy the Highly Placed Person. Holmes, narrowly escaping destruction in a sinister gas chamber in Stepney, finally traps Moriarty, who has disguised himself as a cabbie. And Holmes falls in love with Alice Faulkner.

Conan Doyle on the whole liked Gillette's revision of the play, finding it a rich improvement on his original work, but greatly aggravated by the "love" ending. He did want to meet Gillette in person before making a final commitment. Gillette crossed the Atlantic in May, 1898. Conan Doyle went out in the family trap to greet him at the train station. He was astonished to see descending to the platform a figure dressed in a deerstalker caps† and an ulster, and carrying a silver-topped cane. This man took out a large magnifying glass and minutely inspected Conan

---

* After Paget's premature death, illustrators of the stories, led by Frederic Dorr Steele, tended to base their portrayal of Holmes on Gillette's face and figure.

† An invention of Sidney Paget's. In the stories, Holmes wears a "cap" and a "traveling cap" but not a "deerstalker."

Doyle's face with it. "Unquestionably an author," he said. Conan Doyle's laugh was thunderous. He wrung Gillette's hand and put him in the trap, and the pair of them, no doubt causing great amusement on the way, rode home to an astonished family.

Temperamentally, Gillette was ideal for the part. He did not have to pretent to be taciturn, cold, reserved, and sardonically logical. His humor was acrid and mocking. The opposite sex was no longer of interest to him. With his extraordinary looks and great fame he could have had his choice of women, but his heart had been broken by the death of his wife, the beautiful actress Helen Nichols. He was as eccentric as Holmes. He was a night owl. After a performance, he would take long walks across the city, no matter what the weather, with his gray hat pulled down over his eyes. Frequently, he was discovered by police, sleeping on park benches in the snow in the small hours. On other occasions, he would come home at dawn, soaked with rain. He divided his time between a bizarre log cabin in the mountains of North Carolina and a houseboat.

His cruel logic, extraordinary knowledge of books, and interest in spiritualism—the result of his bereavement—made him a man after Conan Doyle's own heart. They shared, too, a love of miniature railways. Conan Doyle had built a small monorail in the garden at Undershaw, and Gillette was later to construct his own model railway at the castle he designed in Connecticut.

After their meeting, Gillette went back to America, continued a tour with *Secret Service,* and lost his only copy of his own *Sherlock Holmes* in a fire at a San Francisco hotel; since Conan Doyle had also lost his own copy Gillette rewrote the play from scratch, adding a new ending. This was subsequently used only in the French production. In this version, Holmes puts a plaster bust of himself in a window. Moriarty shoots it with an air gun, goes in to inspect the body, and is seized. Conan Doyle later adopted this idea for the story *The Empty House.*

Gillette was always fond of telling how at one stage of the collaboration with Conan Doyle he had cabled him from New York: MAY I MARRY HOLMES? Conan Doyle had cabled back: MARRY HIM OR MURDER HIM OR DO WHAT YOU LIKE WITH HIM.

During the last three years of the dying century, the opposing halves of Conan Doyle's personality became more combative. The Watson in him found expression as he rode to hounds along with Jean Leckie—though he came to disapprove of the sport—played cricket, sailed over Surrey in a balloon, rejoiced in Kitchener's crushing of the Khalifa at the battle of Omdurman, took pleasure in Dewey's destruction of the Spanish fleet at Manila, and gloried in Queen Victoria's Diamond Jubilee, with the potentates of the world paying homage, and millions lining the streets of a flower-decked London to watch her small black-and-silver figure in the open landau ride by. Watson-Doyle played with W. G. Grace at Lord's, and on one occasion scored a century—a hundred runs in a single turn at bat. At past forty, he played soccer. The Holmes in him also gave rise to multifarious activities: he took a passionate interest in murder cases; puffed away at a variety of pipes; examined the properties of certain poisons; studied minutely the latest developments in science—the Curies' discovery of radium and polonium, Ramsay and Travers' discovery of neon, krypton, and xenon, the development of the safety match, and early experiments with steam-driven automobiles and flying machines.

Conan Doyle worked as furiously as ever. He finally finished *Halves*, and it was presented with modest success on the stage. He wrote *A Duet*, a sympathetic novel, at once silly and touching, in the duologue form—filled with sweet glimpses of his marriage to Louise.

As always, though, he was at his best in the horror story. This was a rich period for the tale of terror, with some of the finest work of H. G. Wells and M. P. Shiel being published, and Conan Doyle created quite a stir with his contributions to the genre. In *The Story of the Brazilian Cat* (1898), the heir to a fortune is trapped by his sinister cousin in a cage in a sober country home; the other occupant of the cage is an alarming jungle feline with phosphorescent eyes, which toys with its victim before attempting to tear him to pieces. A touch of the perverse makes the story work: despite himself the prisoner is drawn to the animal, finding its supple, muscular figure painfully alluring. It is clear that the cat is an unconscious symbol of sexuality, at once menacing and attractive, primitive and releasing.

In *The King of the Foxes*, revised in 1903 from a draft written in 1888, Jean Leckie's favorite sport, fox hunting, is given a bizarre literary treatment. At the end of an exciting chase, the "fox" jumps out at the hounds; it is actually a Siberian wolf, a creature the size of a donkey, with a huge gray head, dripping fangs, and tapering jaws, which savages the hounds and sends them squealing for cover. Both these creatures, monsters stalking through a dignified English country scene, were to be echoed in the even more horrendous form of the Hound of the Baskervilles.

Some stories written in this period suggest more extreme and rarefied terrors. In *The Story of the Beetle Hunter* (1898), the entomologist Lord Linchmere and his demented brother-in-law Sir Thomas Rossiter live in a country house crammed with countless specimens of dead beetles, in display cases, which they have brought back from the jungles. The insects suggest a primeval horror which these aristocrats cannot escape. Indeed, Rossiter, obeying some atavistic instinct, prowls through the beetle-filled rooms at night and attempts to smash his relative's head with a hammer. In *The Story of the Japanned Box* (1899), a crazed knight, bereaved by the death of his wife, keeps her dying words on a tin record in a small black portable phonograph, relaying her voice deafeningly through his house at night.

The supernatural is dealt with more alarmingly in the story *Playing with Fire* (1900). In this extraordinary work, the author suggests that beasts, like humans, may survive the grave. At a straightforward séance in London, with little more expected than conventional table raps and flying tambourines, the sitters are dismayed when a vibrating luminous fog swirls through the room and a mysterious form materializes through the mist:

Some huge thing hurtled against us in the darkness, rearing, stamping, smashing, springing, snorting. The table was splintered. We were scattered in every direction. It clattered and scrambled among us, rushing with horrible energy from one corner of the room to the other.

This monstrous unicorn seems to come from the same stable as the great horses of the Apocalypse. And indeed the horsemen were riding when Conan Doyle wrote the story in the autumn of 1899. War was breaking out in South Africa, as the British Empire was challenged by its most vigorous adversary since Sher Ali, of the Second Afghan War.

At her Diamond Jubilee, Queen Victoria had pressed an electric button which released to her subjects around the world a telegraph message expressing her eternal love and good will. Her act can be seen as symbolic of the dawning of a new age, with scientific methods sweeping away the old era. The Boer War, which erupted in October, 1899, was the last of the great conflicts fought with old-fashioned weapons. And it was the first indication of the development of serious fissures in the British Empire, which would finally undermine it. An examination of that war today shows none of the combatants in a particularly good light. It was inspired by greed for territorial rights, and marked by muddle and incompetence on both sides. Its climax was reached with the thoughtless ill-treatment by Kitchener of thousands of women and children who were herded into concentration camps, where they died from epidemic disease.

The war began largely because Joseph Chamberlain, the British Colonial Secretary, was determined to establish British supremacy in South Africa, sweeping aside the claims of France and Germany, and overruling the Boer Dutch colonists and their leaders. Paul Kruger, the President of the South African Republic, opposed the British, insisting that the Boers had territorial authority which they would not allow to be usurped. Cecil Rhodes, of the British South Africa company, who was Prime Minister of the Cape Colony, sought control of areas which were of value to his commercial and colonial interests. In 1895, he unwisely encouraged, and then unsuccessfully tried to stop the Jameson Raid, in which L. S. Jameson led a catastropic attempt at a guerrilla action against Kruger. Convinced that Britain meant to annex the Transvaal, Kruger formed a defensive alliance with the Orange Free State.

In 1897, the British High Commissioner, Sir Alfred Milner, demanded civil rights for the *Uitlanders*, or British settlers, which

Kruger refused to provide. Kruger's inconsiderate attitude toward the British population, and Milner's aggressive attitude, heated the situation to the boiling point. The Bloemfontein Conference of May 31–June 5, 1899, brought Milner and Kruger into a wholly unreasonable confrontation. Jan Christiaan Smuts, States Attorney of the South African Republic, tried to arrange a compromise: the *Uitlanders* would be entitled to conduct business and enjoy civil rights, provided that Britain withdrew her territorial claims within a fixed number of years. Milner turned down this proposition, the conference broke up in near disorder, and the drift into war was inevitable.

At the outbreak of hostilities, in October, 1899, Britain was severely outnumbered in South Africa. She had only 27,000 troops in the area, while the troops of Kruger and his allies numbered 48,000. British morale was raised after initial misgivings by a rapid influx of volunteers and by the arrival in Capetown on October 31 of General Sir Redvers Buller as commander in chief in the field. But Buller turned out to be a great disappointment to everyone. Outclassed by General Louis Botha, he was crushed in a series of bloody defeats in December. Somewhat disgraced, he was demoted and supplanted on December 16 by the remarkable Lord Roberts, a veteran of the Second Afghan War. As Roberts' second-in-command, Horatio Herbert, now Lord Kitchener, proved to be an excellent choice. The post, a reward for his suppression of the dervishes in the Sudan, was greeted with wide approval by the British press.

Conan Doyle, delighted by Kitchener's appointment, nevertheless shared the general feeling of gloom which hung along with the heavy fogs over England that winter. News of Buller's defeat at the front had upset many plans for gaudy celebration of the coming of the new century. It was a century born deformed. The *Times* of January 1, 1900, did not announce the arrival of a new era with glowing anticipation, but instead published a long and damning editorial, condemning by inference Buller and his general staff for their mishandling of the war, and finding praise only for the British soldier under arms. It was felt by several papers (the London *Times* took a rather more sanguine view) that the war was going to ruin the British economy, even though 1899 had brought a surplus in the Exchequer of over £1,500,000.

The last weeks of the dying century offered a remarkable scene in London. Thousands of volunteers obtained leave from their positions of employment and lined up outside the enlistment offices. At the Guildhall, large and resonant, jostling men begged for an opportunity to fight the Boers. Conan Doyle, at forty, realized he stood little chance of obtaining a commission, but since several of his friends were serving in the Middlesex Yeomanry, he took a train to the enlistment center in Hounslow and stood for hours in a queue waiting to be interviewed. The colonel in charge, who had apparently never read a book or an newspaper, had not heard of Conan Doyle, and dismissed him without a second glance because of his age and because he was somewhat overweight.

He returned to Hindhead feeling defeated and profoundly depressed. But a few days later a note arrived which cheered him greatly. The wealthy John Langman had decided to send out to Lord Roberts under the general management of his son Archie, a lieutenant in the Middlesex Yeomanry, a medical unit and traveling hospital consisting of a hundred beds, a marquee, thirty-five tents, and the best medical supplies available. The Langman Hospital, as it came to be known, had as its physician-in-chief the distinguished Robert O'Callaghan, of the Royal College of Surgeons, who was accompanied by two Harley Street doctors, Charles Gibbs and H. J. Scharlieb. The note, from John Langman, offered Conan Doyle the job of senior physician. It also indicated that he and his colleagues would be supported by a hand-picked team of fifty men, including ward-masters, cooks, stewards, and twenty-five orderlies.

Conan Doyle was delighted at the offer, and accepted immediately; Archie Langman was an old friend. He traveled to London at once to discuss the matter with Archie over lunch at the Reform Club. Louise and the children had already been sent off to Naples for the winter. With Major Alfred Wood, his secretary, Conan Doyle began practicing with a rifle, using a special sighting device he had developed himself with the aid of a gun-

smith, experimenting with expanding bullets, and firing so enthusiastically across a lake near Hindhead that he all but shot
down some of the local inhabitants.

Burly and bustling, he joined the Langman Hospital contingent for final inspection at the headquarters of the St. George's
Rifles in Davies Street. The Duke of Cambridge examined the
men, who were dressed in safari hats with small plumes at the
sides, and rather unflattering, loose-fitting special uniforms. The
Duke was extremely uncomplimentary about the deportment and
clothing of the unit, putting Conan Doyle in a thoroughly bad
temper as he and his colleagues set off on their journey to the
Cape.

He sailed with the Langman Hospital on the P. & O. liner
Oriental from Prince Albert Dock on February 28, 1900. As the
unit marched to the ship gangway, brass bands sounded on the
pier. Women ran alongside the columns of soldiers, clutching at
their sleeves and pressing mementos into their hands. Snow swirled
over the decks, followed freakishly by a mixture of rain and hail.
Both Jean Leckie and the Ma'am came to see him off. Jean Leckie
kissed him quickly and ran into the crowd on the wharf. His
parting with the Ma'am was tense. She was furious about the war,
believing that it was inspired only by greed (not an imperceptive
conclusion), and she resented her son's serving in it. He responded
by declaring that his was a knightly quest, and pointing to his
butler, Cleeve, he referred to him as his "squire." She was not in
the least amused.

The crossing to South Africa was on the whole uneventful.
The Langman Hospital and the Royal Scots Regiment formed
rival cricket teams, playing on deck until they lost the cricket ball
overboard. At Cape Verde, they managed to borrow another for
a full-dress landfall game. At night, on swinging decks under the
moon, Conan Doyle gave lectures on his favorite subjects, and
most popularly on Sherlock Holmes.

With all aboard in good spirits, the *Oriental* steamed into a
sun-drenched Capetown on March 21, 1900. Conan Doyle arrived to golden news. Roberts and Kitchener had succeeded in
reversing the unfavorable course of the war. Roberts' inspired
generalship had outmatched Botha's, and his personal legend had

seemingly unmanned the Boers. He and his generals had swept the field, marching in a glorious and unbroken line all the way up to Bloemfontein, capital of the Orange Free State.

While waiting for orders, the Langman Hospital was quartered at the Mount Nelson Hotel, in Capetown. Conan Doyle and Archie Langman paid an official visit to the Boer concentration camps, observing the tight, famished faces behind the barbed wire, passing among the tents and rough-hewn huts dispensing medicine and bluff good cheer. They also visited the famous leper island off Capetown. On March 26, the team was ordered to sail with the *Oriental* to East London. From there, they took a long and tedious train journey to Bloemfontein, arriving tired and dusty on April 2.

Bloemfontein in 1900 was a depressing place. It was a sterile, sprawling, almost featureless jumble of tin-roofed, verandahed public buildings, gimcrack bungalows, and scattered tents, tossed down in the olive-green veldt like trash dropped from the sky. Only clumps of grass, vivid splashes of bougainvillea, and the golden bullets of mimosa on either side of the Orange River broke the dusty monotony of the scene. Union Jacks hung sadly from the breezeless pepper-trees, and little groups of soldiers sat, sweating, in the feeble shade, their beef and biscuit boxes laid out, as they waited for billeting orders. Conan Doyle found windows crudely barricaded with nailed-down wooden planks, the shops drab and virtually devoid of merchandise, almost no lights at night, gas cut off, and paraffin oil and foodstuffs at a premium.

He was somewhat cheered by the military club which provided at least a small source of pleasure. Officers could enjoy books, magazines several months out of date, and billiards at a shabby green-baize table, and they could risk the sun on the wide cast-iron balcony. The day after he arrived, a brass band played military airs in the drill square outside the barracks, a Union Jack specially sent by Lady Roberts was ceremoniously hoisted up a pole, and the Royal Scots and the Langman Hospital unit joined in a parade to the sound of bagpipe and drum.

Conan Doyle, dressed in regulation digger hat, shoulder hol-

ster, and puttees, purposefully set about the task of assisting his
immediate superiors in setting up the field hospital in the pavilion
and grounds of the Ramblers' Cricket Club. Within three days,
the conversion was complete, and Red Cross flags fluttered from
the observation tower and from both ends of the wrought-iron
veranda. Tents mushroomed across the grounds. Everything
seemed ideal to receive the wounded troops from the front line,
except for one detail. There was no water.

Conan Doyle was horrified to learn that the Boers, only
twenty miles northwest of Bloemfontein, had seized the water-
works, and that Roberts, in his headlong rush to conquest, had
neglected to delegate a battalion to secure the water supply. With
this source cut off, Conan Doyle's military superiors had no alternative but to turn to the ancient native wells near the city.
These were contaminated, and within a week a raging typhoid
epidemic was sweeping through the city. The result was that the
Langman Hospital had to take up the overflow from the two
small hospitals in Bloemfontein. The number of patients, in a hospital equipped for three hundred, swelled to over a thousand.
The physician-in-chief, Robert O'Callaghan, threw up his hands
in despair and returned to London. With Gibbs and Scharlieb,
Conan Doyle was left in charge. He and his team were faced
with a terrifying prospect. The patients were unable to sleep.
Rose-colored spots erupted on their chests and stomachs, watery
pimples broke out on their skin, their tongues became dry and
colored black or crimson, the gums rotted, stools poured out like
green-pea soup, and delirium, exhaustion and death inevitably followed. There was still no fresh water.

The stench, as excrement soaked through the beds and onto
the pavilion floors and the parched grass of the cricket field, became unendurable. In the pavilion, a grotesque stage set, for a
Gilbert and Sullivan operetta, provided a strange, incongruous
touch. Attracted by offal and turds, thousands of flies swarmed
in, crawling over the faces of the sick, invading their mouths,
eyes, and ears, and smothering their food and drink.

At first, with invincible British phlegm, Conan Doyle tried
to sustain morale by organizing rival soccer teams among the

medical personnel. Predictably, this gesture soon proved futile. Fifteen of the Langman Hospital team came down with typhoid, despite inoculations on board the *Oriental*. Sixty victims a day had to be buried in shallow trenches, wrapped in hospital blankets because there were no coffins. Even Conan Doyle, with his heroic hardiness, came down with a mild version of the fever. One morning, while he was riding out to breathe for a moment the pure air of the veldt, the wind changed suddenly and the smell of the hospital reached him and made him vomit. Giddy and weak, he made his way back to the Ramblers' Club. That evening, he was bedridden.

At last, a medical relief contingent made it possible for him to take a brief leave of absence. Characteristically, instead of going to the coast for a complete rest, he elected to join a reconnaissance expedition. He felt revived by a long and rather pointless march out of Bloemfontein. The air was sweet and the rain soft, the sunshine was wonderful after the endless hellish nights at the Ramblers' Club. The distant rumble of cannon fire, the stutter of snipers' bullets, vultures wheeling with their strange rag wings, and cattle with their rib cages exposed, all merged in an irresistible chiaroscuro, a *son et lumière* of war. He enjoyed the weight of his rifle on his strong back, the feeling of the ammunition at his belt, the blanket, and the water bottle, which was filled with fresh water now that a water tower had been recaptured. His stallion was a fine beast; he gloried in the sense of being a man among men.

He returned to Bloemfontein much improved in health. Despite recurring bouts of dysentery, he continued with his work until he was released from active service in July, 1900, after only three months of field duty. An injury suffered in a soccer match between the doctors and a local team worried him considerably as he rode up to Pretoria, after his relief arrived, to give Lord Roberts a full report on the conduct of the Langman Hospital, which had been somewhat criticized in the South African, British, and American press.

Roberts was a formidable figure. Brought back from his retirement for his triumphant campaigns, he was a crusty veteran, small and white-whiskered, with a harsh red face and fierce eyes. His voice thrust home like a saber. He cross-questioned Conan Doyle unmercifully, trying to determine whether there was any foundation for the charges of incompetence and insufficient hygiene at the hospital. Conan Doyle provided a spirited defense, and Roberts was completely satisfied by his explanation; but Conan Doyle was greatly irritated by the meeting.

As he left for England on July 11, aboard the S.S. *Briton,* it was obvious that the course of the war had been entirely reversed. The relief of the British siege victims at Mafeking, on May 17–18, had been greeted with great rejoicing in Capetown and London; Johannesburg had fallen to the British troops on May 31. Conan Doyle carried back brightly lit memories to add to his writer's store: Kitchener, coldly detached and proud on a great bay horse, glimpsed in dusty Pretoria riding past the pepper-trees; Lord Roberts, short and grumpy, his pale-blue eyes filmed over with age, still needling his victim; the blare of a brass band and the flourish of the Colors; the flat, sun-baked streets and drab squares of South African towns; copper statues, weeping green rivers in the rain; the veldt, like the rippling flesh of a huge animal; and like a musical theme, subsuming all others, the mingled cries of the typhoid victims giving voice to their terror of death.

Back at Undershaw, Conan Doyle worked day and night on *The Great Boer War,* his history of the war in South Africa, revising it weekly as new reports came in. He also wrote more of the Brigadier Gerard stories, some of them containing episodes picked up from his fellow travelers on the ships to and from the Cape. He began work building a special electric generator in the garden at Undershaw, and enveloped himself in his family. Louise had not experienced a relapse, and seemed to be getting along famously. He saw Jean Leckie whenever he could without his wife's finding out. And Kingsley, his son, was the apple of his eye. An especially good-looking boy, with close-cropped fair hair, perfect features, and flawless physique, Kingsley was becoming an expert cricketer and soccer player like his father. Arthur's younger sister Dodo had married a pleasant, ugly young clergyman, Cyril Angell; Lottie, who had gone out to India as a governess, had married the dashing Captain Leslie Oldham, of the Royal Engineers. Only the Ma'am proved a thorn in Arthur's side. A furious presence, brandishing an ear trumpet or hurtling headlong down country lanes in her pony and trap, she continued to bombard him with criticisms of the Boer War, his interest in spiritualism, and his bringing up of the children.

His involvement in the Boer War had sharpened Conan Doyle's early concern with politics. He had long been a Liberal Unionist—a Liberal in his principles but a firm believer that Home Rule for Ireland was not advisable. The Liberal Unionist party, fighting a somewhat rear-guard action for survival, had long since been forced to join with the Conservatives. Conan Doyle was approached by several members of the party to run as a candidate in the forthcoming "Khaki Election," in which he would compete against a Liberal representative in Scotland. Since he was Scottish by birth, this was thought to be an appropriate venture for him. However, he postponed a definite response.

The Liberal anti-Government position was that the war could only be described as a disgraceful exhibition of incompetence and greed, inspired by Joseph Chamberlain's ambition. Conan Doyle's view was that Kruger's refusal to grant British settlers full voting rights had provoked the hostilities, and that Roberts and Kitchener had done battle to protect those settlers. Unfortunately, his position was weakened at the end of the war by the fact that Kitchener was severely criticized for his scorched-earth policy and his use of concentration camps. The Liberals claimed that having herded women and children into the camps, Kitchener had failed to supply satisfactory hygienic quarters or sufficient medical personnel to prevent a severe outbreak of measles. Conan Doyle was initially shocked by reports from the camps, but upon investigating the matter he concluded that the victims had been put there to prevent them from wandering across the veldt and starving to death, and that the British were not to blame for the epidemic.

In a series of press interviews in London, Conan Doyle had two formidable questions to answer. First, why had Kitchener devastated Boer farms? He answered that Article XXIII of the Hague Convention made it clear that the destruction of enemy property was perfectly allowable when "imperatively demanded by the necessities of war," and that these farmhouses were being used to conceal snipers under the false protection of white flags of surrender. Second, why had there been an epidemic of measles? Conan Doyle replied that the Boers, despite their captors' care, ignored all the elementary rules of hygiene.

He began preparation of a pamphlet which would answer criticisms at home and overseas, not only of Kitchener but of the conduct of the rank and file. Furious at Russian, French and German charges of atrocities and rank cowardice, he wrote, in one impassioned week,* the fifty-thousand-word pamphlet *The War in South Africa, Its Cause and Conduct*. The monarch personally supplied him with five thousand pounds to further his cause, and George Newnes underwrote the distribution of the pamphlet. More than a million copies, at sixpence each, were sold in Britain, and over forty thousand were given away free of charge in France and Germany. The United States, Canada, the Netherlands, Norway, and Denmark were deluged with the first and second printings.

Although Conan Doyle's defenders claim that the booklet counteracted criticism in Europe, the opposite appears actually to have been the case. His special pleading seemed only to emphasize Kitchener's guilt. Though their motives in combating the British interests in South Africa were suspect, to say the least, the Germans had a genuine grievance in claiming that Conan Doyle's combative attitude toward the Boers was extremely provoking. Many humanists in Paris felt that he had papered over some of the vital facts of the war, and in America he was widely accused of concealing specific instances of British cowardice at the front.

In a pause during a cricket game at Lord's some months before the publication of this highly contentious document, John Boraston, secretary of the Liberal Unionist party, shared a lemonade with Conan Doyle and again offered him a chance to air his

---

* Including, as he wrote characteristically to Greenhough Smith, "one day in London"!

controversial views while campaigning for a seat in Parliament. Boraston suggested the central division of Edinburgh, and Conan Doyle accepted at once.

He strode bravely into a tiger pit. Central Edinburgh was a radical hotbed; and he, so firmly a pillar of the upper-middle-class Establishment, was a long way from his proper territory. His sheer charm, humor, and down-to-earth common sense served him well in impressing his potential constituents. His former teacher Joseph Bell, very aged, appeared at several public meetings to give him moral and vocal support, making amusing references to being the model for Sherlock Holmes. And Conan Doyle was friendly and open with employees of factories, gasworks, breweries and foundries. He blamed his failure to win on a religious fanatic who heckled him at meetings and put up posters charging him with being a creature of the Jesuits. He believed that this anti-Catholic defamation in a largely Presbyterian area was fatal. But the real problem was that he represented privilege, that he hobnobbed with the King and the Prime Minister, and that he was not only famous, but rich. In some ways he was relieved when he was defeated. He hated the squalor and the corruption of a political campaign, comparing it to "a mud bath—helpful but messy."

In the eighteen months after his return from South Africa, Conan Doyle kept up many old friendships. He was particularly close to Balfour, who was returned to power, first as Lord Salisbury's right-hand man and then, on Lord Salisbury's retirement, as Prime Minister himself. He was a frequent guest of Edward VII, whose bearded appearance and jovial, amoral character made him, after Queen Victoria's death in 1901, one of the most popular monarchs in English history. He was also very fond of the young Winston Churchill, whom he had met briefly in Bloemfontein, where Churchill had been as a war correspondent. He admired Churchill's energy, bulldog pugnacity, and sheer drive, and continued to see him at intervals for most of his life.

In March, 1901, Conan Doyle's health, surprisingly strong after the Boer War, began to falter. Plagued with his old problems of recurrent fever, diarrhea, and insomnia, he yielded to his doctors' advice and went to Cromer, in Norfolk, for a holiday. Cromer was one of Edward VII's favorite resorts, and it must have reminded Conan Doyle agreeably, too, of his acquaintance in Egypt with the consul general, Evelyn Baring, Baron Cromer. He went yachting and swam, and he played golf at the Royal Links Hotel with a great friend, Fletcher Robinson. A successful journalist, Robinson was a collector of strange legends and country tales. One night, as the two men sat by a cheerful fire in the lounge, with the wind howling outside, Robinson told Conan Doyle a marvelous legend about a gigantic spectral hound which was said to haunt a family in the west of England. The story concerned the Cabell family. Richard Cabell, a seventeenth-century heir to the manor of Brook, was jealous of his wife, and accused her of sleeping with an inhabitant of the nearby town of Buck-fastleigh. Cabell beat her cruelly, and she fled across the moor. He pursued her and stabbed her to death with a hunting knife. Her hound, devoted to its mistress, flew at Cabell's throat and tore it out, while Cabell stabbed the beast to death. According to the legend, the hound still prowled across Dartmoor, howling piteously, and reappearing to each new generation of the Cabell family.

Conan Doyle was intrigued at once. In several stories, as we have seen, he had introduced monstrous animals which emerged from some unknown region to terrorize staid and civilized English homes. At an early stage in his note taking for a story based on this legend, he decided to make it a new Sherlock Holmes adventure. Why did he choose to revive Holmes, when he had in so many interviews declared him irrevocably dead? There can be no firm answer. But it is difficult not to conclude that there was a shrewd commercial reason. William Gillette had opened his play *Sherlock Holmes* at the Star Theatre, Buffalo, on October 23, 1899, and had taken the production by way of Syracuse and Rochester to a triumphant opening at the Garrick Theatre in New York on November 6 of the same year. During Conan Doyle's absence in South Africa, the play had run at the Garrick for 236 performances, closing on June 16, 1900. It had then toured the United States; while Conan Doyle was staying at Cromer, it was still on tour. The production was scheduled to come to London in September.

He must have realized that the British presentation of the play would be a huge success, and that he would be under enormous pressure to produce a new Holmes story. Very well then; he would forestall everyone by timing a new Holmes novella for publication in *The Strand* soon after the play opened.

Besides, he was heartily sick and tired of hearing everyone say he "hated" Holmes. He had only hated the deadlines and the neglect of Louise; he had been afraid that if he did not kill Holmes, Holmes would kill him. This time, he had money; he could write the story at his leisure all through that spring. It would be a holiday job, and if it didn't come off, nobody except Robinson would know it had ever existed. Discussing the tale, the two men took the train to London and thence from Paddington Station to Devonshire.

They stayed at an appropriately Gothic hotel in Princetown, near the wilderness of Dartmoor, a bleak expanse relieved, if that is the word, by the frowning, dark-walled edifice of Dartmoor Prison. Sherlock Holmes had already visited Dartmoor with Watson in *Silver Blaze*, but Conan Doyle had not. He and Robinson walked past Grimspound Bog, with its relics of old tin cans, boots, and the wheels of carts, and its dire legends of escaped prisoners swallowed by its muddy depths. It was a dun-brown fen, pierced with swamp grass, sparkling with phosphorescent glowworms at night, and steaming desultorily under a washed-out sky. They explored Fox Tor Mire, a granite quarry, and Merrivale Hill nearby, watching convicts break stones. They found Brook Manor, home of the Cabells, explored primitive huts, and in their pony and trap rode under storm clouds past gloomy and isolated houses on the fringe of the moor.

Baskerville was a local family name, as well as the name of Robinson's man, who drove the trap, and of the originator of the Baskerville type face, in which several of Conan Doyle's works had been set. He used it for the family in the story. Grimspound Bog, combined with Fox Tor Mire, became Grimpen Mire. Merrivale Hill became Merripit Hill. Dartmoor Prison became Prince-town Convict Prison; by a freakish Doylean joke, an officious warden named Selden became a prisoner of that name. And what about the source for Baskerville Hall, with its two towers and its sprawling sinister gloom? The description of the towers precisely fits Conan Doyle's hated school, Stonyhurst, in Lancashire; the body of the hall is based on Brook Manor.

For the close-knit roofing of leaves, and the long winding drive which led to Baskerville Hall, we need look no further than the entrance to Brook Manor, combined with that of Undershaw. The use of a dog as a villain was a particularly daring and per-verse idea. Since the English worship dogs above almost anything else, the idea of a murderous canine was calculated to give a special *frisson* to the *Strand*'s readership.

Conan Doyle's fondness for dogs is reflected in many of the Holmes tales. Watson says he keeps a bull pup when he is intro-ducing himself to Holmes in *A Study in Scarlet*. Conan Doyle acquired a dog while living in Devonshire Place, and took the animal with him to South Norwood. Conan Doyle's mongrel, half spaniel, half lurcher, was the model for the clever Toby, who helps bring villains to book in *The Sign of Four*. In a later story, *The Lion's Mane*, a counterpart of Conan Doyle's new dog, an Airedale, makes an appearance. By dying at the same place as its master, it alerts Holmes to the solution of the case. There is a spaniel in *Shoscombe Old Place*. Precursors of the evil hound of the Baskervilles appear in *The Missing Three-Quarter* and *The Copper Beeches*.

Dogs inspired two favorite Conan Doyle quotations. In *Silver Blaze*, Inspector Gregory asks Holmes if there is any spe-cial point he wants to note. Holmes directs Gregory's attention to "the curious incident of the dog in the night-time." Gregory replies, "The dog did nothing in the night-time." Holmes ob-serves, "That was the curious incident." The other quotation is in *The Hound of the Baskervilles* itself: "Mr. Holmes, they were the footprints of a gigantic hound!"

The *Hound* is developed in Conan Doyle's richest Gothic vein. The tall, thin James Mortimer, who arrives at Baker Street to tell Holmes the dreadful tale of the ghostly canine, is reminiscent of Fletcher Robinson himself. A long flashback in the Gaboriau manner establishes the history of the family and its accursed ghost. This almost breaks the back of the narrative, but the author is nicely on course again as Watson gropes about the bog and the moor, and a wicked naturalist and butterfly hunter makes attempts on the life of the young heir, Sir Henry Baskerville.

One whole episode in the story is drawn from the visit Conan Doyle made to the "haunted" house with Frank Podmore and Sydney Scott for the Society for Psychical Research. Once more, the sound of sobbing, eerie and echoing, is heard through the house; once more, a minstrel's gallery is the scene of the "haunting"; and in the morning, like the spook hunters before him, Watson notices that a woman's eyes are red with weeping.

One thing Conan Doyle would not do: he would not date the setting of the story past the event at the Reichenbach Falls. This was simply an earlier adventure of the great detective, which Watson had neglected to tell previously. Holmes was still emphatically dead in Switzerland.

Greenhough Smith and George Newnes were beside themselves with excitement when *The Hound of the Baskervilles* arrived at the office of *The Strand* in Southampton Street that summer. They firmly scheduled publication to follow the London production of Gillette's play. The tale would appear in serial form early in 1902. The play, somewhat stronger than in its first draft, opened at Henry Irving's Lyceum Theatre on September 9, 1901. It must have been pleasant for Conan Doyle to remember, as he passed between the tall pillars into the red-plush interior, that this was where he had had his overwhelming taste of great theatre at the age of fifteen, seeing Henry Irving in *Hamlet*.

The first night was not successful. But the play caught on quickly. At the royal performance following the year of mourning for Queen Victoria on January 30, 1902, Edward VII and Queen Alexandra were in a box, and so was Balfour. The stalls were packed with the nobility, and the Conan Doyles had to make do with inferior seats. The crowd was captivated by the play. They loved the use of the new-fangled electric bell as it rang through Moriarty's office; they enjoyed the fact that gas, which would soon be out of fashion for lighting purposes, became the lethal weapon with which Moriarty tried to destroy Holmes; they cheered when Holmes took tobacco out of a Persian slipper and when he escaped from the gas chamber with the help of a well-placed cigar. They hurrahed when Holmes rescued the damsel in distress, and again when he proved to be a gentleman over the embarrassing letters; they thrilled when Larrabee appeared dressed as the Kaiser; and they whispered knowingly when Gillette dropped heavy hints that Holmes's Illustrious Client was none other than the monarch beaming happily in the royal box.

Gillette, almost everyone agreed, was in splendid form. His touch of histrionic extravagance gave an extra dimension to the character. He wore a resplendent rococo purple dressing gown which reminded more than one critic that this magnificent garment was based on Conan Doyle's own. On the stage, Holmes flourished pipes from his impressive collection; he played a Stradivarius with ideal competence; and his slippers were beautifully Persian. At the end of the first act, Edward VII, completely transported, asked Gillette to come to his box, and he kept him talking about the royal parallels in the play for almost an hour. The audience, risking *lèse-majesté,* finally voiced its impatience, and the King was obliged to let his distinguished American guest return to the stage.

At the final curtain, the audience gave the play a rare and prolonged standing ovation. They demanded and got speeches from both Gillette and Conan Doyle. A few catcalls from above indicated that many of the phrases spoken in Gillette's soft accents had been inaudible to the gallery mob, but the aristocrats shouted down their social inferiors with all of the energy of their class-conscious fury.

The play was a tremendous hit, as it had been in New York, and ran for 216 performances, closing on April 11, 1902. On the British tour, and in the London revival in 1905, the part of Billy, the young page boy who represents the Baker Street irregulars, was played by a very young and inexperienced actor named Charles Chaplin.*

One notes with pleasure that a real-life Sherlock Holmes story coincided with the first night. The Marquess of Anglesey was among the many fashionable folk who were there to cheer in the stalls. While the Marquess sat enthralled by the twists and turns of Gillette's plot, his valet, a young man named Julian Gault, was helping a prostitute steal the famous Anglesey jewelry collection, valued at £150,000. The female accomplice arranged to take the jewels to a fence, and promptly vanished in a fog. Gault, escaping the police, fled to Europe, while the desolate Marquess contacted Conan Doyle for help. As a real-life Sherlock Holmes, Conan Doyle helped him to trace some of the jewels, which had been disposed of in London. Working in close consultation with Scotland Yard, Conan Doyle deduced the identity of the thief. The woman was never found, but Gault was arrested and jailed in Paris. Released in 1911, he committed murder during a burglary, and died under the guillotine.

* Chaplin also appeared in a short play about Holmes in which Gillette starred with Irene Vanbrugh. This was *The Painful Predicament of Sherlock Holmes*, presented at the Duke of York's Theatre, in London, in October, 1905, as a curtain raiser for Gillette's ill-fated play *Clarice*. In this spoof, suggested by the fact that Gillette had been criticized for not being audible, Holmes receives a lady client who talks incessantly about her problem, not allowing the great detective to say a single word.

7

HOLMES IS REBORN

The Hound of the Baskervilles, its first installment appearing in the January, 1902, issue of the *Strand*, was greeted with enormous public enthusiasm. It received excellent reviews when it was brought out by Newnes in book form. The continuing run of William Gillette's play at the Lyceum, and the publication *The Great Boer War*, first in 1900, and then in revised and much improved editions in 1901 and 1902, firmly maintained Conan Doyle's reputation as one of the most famous British men of letters of his day. His services to the Crown in the matter of the Langman Hospital, and the publication of *The War in South Africa, Its Cause and Conduct* and of the earlier volume *The Great Boer War*, which was most warmly praised, inevitably led to a knighthood shortly after King Edward VII's accession. Conan Doyle strenuously denied that he was worthy of the honor, insisting that it would impugn the independence of his defense of the British soldier and of Kitchener in his agitatory pamphlet. In view of his friendship with the King, he was doubly sensitive about this possible charge.

Influence was brought to bear on him to change his mind. The Ma'am beseeched him in daily letters to stand firm in the tradition of his noble ancestors. Willie Hornung and Connie were entirely with her in this. His other sisters and brother-in-law, especially his dear friend, the Reverend Cyril Angell, indicated that he must resist his natural modesty and not offend the King. This last appeal really got home to him. When it was reinforced by the Ma'am, and separately by his wife and by Jean Leckie, his resistance finally crumbled.

He was knighted at Buckingham Palace on August 9, 1902,

the ceremony having been delayed because of the King's dangerous operation for appendicitis earlier that summer. At the Palace,
Conan Doyle was distinctly embarrassed by the arrangements for
the potential knights. They were herded into enclosures cut off
by wooden barricades, rather like prize cattle. His only consolation was that his fellow captive on this occasion was Oliver Lodge,
his friend and co-enthusiast for psychical research. Although the
subject was strictly taboo at the Palace, the two men discussed
mediums and séances while they waited to be taken to the in-
vestiture.

Edward VII was especially delighted to be able to touch
Conan Doyle's shoulder with his sword. It is legendary that the
Sherlock Holmes stories were the only works of fiction the monarch was ever able to enjoy, or even finish. At the King's personal insistence, fully supported by Balfour, Conan Doyle was
given a further honor. He was created Deputy Lieutenant of
Surrey. The recipient of this peculiarly futile title was obliged
to wear a grotesque uniform with gold stars on the epaulets and a
vulgar amount of braid; trying it on, Conan Doyle must have
felt rather like a human Christmas tree.

He was widely congratulated on his knighthood. The wireless telegraph brought very welcome Marconi messages from
Wells, Barrie, and Kipling. Jerome K. Jerome was in London,
along with Hornung, Connie, and all the other members of the
family, for a celebration at the Hotel Métropole. Conan Doyle
felt extremely embarrassed by their enthusiasm. When a parcel
containing some exquisite handmade shirts arrived at his suite, he
was pleased until an anonymous note fluttered to the floor. Reading it, he shouted out so loudly that the children present started
to cry. It contained the words, "With greetings to Sir Sherlock
Holmes."

A great honor in 1902 was an invitation from the monarch
to come to Sandringham, where a special presentation was held
for his nephew the Kaiser of *A Story of Waterloo*, with Irving
repeating, at an age now somewhat closer to that of the character,
his performance as the broken-down soldier. The guest list was

extraordinary. Among those present were Prince Paul von Metternich, whose father had obtained over the years a complete collection of John Doyle's political sketches and paintings; Lord Roberts, recently returned from South Africa; Balfour; and the elegant Joseph Chamberlain, with his monocle and the usual orchid in his buttonhole. Irving was in splendid form, and the evening ended with a performance which Sherlock Holmes would certainly have appreciated: Jan Kubelik played German music on the violin.

Despite travel, service in the war, and the experience of public acclaim, Conan Doyle never stopped writing for a day. And he did not neglect the horror story in those years at the turn of the century. In his study at Undershaw, as he gazed out across the rolling Nutcombe Valley, strange visions swirled in his brain. Just before 1900, he had written one of his most extraordinary tales of terror, *The Brown Hand,* which resembles some of Kipling's ghost stories. The narrator this time is a member of the Society for Psychical Research, reminiscent of Podmore, with a wide experience of haunted houses. He is called in to investigate a ghost pursuing Sir Dominick Holden, a distinguished surgeon, reminiscent of O'Callaghan, Conan Doyle's superior in South Africa, who has just been in service in India. Sir Dominick's house, Rodenhurst, in Wiltshire, oddly anticipates Conan Doyle's later home, Windlesham, in Sussex. Surrounded by prehistoric fossils, the house itself is by contrast a microcosm of contemporary science. It is suggestive also of Dr. Bell's rooms in Edinburgh, being crowded with bottles filled with medical specimens: severed organs, distorted bones, bloated cysts, and odious parasites.

Conan Doyle builds the atmosphere marvelously, describing the stench of methylated spirits floating through the rooms, glass cases filled with relics of disease and suffering, and along the shelves at night a spectral Indian gliding with a dangling arm that ends in a useless knotted stump. The dead Indian obsessively returns again and again, looking for his hand, which was amputated by Holden. But the hand has long since been destroyed.

The narrator travels to London to obtain a substitute hand. He secures it at a hospital, and places it in a glass container. Conan Doyle now shows a characteristic touch of macabre humor. The Indian appears, examines the hand, and with a cry of disappointment returns it to its place; it does not correctly match the mutilated arm—it is a *left* hand. Not until the correct member is supplied can the ghost find final satisfaction.

A most significant passage illustrates Conan Doyle's feelings at the time about departed spirits. He tells us that they "are the amphibia of this life and the next, capable of passing from one to the other as a turtle passes from land to water." This curious concept suggests that the dead are condemned to an existence both bloodless and sexless, adrift in a mindless vacuum, impelled only by some overwhelming need.

A bizarre story, *The Sealed Room*, shows a person obtaining a kind of life after death by entirely material means. A young man contacts the narrator in a desperate attempt to locate his father, who has disappeared to Europe, sending letters periodically. At the end of the story, the narrator and his friend burst into a secret room, where they find a ghastly presence. It is the corpse of the father, covered with a layer of dust that has built up over years. Overwhelmed by debts, the father long ago committed suicide, first contriving to give his son the illusion of his continual existence by writing numerous letters which he has arranged to have mailed at regular intervals from the continent.

In *The Great Brown-Pericord Motor*, a story on a somewhat higher level, the terror springs from the transformation into an engine of death of a new invention—the flying machine. The story appeared in *The Pictorial Magazine* in January, 1904, only three weeks after Orville and Wilbur Wright had made the first flight in a heavier-than-air machine on December 17, 1903, at Kitty Hawk, North Carolina. Francis Pericord, a great inventor, has created a weird device with flapping yellow metal wings, which buzzes about with alarming intensity. The implication is that Pericord has violated the code of life by creating a grotesque facsimile of a bird, which can only bring misery to the world. Pericord's reason is affected when his chief mechanic steals his designs. As an act of poetic justice, and at the risk of his own device, he murders the thief, attaches him to the infernal miniplane, and sends him on a last journey:

For a minute or two, the huge yellow fans flapped and flickered. Then the body began to move in little jumps down the side of the hillock, gathering a gradual momentum, until at last it heaved up into the air, and sailed off into the moonlight.

Months later, Pericord is found to be insane, and is confined to a New York asylum, where he constructs new-fangled flying machines in his rare moments of lucidity.

The resemblance to H. G. Wells is obvious, but there is a difference. Though Wells does not ignore the possible menace presented by the new age of science, he at heart welcomes science. In many ways, he becomes its spokesman and apostle. By contrast, Conan Doyle has a more ambiguous attitude. He is fascinated by science, but frightened by it. The Brown-Pericord Motor, a sinister giant metal moth, is seen chiefly as an engine of death; its only act of transportation is to convey a corpse to its last resting place in a moonlit ocean.

In one story a belief that obsessions can drive individuals back from the grave; in another, that the only immortality is achieved through post-dated letters; in a third, that the dead are carried not by angel's wings but by the infernal wings of an airplane: these stories reflect Conan Doyle's constantly changing attitudes toward the survival after death of the human spirit.

His interest in the occult is again reflected in his finest story of the period. *The Leather Funnel* (1900). This tale shows the author's concern with psychometry, a power whereby, supposedly, gifted individuals are enabled to perceive the history of objects when they are close to them. William Denton, Professor of Geology at Boston University in the 1840's, had reported seeing astonishing images of ancient Hawaii after examining a fragment of lava at Kilauea. His wife had examined a mastodon tooth, and in a dream seemed to become the creature itself. Denton's account of his experience must have provided much of the inspiration for Conan Doyle's later novel *The Lost World*. Subsequent examples of psychometry were frequent. Toward the end of his life Conan Doyle compared psychometric impressions to shadows on a screen. He believed that the screen was the ether, "The whole material universe being embedded in an interpenetrated by this subtle material which would not necessarily change its position since it is too fine for wind or any coarser material to influence it."

In *The Leather Funnel,* the occultist Lionel Dacre presents the funnel to a guest for a psychometric experiment. His guest sleeps next to it and experiences a horrifying nightmare, described with all of Conan Doyle's mastery of atmosphere and suspense. He sees a woman, brooded over by black-clad inquisitorial figures, presented with the leather object; it is about to be thrust into her when the dreamer wakens. He has recalled the torture of the infamous Marquise de Brinvilliers, a mass murderess of the period of Louis XIV. Historically, the torture known as the "Question" involved forcing quantities of water by funnel into the mouth and the stomach only. But the author gives this story a typically perverse twist. By not specifying the orifice into which the funnel is pushed, he supplies an unexpected note of sexual terror. The result here is, not for the first time, a hint of Conan Doyle's equation of sexuality and death.

Not surprisingly, Conan Doyle was busy studying spiritualism at the time he was writing these extraordinary works. He was impressed by a book which appeared in the summer of 1903, the posthumously published philosophical work *Human Personality and Its Survival of Bodily Death,* by his friend and esteemed colleague F. W. H. Myers, who had died in Italy in 1901. He called this work (in a letter to his mother, October 17, 1903) "a great root book from which a tree of knowledge will grow." It is impossible to summarize here the contents of over 1,200 pages; but very broadly the theme of the book is that human personality is not simply a combination of physical and mental elements, dependent on the material existence of the body and the brain.

Myers maintained that the personality is essentially supernatural, that the conscious self, lodged in the cerebral tissues, is simply the tip of an inverted iceberg, the rest of the personality being separable from it and superior to it, and connecting with the "soul" of the sentient universe as a whole. Myers was the originator of the term "telepathy," referring to a connection between minds, regarded as linked—like islands in a stream—by a continuing flow of thought and feeling. His study of mediumship had led him to believe that certain human beings, able to release themselves from the confines of the physical bases of subsidiary thought, could establish contact between the islands, as it were, and build up connections with personalities which had survived the physical destruction of the brain.

Fifteen years later Conan Doyle wrote in his book *The New Revelation* (1918):

[Myers'] was an enormous advance. If mind could act on mind at a distance, then there were some human powers which were quite different to matter as we had always understood it. The ground was cut from under the feet of the materialists, and my old position had been destroyed. . . . if the mind, the spirit, the intelligence of man could operate at a distance from the body, then it was a thing to that extent separate from the body. Why should it not exist on its own when the body was destroyed?

Like the Captain of the *Pole-Star* reaching out across the virginal ice, seeking his dead mistress in her whirling snowflakes, Conan Doyle at last was able, once and for all, to reach out through the cold fact of death across the chilly currents of Myers' thought. Now, more keenly than ever, he felt the challenge of a new adventure opening up, like a ski-run across the mountains of Switzerland, an airy, weightless flight into an existence of nonmaterial joy. The idea of survival of the personality excited Conan Doyle as much as cocaine excited Holmes. It was an addiction, providing an elevation of the senses which lifted the addict above the concrete. But the reasoning side of his nature still demanded personal proof. The dazzlement of imagining had to be tempered by the experience of contact with the dead, and this, so far, had not taken place.

It seems charmingly appropriate that Conan Doyle should have brought Holmes back from the dead in this period of hope and reverie. The medium in this case was nobody more spiritual than S. S. McClure, of *McClure's Magazine* in New York. His method of resurrection was simply a presentation of a check for five thousand dollars for six stories, which Conan Doyle could scarcely refuse.* The condition of the offer was that Holmes should be shown to have survived the episode at the Reichenbach Falls; McClure would not tolerate Conan Doyle's placing the stories of the new series in the period before Holmes's visit to Switzerland. Along with the money came a note in which McClure told Conan Doyle that he had not forgotten his generosity some years earlier in lending him the same sum, five thousand dollars, then desperately needed to keep the magazine afloat.

While Conan Doyle wrote the first resurrectionist Holmes story, *The Empty House*, in the summer of 1903, he also occupied himself with a new hobby, which replaced tricycling and its successor, bicycling. He became mad about motoring. He traveled enthusiastically to Birmingham to pick up a spanking-new 12-horsepower Wolseley. Dressed in a long coat that trailed about his ankles, a cap, and goggles, he stepped off the train in Birmingham, only to be mistaken for an attendant. An old lady rapped him on the lapel with her lorgnette and said, "My man, which is the next train to Walsall?"

Conan Doyle made a most perilous journey home to Undershaw from the Midlands. At first, he chugged along cheerfully at a glorious fifteen miles an hour. But the brakes gave out twice, and the automobile took off backward down steep hills while its owner struggled desperately with the wheel; the chain flew off the cogs and at times the car sailed ahead without engine power.

Later, when he took his mother for a ride in the contraption near her home in Yorkshire, he alarmed a cart horse so violently that the beast shied, the cart tilted over and crashed onto one just behind it, and Conan Doyle, his mother, and the two carters were showered with hundreds of turnips. Dragging himself loose, his cap and goggles askew, he was astonished to see the Ma'am sitting bolt upright on a pile of vegetables, calmly knitting a new sweater.

---

* Greenhough Smith offered Conan Doyle a hundred pounds per thousand words to ensure the new Holmes series for *The Strand*.

A less amusing incident took place in 1904. The brakes gave out once again, and the automobile flew up an embankment and tilted over, trapping Conan Doyle under a wheel. The wheel snapped, and (he insisted later) the entire weight of the car— about a ton—settled on his back. He lay for several minutes, entertaining the interesting idea that at any moment his spine might break. He was rescued just in time. In a curious story called *How It Happened,* written in 1913, he imagined what might occur if a person in this situation did indeed die under his machine. Unaware that he has passed on, his character awakens feeling very much as he has in life, and is greeted by a friend who died years before.

The new series of Sherlock Holmes stories began to appear in *The Strand* in October, 1903. They reflect in many instances Conan Doyle's nervous feelings about the contemporary balance of power in Europe. In the Fashoda, or Kodok, incident of September, 1898, Kitchener's confrontation with a new French mission under Marchand in the Sudan had almost led the two countries into war. An uneasy détente had followed, sustained more through the efforts of the French Foreign Minister, Théophile Delcassé, than through the uncertain diplomatic skills of Joseph Chamberlain. An alliance of France and Italy brought fears that Britain would be pushed into a corner. Conan Doyle apparently believed, after the Boer War ended with the Treaty of Vereeniging on May 31, 1902, that France, Russia, Germany, and Italy would constitute a quadruple threat. The insistent theme of terror of foreign powers recurs in his work all the way up to World War I.

In the new stories, Holmes's position like, his creator's, has radically changed. Now he is no longer chiefly concerned with the personal problems of the upper middle class. He is being approached more often by people at the highest level of society. Like Conan Doyle, with his frequent visits to the homes of Balfour and the King, and his great friendship with Joseph Chamberlain, he is consulted on matters of national moment. His participation in these affairs is even greater than his author's, since he is asked, on occasion, to settle situations which might imperil world peace. He is one with Conan Doyle in looking toward the future with alarm, foreseeing the end of the Empire as a not-too-distant possibility.

In the first story of the new cycle, *The Empty House*, Holmes materializes in disguise, having disappeared from the Falls because of mysterious threats from his enemies. Amusingly, Conan Doyle has Holmes spend part of his long journey around the world visiting the Khalifa in the Sudan, and communicating his findings to the Foreign Office. Holmes returns to solve the mystery of the murder of the Honorable Ronald Adair. Adair had been killed by a dumdum bullet from an air gun. His killer is Colonel Sebastian Moran,* "the second most dangerous man in London," a monstrous big-game hunter from India.

The parallels here are immensely diverting. The dumdum bullet had been a subject of recent public controversy. In *The War in South Africa, Its Cause and Conduct*, Conan Doyle had strenuously denied that it was used by British troops in South Africa. Sebastian Moran, with his background in India and his menacing manner, is agreeably reminiscent of Lord Roberts. And who, in life, was "the second most dangerous man in London"? Almost certainly the famous master criminal Max Shinburn.

The criminologist Charles Kingston wrote of Shinburn in *Dramatic Days at the Old Bailey* (1923): "His courage was immense, his brain-power enormous. He controlled a turbulent gang with the same ease as he repressed himself."

Like the most dangerous man in London, Adam Worth, with his grandiose flat in Piccadilly and his host of aristocratic friends, Shinburn lived splendidly in London, New York, and Brussels, robbing banks of millions on both sides of the Atlantic, forging letters of credit, and engineering major thefts, including the brilliantly contrived robbery of the Verviers mail train on November 27, 1886.

This new series of Holmes stories makes clear Conan Doyle's extraordinary reliance on past experiences as a source of inspiration, and his great capacity to create high-quality entertainment out of his reading and research. *The Second Stain* is crowded

---

* The name is "Morstan" with the "saint" removed.

with abstruse elements which help to form a strong and convincing narrative. Two very imposing gentlemen arrive at Holmes's rooms in Baker Street: Lord Bellinger, clearly suggestive of Lord Salisbury, and the Right Honorable Trelawney Hope, equally suggestive of Joseph Chamberlain. The visitors report the loss of a document so important that if it were to fall into the wrong hands it would precipitate a European war. Holmes is asked to find it. Obliquely, the author suggests that the document involves accusations of British atrocities in South Africa, of the kind which Conan Doyle had sought to refute in his book. It is not clear which foreign power would most benefit from obtaining the document. But given Conan Doyle's knowledge of foreign affairs, it is likely to have been Germany. The implication is that if the letter, presumably denouncing the treatment of the Boers, were to be incorrectly used, a conflict would be inevitable. Oddly enough, in November, 1908, an episode was to occur which presented a near parallel with the story: another attempt to suppress a document dealing with public affairs. The Kaiser gave a notorious interview to the London *Daily Telegraph*, saying that while he personally was friendly with his uncle Edward VII, and greatly admired the British people, most Germans were violently anti-British. His Chancellor, Bernhard von Bülow, tried to prevent publication of the piece, but was unable to do so, and was accused of having arranged the interview. As a result, he was forced to resign, and the Kaiser was told by an infuriated Reichstag that his power would be limited in the future.

Holmes in *The Second Stain* discovers that the crucial document has been stolen by a beautiful woman who has been blackmailed by a man named Lucas; he has promised to return to her a letter impugning her reputation if she will obtain the crucial document for him. She confesses her action to Holmes, the controversial document is returned to the appropriate dispatch case, and war is avoided.

The complex origins of the plot can be traced in part not only to elements in *A Scandal in Bohemia*, and oddly enough, in Gillette's play, but to Poe's story *The Purloined Letter*, in which a document of equal importance, belonging to a very highly placed person indeed, is stolen by a "Minister D———." There are also indirect references to a number of important divorce cases in which incriminating letters formed crucial pieces of evidence. Among these was the famous Hartopp divorce case of 1895, in which Lady Hartopp, daughter of Charles Wilson, M.P., betrayed her husband, Sir Charles Craddock-Hartopp, with Sir John Willoughby, who had figured in the Jameson Raid, and with whose career Conan Doyle was closely familiar. Like the similarly named Lady Hilda Trelawney Hope in *The Second Stain*, Lady Hartopp was a reigning society beauty, and the divorce case, in which several incriminating love letters were produced, was a sensational affair, with many titled figures giving evidence. Clearly, Conan Doyle was imagining the sort of situation in which a blackmailer might have been threatening Lady Hartopp, as the press suggested at the time of the case.

The theme of blackmail recurs in the excellent story *Charles Augustus Milverton*. Lady Eva Blackwell, also remarkably similar to Lady Hartopp in her beauty and social distinction, has written indiscreet letters which have fallen into the hands of Milverton, a plump, dandyish blackmailer. Milverton, described as a snakelike blackmailer, reminds one of Thomas Wainewright, the forger and poisoner, who was said to have snakelike eyes and an expression at once repulsive and fascinating, and who lived in great luxury, hobnobbing with the aristocracy and collecting *recherché* books and priceless engravings. There are also reverberations of the notorious moneylender Henry Padwick. He tried to ruin the lovely Lady Florence Paget, known as the "Pocket Venus," who deserted her lover Henry Chaplin for the Marquess of Hastings. Padwick, to quote a contemporary account, "would destroy his victims with a smile." In describing Milverton, Conan Doyle says, "With a smiling face and a heart of marble, he will squeeze and squeeze until he has drained them [his victims] dry."

Concerning the physical appearance of Milverton, we are told:

[He was] a man of fifty, with a large, intellectual head, a round, plump, hairless face, a perpetual frozen smile, and two keen gray eyes, which gleamed brightly from behind broad, gold-rimmed glasses.

Above: London in the early 1870's. Engraving by Gustave Doré.

On the facing page, above: Charles Altamont Doyle,
Conan Doyle's father. Photo taken in the 1840's.
Below: Arthur at age five, in a portrait by his uncle,
Richard Doyle.

The real Sherlock Holmes: Dr. Joseph Bell of Edinburgh University.

Group photo taken aboard the whaler *Hope*, in 1880. Conan Doyle is third from left.

Conan Doyle as a young doctor in his study at South Norwood, about 1892.

Arthur and his wife Louise on a tricycle in South Norwood,
1892.

Louise and Mary Conan Doyle at South Norwood, 1893.

Greenhough Smith, literary editor of *The Strand Magazine*, in his office, 1892.

Ludmilla Hubel, Austrian singer and actress, before her disappearance in 1891. She was probably the model for Sherlock
Holmes's favorite woman, Irene Adler.

Dr. Conan Doyle in the great Boer War at the Langman Hospital, 1900.

The famous actor William Gillette as Sherlock Holmes,
1899.—*The Stowe-Day Memorial Library and Historical Foundation, Hartford, Connecticut*

Conan Doyle, the now celebrated and successful author in his study; circa 1915.

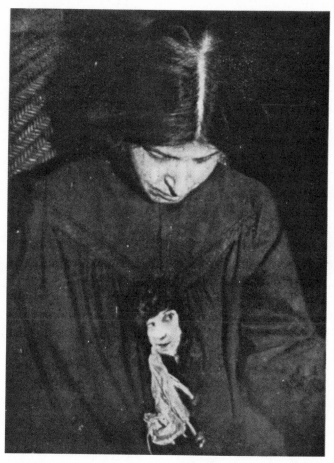

Eva C., famous ectoplasm medium in Paris, 1915.

Facing page, top to bottom, Conan Doyle's homes: Undershaw, Hindhead, Surrey; Windlesham, Crowborough, Sussex; Bignell Wood, New Forest, Hampshire.—*Tony Rayns*

Above left: Conan Doyle on his spiritualist quest, 1922. *Above right:* Baker Street at the time of the Sherlock Holmes adventures, complete with hansom cab. —*William Gordon Davis*

Left: Conan Doyle's grave in New Forest. —*Tony Rayns*

Conan Doyle and Houdini in Atlantic City, 1922.

Compare this description of James Bloomfield Rush (one of the murderers Conan Doyle had seen represented in the Chamber of Horrors at Madame Tussaud's), which appeared in 1882 in Joseph Forster's *Studies in Black and Red:*

His eyes are well-opened, deep-set in the head and very bright. His mouth is large, prominent, and sensual, the lips being very thick; his complexion sanguine, the brow full and the brain well-developed.

In his portrayal of Milverton, Conan Doyle goes on:

There was something of Mr. Pickwick's benevolence in his appearance, marred only by the insincerity of the fixed smile and by the hard glitter of those restless and penetrating eyes.

Forster describes Rush further:

To the superficial observer, his countenance is not unpleasant, but there is danger in the face; a face of dogged obstinacy and implacable resentment when thwarted or opposed.

Like Rush, Milverton favors astrakhan coats and is in his fifties. Like Padwick, he gains his pleasure from humiliating his victims. Like Lucas in *The Second Stain,* he is done away with; while Holmes and Watson watch from behind a curtain, Milverton's aristocratic lady victim shoots him and grinds her heel in his upturned face.

Once again, life imitated art, or Conan Doyle revealed gifts of prophecy. An almost identical episode took place on March 16, 1914. Mme. Joseph Caillaux, wife of the Minister of Finance of France, and a leading society woman, visited the offices of the newspaper *Figaro,* to see its celebrated editor, Gaston Calmette. She was infuriated by vicious articles attacking her husband, and now Calmette threatened to publish love letters written to her by Caillaux while he was still married to his former wife. She walked into Calmette's office and shot him dead to prevent him from carrying out his threat.

Yet another companion piece is *The Abbey Grange.* Lady Brackenstall, similar in name to Lady Blackwell, of *Charles Augustus Milverton,* and in appearance to the "Pocket Venus," is a reigning society beauty. She is involved with a sailor, but is unhappily married to the heavy-drinking Sir Eustace Brackenstall, a sadistic monster who has even set fire to her dog. She is assaulted and her husband is killed during a burglary, apparently committed by the members of a family gang only one step removed from the real-life Bertha Weiner burglary gang of 1901, which in similar circumstances robbed a Palladian mansion in a London suburb. Conan Doyle, as in *Charles Augustus Milverton*, allows Holmes to be judge and jury, and the killer—who turns out to be the sailor who loves Lady Brackenstall—goes free. The implication is that like the French, his ancestors on one side of his family, Conan Doyle believes that a *crime passionnel* can in certain circumstances be forgivable.

The story *Black Peter* is particularly rich in personal allusions. There is reference to a whaling voyage, reminiscent of Conan Doyle's on the *Hope;* a murder committed by harpoon recalls the author's revulsion at the mass killing of wild life in the Arctic; and there is an episode involving a stormy crossing to Norway, like the one he made with Louise, Connie, and Jerome K. Jerome. The word "Peter" in the title suggests Peterhead, the port from which Conan Doyle embarked on the whaling journey; the name of the Captain in this instance—Carey—is almost an anagram of the name of Captain Gray, of the *Hope* (the publication of the story brought an angry letter from Gray to *The Strand*). A stonemason named Slater appears in the story. This is very odd, for later Conan Doyle was to be involved in the defense of an Oscar Slater, whose punishment for a crime he had not committed was to break stones at Peterhead jail. Though Conan Doyle rejected "Sherringford Hope" as the name of his detective, he recalled his old ship in the names of Jefferson Hope in *A Study in Scarlet*, and Trelawney Hope in *The Second Stain*. It may also be noted that *Black Peter* has an extraordinary personal association for the writer. In the story, a man named Neligan is drowned at sea. Shortly before Conan Doyle's death, the secretary to my father, Sir Charles Higham, suffered the death of her husband Neligan at sea. Soon after that, she became my stepmother.

In *The Missing Three-Quarter* there are details drawn from Conan Doyle's sporting background. *The Priory School* recalls his prep school, Hodder; and Thorneycroft Huxtable, M.A., Ph.D., is reminiscent of Father Purbrick, the head teacher at Stonyhurst. While Conan Doyle was at Hodder, there was a to-do—nostalgically recalled in this tale—about the son of an Italian Catholic count running away, and a missing examination paper. *The Three Students* evokes the atmosphere of Conan Doyle's life at Edinburgh University. And it is nice to note the locale of *The Norwood Builder*. In this story, about a strange old man who hides in a secret room in a house not unlike 12, Tennison Road in order to fake his own murder and frame an innocent victim, a theme which recurs later in *Thor Bridge*, there is much play with the nascent science of fingerprints. Conan Doyle wrote the story in 1903, and coincidentally with its publication, an episode occurred which could have been in one of his own stories: the bloody thumbprint of a thief on a safe led to his arrest by Scotland Yard. Another curious episode that year involved a burglar who broke into a Clerkenwell warehouse, and alarmed by a sound of the constable on the beat, fled, catching his wedding ring on a spike as he jumped over a fence. The finger snapped off. The police examined the finger, took an impression of the print, and found one in the files which corresponded to that of the criminal.

The most bizarre allusion in this group of stories occurs in *The Dancing Men*. In this excellent story, an English squire, Hilton Cubitt, discovers that his American wife is being terrorized by a series of cryptograms inscribed on various places, among them a tool-house door and a sundial. The cryptograms consist of tiny, spidery black figures of men, dancing in regular lines. Each man represents a separate letter of the alphabet. It is interesting to note that in the children's magazine *St. Nicholas* for May, 1874, there was published a similar cryptogram, under the heading "The Language of the Restless Imps." The following comparison indicates the resemblance.

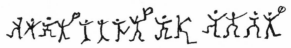

From *The Dancing Men:* "Come here at once."

From *St. Nicholas*, May, 1874: "Little drops of water, . . ."

The first two lines of the *St. Nicholas* puzzle mean, "Little drops of water,/Little grains of sand." (For the full solution, see the Appendix.)

During these months of literary activity, Conan Doyle was happier than ever with his working relationship with Greenhough Smith at *The Strand*. Disputes were infrequent; Conan Doyle did object to instances in which illustrations caused certain of his stories to be printed two words to the line either side of them. Referring to *The Leather Funnel*, he wrote, "It's bad economy to spoil a 200 pound story by the intrusion of a three guinea engraving." He was also annoyed when a picture of Napoleon lying dead preceded a Brigadier Gerard story, since the whole point of the narrative was to give the reader a shock on discovering Napoleon's demise in the last pages. Smith insisted on a complete reworking of *The Solitary Cyclist*, feeling that Holmes had far too little to do in it, and the correspondence between the two men shows that it was quite extensively revised.

Although he had an agent, Conan Doyle himself continued to set the prices for his work until the end of his life. His requests were acceded to, not always happily, because of his contract (a gentlemen's agreement rather than a firm written commitment) to give *The Strand* all of his writing of appropriate length. He only demurred when, later on, *The Strand* wanted his spiritualist writings; he felt that these were unsuitable for the magazine's broad family readership.

His letters show that he maintained a very friendly relationship with Newnes as publisher, and later with John Murray. Once broad figures were agreed upon, he did not haggle over exact amounts, and the continuing huge success of the Holmes stories, selling hundreds of thousands of copies in collected form as the century progressed, made him the apple of his publisher's eye. His grumbles were generally handled well, and his agent dealt expertly with translation problems.

By 1903, Conan Doyle was on his way to becoming a rich man. Unfortunately, he was not very wise in his investments. He tended to spend heavily on harebrained treasure-hunting expeditions and salvage operations which satisfied his romantic, adventuresome side of his nature but seriously unsettled his bank manager.

The William Gillette play was a major triumph in Paris. At the Théâtre Antoine, Firmin Gemier gave a remarkable performance as Sherlock Holmes, in a version written by Pierre de Courcelle which includes some interesting changes. The character Larrabee is now called Olebarre, his new name virtually an anagram of the original. The safe-cracker, formerly Sidney Prince, becomes John Alfred Napoleon Bribb—the name caused hoots of laughter at the Antoine whenever it was mentioned. Alice Faulkner becomes Alice Brent, since the original name proved extremely difficult for the French actors to pronounce. The gas chamber in Stepney becomes *la chambre de sommeil.*

The ending was broadly adapted from Gillette. Bribb, not Moriarty, appears as a cabbie and is handcuffed. And Courcelle restored the original finale. As the curtain goes up, the stage is seen to be divided into three parts: on the left, the study at 221B, Baker Street; in the middle, a London thoroughfare filled with fog; and on the right, a room in an empty house. In the eerie half-light of the room in Baker Street, the figure of Holmes gradually becomes visible, sitting in profile in a chair by his own window. Moriarty and an assistant fire from across the street with an air gun, and utter the words, "Adieu, Sherlock Holmes"; the figure falls to the floor. But at that instant Holmes himself enters the room across from 221B, Baker Street. Moriarty is arrested, and the figure in the chair is found to be a beeswax dummy.

While creating and solving new Holmes puzzles, Conan Doyle was also busy answering hundreds of letters from readers, with the aid of his secretary, Major Alfred Wood. The bookstores were besieged with customers, rushing in to buy *The Strand* by the thousands. On publication day each month, long queues formed in Southampton Street. Circulation zoomed again to well over half a million. Conan Doyle received countless suggestions for new stories, many of them addressed to Holmes or Watson. One letter, followed by several others to the same effect from different individuals, said, "There is a serious mistake in *The Priory School*. It is quite impossible for you, Mr. Holmes, to have known in which direction the bicycle was heading simply by looking at his track on a damp moor." Before replying, Conan Doyle waited for a wet day and then took his bicycle out to the Devil's Punchbowl, a valley near Hindhead, rode it, and examined the track. He was alarmed to discover that his correspondents were right. He had imagined that the track of the hind wheel overlaying the track of the front wheel when the machine was weaving in mud would indicate the direction. He did not immediately admit to his misdemeanor, but confessed it in *Memories and Adventures* (1924).

A woman wrote to "Sherlock Holmes, Hindhead, Haslemere," asking, "Can you help me? I am very puzzled. In one week I have lost a motor horn, a brush, a box of golf balls, a dictionary and a boot-jack. Can you explain it?" Conan Doyle wrote back, "Nothing simpler, my dear lady. It is clear that your neighbor keeps a goat. SHERLOCK HOLMES." One woman insisted on writing to him from Warsaw, beginning her letters "Good Lord." He was about to reply to the fourteenth such letter, which indicated its author was an invalid, when he ran into Willie Hornung in the Strand. Hornung produced fourteen identical letters from his pocket, addressed to him.

The letters continued in later years. One, from a lady in Bournemouth, read: "Will Mr. Sherlock Holmes require a housekeeper for his country cottage at Christmas? I know someone who loves a quiet country life, and bees especially—an old-fashioned, quiet woman." Another communication ran:

Dear Sir,

I am a professional lecturer on the subject of bees. I see by some of the morning papers that you are about to retire and take up bee-keeping. I know not if this be correct or otherwise, but if correct I shall be pleased to render you service by giving any advice you may require. I make this offer in return for the pleasure your writings gave me as a youngster, dear Mr. Holmes; they enable me to spend many and many a happy hour, therefore I trust you will read this letter in the same spirit in which it is written.

Another letter, asking Holmes for his autograph, offered the post-script: "Not being aware of your present address, I am taking the liberty of sending this letter to Sir A. Conan Doyle, asking him to be good enough to forward it to you."

Conan Doyle frequently sent his reply on a post card without a stamp, requiring his correspondent to meet the cost of postage upon receipt. Typically, the card would read: "I was interested to receive your communication addressed to Mr. Sherlock Holmes. In the words of Mrs. Gamp, 'there ain't no such person,' but thank you for your interest." The post card was signed in each instance, "Dr. John Watson."

Conan Doyle was pleased by a story about a group of French schoolboys who were brought to London on a sight-seeing tour. They were asked by their English guide, "Would you prefer to see Westminster Abbey or the Tower of London first?"

"Neither," replied the group leaders. "We intend to begin the tour with 221B, Baker Street."

One day Conan Doyle received a tradesman's bill addressed to Mr. Holmes. Astonished, he was told by the tradesman that it was bona fide. The man said that he understood that since Conan Doyle had been knighted, he had changed his name. Conan Doyle enjoyed telling this story on himself for years.

There were many stories in circulation about Sherlock

Holmes and his author, and Conan Doyle was particularly fond of two of them. In the first, an apocryphal variant on the true story of the Boston cabman, a French cabbie says to him, "I perceive from your appearance that you have recently been in Constantinople. I have reason to think also that you have been at Buda, and I perceive some indication that you were not far from Milan."

"Wonderful," Conan Doyle is supposed to have replied. "Five francs for the secret of how you did it."

"Elementary, my dear Monsieur Doyle. I looked at the labels pasted on your trunk."

The other story is one which Conan Doyle mentioned only over brandy and cigars after dinner, when the ladies had repaired to the drawing room. Sherlock Holmes arrives at the pearly gates. St. Peter greets him with great effusiveness, and says that there is a puzzle in heaven which only Holmes can solve: Adam cannot be identified among the countless millions of men up there. Holmes instructs every man in Paradise to remove his clothes, and without difficulty finds Adam. St. Peter is astonished. "How did you do it?" he asks.

"Elementary, my dear St. Peter," Holmes replies. "He is the only one of the millions who lacks a certain *je ne sais quoi* in the middle of his stomach."

In 1903, Conan Doyle started work on a new historical romance, *Sir Nigel*, dealing with events which took place before the beginning of *The White Company*. It is the heroic story of a brave knight who has to perform three deeds before he can win the hand of Lady Mary (her name a gracious reference to Conan Doyle's mother and daughter). The childhood scenes are interesting for their veiled portrait of young Conan Doyle and his mother studying heraldry together. The Lady Ermyntrude, grandmother of Sir Nigel, is clearly based on the Ma'am as she was in 1903. The book opens with one of the finest passages in all of Conan Doyle's work, a magnificent evocation of the arrival in medieval England of the Black Plague. Here his macabre imagination is most keen, describing rain as thick as blood, and foul toadstools and lichens bursting out as though the world itself were sick. The purple cloud hovering over a beautiful British landscape is uncomfortably reminiscent of M. P. Shiel's novel *The Purple Cloud*, and the rest of the novel is conventional boys' stuff; but these early passages still retain their power.

During the year 1904, he buried himself in his study at Undershaw, to write an attractive book of essays, *Through the Magic Door*, in which he discussed many of his childhood favorites in the light of his mature knowledge. In his forties, he became more painfully aware while working on the book of the vanishing of a simpler and more innocent time. Louise was failing fast, and the doctors could no longer offer hope. The Victorian age was already gone, and the Edwardian age, with its motorcars and telephones and airplanes, was upon him. The most painful knowledge was that the structure of his political world was breaking apart. Firmly attached to the Conservative cause, which by now was more or less blended with that of the Liberal Unionists, he witnessed the political career of his friend Arthur Balfour decline sharply.

By importing mass Chinese coolie labor into South Africa at the end of the Boer War, and by espousing tariff reform, which would mean abandoning free trade with Europe in favor of preferential treatment of imports from the colonies, Balfour alienated the public. The British people were sympathetic to the twentieth-century concept of open trading arrangements, and refused to tolerate the use of anything resembling slave labor. Balfour, honorable as he was, could not help remaining a man of the nineteenth century.

Despite his fascination with machines, Conan Doyle tended to be old-fashioned politically. He supported tariff reform most earnestly, and would soon be a radical opponent of women's suffrage. He stuck to Balfour loyally. Balfour seemed hopelessly out of place in the age of Edward VII, a king who was openly hedonistic, who enjoyed food, wine, and women without guilt. Balfour lacked the common touch. In 1906, he was resoundingly defeated at the polls. Joseph Chamberlain was swept away in the deluge, and so was Conan Doyle, who ran unsuccessfully for a Scottish seat, The Hawick Burghs, in support of Balfour.

Sir Henry Campbell-Bannerman, the witty and worldly Liberal who succeeded Balfour as Prime Minister, proved to be ideally suited to the spirit of the new age. Very rich, and not ashamed of it, he lived splendidly, in great and tasteful opulence; the King, who at first thought he might be a bore, warmed to him unexpectedly, and approved his style and his grand manner wholeheartedly. When Lloyd George, a passionate fighter for justice, was appointed to the Cabinet, it was obvious that the nineteenth century had been buried once and for all.

As if these social and political changes were not enough, Conan Doyle had to cope with some devastating scandals involving spiritualists. Eusapia Paladino, the gross Italian medium, was exposed several times when inquisitive sitters grabbed her feet and found she was using them to move luminous objects, and substituting them for her hands in supposedly controlled séances. The philosopher Josiah Royce wrote a poem about her which was widely circulated:

> Eeny, meeny, miney mo,
> Catch Eusapia by the toe,
> If she hollers, then you know
> James's theory is not so.

The reference was to the spiritualist William James, the American pioneer in psychology and founder of pragmatism, whom Conan Doyle knew and admired. Leonora Piper, the famous Boston medium, had admitted that she had never been in touch with spirits, and that all of her many remarkable messages stemmed from telepathy. She tried to retract the statement later, but the effect of it stuck.

Closer to home, Conan Doyle was faced with an unfortunate incident involving the medium Frederick Foster Craddock. At the invitation of the spiritualist Admiral Moore, Conan Doyle visited Craddock's séances at Pinner, near London. He was a trifle dubious because Craddock's spirit control, Rosetta, had been seized at a previous séance, and had been revealed to be the medium himself, wearing a white nightshirt, a wig, lipstick, and high-heeled shoes. The room in the house at Pinner was lit dimly by a red photographic lantern. From the cabinet in the corner, with its mauve-velvet curtains, a series of figures floated out successively, in a variety of garments, their faces glowing sepulchrally through small squares of gauze stretched on wooden frames, which they held in front of them. They moved among the sitters, bowed or curtsied, and announced themselves as Dr. Graem, Dr. Arnold (presumably of Rugby), Sister Amy, La Belle Cérise, Sheik Abdullah, and Joey Grimaldi. As a form approached a lady in the circle, she said to her husband, "It's your father!" and her husband replied, "No, it's your mother!"

Highly suspicious, Admiral Moore seized the figure, which indeed appeared to be the subject's father—it had a mustache. A struggle followed, and the phantom's sex now became indeterminate. The mustache came away in the Admiral's hand. With a flurry of robes, the figure made its way toward the fireplace. It picked up a coal shovel and made an alarming movement in the Admiral's direction. An assistant turned on the lights, and disclosed, to everyone's astonishment, that again the figure was actually the medium, this time grotesquely disguised in a sheet, a rubber mask, and a head handkerchief wrapped like a turban.

A further scandal involved one of Conan Doyle's acquaintances, Cecil Husk, a former member of the Carl Rosa Opera Company, who offered singing by spirits as a main feature of his séances. He and his control, the tall and bearded John King (inherited from, and presumably shared by, Florrie Cook) were exposed as one and the same person when a sitter brought a tiny electric bulb fixed to a tiepin into the séance room and revealed Husk busily painting his face with a phosphorescent substance. Husk screamed and vanished into the cabinet; his efforts to dissemble proved futile.

There were numerous instances of séances in which bluish figures, casting an eerie glow, were clasped by the sitters because they seemed attractive, and responded in a way that was, to say the least, earthy.

Despite these unfortunate episodes, there can be no question that Conan Doyle's essential sympathy toward spiritualism remained unchanged. Very broadly, his position was that while it was true that many mediums were of poor character and poor breeding, and were guilty of constant acts of fraud, a proportion of the phenomena at their séances could possibly be regarded as genuine. Paladino, like Florrie Cook, had as a control John King, who spoke to her only in Italian; this was considered suspicious, although many people claimed that King brought convincing messages from the spirit world, and had "learned Italian there." But along with the many instances of Paladino's evident fakery, there were others in which what she did was apparently inexplicable. In the 1880's, Dr. Ercole Chiaia had declared that Paladino could attract furniture to her, making it move toward her without touching it, that flashes of electricity shot from her body, that she could draw figures on a card merely by pointing it, and that she could levitate and take strange forms. While tied hand and foot, she could apparently make bells fly through the air, and she could materialize strange figures or mysterious black nodules as the curtains of her cabinet billowed out to her command. Years later, amidst a series of disastrous sittings, she still apparently produced a variety of phenomena; in Genoa in 1902, after she had been tied to a camp bed with sticking plaster, six ghostly figures appeared in the door of her cabinet, one of them that of a woman with a baby in her arms.

Even the skeptical Frank Podmore was impressed in 1908, when, before two conjurers in a locked room of the Hotel Victoria in Naples, Paladino, tied hand and foot, produced from the cabinet curtain disembodied hands and heads which brushed against the sitters.

Despite her disclaimers, Leonora Piper also had a remarkable record. She did not produce physical phenomena, except in rare instances when she apparently succeeded in withdrawing the scent from flowers and causing them to wither in a matter of minutes or seconds. Although she was subject to criticism—for example, when she claimed to be in touch with the spirit of Hannah Wild and the spirit's voice could not identify the contents of a sealed envelope—her mediumship was unhesitatingly accepted by William James, the philosopher, psychologist, and orientalist Professor William Romaine Newbold, the University of Pennsylvania, and other savants. In 1906, Mrs. Piper traveled to England to undergo an investigation by the Society for Psychical Research into her involvement in cross correspondences, in which mediums receive connecting or equivalent messages from the same departed people. It was believed that Edmund Gurney, F. W. H. Myers, and Richard Hodgson, all famous investigators of psychic phenomena, were returning with intricate messages conveyed through a variety of mediums. A Society report asserted that at seventy-four sittings with Mrs. Piper, and an almost equal number with Mrs. A. W. Verrall, wife of a well-known classical scholar and herself a lecturer in classics at Newnham College, and with the pseudonymous "Mrs. Holland," definite evidence of communication with these well-known men had been established.

Conan Doyle was in the position of having to weigh the grotesque, blasphemous yet bizarrely comical episodes of mediumistic fraud against the numerous carefully checked and scientifically recorded episodes involving apparently genuine phenomena. There can be no question that he spent more time minutely studying the journals and proceedings of both the British Society for Psychical Research and its American counterpart than he did examining any other matter. He became totally absorbed in the quest for a final proof of survival after death. Why did he not now accept it as proved, since a fair percentage of the phenomena he had observed in other people's records appeared to be genuine?

The answer is twofold. First of all, many people, most notably William Crookes, averred that the phenomena which had been observed could well be caused by transcendental entities, not by the spirits of the dead. Second, Conan Doyle could not believe in survival of the human personality until he had actually communicated with a surviving personality himself. One is forced to the conclusion that despite the numerous séances he attended, he was not convinced by messages from the dead at that time, or indeed until 1916.

8

CONAN DOYLE AS SHERLOCK

IN THE summer of 1906, Louise's health failed rapidly. On June 30, Conan Doyle wrote to his mother and brother Innes indicating that the end was near. Louise's mother and the housekeeper kept vigil with him. Louise passed away at three o'clock on the morning of July 4. She was forty-nine years old.

Conan Doyle was devastated. It is not known whether he attempted to contact her through mediums, but he seems unlikely to have done so, since at that time he was still uncertain about the possibility of communication with spirits. The funeral was simple. Louise was buried under a stone cross at Hindhead, with sculptured vine leaves trailing over the grave. After Louise's death, Conan Doyle became ill from exhaustion and anxiety, and was barely able to pursue his normal schedule of work. It was during this painful period, toward the end of 1906, that he picked up a newspaper called *The Umpire*, containing articles of general interest as well as sporting items, and noticed an article by George Edalji, the son of a vicar in Great Wyrley, a mining village in Staffordshire.

Edalji's story was a remarkable one. It had begun in 1874, with the marriage of his father, a Parsee Indian, to an English girl. George had been born in 1876. The family, happy in the small parish, had lived a quiet and uneventful life until 1888. In that year, a series of vicious and obscene messages about the Edaljis, obviously inspired by racial prejudice, were inscribed on the walls of outbuildings in the parish. A disaffected servant girl was arrested and charged with libel, but she was released for lack of sufficient evidence. Soon after her departure from Great Wyrley, more messages began to appear. These, in a different handwriting, were thrust through windows onto sitting-room floors. Tradesmen received orders for goods, supposedly from the Edaljis, and when they made their deliveries, the Edaljis, who were unable to pay for them, denied they had ever sent the orders. Controversial letters appeared in the Staffordshire newspapers, attributed to the Reverend Edalji but not written by him.

In 1892, a key which had been stolen from Walsall Grammar School suddenly turned up on the doorstep of the vicarage, and the local chief constable, the Honorable G. R. Anson, accused the sixteen-year-old George Edalji, who was a pupil at the school, of stealing it. Edalji protested vainly that if he had stolen the key he certainly would not have left it on his own doorstep, but he was not cleared of suspicion. Letters continued to appear at the Edaljis, vilifying George's parents; and Captain Anson accused him of being their author.

In February, 1903, Great Wyrley was back in the news. That night, a local farmer found one of his horses hideously mutilated, its stomach slit down the middle, almost exposing the entrails. In April, a cow, a horse, a sheep, and other cattle were found butchered in the same way. On August 17, a pit pony was found identically killed. The police arrested George Edalji and accused him of the crimes. From jail, awaiting trial, Edalji wrote letters to the press offering his life's savings of twenty-five pounds to anyone who could supply a clue which would lead to the discovery of the guilty party. The sensitive, rather effeminate young man frequently cried in his cell; and his parents, under severe criticism by the Church of England, suffered unbearably. His coat was examined, and the police announced it had animal bloodstains on it. His razor was supposed to have tiny adherences of animal hair. A police surgeon later claimed he had picked twenty-nine horsehairs from Edalji's coat sleeves. These, he said, matched the hair on the hide of the multilated horse. Edalji's boots were examined, and the heels were supposed to have mud on them which matched the soil near the scene of one of the crimes.

A hysterical farmer's son named Harry Green confessed to the crimes, but the police rejected his statement and apparently arranged for him to leave at once for South Africa because his presence was inconvenient. Edalji was sentenced to a long term of imprisonment, and a handwriting expert positively identified the writing on the numerous vicious notes as matching Edalji's own.

Conan Doyle read the article describing these events, written after Edalji's release from prison for good behavior, with the utmost astonishment. He immediately concluded that Edalji was innocent, and decided to see to it that the young man was exonerated and reinstated in his job as a junior barrister. In January, Edalji came to London to meet Conan Doyle at the Grand Hotel, Charing Cross. Conan Doyle arrived late, delayed by lunch at the Reform Club. He saw the young man sitting in the lobby, reading a newspaper. A significant detail immediately caught his attention. Edalji was peering at the paper painfully through thick pebble glasses, obviously only just able to make out the words. The mutilations had all taken place at night. Conan Doyle knew that Edalji could not have effectively overpowered large animals and aimed a razor precisely at the vulnerable points, even with the aid of a light, if he was almost blind. It was the oculist as well as the detective in Conan Doyle that made him observe this detail.

He studied Edalji intently as they conversed. A shrewd judge of character, he concluded that his companion was an honest man. His myopic eyes filled with tears behind his glasses, his small body trembling, Edalji was an object of pity. Conan Doyle, to make sure he was not faking, questioned him closely on the movements he had made on the nights of the crimes. His alibis seemed watertight. Moreover, when Conan Doyle took Edalji to see eye specialists in Wimpole Street, their verdict confirmed Conan Doyle's diagnosis: the young man would have great difficulty in moving about at night.

Impressed by Edalji's sweet character, Conan Doyle traveled of Great Wyrley to investigate. He was moved by the parents; grief-stricken, they were eager to help him in any way they could. He decided to follow the course which Edalji would have taken to reach the spot where the last animal victim, a horse, had been butchered. The place could be reached only on foot, but one of three routes. The direct route involved crossing the tracks, rather badly grown with grass, of the North-Western Railway. Conan Doyle, taking a light, walked down the vicarage garden, over a grass mound, and across the tracks, which almost tripped him as he went. He found that he had to traverse hedges, climb over half-hidden ditches, and make his way through an overgrown meadow. It was a long and difficult walk which took up much of the night, and which Edalji most certainly could not have managed.

Conan Doyle returned to the vicarage, and at breakfast, told the parson and his wife about his observations. Their gratitude was touching. He next walked across the alternative routes, and came to the same conclusion: only a man with good eyesight and a robust constitution could have made the journey on a storm-swept night and attacked a powerful farm horse.

He then went to the local police station, taking a written authorization, the nature of which was never disclosed by him, from Scotland Yard. This permitted him, no doubt to the fury of the local constabulary, to make an investigation of Edalji's "incriminating" clothes. He examined the horsehair on the coat sleeves and was appalled to discover that for the inquiry the coat had been bundled together with a severed portion of the horse's mane. He analyzed the bloodstains and found that they came from undercooked meat which Edalji had eaten on the night of the crime. The wet condition of the coat and boots was of no significance, since Edalji admitted that he had taken a short walk that night. Conan Doyle took samples of the mud on the boots and found that, contrary to the police statement, it did not match the loam in the meadow. The hair adhering to the razor was not animal but human, and matched that of Edalji's father.

The problem now, apart from having Edalji cleared, was to identify the real culprit. Conan Doyle convinced that a former fellow pupil of George Edalji's was responsible, made detailed inquiries at the local school. He then proceeded to London and published in the London *Daily Telegraph* a series of devastating articles, later issued in book form. These caused an extraordinary sensation, proving as they did that Conan Doyle was capable of using Holmesian deductive methods in real life.

Conan Doyle began to receive poison-pen letters himself; the writing in these was matched to that of a former sailor. Attempts to obtain retrial for Edalji were unsuccessful. Officialdom stood firm. Conan Doyle never did secure reparation for him, but his efforts excited public feeling and succeeded in informally clearing his name. Following the unsatisfactory report of the Gladstone Commission on the case, national criticism was so widespread that eventually the result was the creation of the Court of Criminal Appeal.

Conan Doyle was convinced that the cattle mutilator was a man named Royden Sharp, a school mate of George Edalji who, Conan Doyle believed, had built up a grudge against him. Sharp's voyages as a sailor coincided with the periods in which the threatening letters did not appear in Great Wyrley, and there were other indications of Sharp's guilt. However, until very recently, this information was not made public. It appeared in a critical study of Conan Doyle's work by Pierre Nordon in 1966, and in a BBC recreation of the Edalji case in the early 1970's.

After his fine work on this case, Conan Doyle was frequently asked to solve puzzles of various kinds. One case that came his way particularly fascinated him. He always refused to disclose the names of the people concerned; the names are invented in the following account.

Conan Doyle was contacted by a Mrs. Bellew, who said that her favorite cousin, Henry Armstrong, had disappeared. He had left the Langham Hotel in London after attending a musical performance, had been seen entering his room late at night, and had not been seen leaving it. Conan Doyle wrote by return mail:

Dear Mrs. Bellew,
Your cousin is in Scotland. Look for him in Glasgow or Edinburgh, and I will guarantee you will find him.
ARTHUR CONAN DOYLE

He had deduced the solution in an hour. He determined by telephone that the man had withdrawn his money from a bank. He deduced that the man could not have left the hotel after midnight, because the hall porter locked the door at that time and would have seen anyone who came through it. Why did Armstrong choose to leave at a late hour unobserved, but not after twelve o'clock? Obviously, because he was catching a train. He could not be going to a modestly sized town, where he would easily be recognized. The train for Edinburgh and Glasgow left at midnight. Conan Doyle's deduction proved to be correct, and the man was found.

A much more important event occurred in 1907. In the stories *The Musgrave Ritual, The Blue Carbuncle,* and *The Beryl Coronet,* Holmes had been shown solving the thefts of precious objects. Now, Conan Doyle was faced with a remarkably similar problem in real life. For many years, his mother had kept in touch with a second cousin, Sir Arthur Vicars. As Ulster King of Arms, Vicars was in charge not only of the heraldic records maintained in Dublin Castle but also of the valuable Irish crown jewels, consisting of a diamond star, a diamond badge, and five collars studded with precious gems. The jewels had been presented by William IV in 1830 to the Order of St. Patrick, to be worn on state occasions by the Lord Lieutenant of Ireland as Grand Master of the Order. Vicars' predecessor, Sir Bernard Burke, had supplied the Ma'am with details of her family heraldry, and has passed on many of her requests for information to Vicars.

The combined worth of the Irish crown jewels was £100,000, the equivalent of over £500,000 today. Early in July, Conan Doyle was astounded to read in the paper that the jewels had been stolen from under the noses of Vicars and his nephew and assistant, known as the "Cork Herald," Peirce Mahony. They had been taken from a safe housed in the Bedford Castle tower, and the only man who had the keys was Vicars himself. Vicars was engulfed in a major scandal. In the first place, it emerged that he had removed the jewels for "inspection" a month earlier, and had failed to lock them up properly when he returned them to the library where they were stored. It was impolitely suggested that actually he had not put them back into the safe, but had put them into a simple iron box, for the feeble reason that the lock of the safe was rusted. It was also pointed out that when the loss of the jewels was discovered, for some reason best known to himself he had not reported the matter to the police immediately.

Seriously embarrassed, Vicars wrote to Conan Doyle seeking advice. Could the robbery be an imitation of the recent theft of the Ascot Gold Cup? Was there a political motivation? Was the theft the act of Irish rebels?

Conan Doyle sifted through all the available evidence. He discovered that there was a curious little group surrounding Vicars; all of its members bore the pretentious title "Herald," and in some cases they were possibly homosexual. The Dublin Herald—the second in command to Vicars—was Francis Shackleton, brother of the famous explorer Ernest Shackleton, who was at that moment preparing his expedition to the Antarctic and the South Pole in the *Nimrod*. Conan Doyle had met Francis Shackleton in South Africa and had heard about his gambling debts, his bisexual relationships, and his outrageous behavior in public. By a process of deduction, Conan Doyle concluded that Francis Shackleton had had access to the keys and could have made an impression of them. Since Shackleton was already known as a criminal, the conclusion was obvious. Conan Doyle also felt that Shackleton must have had an accomplice, and he decided that this would have to be Peirce Mahony.

While Conan Doyle was unraveling the details, a peculiar event took place in Ireland. Francis Shackleton returned to Dublin, ostensibly to help in the recovery of the jewels. Apparently a spiritualist, he arranged a séance at Sir Arthur Vicars' handsome house in Dublin. While a society audience sat enthralled, and police watched skeptically, a medium sank into a deep trance and announced that the crown jewels were to be found in one of two graveyards near Dublin. Vicars, grabbing at any straw, set out with Shackleton on a bizarre expedition to dig up the graveyards. Needless to say, they found nothing, and the comments of the Dublin press were, to say the least, unflattering. In England, led by the novelist Marie Corelli, the press had a field day, describing the anxious knight and his flustered helper combing their way through bones, tin cans, and rubbish of all kinds, scrabbling on all fours in the rain.

Edward VII did not find the spectacle amusing, dismissed Vicars, and allowed the odd little group of Heralds to resign. Conan Doyle's investigations continued. The police also were on the trail. Then, without warning, the entire matter was dropped.

It had been found that Shackleton, who had lived on terms of suspicious intimacy with Vicars in London, was also very close to the Duke of Argyll, the King's brother-in-law, and that Shackleton was involved in a homosexual ring in Dublin and London. Evidently, Edward VII was afraid that if Shackleton were arrested, he would disclose under cross-examination that homosexuality was to be found extremely close to the Throne. The consequences of this revelation would, of course, be especially serious. Vicars was ruined, and Francis Shackleton died destitute in 1925, destroyed by gambling and blackmailers. In 1914, Peirce Mahony died mysteriously. He was supposed to have been shooting birds on a lake. Apparently, as he climbed over a wire fence, he accidentally tripped the trigger of his gun, and was shot dead. Many people believed that he had been killed because he knew too much about the crown-jewel robbery, and his demise had been expertly arranged to look like an accident. In 1921, Vicars was called from his house and shot down. He probably knew too much. The jewels have not been recovered to this day.

If this was a case of art imitated by life, then, as so often before, Conan Doyle again turned life into art. He thinly veiled the entire episode in his Holmes story *The Bruce-Partington Plans*. Sir Arthur Vicars becomes Sir James Walter, keeper of official papers in London. Francis Shackleton becomes his brother, Colonel Valentine Walter, his first name an extremely subtle reference to the gossip that Shackleton was Vicars' lover. A man named Cadogan West is found dead, his murder made to look like an accident. Quite obviously, he is modeled on the unfortunate Peirce Mahony.

The theme of *The Bruce-Partington Plans* is the theft not of jewels, but of submarine plans, a theft which may lead to war with a foreign power. It is quite extraordinary that Conan Doyle should have brought up this subject so early. True, since the passage of the first German Navy Law in March, 1898, the expansion of the Kaiser's navy under Admiral Alfred von Tirpitz had caused some concern at the highest level in Britain. True, also, the Pact of Cartagena of May 16, 1907, between Britain, France, and Spain, designed to maintain the *status quo* between the Mediterranean and the east Atlantic powers, had emphasized the need for a British naval force equivalent to Germany's. But submarine warfare, though occasionally discussed, was not seriously considered at the time. One can only speculate on Conan Doyle's source of information. Since presumably he was not, for all his talents, gifted with second sight, it must be deduced that his friendship with Edward VII, and with the new Prime Minister, Herbert Asquith, gave him access to privileged material which he slipped into his stories in disguised form. The subject of submarines was to come up again at the outset of World War I, when he was accused of inadvertently supplying the Germans with the idea of a submarine blockade in his story *Danger!*

On September 18, 1907, Conan Doyle married Jean Leckie. The entire Doyle family wholeheartedly approved the match. Conan Doyle dreaded crowds, brass bands, and fuss, and he refused to tell the press where the ceremony would be held. But of course, the location was discovered immediately—St. Margaret's, Westminster, right next to the stately gray pile of Westminster Abbey. Arthur and Innes, who was best man, arrived in a hansom; all of his sisters came, except Lottie, who was in India; and Dodo's husband, the Reverend Cyril Angell, officiated. Kingsley, a well-knit, handsome blond boy of fifteen, and Mary, a sweet and attractive girl of eighteen, were there, and welcomed their new stepmother warmly. Conan Doyle, in black frock coat, white chamois waistcoat, striped trousers, and spats, looked uncomfortable; Jean, in white silk appliquéd with handsome white Irish lace, was exquisite, but extremely nervous. After the ceremony, the guests went by carriage to the Hotel Métropole. Jean was so badly hampered by the long train of her gown that

Arthur swept her off her feet and carried her, in one long powerful movement, all the way up the red-carpeted stairs to the Grand Reception Room. Among the well-wishers present to enjoy the champagne, caviar, and smoked salmon were Jerome K. Jerome, Bram Stoker, now famous as the author of *Dracula*, George Newnes, Greenhough Smith, John and Archie Langman, and George Edalji.

The honeymoon trip was leisurely; they cruised in the Mediterranean, visiting the Greek islands, Egypt, and Turkey. In Egypt, Conan Doyle was disappointed to find that no one was left on his old hunting ground. Sir Eldon Gorst, who had just taken over from Baron Cromer as Egyptian consul general, was most gracious to the Conan Doyles, but he was distracted by his new responsibilities and could not give the honeymoon couple much attention. In Sophia, they were given permission to attend the sacred festival of the Night of Power. Conan Doyle wrote: "It was the most marvelous spectacle as from the upper circle of pillared arches we looked down upon 60,000 lighted lamps and 12,000 worshippers, who made, as they rose and fell in their devotions, a sound like the wash of the sea." A young woman in the party perched on the parapet and waved at the twelve thousand men below. No woman was permitted to behave in this fashion, and a sea of faces, livid with anger, turned up toward the group. Conan Doyle wrote: "I heard a low deep growl . . . it only need one fiery spirit to head the rush and we should have been massacred—with the poor consolation that some of us had really asked for it. However, she was pulled down, and we made our way as quickly and as quietly as possible out of the side door. It was time, I think."

In early November, in Constantinople, Sultan Abdul-Hamid arranged for Conan Doyle to receive the Order of the second class of the Medjideh, and Jean was awarded the second class of the Niehan-i-Chafahat. The Sultan revealed through his Chamberlain that like other crowned heads of Europe, he was completely captivated by the Sherlock Holmes stories.

Back in England in December to spend Christmas with the children, the Conan Doyles looked extremely fit and happy. The easygoing Mediterranean cruise, the quiet strolls through different ports, had added to the intense pleasure of personal fulfillment after a decade of self-denial. On their return, Conan Doyle made arrangements to lease Undershaw, so that they could buy a house where they would be near Jean's family. He settled on Windlesham, a handsome estate only minutes from the house at Crowborough in which her parents and her delightful brother Malcolm were living after moving from Glebe House, Blackheath.

Conan Doyle was so badly cheated in the deal for the house that it became known, from that moment on, as Swindlesham. It was situated near an extremely quiet, tree-shaded country road. The road ran south of the house, which was sheltered by a tall privet hedge; rolling lawns ran up to the front door. Near the entrance stood a small gardener's cottage. To the west of the house lay a rather overgrown garden, which Jean soon converted into a series of rose bowers, with canopied shadowy walks which she loved to stroll through on warm afternoons.

It was a much more imposing residence than Undershaw. Guests arriving at the front door were greeted by a page like Billy in the Gillette play, in brass buttons and a cap, who ushered them into the hall. A tremendous flight of stairs swept up to the first-floor landing. To the right, under the shadow of the stairs, was the study-office of Conan Doyle's secretary, Major Wood; farther along, beyond a special door, lay the completely separate servants' quarters. The dining room was at the back of the house, with windows looking over the garden; and beyond it again was an immense billiard room, stretching the entire width of the house. At the northern end was a nursery, which was later used as a séance room.

The hall stairs led to Conan Doyle's study, at their left. This room, handsomely appointed, occupied the southwest corner of the upper story, for the length of two of the four gables. Walking northward along the corridor, the visitor could see a small guest room, then Jean's room, above the western end of the billiard room. It was the most beautiful part of the house, and from it Jean could look out on the rose bowers of her exquisite garden. A connecting door led into Conan Doyle's bedroom.

A mud-encrusted cricket bat hung in the place of honor in

the hall, commemorating Conan Doyle's first century on a wet wicket at Lord's. The drawing room offered a handsome statuette of Lord Roberts, a gift from the members of the Langman Hospital in recognition of his sterling work at Bloemfontein. In his bedroom was a silver bowl given to him as a farewell present by his neighbors and their gardeners and grooms at Hindhead. The hall offered a haversack containing a chessboard and chessmen he had found near Capetown, and a blood-encrusted bandoleer taken from a dead man near Pretoria. There were sporting trophies everywhere, including a magnificent stag's head, and photographs of celebrated boxers. In a study window stood a bust of Sherlock Holmes, with an air gun ironically laid beside it.

The house, which Conan Doyle was to retain until his death, was infused with his personality; spacious, warm, glowing with good cheer, it was an Englishman's castle to the last brick. He was very happy there.

It was in this period that Conan Doyle became fascinated by a new subject: the extraordinary case of "Eva C." He had read reports about her by Dr. Charles Richet, Professor of Physiology at the Faculty of Medicine in the University of Paris and honorary President of La Société Universelle d'Études Psychiques. In April, 1906, Richet published, in the *Annales des Sciences Psychiques*, details of some extraordinary occurrences at the Villa Carmen in Algiers, a rambling white building, owned by a General Noel of the French Resident Army. These had begun in the 1890's. Almost every night during that decade, the General and Mme Noel held séances, presided over by their medium, Ahmed, an elderly Arab servant who appeared to have a flair for evoking psychic manifestations. It was said that at his behest the spirits on one occasion carried a stone weighing seventy kilograms from the garden into the house, and on another changed tea in a cup to coffee.

Ahmed claimed to be in touch with a spirit known as Bien-Boa, a Brahmin Hindu who announced that he had died exactly three hundred years before and had been appointed, he did not say by whom, as a ghostly guide to the Noels. He caused table movements, spirit writing on papers and slates, and a pretty exhibition of whirling colored lights in the darkness of the villa.

In 1899, "Eva C" or "Eva Carrière," entered the picture. Her real name was Marthe Beraud. Dark-haired and rather plain, she still had a considerable power to attract, and many people who attended séances she conducted mentioned her magnetic force. Her family—she was the daughter of a French army officer un-der General Noel's command—had sworn her to secrecy about her identity in 1897. The first we hear of her is that she became engaged to Noel's son Maurice in August, 1899.

In July, 1900, Maurice went to the French Congo as a com-mercial agent. He died of a tropical disease in 1904. By now, Ahmed had been fired, since he had been caught by a visitor peeping out from behind a curtain, with a luminous mask. He was replaced by another medium, known as Ninon. Bien-Boa ap-peared again, helmeted and heavily bearded, at Ninon's séances. He was accompanied by his sister, Bergolia, who announced in a silvery voice that she and her brother had been dear friends of Mme Noel's in a previous incarnation. Mme Noel wrote to her legal adviser, an Algerian lawyer named Marsault, that Bergolia drank tea with her, "talking in the most feminine way imaginable, while rummaging about in a box of sweets."

Most marvelous of all, Mme Noel saw her son Maurice. He embraced her, and when he withdrew into the cabinet she could still feel on her forehead the icy imprint of his reading glasses. But soon after, Mme Noel received a disagreeable shock. Eva C. caught Ninon in a wig, spectacles, and mask which exactly dupli-cated the appearance of Maurice Noel. "Ninon had better not impersonate my fiancé to me, or I'll jump in his face!" she told her horrified hostess.

After that, Ninon disappeared discreetly, and Eva C. took over as the only medium at the Villa Carmen. A cabinet was built to her specifications, and the room used for séances was lit only by subdued red light. She would retire to the cabinet. A few minutes after, as the curtain swung into place, a figure dressed in white would emerge and drift through the audience. This was Bergolia. Often she would be joined by Bien-Boa, and Maurice

Noel would materialize, his spectacles shining faintly in the glowing red light of the lamp. Mme Noel published a detailed account of these séances in the French spiritualist magazine *Revue Scientifique et Morale de Spiritisme*.

Understandably intrigued, Professor Richet arrived at the Villa Carmen in 1904, and remained as a house guest for two years. The séances held for Richet took place in a specially prepared room over the stables. The black maid, Aischa, sat next to Eva C. in the cabinet. Sometimes Eva C. would cry out from the cabinet that in the burning heat of the North African summer, she could not endure the odor of the Negress; after that, an understandably grieved Aischa would rush out of the cabinet and disappear down the corridor, wringing her hands. After a two-hour wait, Bien-Boa would finally emerge from the cabinet. Richet swore that Eva C. and Bien-Boa were not one and the same. An intruding neighbor gossiped that he had seen Areski, the Arab coachman, dressed up in a mask and false beard. Shortly after, an Algerian physician, Dr. Rouby, exhibited Areski in his impersonation of Bien-Boa to the local theater.

Richet brought a flask of baryta water to one séance, to see if the phantom would exhale carbon dioxide. It did. Bien-Boa blew so vigorously into the tube that bubbles were seen. Richet became suspicious after this: surely Bien-Boa must be human? At another séance, ectoplasm made an appearance. Richet saw a white vapor, like a small scarf or handkerchief, rise up and form itself into a little man, dressed in a turban and white mantle, who moved with a slight limp from right to left in front of the curtain. Then the head rose from the shoulders and executed a circle in mid-air. Richet had his suspicions. The beard and mustache of the little figure looked artificial, and between the curtain and Eva C.'s black skirt were two small white rods which could have held up a simulacrum of a head and shoulders. He noted also that Eva C.'s left sleeve was empty; was she an expert in glove puppetry? As Richet prepared to leave Algiers, Bien-Boa said to him, "Stay! You will see her whom you desire!"

"It will be easily understood," Richet added, "that I stayed."

The next day, there appeared in the cabinet the face of a

lovely young girl, with a gold crown and pearly teeth. General Noel said to Richet, "Put your hand behind the curtain and you can touch her hair." Richet, quite carried away, obeyed, but withdrew his hand immediately. "It's more like horsehair," he said with disgust.

The young girl's hand tapped him reprovingly. "Bring scissors tomorrow," she said. Richet complied. The girl emerged and announced that she was Cleopatra. "Did you bring the scissors?" she asked. Richet nodded and grabbed a large chunk of hair. As he cut it, a hand emerged and slapped his down. "That's quite enough," she said.

The hair was very fine and silky, and turned out to be genuine. Ruling out a wig, on the peculiar basis that the Noels couldn't afford one, he returned to Paris excitedly to publish his immense study of Eva C. in the *Annales des Sciences Psychiques* in April, 1906. Meanwhile, the lawyer, Marsault, and the physician, Dr. Rouby, issued a report in the Paris magazine *Les Nouveaux Horizons* which threatened to ruin both Richet and Eva C. Marsault disclosed that Eva C. had told him both Bergolia and Bien-Boa were pure humbug. He also revealed that Eva C. and her black servant liked to dress up as men in masks and beards. Eva C. said she had become a medium to satisfy Mme Noel who was fascinated by spirits. When she heard Richet was coming, she arranged further disguises and the installation of a series of trap doors.

The bizarre events at the Villa Carmen intrigued Conan Doyle enormously. Convinced that Marsault was disaffected, he ignored the lawyer's report, and wrote to Richet telling him that he was dazzled by his discoveries in Algiers. The whole episode appealed to him on a deeply romantic level; his love of the bizarre completely overruled his sense of logic, and he desperately wanted to know more. It turned out that Eva C. had now come to Paris, at the invitation of the dramatist and socialite Alexandre Bisson, author of the melodrama *Madame X*, whose wife was a fashionable sculptress.

Richet wrote to Conan Doyle describing Eva C.'s new series of séances. Mme Bisson frequently spent the séances in the cabinet with Eva C., a highly suspicious fact which a few were rude enough to refer to. Bien-Boa and Bergolia had presumably been left behind in Algiers, since they did not materialize in Paris. Eva C. produced ectoplasm, vague shapes of arms, hands, and fingers, and finally a fully materialized female head. Baron von Schrenck-Notzing, a leading psychic investigator, arrived from Munich to examine Eva C. and her phenomena and record them by camera. Conan Doyle was astounded by the photographs which arrived from Paris. He wrote, "Isn't this, without a doubt, the most fantastic thing the mind can conceive? Before such results the brain, even of the trained psychical student, is dazed. While that of the orthodox man of science, who has given no heed to these developments, is absolutely helpless." He evidently overlooked the possibility that the various shapes might have been modeled in soft material by Mme Bisson, who was, after all, a practiced sculptress, and that Eva C. might have regurgitated certain substances.

In the world of the rational, Conan Doyle was as busy as ever. He wrote a series of tales set in ancient times, which were published in 1911 as *The Last Galley*. The title story, thinly disguised as an account of a Roman naval onslaught on an impotent Carthage, was an early critique of Britain's naval unpreparedness in time of possible war. On the face of it, the warning seemed inappropriate, since Britain was then following a program of building dreadnaughts. Presumably, Conan Doyle was again referring indirectly to the danger of foreign submarines, and perhaps to the notorious weakness of the plating below the water line on British vessels.

During the writing of this series of tales, his health again began to fail. In January, 1909, his recurring intestinal problems became so serious that he was bedridden. He appears to have had an intestinal blockage, which called for an operation on January 11. Daily bulletins in the London *Times* indicate that he was in very serious condition, and for three days was on the danger list. Evidently the memory of this close brush with death was deeply painful, for he did not mention it in the memoirs he published in the 1920's. Because of his pressing commitments, he was unable to take a convalescent vacation until September, when he and Jean cruised to Lisbon and the Mediterranean.

Despite his illness, Conan Doyle managed to try his hand at a new form—an original play. His earlier ventures into drama—his stage adaptation *Halves,* and *Brigadier Gerard* for the handsome matinee idol Lewis Waller—had been only minor successes. Now he began a new series of vehicles for Waller, all of which he scrapped. He finally settled on writing a play based on *The Tragedy of the "Korosko."* Called *The Fires of Fate,* "A Morality Play in Four Acts," it starred Waller as a gallant colonel who, given a short time to live by a London doctor, travels to Egypt and becomes the shepherd of a flock of river-boat tourists.

Determined to allow nothing to interfere with the production of this work, Conan Doyle took a lease on the Lyric Theatre and financed the undertaking himself. He scrupulously oversaw every detail of the sets and costumes, driving both designers and costumiers almost mad with his insistence on authenticity. He was recreating his experience in Egypt, and his memory was perfect. He even insisted that when the dervishes captured the little party of tourists, they should beat them with real cudgels and whips. The unfortunate cast was black and blue by opening night, and as noted by more than one keen-eyed spectator, they hobbled onto the stage when the curtain rose. At the end of the scene, Conan Doyle stood over the performers as they were dragged off stage, tied hand and foot. One actress said, "If you are quite finished, I should like to attend to my toilette."

The play opened on June 16, 1909. The audience was very excited by the capturing of the tourists, and when the dervishes wailed an eerie song of triumph through the theater, responded with a standing ovation. Lewis Waller's spaniel-eyed, pallidly handsome hero was greeted with eight curtain calls. An extraordinary episode took place during Act III: a young captain in the Welsh Guards, seeing the ladies on stage being manhandled by the grinning dervishes, cried out, "You cads! How dare you treat our English women so!" Pulling out his gun, he ran up to the stage, tried to take a flying leap over the orchestra, and was only just restrained from firing at the astonished actors.

Conan Doyle answered calls of "Author!" and, very embarrassed but gently urged by Jean, walked onto the stage and gave an amusing speech about experiences in Egypt in 1895. Another standing ovation greeting him, punctuated with cries of "More Holmes, please!"

He did not quite understand the significance of this request at first, but the blazing summer of 1909 showed that it would take a Sherlock Holmes to get people to brave the heat of the Lyric Theatre. *The Fires of Fate* had to go on the road very quickly to save Conan Doyle from a heavy loss. By now, undaunted, he had written another play, *The House of Temperley,* and he leased the Adelphi Theatre for the presentation of this work. Subtitled "A Melodrama of the Ring," *The House of Temperley* was originally sketched out as a precursor of *Rodney Stone.* It dealt with the complicated affairs of Sir Charles Temperley, whose reckless gambling has compelled him to stake the remnants of his fortune on a boxing match. Again, Conan Doyle spent heavily to ensure that the settings—this time, of the Regency period—were authentic and resplendent. He cast Ben Webster as Sir Charles, and in a small part as a pugilist, a young actor named Edmund Gwenn appeared. With his background in boxing, Conan Doyle was determined to see that the boxing match was staged authentically: the "fancy" eagerly watching, the combatants fighting with bare fists. And, of course, Conan Doyle saw to it that they really did box each other. Their bruises had to be covered with make-up for each performance. They were supervised by Fred Binnington, boxing instructor to the London Rifle Brigade. The director, Herbert Jarman, helped Conan Doyle in the actual staging of the fight.

The first-night audience loved the play, shouting approval when the bullying boxer set up against Sir Charles Temperley's man was defeated, cheering Sir Charles when he retrieved his fortune, and greeting Conan Doyle's curtain speech with a prolonged huzzah that lasted eight minutes.

But once again, the author's theatrical adventure proved ill-fated. No sooner had the run started than it was announced that Edward VII was ill; and his death curtailed attendance. Conan Doyle, personally distressed by the demise of his friend, attended the state funeral, and then set to work petitioning the authorities to change the wording of the Coronation Oath for his successor, George V. Although himself a lapsed Catholic he was determined to have the slighting references to Catholics in the Oath eliminated, and he succeeded in obtaining this revision.

His third play, written for the Adelphi and opening on June 6, 1910, was *The Speckled Band*, based with some modifications on the story of the same name. As always a stickler for realism, Conan Doyle engaged the admirable H. A. Saintsbury, who had toured with the Gillette play, as Holmes; Lyn Harding, a good character actor of leering villians, as Dr. Grimesby Roylott; and a real snake for the title role. This caused Christine Silver, whose jitters as the heroine were not entirely simulated, considerable alarm. Unfortunately, the snake proved to be a less than adequate performer. A rock boa, it insisted on hanging down the wall like a piece of rope instead of slithering about in the prescribed manner, and moved only when somebody in the cast or backstage surreptitiously pinched its tail. Conan Doyle was furious when a critic said that the boa was "palpably artificial," and he replaced it quickly with a clockwork creature.

The play was a success, paying off most of the debts resulting from *The House of Temperley*. Conan Doyle's thunder was stolen for once by Lyn Harding, who appeared for his curtain speech with the real snake wrapped around his neck, and giving it a vigorous pinch behind the head, forced it to take a bow.

The Speckled Band ran for 169 performances, transferring to the Globe on August 8. It went on a very satisfactory tour, but the New York production, clumsily produced, was not a success. Conan Doyle never felt satisfied with the play, and indeed time has proved it to be quite inferior. Holmes makes a very late appearance, at least one key element in the solution is left absurdly to Dr. Watson, and the dénouement is an extravagance of melodrama.

Conan Doyle wrote a good many ghost stories in those years. His overstrained mental state, brought on by excessive hours of work, is reflected in *The Silver Mirror*, which in its diary form is reminiscent of *The Parasite*. The narrator is a hard-pressed junior partner in a law firm, who, under extraordinary pressure, has to check out a malfeasance by examining the records of accounts in a musty office:

> I get nervous and highly strung when I sit alone at my work at night. It is not a pain—only a sort of fullness of the head, with an occasional mist over the eyes.

Like his creator, the narrator is heading for a breakdown; and one night, he discovers that he is being haunted. A silver mirror irresistibly attracts his attention. At first, it seems to contain nothing more than a reflection of the room. But then "with a thrill of interest rather than fear"—a statement deeply revealing of the author—he becomes aware that two eyes, filled with anger or terror, are looking out into the room at him from the glass, and they are not his own. They are the eyes of a beautiful woman. He becomes obsessed with them; the mirror itself is "a sort of barometer which measures my brain-pressure."

Bit by bit, details emerge in the mirror, like portions of a painting which is being cleaned. What appears to be a bunch of white ribbons turns out to be a hand, a figure like an animal clutching at the woman's skirts turns out to be a courtier in the grip of terror. One by one, the macabre details emerge, until at last the whole is clear: it is a murder scene in Scottish Stuart costume later recognized as the killing by Darnley of Rizzio, the lover of Mary, Queen of Scots. Conan Doyle's father had worked at Holyrood Palace as a member of the Office of Works; the story suggests the delirium which Charles Doyle experienced as an epileptic and alcoholic.

Another story in diary form, reflecting a mind strained close to breaking, is *The Terror of Blue John Gap*, written in 1909. The narrator is a neurasthenic bachelor, staying with two ladies at a farm in northeast Derbyshire. It is a strange, primitive region, with huge caves and beetling crags. Sheep have disappeared near a large cleft in one rock known as Blue John Gap, and have been found bloodied—a detail recalling the Edalji case. The narrator, summoning up his courage, explores the Gap, and finds huge footprints, suggestive of a gigantic bear. One night, he slithers down the stones of a mountain stream, and, his candle extinguished, hears something inhuman padding by, "an enormous weight, carried on sponge-like feet." He fires at the creature, but it vanishes; the hitherto skeptical villagers, finally convinced of its existence, use rocks to wall it up alive in its cave.

The encounter is vividly described; the beast, its eyes glaring like electric bulbs, suggests not only something monstrous from the abysmal prehistoric past, but something threatening from the scientific future. It is probable that the idea for the story stemmed in part from a contemporaneous discovery near Windlesham of the footprints of a prehistoric animal, apparently an iguanodon, of which Conan Doyle kept casts in his study.

Two Holmes stories of those years indicate Conan Doyle's assiduous reading of everything current. *The Red Circle* is a story of ritual vengeance, reminiscent of *A Study in Scarlet*, and in its opening evocation of a stranger pacing up and down a lodging-house room to the consternation of his landlady, prefiguring *The Lodger*, by Mrs. Belloc Lowndes (1913), and echoing *The Passing of the Third Floor Back* (1908), by Jerome K. Jerome. The secret society which appears in the story is obviously based on the Black Hand, the precursor of the Mafia, which at the time Conan Doyle was working on the tale, had been the subject of many magazine features on both sides of the Atlantic. There had been an extraordinary trial of several members in Viterbo, and the Black Hand had recently caused the murder of the "Sherlock Holmes of America," Lieutenant Joseph Petrosino, in Palermo, Sicily.

Wisteria Lodge had as its theme the appearance in England of a cruel Latin-American tyrant. Once again, the story was related to current news. Magazines and newspapers referred frequently to the resignation of José Santos Zelaya, the heartless President of Nicaragua, whose regime of terror had made him the most hated man in Central America. Zelaya's departure for New York closely paralleled the departure to Barcelona of the Tiger of San Pedro, Don Murileo, in Conan Doyle's story. There is a strong emphasis in the tale on voodoo artifacts; Haiti had just been in the news, and voodoo artifacts had been connected with a bloody insurrection in that island.

Conan Doyle's greatest joy in the last years of the decade was that Jean became the mother of two sons, followed by a daughter. The eldest, Denis, was a handsome, athletic boy, rather like Kingsley in temperament. The second son, who was then called Malcolm but later preferred to use his first name, Adrian, was more mischievous in character, odd and unpredictable, and something of a rapscallion in family games. The daughter was named Jean Lena Annette, after her mother, her maternal grandmother, (Selina Leckie), and her aunt and great-aunt. She disliked "Lena" and "Annette," and Conan Doyle, who wanted his children to make up their own minds very early, allowed her to pick a name at age six. She chose "Billy," after a favorite comic-book character. Conan Doyle's book about his children, *Three of Them*, was so excessively affectionate, for all its charm, that it proved quite embarrassing to his offspring at school.

Conan Doyle continued, at just past fifty, to maintain his grueling schedule, working from 6:30 A.M. to 3 or 4 A.M. when at home. He wrote while riding on trains, while waiting for trains, and even when stopping for a traffic light in his car. His restless mind was easily stimulated by many subjects, but in 1909 and 1910, one in particular eclipsed almost all others—the Congolese question.

The matter of reform in the Congo Free State had been a political issue in England since 1903, when Roger Casement, the young and ardent British consul, reported a series of atrocities by the Grand Lacs Company and by various concerns which ran rubber plantations in the area, then under the sovereignty of King Leopold II of Belgium. Though it now seems that these reports were exaggerated, and colored by Casement's extravagant paranoid fantasies and homosexual involvements with some of his black employees, they were of the utmost importance in drawing attention to the exploitation of black labor in the Congo. In 1908, Belgium annexed this vast country, the size of Europe, and a token attempt seems to have been made to alleviate the torture and bloodshed which had shocked the world; but this was not enough for Edmund Dene Morel, a radical journalist and agitator, who whipped up a public outcry in England against Belgium.

This stimulation of public feeling proved embarrassing to moderates in the Foreign Office, since it was widely feared that criticism of Belgium would force Leopold II into a close alliance with Germany, which would affect the struggle for power in Europe. Generally, though, the Government and the Opposition joined in approving Morel's crusading campaign. As secretary of the Congo Reform Association, with Lord Beauchamp as president, Morel obtained the unqualified support of Lord Cromer, and a hundred Members of Parliament.

In his attempt to obtain help from every major public figure, Morel inevitably turned to Conan Doyle, who was greatly impressed with his sincerity and his almost naïve faith in the ultimate triumph of human goodness. Conan Doyle saw that apart from giving lectures and writing letters to the *Times*, the best way for him to tackle the problem would be to exercise his talents as a pamphleteer and issue a booklet along the lines of *The War in South Africa, Its Cause and Conduct.* The difference would be that on this occasion the work would be accusatory rather than defensive.

The Crime of the Congo, a brief and impassioned plea for justice and decent treatment, is one of Conan Doyle's most deeply felt works—but its timing could not have been less fortunate. It was written too late. It appeared just before the death of Leopold II, so that its violent attacks on that monarch seemed tasteless. It ignored the pioneer reforms of the Belgian Jules Renkin in the Congo basin, and it relied too heavily on Casement's hysterical reports, treating most cavalierly the subsequent, far more balanced report of the Belgian committee set up to investigate the troubled region in 1904.

Badly timed or not, the document did have the effect of shaking Belgian complacency about what had been achieved since the annexation, and probably sharpened international pressure for further reform. In one respect it seems almost shocking today. Conan Doyle implied that war with Belgium might be necessary, suggesting most rashly that the Congo should be taken from Belgium and divided among France, Germany, and Great Britain. He made the exaggerated statement that Belgium was guilty of "the sack of a country, the spoliation of a nation, the greatest crime in all history."

The publicity for the Congo campaign was underlined in the autumn of 1909 by a major demonstration at the Albert Hall, almost coincidental with the publication of Conan Doyle's book, and presided over by the Archbishop of Canterbury. Conan Doyle traveled the length and breadth of Britain lecturing for the cause. The whole campaign reached its climax at a meeting in the Whitehall Rooms on May 29, 1911, presided over by Lord Cromer. Conan Doyle gave Morel a four-thousand-pound check and a bronze statue of a Congo chief by Herbert T. Ward; he presented to Mrs. Morel a portrait of her husband by William Rothenstein. By 1913, the reform of the Congo was virtually complete. Blunt though his weapons may have been, Conan Doyle had established, once and for all, his reputation as a crusader for social justice.

9

SUBMARINES AND SCIENCE FICTION

CONAN DOYLE continued to be active in his role as a real-life Sherlock Holmes. During his illness in January, 1909, he had first become aware of a case which was to preoccupy him as much as the Congolese question.

The Oscar Slater case fascinated Conan Doyle perhaps even more than the Edalji affair. It began with a murder. The setting of the great crime was Queens Terrace, a sober, gray street in Glasgow. Marion Gilchrist, a spinster of eighty-two, lived on the first floor of Number 15, in a modest but comfortably furnished flat. The ground-floor flat, which had been combined with the ground-floor flat of number 14, the intervening wall having been knocked down, was occupied by a family named Adams. The top-floor flat was empty. Miss Gilchrist's only companion was a twenty-one-year-old maid, Helen Lambie. Miss Gilchrist lived a sedentary existence, her only interest being her jewelry collection, valued at three thousand pounds. Terrified of robbery, she had three locks of three different makes on her front door.

The household was run with Scottish regularity. Each evening at exactly seven, Helen Lambie would leave to buy the Glasgow papers for her mistress and do any shopping that was necessary, and would return promptly. On the night of December 21, 1908, according to her own testimony, she went out, locked the door, and took the keys with her. She stopped to talk to a constable on the beat, and when she returned from an expedition that took no more than ten minutes, she noticed a single muddy footstep on the front porch. When she had climbed up the stairs to the first-floor landing, she saw Mr. Adams, the neighbor from the flat below, standing there ringing Miss Gilchrist's doorbell. Adams said, "I heard a loud bang on the ceiling followed by a chopping sound."

The maid replied, "Oh, that would be the pulleys [clotheslines] in the kitchen."

She unlocked the door. To her astonishment, a man darted out, and down the stairs. She insisted later that no man had been in the apartment when she had gone out. Her next action seems a trifle odd in the circumstances. Instead of looking to see if her mistress was all right, or even calling out to her, she went into the kitchen and found that the clotheslines had not fallen down. Then she and Adams, instead of going into the sitting room, where she had left Miss Gilchrist, went into the dining room. There they found Miss Gilchrist, lying face down not far from the fireplace, with a rug over her head. Her face and the back of her skull had been smashed with terrible violence, in a manner which recalled the murder of Lizzie Borden's parents some seventeen years earlier in Massachusetts.

The police arrived, believing that the murder had been committed for Miss Gilchrist's jewels. But the jewels had scarcely been touched. Aside from a diamond brooch, nothing of significance had been taken. But a box containing various documents, including Miss Gilchrist's life insurance and a recently altered will, had been broken open and rifled.

From that moment, the handling of the case by the Glasgow police was nothing short of a disgrace. They did not conduct a satisfactory search of the flat upstairs; they did not adequately question Adams about his background, or his relationship with the deceased woman. They neither published nor even obtained an exhaustive account of Miss Gilchrist's family, which might have disclosed a motive and perhaps a murderer. It seems clear that from the beginning they wanted to protect the killer, and one is led to the conclusion that he was either connected with the force in some way, or was so highly placed that an investigation of him would have seriously embarrassed senior officials in Glasgow.

Helen Lambie testified later, long after her statement could help a falsely accused man, that the police had compelled her to make an incorrect identification. At the time of the investigation, she and Adams agreed that the man who left the flat was between twenty-five and thirty-nine years of age, 5 feet 8 or 9 inches tall, dressed in a light-gray overcoat and cloth cap. A fifteen-year-old girl named Mary Barrowman said she had encountered a man running out of the house so fast he had almost knocked her over. But there was an odd discrepancy between her description and theirs. She said the man was tall and had a twisted nose. Both Helen Lambie and Adams agreed that he was of medium height and that his nose was normal.

The police told reporters that Miss Gilchrist must have heard the doorbell ring, opened the door, and sat down, waiting for someone to come in. This was an absurd hypothesis in view of her avowed terror of burglars. The much likelier theory, that the man had been admitted by the maid and was known to the victim, was completely overlooked.

On Christmas Eve, 1908, the police determined that a certain Oscar Slater, a German Jew, who was a pimp and possibly a criminal, had attempted to pawn a brooch very similar to Miss Gilchrist's missing ornament. When constables arrived at his flat, they found that he and his mistress had left the country on board the S.S. *Lusitania*. He became the perfect scapegoat. He was arrested in New York and charged with the murder. Adams, Helen Lambie, and Mary Barrowman, the three witnesses, were taken across the Atlantic, and at a police line-up, unhesitatingly identified him as the man they had seen. Slater became hysterical, insisting that he had never heard of Miss Gilchrist or been anywhere near her house on the night of the crime.

Presumably hoping that his action would prove his innocence, Slater did not wait for extradition, but voluntarily returned to Glasgow to answer further questions. While he was in jail, the brooches were definitely established to be different in setting and radically different in design. It was also established that Slater had made the bookings on the *Lusitania* several weeks earlier. His alibi was watertight. He had been seen by several people playing billiards at the time Miss Gilchrist was murdered. Moreover, he wore a mustache; all three witnesses had declared that the man they had had seen was clean-shaven.

At the trial, several experts testified that the head of a hammer found in Slater's belongings matched the indentations in Miss Gilchrist's head. Other experts said that the hammer was far too small to have administered the blows. The three key witnesses stuck religiously to their original stories. All insisted that the man in the dock was unquestionably the person they had seen. The jury, further influenced by a biased summing up by the judge, Lord Guthrie, brought in a verdict of guilty. Slater made a hysterical appeal for mercy, but he was sentenced to be hanged. Apparently some highly placed people had grave doubts of his guilt, and twenty thousand signatures were obtained on a petition for a reprieve. Only two days before the scheduled execution, the prisoner's sentence was commuted to penal servitude for life. He was sent to Peterhead jail, where he broke stones for eighteen years.

Conan Doyle became interested in every detail of the case. When he received a letter from Slater's lawyers begging him to try to solve it and gain the release of their client, he turned all of his formidable intellect and strength toward the problem. He was satisfied immediately that Slater was not guilty. There was not a shred of proof that Slater knew Marion Gilchrist or Helen Lambie, or had the opportunity or the knowledge to obtain an impression of the keys and have them duplicated. Conan Doyle was convinced that the keys had been duplicated and that the police knew the murderer. He fastened his suspicions on a relative of Miss Gilchrist's who had been written out of her will. But he dared not name the possible culprit.

On March 30, 1914, Conan Doyle received a letter from a Glasgow solicitor, David Cook, revealing that a member of the police force, Detective Lieutenant Trench, had, after searching his conscience, disclosed that he was convinced that Mary Barrowman had lied when she said she had seen Slater dashing out of the house, that the police had made her lie, and that Slater had been proved to have more witnesses to his presence elsewhere than the police had been prepared to admit. But the most extraordinary information Cook had to convey was that Helen Lambie had actually identified the killer; she had given his name to Miss

Gilchrist's niece, Miss Birrell. Conan Doyle believed that the police had ignored her statement and had made her concoct another version of the facts, for reasons to be determined.

In response to agitation by Conan Doyle and others, an inquiry was held under the Sheriff; but Slater was refused an opportunity to give evidence, or even to be represented by counsel. The public and the press were excluded, and the witnesses were interviewed most desultorily. Helen Lambie denied that she had ever named the killer to Miss Birrell, and reiterated her identification of Slater. Miss Birrell denied that she had heard the murderer's name. Mary Barrowman repeated her story, complete with the differences from the descriptions by the other witnesses. Adams did not vary an inch from his earlier account. The police denied that Miss Birrell had ever disclosed the identity of the murderer to them. The Sheriff bullied Trench, who, though threatened with ruin, courageously stuck to his story. The result of the inquiry was that Slater's guilt was reaffirmed, and Trench was disgraced. There the matter lay. Even Conan Doyle's admirable pamphlet *The Case for Oscar Slater*, published as early as 1912, had failed to shake the obstinate Scottish judiciary. The Slater case was not heard of again until almost the end of Conan Doyle's life, in the late 1920's.

On July 10, 1911, Conan Doyle was in Germany to take part in the Prince Henry Automobile Race, in which fifty German cars were pitted against fifty representatives of the Royal Automobile Club. With Jean at his side, and a German cavalry officer along for the ride, he chugged along in his handsome, green-painted 20-horsepower Dietrich-Lorraine automobile. The purpose of the race was, presumably, to indicate Germany's feelings of good will toward Britain. The prize was a carved ivory statue of a woman carrying the dove of peace. With a roar of motors, and in a cloud of dust, the procession of cars took off from Homburg, rattled through Cologne, Münster, and Bremerhaven, and then proceeded by steamer to a resumption of the race in Southampton. The race continued, watched by large crowds, through much of England and Scotland, ending in London. The

British team won, and the two teams joined in toasting the Kaiser at the Royal Automobile Club.

Conan Doyle was convinced that the contest was a deliberate blind, to distract attention from German behavior in the Moroccan crisis. In 1909, the Germans and the French had reached a shaky agreement on their separate claims to special territorial interests in Morocco; but the French had flagrantly disregarded the terms of the agreement, and had refused to make compensation to the Germans. In June, the French, who were supposed to restrict their activities to policing specific areas, in effect achieved a military occupation of Fez. This was intolerable to the Kaiser and his Chancellor, Theobald von Bethmann-Hollweg. They announced that the French action was in direct violation of the Act of Algeciras. The French ambassador in Berlin, Jules Cambon, at a meeting with the German Foreign Secretary, Alfred von Kilderlen-Waechter, failed to make a satisfactory explanation of the Fez affair. Because the French government was in the midst of a cabinet change, which resulted in Joseph Caillaux's new ministry on June 28, 1911, Cambon was handicapped in making any definite statement. On July 1, the German gunboat *Panther* arrived at Agadir, on the Atlantic coast of Morocco, as a warning to the French that they must no longer exercise an improper control of Moroccan territory.

Conan Doyle mistakenly assumed that Germany was acting iniquitously in the matter, and decided that the episode was proof that she was contemplating war. Actually, the Kaiser, and his nation, were anxious to remain friendly with Britain, but feared that following Britain's build-up of the dreadnaught fleet, Germany would be seriously imperiled. Britain also felt a sense of suspicion and fear, because of Germany's arms build-up. After the Agadir incident, the British followed a somewhat ambiguous policy, nervously seeking neutrality without believing that it could permanently exist.

Conan Doyle himself shows unusual ambiguity in his writings at the time. On the one hand, he felt that he was wrong in doubting Germany's aspirations for peace; on the other, he made it clear that one part of him had feared the Germans from the beginning of the century. Actually, with his extraordinary instinct, he was foreseeing the outbreak of World War I; but with characteristic oversimplification of the facts, typical of upper middle-class Englishmen of his time, he saw the drift into war as being brought about solely by an aggressive Germany.

His letters to the press, indicating that Germany was acting most improperly in Morocco, were ill-timed, given the international situation. In view of his great fame and influence, they seriously handicapped the moderates, while undoubtedly reflecting the official attitude of his friend Sir Edward Grey, the Foreign Secretary.

Conan Doyle was on safer ground in 1912, when he collided with George Bernard Shaw in the famous *Titanic* controversy. After the S.S. *Titanic* was ripped open by an iceberg on April 14, taking with her an old friend of Conan Doyle's, the controversial editor and spiritualist W. T. Stead, Shaw announced that the ship's captain had been inefficient, that the officers had handled themselves badly, that there had been panic on board, and that the steerage passengers had been denied a chance to escape. His articles in the London *Daily News and Leader* caused widespread comment. Conan Doyle, feeling yet again that British honor had been impugned, rushed to the defense of the late Captain Smith and his gallant officers and crew. Both Shaw and Conan Doyle, flying to extremes, overlooked the one really crucial factor in the *Titanic* sinking—the weakness of the famous vessel below the water line.

In his memoirs, published after World War I, Alfred von Tirpitz revealed that the sinking of the *Titanic* confirmed his belief that British ships, with their comparatively thin hull-plating, and their watertight doors between the watertight compartments, laid themselves wide open to U-boat attack. In fact, he disclosed that after this disaster he had seen to it that all German battleships and cruisers were constructed with substantial plating and with walls instead of doors between the watertight chambers, and that specially built test portions of the warships were subjected to attacks by a wide variety of torpedoes before they were passed for completion.

There can be no question that although he apparently did not see the direct significance of the *Titanic* sinking, Conan Doyle was very much aware of the U-boat threat in 1912. Indeed, the purpose of his story *Danger!* was to alert Britain to this threat. And it cannot be an accident that Conan Doyle wrote the story only a few weeks after Winston Churchill, newly appointed First Lord of the Admiralty, made a statement at the 118th meeting of the Committee of Imperial Defence (July 18, 1912):

If ever there was a vessel in the world whose services to the defensive will be great, and which is a characteristic weapon for the defence, it is the submarine. But the German development of that vessel is, from all the information we have, to be changed into one of offence, that is to say, they are building not the smaller classes which will be useful for the defence of their somewhat limited coastline, but the large classes which would be capable of sudden operations at a great distance from their base across the sea.

Danger! is told in diary form by Captain John Sirius, a submarine commander of a minor European power. There has been tension in the colonies; an ultimatum expires following the death of two missionaries—a direct reference to the Congolese situation. Sirius is given the task of bringing Britain to her knees. When the dreadnaught fleet of which he is a part is sunk at Blankenberg (read "Spitsbergen"), Sirius is convinced the war can still be won. In command of eight submarines, he sets out to destroy the British fleet. He sinks five British vessels off Maplin Sands and the Nore, thus proving the efficacy of the new weapon, the submarine torpedo.

It is fascinating to compare Conan Doyle's detailed description of the Sirius submarine fleet with the actual specifications of U-boats, not released until after the war. In Sirius' small group are eight vessels, each with a displacement of 800 tons, and an engine of 1,600 horsepower, managing 18 knots on the surface and 12 when submerged. In 1912, Tirpitz's fleet consisted of nine submarines (increased to fifteen by late 1913), each with a displacement of 900 tons, and an engine of 2,000 horsepower, managing 16 knots on the surface and 11 when submerged. Conan Doyle's description of the Sirius torpedoes, the Bakdorfs, is astonishingly similar to official descriptions of the Schwartzkopf torpedoes of the U-boats; and the antiaircraft guns of the Sirius and the U-boat fleets are virtually identical.

It hardly seems possible that all these resemblances were mere coincidences. One is forced to the conclusion that Conan Doyle, perhaps through his friendship with Sir Edward Grey, King George V, and Asquith, was given access to privileged information supplied by British spies. He may have been used as a mouthpiece by individuals who felt it advisable for England to be aware of the build-up of the U-boat fleet.

In an article, "Great Britain and the Next War," he asserted that Germany was planning a U-boat blockade. The article, and his busy campaigning in letters and speeches through 1912 and 1913 for effective anti-U-boat surveillance and protective devices, were largely opposed in official circles. His one strong public supporter apart from Churchill was Admiral Sir Percy Scott, who warned repeatedly of the weakness of British vessels below the water line, and of the very real danger of a blockade.

Critics of Conan Doyle, Scott, and the anti-U-boat lobby insisted until the outbreak of war in August, 1914, that torpedoes had an insufficient range, that submarines could only manage 10 knots against the 30 knots of light-armored cruisers and the 25 knots of battleships, and that submarines were highly vulnerable when surfaced. Sir Percy Scott begged for additional submarines, writing to the London *Times* that with a flotilla commanded by dashing young officers, he would undertake to slip past any harbor boom and sink or materially damage all the ships in that harbor. His and Churchill's urgent requests were, to the lasting disgrace of the government, not acted upon until it was almost too late.

As soon as war broke out, a real-life Captain Sirius emerged in the person of Captain Weddigen, the daring commander of the U-9, who in the North Sea on September 22, 1914, sank three British ships, all very weak below the water line—the *Hogue*, the *Cressy*, and the *Aboukir*. On February 4, 1915, the German government announced that a submarine blockade of Great Britain would begin on February 18, just as Conan Doyle had predicted. On May 7, the *Lusitania*, extremely vulnerable below the water line, was sunk with the loss of 1,198 persons, including Conan Doyle's friend Charles Frohman.

Conan Doyle had been vindicated completely. But a curious series of events followed his vindication. On February 18, 1915, the day the submarine blockade was to commence, an article appeared in the *Times* in which an anonymous American journalist described his interviews with officials in Germany on the question of the blockade. One of them had told him:

We had the idea ready-made in England. Conan Doyle suggested the outline of a plan which every German had hoped would be used. His story *Danger!* will tell you far better than I can what we intended to do. We have the U-boats now, and as we believe that England is attempting to starve us, we must show her that two can play at that game.

The writer added, "This was said to me with all seriousness, and I heard Conan Doyle's story referred to repeatedly in defense of the blockade." On May 1, 1916, the Reichstag held a special meeting to discuss the naval war. The Secretary of the Navy, Admiral Capelle said, "Admiral Gelster is generally accredited as the inventor of submarine warfare. He never mentioned it. The real and only prophet was Sir Arthur Conan Doyle."

After publication of this statement in *The New York Times*, Conan Doyle gave a press conference at which he said, "I need hardly say that it is very painful to me to think that anything I have written should be turned against my country. The object of the story was to warn the public of a possible danger which I saw overhanging this country and to show it how to avoid that danger."

In 1910, Conan Doyle had become very friendly with a young lawyer, Edward Marshall-Hall. Though suffering from recurrent illnesses, and from excruciating back pain, Hall was a charismatic figure at the bar. Like Arthur Balfour, he had become interested in spiritualism following the death of the woman who meant most to him in the world. His wife Ethel had never been in love with him. When he neglected her for his legal duties, she entered into an adulterous relationship with a young officer. Becoming pregnant, she had gone to an abortionist, Albert Laermann, who drugged her with wine, and while an assistant operated on her, played the piano to drown out her screams. Ethel Marshall-Hall had died as a result of the operation. Laermann was sentenced to fifteen years of penal servitude.

Moved by the horrifying story, Conan Doyle was drawn to the tragically bereaved husband. Hall told him of a curious episode which had taken place in 1894. A Miss Wingfield was receiving messages in automatic handwriting, and Hall decided to test her powers. His brother, John Cressy Hall, was a remittance man living in South Africa. Hall had recently received a rude letter from his brother; he sealed it in a blank envelope, handed it to Miss Wingfield, and asked her to identify the author. Her hand began to move. The following words were spelled out: "The writer of this letter is dead."

Hall asked, "When and where did the writer die?"

The reply was, "He died yesterday, in South Africa."

He dismissed the matter from his mind. He was convinced that the message was absurd; his brother was alive. But only a few days later, he learned that his brother had in fact died on the day in question, or possibly just a few hours later. Hall regarded this episode as conclusive, and from that moment on became a convinced spiritualist.

In the years just before the war, Conan Doyle's imagination was on fire. His Holmes stories of the period are among his finest achievements. *The Disappearance of Lady Frances Carfax* was suggested by an actual episode in Lausanne, where Kingsley Doyle was studying medicine; a lady mysteriously disappeared from a local hotel, leaving several unpaid bills. In the story, Watson goes to Lausanne to unravel the puzzle in aid of Holmes. It emerges that Lady Frances has been abducted by an Australian criminal, possibly modeled on the late bandit Ned Kelly, who takes her to London, hides her in a room, and then attempts to murder her by burying her alive in a coffin over the body of an old woman.

In *The Devil's Foot*, Holmes and Watson, in Cornwall, trying to unwind from weeks of heavy work (a reference to Conan Doyle's trip to Devon with Fletcher Robinson) are faced with a horrible puzzle. In a farmhouse, several members of a family are found—one dead, the others driven mad—their faces livid with terror. There are suggestions of the famous west-country legend of the Devil's Footprint; this calamity has been caused not by a mysterious one-legged demon, but by poisonous smoke resulting from the burning of a tropical plant. In this respect the story recalls the notorious Hanoi Shan case in Paris of 1906, in which the victims were found staring and dead, killed by poisonous emanations of another plant. The theme of vengeance echoes *A Study in Scarlet;* the strange explorer-killer suggests the murderous big-game hunter of the earlier story *The Empty House.*

And Conan Doyle seems to be alluding as well to yet another actual event. In August, 1910, his friend and fellow in psychic research Frank Podmore had disappeared from a house at Malvern Wells. Podmore was last seen at dinner, then wandered off on the moors with a young man he knew, never to return. He was discovered after several days of searching, lying in a shallow pond with a look of terror on his face. His death was officially recorded as an accident, and despite some suspicion attaching to his friend, the question of murder was never seriously considered.

In 1911, Conan Doyle had casts made of the previously discovered iguanodon footprints. Almost as though he were practicing psychometry, he was inspired by them to create perhaps his finest work in fiction, *The Lost World,* for which he consulted with the eminent zoologist Edwin Ray Lankester. The narrator of the adventure story is Edward Dunn Malone, clearly modeled on Edmund Dene Morel, an affectionate compliment to his fellow campaigner. Malone is a somewhat naïve but impassioned journalist who has to interview the bizarre Professor George Edward Challenger, author of "Some Observations Upon a Series of Kalmuck Skulls" and "The Underlying Fallacy of Weismannism," and recently returned from a mysterious expedition to South America. Rude, violent, and physically primitive, Challenger is drawn from Conan Doyle's old teacher the Assyrian-bearded Professor Rutherford, of Edinburgh University.

Despite an ill-tempered letter from Challenger, Malone decides to brave the lion in his den at Enmore Park. Challenger presents an astonishing spectacle to his visitor: his head is enormous, almost macrocephalic, his shoulders and chest are equally Doylean, but his body is that of a stunted Hercules. Exasperated by Malone, he grapples with him; they go hurtling downstairs, locked together in a fury. Challenger insists that his victim return upstairs; still flaying Malone with insults, he shows him a drawing which makes his head reel. The picture is of a creature with a fowl's head, a lizard's body, a fringed back, and a spiked tail. It is a prehistoric monster that has been seen on a plateau in South America, a denizen of a lost world of primitive creatures. Challenger is organizing an expedition to investigate this world. Malone becomes Watson to Challenger's Holmes.

Two new members later join the expedition, as well as Malone, who is assigned to cover it. These are Professor Summerlee, thin, gaunt, and acid-tongued, always puffing at a pipe, who is reminiscent of Dr. Joseph Bell; and Lord John Roxton, the spare, handsome, exquisitely dressed battler for the underprivileged natives of the Congo and the South American hinterland, who is modeled on Roger Casement.

The book is a masterpiece of imaginative fiction, reminiscent of Jules Verne but not suffering from the comparison. After the funny and grotesque opening, the arrival at the Amazon basin is wonderfully described. When the travelers enter the jungle, we are reminded of the journeys of Darwin:

During the hot hours of the day only the full drone of insects, like the beat of a distant surf, filled the ear, while nothing moved amid the solemn vistas of stupendous trunks, fading away into the darkness which held us.

The vault of interlacing leaves, the emerald river, the black-velvet chittering monkeys and green-eyed pumas, the brilliantly colored wings of birds—the vision of the wilderness brings out the poet in Conan Doyle, while the long, dreamlike, thrusting journey to the mysterious lost plateau excites the adventurer in him.

Gradually, the romantic image of forest and stream changes into a nightmare; we move from Hudson and Rousseau to Dante and Doré as we see the rookery of pterodactyls, with their red eyes and flapping spined wings, their yellow eggs and disgusting fetid odor. The tortured cry of an iguanodon echoes through the forest; ape men dart among the trees; a huge toadlike face stares through the leaves; and the night has the flat, static terror of a drug-induced hallucination:

I stood and glared with starting eyes down the moonlit path which lay behind me. All was quiet as in a dream landscape. Silver clearings and the black patches of the bushes—nothing else could I see. Then, from out of the silence, imminent and threatening, there came once more that low throaty croaking. . . .

The story is humanized by the fantastic bitter humor of the explorers, scoring points off each other as though in a London club; and the climax at the Queen's Hall reaches extraordinary heights of comedy and terror. As Professor Challenger delivers his lecture, he presents a mysterious box:

"Come then, pretty, pretty!" [he said] in a coaxing voice.
An instant later, with a scratching, rattling sound, a most horrible and loathsome creature appeared from below and perched itself upon the side of the case. Even the unexpected fall of the Duke of Durham into the orchestra, which occurred at that moment, could not distract the petrified attention of the vast audience.

The Duke of Durham's mishap is, of course, the master touch; the incongruous note of farce makes the apparition of the monster all the more unsettling. As the pterodactyl flaps around the hall, with its putrid odor and its hump-backed, shawled look, it is like a devil returned from the black past to terrorize London. Later, it appears before a sentry like a demon flying across the moon. The crowd outside, stretched from the Langham Hotel to Oxford Circus, recovers from its panic to cheer the explorers in triumph. But there is a twist in the tail, typical of Conan Doyle's sardonic wit. Malone had been impelled to accompany the expedition largely because a certain challenging young woman wanted to see him prove himself as a hero and man of adventure. He rushes off to her house in Streatham to claim her, as a knight would claim his lady, and is horrified to discover she is married to a mediocre solicitor's clerk who has never been anywhere.

The reviews—and sales—of *The Lost World* were excellent. The inexhaustible author posed for publicity photographs dressed up as Challenger, with friends costumed as Summerlee, Roxton, and Malone. He liked his Challenger impersonation so much that he wore the disguise around London and frightened Willie Hornung with it; Jean had the greatest difficulty in persuading him not to wear it to bed.

Delighted that so many critics enjoyed the adventure of his story, but disappointed that they did not note the ironical humor, Conan Doyle plunged almost immediately into an other Challenger tale, which in sheer imaginative force very nearly equaled the first.

The Poison Belt, published in 1913, is reminiscent of Poe and M. P. Shiel. Malone is intrigued by reports of disturbances in the ether and the color spectrum, and decides to visit Challenger at his house near Rotherfield, Sussex, to join him in investigating the phenomenon. Challenger sends a brief telegram: BRING OXYGEN. On the way to Sussex, Malone runs into the other members of the Lost World expedition, who have also been asked to bring oxygen. Challenger's house, as described by Malone, appears exactly like Windlesham, with a perfect view of the South Downs. Challenger, it seems, has become more erratic than ever. He has bitten the leg of his chilly, aloof housekeeper, sending her screaming from the room; he has narrowly resisted startling his wife to death by jumping out at her from the stairs. He reveals to his former companions that the earth has swung into a poison stream in the ether, that he is among the first to be mentally affected, and that mankind is doomed. He says to his manservant:

> "I'm expecting the end of the world today, Austin."
> "Yes, sir, what time sir?"

He reassures his wife that death will be pleasant, no more painful than inhaling gas at the dentist's; and he asserts a Doylean belief in the hereafter. In Mrs. Challenger's airtight boudoir, the scientists enjoy claret and a fine dinner, while outside the windows the world withers and dies. They are no politer to each other than they were in South America:

> "I was working at a book of verses."
> "Well, the world has escaped that, anyhow."

They leave the house equipped with oxygen tanks, and observe a peaceful frieze of death: a cheerful group in the open tonneau of an automobile, a servant with a gas hose, a whole population fixed at its tasks and pleasures. Conan Doyle may have obtained this extraordinary image from a visit to Pompeii which he had made some years before. The scientists discover an amusing contradiction of the rule of the survival of the fittest; on the way to London, the only living person they encounter is an old woman who has been taking oxygen for her asthma. They tell her that the world is at an end. Her response is wonderfully English:

"Gentlemen, I beg that you will be frank with me. What effect will these events have upon London and Northwestern Railway shares?"

At the end, Conan Doyle gives the reader a pleasant surprise: the people of the world are not dead, but merely in a trancelike state, and like clockwork figures the seeming corpses scattered across town and country click into action again. The release of the millions is exquisitely described. More than one survivor is furious, longing to return to the bliss of death. Here again, the master ironist is at work, making one see the absurd and touching paradoxes of the human mind.

One of Conan Doyle's ventures into imaginative fiction at the time reflected an increased interest in air travel following the nightmare vision several years earlier of *The Great Brown-Pericord Motor*. This new story is *The Horror of the Heights*, inspired by reports of a new altitude achievement, by his own recent flights from Hendon airdrome, and perhaps by his fear of future war in the air. The story begins ominously with a farmer's discovery of a brier pipe and a pair of binoculars in an area not far from Windlesham. Pages from a record book indicate that these pathetic relics belonged to a poet-flier, Joyce-Armstrong; the pages tell the story of his flight in a monoplane five thousand feet above Salisbury Plain.

The dead man's word are disturbing; they describe an ascent through strange, shifting clouds and eddies of air, and then, in the sea-like upper atmosphere, encounters with a jellyfish larger than the dome of St. Paul's, more strange drifting creatures, and at last a horrific adversary, a kind of air-borne squid. The airman's strange attraction to the beauty of the floating monsters reflects the author's love of the bizarre, the inversion of ocean and air is an interesting idea, an echo of the image of the poisonous stream in the previous work. The giant jellyfish and squid are probably meant to symbolize the Zeppelins which would soon bomb London, and which were to horrify Conan Doyle more than any other artifact of war.

In 1912 and 1913, he was tirelessly agitating for many kinds of reform. He was very much behind a movement to ban the use of feathers in women's hats and clothing; the "plumage issue," as it became known, was a subject of numerous meetings right up until the middle of the war. He was also president of the Divorce Reform Association, making it clear that he believed couples who were incompatible should be permitted to sever their relationship legally on that ground alone. He also urged improved oral teaching of the deaf and dumb, and delivered a brilliant lecture on the subject at the Carlton Rooms, in London, on July 17, 1912.

A major concern was the construction of a Channel tunnel. In several letters to the press from Windlesham in 1913, he urged the government to begin building a tunnel across the English Channel, for a two-way railway connecting England with France. The purpose of this construction would be to prevent a blockade from being effective, and to ensure a continuing flow of food supplies in time of war. The tunnel would put Britain in communication with the whole Mediterranean basin through Marseilles. It would also permit the easy movement of troops to and from the continent.

Conan Doyle completely rejected the view that it would be possible to invade Britain through a hole twenty-six miles long and twenty-six feet wide. He wrote to the London *Times:*

An enemy, to use the tunnel, has to hold both ends of it. In the unlikely event of a quarrel with France it is surely not difficult to seal up our end . . . the tunnel should open within the lines of an entrenched camp at Dover, and the end of it should be commanded by heavy guns from the heights.

It is perhaps fortunate that Conan Doyle's idea was not acted upon. In the event of France's complete collapse, a Channel tunnel would have given Germany a direct link to Britain. It is possible that if the psychological block created by the existence of a body of water had been removed in World War II, Hitler might have been encouraged to undertake an invasion.

Very oddly, a film version of one of Conan Doyle's finest stories was shown in Berlin only six weeks before the outbreak of war, and members of the German royal family, including Prince August Wilhelm, Prince Friedrich Sigismund, and Prince Friedrich Karl, saw it and enjoyed it enormously. This was Richard Oswald and Rudolph Meinert's *Der Hund von Baskerville*, said to have been a nicely creepy version, and the best Holmes film to date. Generally speaking, the previous versions had been indifferent; a long series made in Denmark was very feeble, and Italian and Hungarian versions had not been inspiring. The only tolerable films had been those of the Éclair series, made by a French company in England and starring Georges Tréville as Sherlock Holmes. Some of these had been shot on the sand dunes of Bexhill-on-Sea, and Conan Doyle had gone down to watch them being made.

In early 1914, Conan Doyle responded to an invitation from the Canadian government to visit several national parks. He and his family sailed to New York on the White Star liner S.S. *Olympic* in May. One wonders if it was a touch of sardonic humor, or simply his characteristic daring, that made him book passage on the sister ship of the *Titanic*, and on the very edge of a world war. It is amusing to note that one of his fellow passengers at the Captain's table was a Henry Baskerville.

He reveled in his surroundings on the *Olympic*, a marvel of extravagance: she offered the first swimming pool ever installed in a liner, a Louis Seize dining room seating 114, Turkish baths with cooling rooms like Arabian bordellos, and first-class suites crowded with French antiques. After a rough crossing, the *Olympic* steamed into New York amidst a Gothic thunderstorm. It was an exhibition worthy of Doré, as lightning forked over the skyscrapers, and thunderclaps sounded like bursting planets. Conan Doyle enjoyed the spectacle, and the more mundane pleasure of seeing the reporters, who boarded on a Jacob's ladder from the press launch off Ellis Island, soaked to the skin.

He gave them their drenching's worth. He told them there would shortly be war with Ireland, that he now supported Home Rule, that if militant suffragettes kept disrupting London they would be lynched by an angry public, and that the former President Teddy Roosevelt was a magnifico among men, his work in discovering a new river in South America an achievement worthy of Professor Challenger himself.

He said that the American he most wanted to see was the controversial policeman William J. Burns, who had inherited Joseph Petrosino's title of the "Sherlock Holmes of America." Burns had visited him in England; Conan Doyle admired him for his work on the Leo Frank case in the Deep South, and on the Los Angeles *Times* bomb-explosion affair. Burns met the Conan Doyles at quarantine, a plump, ill-kempt figure in a bowler hat and loose-fitting overcoat, his umbrella turned inside out by the storm. Conan Doyle posed with him for the photographers, looking more like a benevolent sea lion than ever, alongside a visibly nervous Jean.

Burns then took the couple by automobile with a small police escort to the Plaza, which with its marble mosaic pavements, silvered ceilings, infoliated bronze columns, and counters of Mexican onyx was a delight to the eye. The large and airy suite on the seventh floor overlooked Central Park, and Conan Doyle was greatly taken with the tranquil view of leaves after the storm, the glitter of new skyscrapers—the *World* building had been the tallest in the city in 1894—the much-improved police, and the sparkle and efficiency of the Plaza staff. A founder of the Pilgrims, dedicated to Anglo-American friendship, he attended a Pilgrims' luncheon in his honor at the Whitehall Club, presided over by Joseph H. Choate and Admiral Robert E. Peary, the Arctic explorer. He gave a tongue-in-cheek speech in which he referred to the recent crime wave, saying, "I believe the history of America would be better if you would get a shipload of

Sherlocks over here." He introduced a characteristic touch when he reported that strange high-frequency messages had been received from space by Marconi-gram at sea, and he amused the audience by saying that a mid-ocean message from the Pilgrims was "more easily decipherable." He brought the house down with:

In the past, the kit of a wandering Pilgrim consisted mainly of a staff and an empty wallet. I have a good substitute for a staff in the shape of a good, stout English umbrella. As to my wallet, Mr. Lloyd George has seen to it that it is empty!

He could not resist mentioning his horror of the impresario Major Pond on his previous visit; he expressed his love of America and his regret that Asquith had not agreed to have Britain participate in the recent Pan-American Exhibition; and he concluded with one of his sure-fire dinner-table stories:

A Cornish fisherman was the worst critic I ever had. He told me, "Well, sir, Sherlock Holmes may not have killed himself falling over that cliff. But he did injure himself something terrible. He's never been the same since!"

As he had in England, Conan Doyle greatly enjoyed the company of William J. Burns, with his burly common sense and his fine deductive ability. Burns and other members of the police force took Arthur and Jean to the Tombs prison, which, the author observed, "would be just the place for the suffragettes." He took a special interest in "drug fiends' row" and asked to see the recently condemned Lieutenant Becker, a request that was promptly denied; he lunched with Mayor John P. Mitchel at City Hall; he watched the Yankees and the Athletics play baseball—his first, exhilarating experience of the great American game.

He went up to Ossining to see Sing Sing. Warden Clancy locked him up for five minutes in a cell; he emerged beaming, to declare that it was the first restful moment he had enjoyed since his arrival, since there were no reporters in there yet. He applauded the absence of steam heating in the prison. He sat cheerfully in the electric chair, fitted the steel cap over his head, said it was "a little small," and smoked a pipe, noting that the experience as a whole was "quite comfortable." Asked by a *New York Times* reporter what he thought of Sing Sing, he said, succinctly, "Burn it down!"

He gave interviews at the Plaza for days on end, reiterating a favorite theme: birds should not be plucked for ladies' plumage, and it was a disgrace that the Queen of Denmark had ridden down The Mall in London with egret plumes in her hat:

Just as the white feather of cowardice is the worst thing that a man can show, so the white feather means slaughter of the mother bird is the worst thing with which a woman could decorate her hat.

Conan Doyle went with fifteen friends, including Burns, for a Sunday outing at Coney Island. Like a big schoolboy, he rode the scenic railway, absorbed the dips and drops, roared happily at the chute-the-chutes, had his fortune told, went by trolley to the end of Steeplechase Park, strolled along the "Bowery" and nibbled frankfurters, and stood rigidly to attention as a brass band played the British and American national anthems and the crowd cheered him lustily. He reveled in Crazy Village, with its tilting walls, unexpectedly sliding floors, and jigging sidewalks; he sat solemnly on a bench in a little house as it turned upside down, until he found himself sitting on the ceiling. And he wound up the evening watching the maxixe and the one-step performed by dozens of couples at the Castle House, under strings of multi-colored fairy lights.

The Conan Doyles took off for Canada. They were delighted by Niagara Falls and by Lake Champlain, went up the Richelieu River, traveled across the Great Lakes, saw the ill-fated *Noronic* at anchor, enjoyed Fort William and Port Arthur. They were especially dazzled by the prairie, as this passage from *Memories and Adventures* indicates:

It was wonderfully impressive to travel swiftly all day from the early summer dawn to the latest evening light, and to see always the same little clusters of houses, always the same distant farms, always the same huge expanse stretching to the distant skyline, mottled with cattle or green with the half-grown crops.

Conan Doyle loved the emptiness of the Canadian wilderness; he was reminded at every moment of his childhood idol Mayne

Reid. The highlight of the trip was Jasper National Park, reached by a beautiful private car on the Grand Trunk Railroad. He saw the cinnamon bear, less terrifying than the monster of Blue John Gap, and the friendly porcupine. He was enthralled by the whole American experience, and returned to England in a very good humor.

He was back at Windlesham only two weeks before war broke out. The local plumber sent him a note saying, "Something should be done," and something was; within a week, Conan Doyle had distributed leaflets and formed the Civil Reserve, a local branch of the First Battalion of Volunteers. They elected their own officers at a meeting at the Crowborough drill hall, watched by a fascinated William Gillette, who was appearing in London. Conan Doyle and Major Wood worked like Trojans sending out temporary books of rules to villages across the country, but after two weeks of work the War Office announced that the local branches must be disbanded immediately, and re-formed on more official lines.

Meanwhile, the authorized First Battalion of Volunteers, promoted by an energetic young advertising man named Charles Frederick Higham,* was formed in London under the chairmanship of Lord Desborough. Conan Doyle worked alongside Percy Harris, the secretary, and Charles Higham, the fund raiser; the Crowborough company became part of the Sixth Royal Sussex Volunteer Regiment. Conan Doyle got a tremendous kick out of the route marches, target practice, "captures" of defended farms, and evening sing-alongs; seeing the war with a Boy Scout cheerfulness, he found it almost as enjoyable as the trip to Coney Island. In "Merry England in Wartime," appearing in *Collier's* on October 2, 1915, he wrote:

There is just time to get a black cloak and rubber-soled shoes, and there follows an hour of the most interesting of games, skulking in the shadow of the hedges, creeping down the darkest side of walls, waiting breathlessly while the dark sentry passes, and then hurrying swiftly on to make ground before he turns on the beat.

A constant background to the maneuvers, day and night, was the

* My father, later Sir Charles Higham.

distant roar of guns, "calling, calling with their terrible voices, to me, to you, to all of us, to be up and ready, for what the future may send." As Jean pruned the roses in the bowers of her garden, laying the long-stemmed beauties in her wicker basket, she would look up and listen to the sound of war brought by the wind from across the Channel. When Arthur retired to bed, long after midnight, he would hold her close, hearing the same recurrent refrain and looking out at a late-summer sky filled with stars.

With the approval of Asquith and the War Office, Conan Doyle began at the outset working on a history of the war, *The British Campaign in France and Flanders*. Handicapped by the inaccessibility of adequate maps and the somewhat scattered information received from the front, he still managed to write a bold and handsome multivolumed account of the events of the first years. Jean began a Belgian refugee home in a converted house near Windlesham; Mary worked on the assembly line making shells at the Vickers factory, and in the evening doled out food and cups of hot tea at an army canteen. Conan Doyle was detailed to take charge part-time of war prisoners at Lewes Jail: he found the Germans "capital chaps, subdued and decent." One day the remains of an aviator, in circumstances rather like those described at the beginning of *The Horror of the Heights*, were found scattered about a wheat field at Cross-in-Hand, near Crowborough. In the *Collier's* article, Conan Doyle wrote:

The accident, whatever it may have been, occurred high above the clouds. He fell like a stone 2000 feet or more. Ah, what a terrible, and, on second thought, what a glorious end! One can picture it— the sudden snap which showed that something had broken, the peremptory death-call coming so quickly that the soul hardly had time for one flutter of apprehension . . . a huge, switchback swoop ending in euthanasia.

To the outside observer, these must have seemed extraordinary words for a writer at the height of his fame, a bluff and hearty family man and cheerful volunteer soldier. Clearly, the side of Conan Doyle that was weighed down by the world, that ached with the burden of his heavy structure of flesh and bone, the torture of day-to-day problems, had again become paramount. His early childish delight in war games gave way before the horrifying news from the front. First came the sinkings, predicted by him, of three British cruisers in the North Sea. German battle cruisers shelled Yarmouth, Scarborough, and Hartlepool; there was the grim naval battle of the Dogger Bank. The news of the battle of the Falkland Islands, in which German ships under Admiral Spee were sunk, brought temporary good cheer. But there were desolating accounts of butchery in the trenches—at Mons, the Marne, Nieuwpoort, Verdun, and Ypres.

In those difficult months, Conan Doyle found escape in writing a new Sherlock Holmes novella. This was the remarkable work *The Valley of Fear*, published in 1915, in which Professor Moriarty, a somewhat shadowy figure in *The Final Problem*, emerges in much stronger colors.

Holmes and Watson arrive in Sussex to investigate the death of a certain John Douglas, who is none other than Conan Doyle in very thin disguise. With forgivable vanity, the author describes Douglas:

[He] was a remarkable man, both in character and in person. In age he may have been about fifty, with a strong-jawed, rugged face, a grizzling moustache, peculiarly keen gray eyes, and a wiry, vigorous figure which had lost nothing of the strength and activity of youth. He was cheery and genial to all, but somewhat offhand in his manners, giving the impression that he had seen life in social strata on some far lower horizon than the county society of Sussex.

Slightly less flatteringly, the author suggests that his alter ego is very secretive about his past. The story, most intricately constructed, reworks themes found in *The Norwood Builder* (John Douglas, it turns out, is not really dead, but hidden in his house) and in *A Study in Scarlet* and *The Five Orange Pips* (an American organization comes menacingly to England; in this case, it is not the Mormons or the Ku Klux Klan, but the "Scowrers"—the name an old Scottish word for "scarers," the organization recalling that of the Pennsylvania coal-field agitators, the Molly Maguires).

Conan Doyle saw to it that Holmes apprehended a German spy in *His Last Bow*. He bombarded the London *Times* with

letters calling for reprisals against the Germans for their treatment of war prisoners, and their use of the Zeppelin in air raids.
He called attention to the threat of drink to the efficiency of the
ranks. He wrote words of praise for Lord Roberts, who died in
1914, and for Charles Frohman, who went down with the
Lusitania. He lectured at the Connaught Rooms, the Queen's
Hall, and His Majesty's Theatre on the battles in Flanders, using
up-to-date photographs and lantern slides supplied by the War
Office. He urged the use of body armor at the front, conjuring
up images of medieval warfare; he submitted suggested designs
for protective steel helmets and shields; he pressed for inflatable
rafts for ships; and he even designed the swimming collar which
became the basis of the inflatable life jacket later on.

In the midst of all this activity, Conan Doyle never ceased to
collect news items relating to crimes. Just before the war, he had
read of the death of a Mrs. Williams in Herne Bay. She had died,
apparently of a fit, in her bath. He preserved the item and pasted
it into one of his books of clippings. With Holmesian doggedness
he dug into the matter, discovering that through a solicitor, her
husband, Henry Williams, had managed to have himself desig-
nated the sole recipient of his wife's income, and had then abandoned her. Mrs. Williams had gone to live in the Somersetshire
watering place Weston-super-Mare. On March 14, 1913, she had
seen her errant husband walking on the sea-front esplanade. She
forgave him at once, and foolishly rejoined him; they moved
together to Herne Bay. Williams now arranged to obtain not
merely the interest on his wife's property but her capital as well.
She died in her bath soon after she had rewritten her will.

Conan Doyle, examining the evidence given at the inquest,
felt there was something decidedly suspicious about it. He went
to Herne Bay and interviewed witnesses. He discovered that
Henry Williams had changed his name to John Lloyd. Further
digging convinced him that Mrs. Williams had not died accidentally. He contacted his friend, the Lestrade-like Inspector Neil
of Scotland Yard, alerting him to a matter which soon blew up
into one of the great *causes célèbres* of the century—the Case of
the Brides in the Bath.

On December 18, 1914, John Lloyd found his new bride

dead in her bath. He told police he had been "out buying tomatoes." The landlady at the boarding house where he was staying said she had heard a loud splashing sound, followed by someone playing "Nearer, My God, to Thee" on the small pedal organ in the Lloyds' sitting room. The coroner's jury, impressed by Lloyd's show of grief, declared him innocent of an act of murder. But Neil was ready to pounce, and only a few hours later witnesses who had read the account of the inquest in the press began calling the Yard. A Mrs. Heiss revealed that she knew Lloyd, and believed him guilty of a murder of a third woman. Within days, Neil had arrested George Joseph Smith, alias John Lloyd, alias Henry Williams, on a charge of murder. Smith was tried and hanged.

Conan Doyle was also interested in a matter involving an old friend—the trial of Roger Casement. Casement, the hero of the campaign for reform in the Congo, had suddenly become a figure of public contempt. A fierce Irish nationalist, he strongly opposed the involvement of Ireland in the war, and traveled to Berlin in November, 1914, to attempt to obtain German assistance in winning Irish independence. In 1915 he circulated violently agitatorial anti-British pamphlets, and tried to recruit a brigade of Irish prisoners of war in Germany to serve against England. In April, 1916, he left Germany for Ireland on a U-boat; he was intercepted at Banna Strand and arrested, and stood trial for treason before the Lord Chief Justice in London. His notorious Black Diaries were used against him, since they contained evidence of his homosexuality.

For several years, Conan Doyle had enjoyed a complex intellectual relationship with Casement. They had met through their mutual friend Edmund Dene Morel, and had gone together to see *The Speckled Band* on the fourth night of its performance. Casement had been influential in converting Conan Doyle from Unionism to Home Rule for Ireland; but in an article for *The Fortnightly Review* in 1913, Conan Doyle had made clear his belief that regardless of whether Ireland was independent, she must certainly share in the responsibility for the defense of Great Britain should Germany prove threatening.

Conan Doyle sent the proofs of the article to Casement, who was at that time staying in Majorca. Casement disagreed radically with Conan Doyle, and published a vigorous reply in the pages of *The Irish Review*, in which he asserted that Ireland would in fact benefit from the conquest of Great Britain. This article greatly unsettled Conan Doyle, and when, toward the outbreak of war, Casement continued to send him a stream of anti-British letters, their friendship dissolved.

On the face of it, one would have expected Conan Doyle, with his strong involvement in military affairs and his knightly ancestry, to be the last person on earth to support Casement. But he had never forgotten Casement's work for the Congo Reform Association. With his customary decency and sense of justice, he measured Casement in the balance and did not find him wanting. He believed that Casement was a genuine Irish patriot, that his act in going to Germany had been partly a result of authentic patriotism and partly the result of mental disturbances brought about by the tropical conditions of the Congo and the Putumayo.

When Casement was condemned to death, Conan Doyle approached the Prime Minister, Asquith, and was advised to prepare a petition for a reprieve. He immediately telephoned all the important persons he knew in order to obtain their support. Among those who signed the petition were G. K. Chesterton, John Galsworthy, Arnold Bennett, Israel Zangwill, John Drinkwater, the Bishop of Winchester, C. P. Scott, editor of the Manchester *Guardian*, H. W. Massingham, of *The Nation*, and the presidents of the National Free Church Council, the Baptist Union, and the Royal College of Physicians. Morel, already threatened with public calumny over his advocacy of appeasement toward Germany, declined to be a signator; and the Archbishop of Canterbury refused on the ground that he should not bring to bear specific pressure for mercy, in view of his close association as head of the Church of England with the royal family. George Bernard Shaw regretfully withheld his signature for the peculiar reason that if the leading intellectuals saw his name on the petition, they might refuse to sign it.

The petition proved ineffectual in swaying the Home Secretary. When it failed, Conan Doyle tried a new tactic; he sought to persuade Asquith that Casement should be treated as a prisoner of war. This attempt also failed. It is characteristic of Conan Doyle that, disapproving of Casement's private life, he did not visit him in jail, simply seeing his situation as an abstract example of man's injustice to man. With remarkable dignity, Casement went to his hanging at Pentonville on August 3, 1916. An ironical footnote to the story is the fact that that although Conan Doyle was by far the largest contributor to Casement's defense, spending no less than seven hundred pounds, and although he was the organizer of the appeal, Casement's diaries disclose that he thought of Conan Doyle with nothing but contempt. He was infuriated that Conan Doyle, in the pages of the London *Daily Chronicle*, indicated a belief that he must have lost his reason. He wrote of Conan Doyle as his "friend" only in derisory inverted commas. It was not to be the last time that Conan Doyle would be treated ungratefully by a man he had sacrificed his own time and money to defend.

Besides the execution of Roger Casement, Conan Doyle had to face the severe blow of the end of his friendship with Edmund Dene Morel. Up to the outbreak of hostilities, Morel had sought the adoption by Britain and Germany of less combative and more rational attitudes toward each other. Pointing out that there had been gross errors on each side in the manipulation of international events before 1914, he zealously campaigned for conferences which would iron out mutual difficulties. But he reckoned without the irrational pugnacity of both the War Office and the Reichstag. When war broke out, Morel, in association with Ramsay MacDonald, the author Norman Angell, Charles Trevelyan, and the left-wing Arthur Ponsonby, formed an organization known as the Union of Democratic Control, with himself as secretary and treasurer. The UDC followed an appeasement policy, maintaining that Britain, France, and Germany were equally responsible for the war, and urging an armistice and a forgiveness of mutual aggressions.

Unhappily, Conan Doyle, steeped as he was in the ethos of empire, and in the principle of single-minded destruction of an enemy, was appalled by the UDC, particularly because it opposed the reprisals against the Germans which he so eagerly sought in the correspondence columns of the popular press. In August, 1917, following the publication by Morel of a stream of pamphlets described by several right-wing critics as indicating that he was Germany's agent in Britain, Morel was put on trial. The official reason was that he had sent pamphlets to Switzerland, to the distinguished French novelist Romain Rolland, an act considered treasonable because the material was delivered by hand to a resident of a neutral country.

Morel was imprisoned for six months alongside ordinary criminals, and Conan Doyle refused to intercede or indeed to speak to Morel henceforth. In view of their close association and friendship during the campaign for reform in the Congo, this behavior can only seem harsh. But Conan Doyle, rigorously principled in the matter of Roger Casement, whom he saw as wronged because, being an Irishman, he could not be considered a traitor, was equally rigorous in the matter of Morel, whom he saw as a British subject who failed to support his country in time of war. In his view, Morel's pamphlets were subversive, seditious, and dangerous, and he had nothing to do with Morel ever again.

With so many relatives and friends at the front, including his son Kingsley, his brother-in-law Malcolm Leckie, and his brother Innes, Conan Doyle was most eager to visit France to see the action at first hand. Moreover, his continuing war history required descriptions written on the spot. Lord Newton, of the Foreign Office, suggested he go to Italy to report to the British public on activities at the Italian front line. He agreed only on condition that he be allowed to go to France first. Since he was not authorized to wear his Volunteers uniform, he elected to make his journey as Deputy Lieutenant of Surrey.

In the company of an old friend, General William Robertson, he sailed across the English Channel on the destroyer *Zulu*, and took a train to a point not far from the front line. He was impressed by the brown, healthy faces of the troops, the resilience and humor of the survivors of Mons, and he looked compassionately at the faces of dead Germans by the roadside. He attended a ceremony at which soldiers were decorated in a grimy town square, drove across a vast plain slashed with trenches and pitted by recent bombs and shells, and gazed down an incline at the Ypres salient, which held a special fascination, with its ceaseless searchlights, thudding cannons, and stench of death. The poet in him observed a shell hole, in *A Visit to Three Fronts* (1916): "It has filled itself with forget-me-nots, and appears as a graceful basin of light blue flowers, held up as an atonement to heaven for the brutalities of man."

Traveling through the shattered, olive-green landscape, with its puffs of smoke and flames in the sky, its distant thunder of gunfire, he felt a growing shame. The old soldier hated to be crouching and darting and scribbling in dugouts while handsome, brave young men were dying by the thousands not far away. He was consoled to some extent by seeing Innes, now a good-looking, vigorous forty-year-old, the assistant adjutant general of the Twenty-fourth Division. They drove together into the central square of Ypres, where the dead lay in the broken streets and over the steps of the great cathedral. He was reminded once more of Pompeii.

A curious incident took place during the tour. A French general asked him how Sherlock Holmes was progressing in the services. Conan Doyle scarcely knew what to reply, and finally said, "He's too old to be in the war."

He was even more delighted to meet Kingsley, a medical officer and acting captain in the First Hampshires. With his close-cropped, fair hair, classic features, and superb physique, Kingsley cut a splendid figure in his uniform. Conan Doyle was eternally grateful to the commander-in-chief of the British forces, Douglas Haig, for arranging the meeting. His heart swelled with pride; and he was very warmed too by an encounter with his secretary, Major Wood, who was in the Fifth Sussex Territorials, and had become honorary town mayor of Beauquesne.

He found Paris deserted, gray, and lifeless, the Hotel Crillon a desolation of nailed-up boards and barbed wire. He traveled to Padua, visited the trenches near Udine, and almost ran into an ambush at Ronchi. A shell narrowly missed his small motor convoy, and he was forced to beat a retreat from Monfalcone. Back in Paris again, he was appalled to learn of the death of Kitchener, who had been on a secret mission to Russia and had drowned when the H.M.S. *Hampshire* was torpedoed off the Orkneys. He learned later that Kitchener had been seen standing all alone just before the sinking, his face set in an iron stillness.

At the invitation of the Australian government, Conan Doyle returned to the front to inspect and report on Aussie troops and their movements. He was impressed by the hawk-faced and bronzed men, with their digger hats and their raw humor. He made a great friend of the Australian commander, Joseph Cook, former leader of the Fusion party. There was a horrifying encounter that remained with him for the rest of his life. In *A Visit to Three Fronts* he wrote:

. . . a tangle of mutilated horses, their necks rising and sinking, beside them a man with his hand blown off was staggering away, the blood gushing from his upturned sleeve. . . . beside the horses lay a shattered man, drenched crimson from head to foot, with two great glazed eyes looking upward through a mask of blood.

Conan Doyle returned to England in the late summer of 1916 with an overwhelming sense of the decency and forthrightness of the British soldier under arms, a respect for the German prisoner of war, and a horror of the realities of the front line. His subsequent volumes of war history gained considerably from his experience. His writing noticeably sharpened and deepened when he dealt with the Ypres salient. Behind every line can be sensed an agonized yearning. It is clear in these pages, more than in any of his other works, that he longed for service more than for anything else. Those who believe that an excess of pacifist feeling about the mass deaths at the front later drove him into spiritualism have entirely failed to understand the man.

Conan Doyle was aware, both in France and back in England, that the world had become interested in spiritualism to an unprecedented degree. With tens of thousands of fine young men killed at the front, the public most desperately needed to find assurance that there was a life beyond the grave. The seemingly endless photographs in the press, of mud and rain and barbed wire and rats and smashed bodies, made people more acutely conscious of death than they had been since the Boer War. Moreover, there was the fear that the lines would be broken and Britain would be invaded. Scarcely a family in England was not deeply bereaved. The churches were filled with men and women in deep mourning. Zeppelins like enormous sinister cigars buzzed and spluttered over London, bringing a hail of death. It was a time when even the Christian religion did not seem to provide sufficient consolation.

But people of all classes could obtain this consolation from spiritualism. It retained the Christian belief in God. It supplied proof, or so it seemed, that these glorious young men, in replicas of their earthly bodies, had reached a sphere that was without pain or any physical suffering and that offered the joys they had known in life. In another dimension, their etheric forms could play games, could run and laugh and jump and shout. It is hard today to imagine accepting such a simple and noble concept. But to a generation that had been raised to believe unquestioningly in Christ, and that attended church unfailingly every Sunday, it was most attractive.

Spiritualism—or, more accurately, "spiritism"—was in fact a religion or philosophy in itself. No matter how infamous most mediums were revealed to be, the belief retained its romantic and poetic appeal. Conan Doyle felt more strongly urged toward it than ever, haunted by reports, spreading like an epidemic, of strange wartime events, portents, prophecies. Families said they had seen their dead standing beside them in graveyards, or strolling through the house at night, glowing with an eerie light; photographs of war cemeteries showed the faces of departed soldiers hovering over the tombstones or simple wooden crosses; ghosts were seen among the troops at the front.

A Captain W. E. Newcombe reported in *Pearson's Magazine* that during the advance of the Second Suffolks on Lewes, a white, semitransparent figure of an old soldier had risen from a shell hole and marched between the British and German troops, silencing the gunfire and making the soldiers doff their helmets in a moment of religious awe. Many claimed that the figure was Kitchener; Newcombe was convinced it was Lord Roberts. Soldiers claimed they saw the famous Angel of Mons (actually an invention of the author Arthur Machen). A William A. Speaight claimed that he saw his best friend appear in a dugout at the Ypres salient and point at a spot on the floor boards. When Speaight dug down three feet at the spot, a narrow tunnel was found, and in it was a land mine timed to explode in a few hours. Conan Doyle brooded on these happenings, wondering if they were true.

A constant house guest during the war was a sweet-natured but sickly young woman, Lily Loder-Symonds, who was Jean's closest friend. She had been her bridesmaid at the wedding, and had often sat with her while Arthur read aloud, page by page, his latest book. She was a strange person, with a bizarre way of dressing—as likely as not to put her hat on back to front.

With no money of her own, she was given the job of helping the nanny take care of the children; but she was so delicate, suffering severely from bronchial trouble, that the work tired her too much. She was kept on at the house because of Arthur and Jean's kindness.

Bedridden part of the time, Lily had developed the art of automatic writing. Her pen was seemingly propelled by invisible entities, bringing back, in clear script, word of life on the Other Side. At first, Conan Doyle was unimpressed by these messages, and Jean, embarrassed, tried to discourage Lily from proceeding with them. The nature of their content—a bewildering mixture of true and false information about departed friends—suggested that they flowed from Lily's subconscious mind. But Conan Doyle was interested when, on the day the *Lusitania* was sunk, a message came through saying, "It is terrible. Terrible. And will have a great influence on the war." He believed that the message indicated the United States would join the struggle.

Three of Lily's brothers were killed at the Ypres salient in April, 1915. Jean's brother Malcolm, always a great favorite of the Conan Doyle family, died at the battle of Mons on August 23,

1914. Lottie's husband, Captain Leslie Oldham, and Connie and Willie Hornung's son Oscar also died at the front. After this series of shocks, Lily Loder-Symonds' condition worsened. In the fall of 1916 (not May, as Conan Doyle later stated), she produced what seemed to be messages from her brothers giving details of the life of a combat soldier. Since press reports about Ypres had been extremely full, and Conan Doyle himself had written pages describing conditions at the front, there was nothing especially remarkable about these messages. But because of his fondness for Lily, he decided to ease her mind by giving them his most serious consideration.

At last an unnerving thing happened. While he was sitting with Lily one day, she started writing in a hand remarkably similar to Malcolm Leckie's. As her pen raced across the paper, Conan Doyle began asking questions. He wanted details concerning an extremely personal conversation he had had with Malcolm some years before. The reply astonished him. It specified exactly what he and Malcolm had discussed. At that instant, he decided that spiritualism was genuine, and that he must dedicate the rest of his life, every ounce of his energy, to bringing the world the greatest consolation it had ever known.* In his *History of Spiritualism* he said:

. . . the sight of the world which was distraught with sorrow, and which was eagerly asking for [my] help and knowledge, did certainly affect [my] mind and cause [me] to understand that these psychic studies, which [I] had so long pursued, could no longer be regarded as a mere intellectual hobby or a fascinating pursuit of a novel research.

He wrote two books, *The New Revelation* and *The Vital Message*, which launched him on his career as an exponent of the spiritualist philosophy. The first, and more impressive, of these was published in 1918. It was dedicated to "all the brave men and women, humble or learned, who have had the moral courage during seventy years to face ridicule or worldly disadvantage in order

* He revealed the precise moment of his conversion only once, in a lecture in Sydney, Australia, reported in the Sydney *Morning Herald* in 1920.

to testify to an all-important truth." He recorded the history of his interest in the subject from his early experiments with Major General Drayson, through his study of communications from dead people to such figures as W. T. Stead and Oliver Lodge, all the way to an examination of psychic phenomena in wartime. Though he did not deny the existence of fraud at séances, he asserted that mediums were largely genuine, only resorting to deception when they felt they must not disappoint their sitters.

In books and articles, Conan Doyle analyzed the nature of the Future World. He said that after death a man could be briefly unconscious, then wake to find that he could not at first communicate through the ether with human beings, who were attuned to much coarser stimuli, unless they were mediums. Gradually, the departed person would become aware that there were others in the room or garden where he stood, besides those who were alive. Seeing figures as substantial as those of the living, he would realize that these were people he had loved and lost. He would be embraced, or his hand would be taken, and with the aid of a radiant and angelic guide, he would be helped to move through walls and the trunks of trees into his new life.

Conan Doyle did not believe that the dead person was a potential angel or devil, but felt that he carried with him his baggage of strength and weakness, his wisdom and folly. He dismissed the idea of Hell, believing it to be blasphemous in its view of an avenging God. But he accepted the idea of the punishment of grosser souls by the purifying agony of Purgatory, in which the criminal would see his sins, and the suffering of those he had killed. Thus, even the criminal would be helped to cleanse himself, and reach a condition of Eternal Joy. Conan Doyle was fond of quoting the statement by Julia Ames, apparently given to her friend W. T. Stead after her death, that "the greatest joy of Heaven is an emptying Hell."

Conan Doyle believed that the continuing life after death was pre-eminently a life of the mind, just as earthly existence was a life of the body. Food, money, and sex no longer existed. But the arts of music, painting, and the composition of poetry and fine prose were practiced. The dead lived in communities, and marriages were purely spiritual. In this other world—weightless, unphysical, pure and holy—the happiness which eluded most mortals could at last be found.

In *The New Revelation* (1918), Conan Doyle wrote, "The objective side of it ceased to interest, for having made up one's mind that it was true, there was an end of the matter." That is a very significant sentence indeed. As a lapsed Catholic, and a Celt to his fingertips, with a lifelong interest in ghosts, goblins, and fairies, Conan Doyle found it relatively simple to embrace and propagate a faith that had an intense moral and emotional appeal. Given his puritanical turn of mind, and the elevated love he felt for Jean, it is easy to see how warmly he would have welcomed an existence which was free of the demands of the body. For a man raised, like so many of his generation, to regard sexuality as coming from some baser part of the being, an asexual suspended existence would be irresistibly attractive. Moreover, quintessentially English, he had no gourmet taste in food; he would miss nothing once his body had been extinguished. As an obsessive writer, he clearly liked to feel that he could continue to work into eternity, and he must have found most appealing the prospect of being able to convey his compositions from mind to mind, without the crippling limitations of ink, pen, paper, and publication.

It is fortunate that Conan Doyle became converted when he did. Otherwise, two tragedies which came at the end of the war might have proved crippling. Both his beloved brother, Innes, and his son Kingsley, the very center of his existence, died of pneumonia. When Conan Doyle received word of Kingsley's death, he was mounting a lecture platform. Had the news reached him before Lily Loder-Symonds brought the message from Malcolm Leckie, he might have broken down completely. But instead he hesitated only for a second, reminded himself that Kingsley was much happier now, and proceeded to give the lecture without more than the slightest show of grief. And just a few hours later, he believed that he contacted Kingsley through a medium, and learned of the boy's brave soldierly journey through the mists of death.

For the rest of his life, he was convinced that he remained in touch with Kingsley and Innes. A constant flow of messages, sometimes confirmed by apparitions of the two beloved forms at séances, buoyed him up through his declining years. In 1919, at the age of sixty, he was a happier man than he had ever been before. Denied his chance to be a military figure, Conan Doyle felt himself at last presented with the most important challenge of his career: the opportunity to put before the world the facts relating to spiritualism. He did this not in an evangelistic effort to enforce his views, but simply in the hope that the philosophy would be accepted by millions of people, who would thereby obtain an increased understanding of the nature of the life after death. He was aware that with his immense public he was uniquely equipped to attract popular interest to his conviction. He did not just think his views were correct—he *knew;* it was a question now of presenting that knowledge to the world.

All clear profits from his lectures went to the spiritualist cause. Moreover, it has been estimated that he invested in it more than £250,000 of his own money.

Lily Loder-Symonds suffered from severe bronchial attacks toward the end of the war. Jean sent for a patent medicine which claimed to cure colds, believing it might help; but after taking the medicine, Lily became seriously ill, and died. Jean was overcome by mental anguish, wondering if the medicine had killed her closest friend.

After Lily's death, Jean's last resistance to spiritualism disappeared, and she acquired her late friend's gift of automatic writing, which she practiced partially in order to get in touch with Lily.

Conan Doyle lectured energetically across the length and breadth of England. He combined a presentation of the facts about spiritualism as he understood them, with some perhaps unfortunately severe criticisms of organized religion. He asserted that religion was breaking down because of the "windy words and dogmatic assertions" of the sermon delivered by the average clergyman. He was surprised that the church would attack spiritualism, which provided proof of the survival of the human after death. Inevitably, he ran into flak. In London in 1919, the Bishop of London criticized Conan Doyle and his friend Oliver Lodge for attempting to communicate with departed people. In the pages of several magazines, severe critics of Conan Doyle, led by his former friend Jerome K. Jerome, denounced the whole atmosphere of mediumship, their view being, in Jerome's words, that "the darkened room, the ubiquitous tambourine, the futile messages, proved frequently to be 'concoctions', vague prophecies of the kind that we can read in any Old Moore's Almanac."

In 1919, Conan Doyle set out for Belfast to attend a series of séances with a working-class family named Goligher—a father, four daughters, a son, and a son-in-law. All were mediums, but Kathleen Goligher, then twenty-one years old (and still alive at the time this is written, in 1976), was considered to be the most effective. Every night for four years the séances had taken place either at the Goligher's home or at the home of their friend and chief supporter, the widely respected Dr. J. W. Crawford, a lecturer in mechanical engineering at Queens University. The séances were of a very peculiar character. The members of the family would sit around the table with Crawford, while what they claimed was ectoplasm fell down from their chests or thighs onto the floor. Photographed, this looked very much like cheesecloth. They also appeared to extrude rods, which lifted the table or gripped various objects with a podlike formation at the end that felt rather like chilly dead flesh.

In consultation with Crawford, and at the séances themselves, Conan Doyle made detailed records of the activities of the circle; he was convinced that the rods were "teleplastic"—that is, of psychic origin. Critics claimed that they were collapsible devices concealed within the vaginas of the female sitters, or the rectums of the male sitters, but this was never proven. One particular analyst, Dr. E. E. Fournier d'Albe, claimed that all of the séances were fraudulent. On July 30, 1920, Crawford flung himself from a cliff near Belfast, leaving a suicide note in which he stated that his death did not disprove the veracity of the Golighers, and then went on to say, "I have been struck down mentally. I was perfectly alright up to a few weeks ago. It is not the psychic work. I enjoyed it too well. I am thankful to say that the work will stand. It is too thoroughly done for any material loopholes to be left."

Conan Doyle's tours on behalf of the spiritualist cause seriously embarrassed many of his highly placed friends. King George V, Lloyd George, who had followed Asquith as Prime Minister, and Winston Churchill entirely failed to share his beliefs. He was, in fact, denied a peerage because of them. He was crucified publicly by magicians, who were at once amused and horrified by the fact that he was taken in by the most obvious mediumistic deception. They liked to show him, with a degree of sadism, that the appearance of materialization could easily be achieved with magical means. They frequently exposed mediums as they were in the course of producing their phenomena, and ruined several careers.

In 1910, at a séance in New York, Eusapia Paladino had again been caught cheating by magicians. They had slithered along the floor in skin-tight black leotards; when one of them grabbed her foot, which was up to its usual mischief in the cabinet, she had given a scream like an ambulance siren, and afterward she was in a fainting condition. There had been numerous other examples just before, during, and after the war years, when magicians turned out to be the mediums' worst enemies.

In 1920, the greatest magician of all, Harry Houdini, was touring Britain, delighting audiences by escaping from a locked trunk, releasing himself from a straitjacket, and appearing to swallow sixty needles and ten yards of thread, washing them down with water from a large tumbler. He would then pull out the needles, now on a single length of thread which he would string across the full length of the stage.*

Learning that Houdini was performing at Portsmouth, Conan Doyle took his family to his old home town to see the show. He was dazzled by the magician. Small, stocky, with curly, wiry hair parted in the middle, piercing eyes, a thin determined mouth and a rock-hard jaw, Houdini had a superbly co-ordinated and perfectly proportioned physique. Not only was his body an ar-

* Hastings or Brighton, according to various sources.

senal of concealed devices, he had controlled every muscle of it with an almost swami-like degree of discipline and understanding. He was a religious man without a religion.

The secret of his success was an almost incredible mental alertness, a refusal to panic in moments of danger, and constant and ruthless training. Fascinated by spiritualism—his beloved mother had died, and he longed most desperately to bring her back—he nevertheless did not believe in its validity and was horrified at what he felt to be the blasphemy of mediums and their followers. It was his life's purpose not only to entertain the public but to prevent it from being deceived by those who claimed they could talk to the dead. He believed that the art of illusion should be restricted to theatrical performances. Used in the séance room and on the lecture platform, it became sheer deviltry.

He was at once conjurer and witch-hunter, illusionist and disillusionist. He was, in fact, the last person in the world to whom one would have expected Conan Doyle to be attracted. And Conan Doyle was far from being the kind of man one would expect Houdini to like. But from the moment of the performance in Portsmouth, they were inexorably drawn together. One had intellectually crossed—or thought he had crossed—the Styx; the other longed to cross it, but in his hearts of hearts feared that it could not be done. One believed he talked with the dead; the other thought that such conversation was forbidden. One felt he could supply a bridge across the gulf; the other wanted to seek that bridge. Despite their constant collisions over the genuineness of mediums, they both had a touch of the mystic.

Conan Doyle rushed backstage after the Portsmouth performance to congratulate Houdini most warmly. It is typical of him that he believed Houdini achieved his effects by mediumistic means. Houdini was amused by this, anxious to preserve his secrets, and half pleased that Conan Doyle regarded him with such seriousness. The aging sportsman-writer, and the small, bouncing, burningly intense escape artist talked far into the night. Shortly afterward, Houdini visited Windlesham, and performed more tricks for the Conan Doyle children. The whole family was fascinated by him, and deeply flattered that he should honor them with a personal appearance. Conan Doyle told him of frequent conversations with Kingsley and Innes; and Jean disclosed her achievements in automatic writing. Houdini was far too impressed with the distinction of his host and hostess to criticize them to their faces.

Houdini went on to appear in Bristol, where he was packed into a box by a local firm of movers, and burst out of it in just under seven minutes. Conan Doyle telegraphed him, congratulating him on his achievement in dematerializing himself, praising him for his occult powers, and suggesting that he stop pretending and announce his possession of supernatural gifts to the public at large. Houdini's method of escaping from the box was perfectly simple, and did not depend on any supernatural powers; he denied Conan Doyle's interpretation of his feat, but they continued to correspond.

Within a few weeks of Houdini's visit to Windlesham, a new and exciting occurrence swept aside all of Conan Doyle's other interests. Early in May, he received a letter from a spiritualist friend in London, Felicia Scatcherd, saying that somebody in Yorkshire had proved the existence of fairies by photographing them. Conan Doyle was ecstatic. Ever since his Uncle Richard had interested him in fairy lore, he had been collecting material on the subject. He had read the writings of the Reverend Sabine Baring-Gould, who described how at the age of four, in 1838, he had seen goblins running beside the horses on a country estate. Baring-Gould also described how one of his sons had seen a little man, wearing a red cap, a green jacket, and brown knee breeches, among the pea pods in a vicarage garden. Other accounts of fairies had been given by the well-known novelist Violet Tweedale, who was a friend of Gladstone's, and by the English seer Vincent Newton Turvey.

Conan Doyle immediately decided to investigate the matter of the Yorkshire apparitions. He contacted a friend of his, the theosophist Edward L. Gardner, and asked him to make a thorough examination of the case. Gardner sent for the photographs, and found that they showed tiny female figures dressed in party gowns fashionable in 1917 and displaying fluttering transparent wings. They had been photographed by two young girls, Elsie and Frances Wright. Their father was an amateur photographer, with his own darkroom. The girls were supposed to have cried out, as their father developed the plates, "Oh, we can see the fairies!"

The Wright sisters became almost as famous as the Wright brothers in England that summer. Conan Doyle had the negatives taken to the Kodak laboratories in the Strand and examined for genuineness. The Kodak technicians understandably refused to commit themselves. A representative of the Eastman Company, interviewed separately, said firmly that the pictures were "visibly fake." An Eastman laboratory man said that it was rather curious that the fairies should be wearing recent Paris fashions. Another said that they had more than a slight resemblance to the fairies in advertisements for a certain brand of night light.

Gardner, quite astonished by these disclosures, traveled to Yorkshire to interview the young girls. He questioned them closely. They said that the camera they used was a Midg; the photos had been taken in July, 1917, at 3 P.M. and in September, 1917, at 4 P.M., on clear, sunny afternoons. The girls said that the fairies' wings were pale green, pink, and mauve, and their bodies were white. They also claimed to have seen a gnome, which they did not photograph until later. He was camera-shy. He wore a reddish-brown jersey, a red pointed cap, and smart green tights. Gardner wrote to Conan Doyle saying that he was now convinced the fairies were genuine.

Conan Doyle examined the photographs with renewed interest. He noted the fairies' double pipe, traditionally associated with elves, the elegance of the dancing movements, the mothlike delicacy of the wings. He wrote in his book *The Coming of the Fairies* (1922):

Other well-authenticated cases will come along. These little folk who appear to be our neighbors, with only some small differences of vibration to separate us, will become familiar. The thought of them, even when unseen, will add a charm to every brook and valley.

He was greatly disappointed that because he was getting ready for a spiritualist crusade in Australia, he could not go to Yorkshire to talk to the Wright sisters himself.

When he returned from the Antipodes, he faced a barrage of hostility and public censure. His old favorite, *The Westminster Gazette*, published a damning critique of the pictures after they appeared together with an article by him in *The Strand* in the winter of 1920. The well-known literary journal *John O'London's Weekly* published an article by the novelist Maurice Hewlett, author of *The Forest Lovers*, who said, in effect, that Conan Doyle, like the fairies, had two legs, one of which was being pulled.

Meanwhile, Conan Doyle had rashly allowed Houdini to take the pictures to the United States. They were published in the New York *Herald Tribune* along with two more fairy pictures and one other, showing a no longer camera-shy and in fact extremely conceited gnome. The *Herald Tribune* had them analyzed by experts, who declared that the fairies were actually dolls. The New York *World* ran a letter in which the correspondent said, "When Peter Pan called out to the audience in London at a recent performance the famous question about fairies, Conan Doyle was the first to give an affirmative."

The London *Star* asserted, "Messrs. Price and Sons, the well-known firm of candlemakers, inform us that the fairies are an exact reproduction of a famous poster they have used for many years, to advertise their night lights."

Cruelly, the *Star* published a photograph of Conan Doyle with the fairies dancing around his head. His response to this is not known, but one assumes he brushed it aside as an example of yellow journalism. Actually, upon close examination, the appearance of the photographs, which are palpably fake, suggests that rather shaky copies of the Price night-light fairies were pasted onto the negatives. Whatever the technique, the fabrication was done with extraordinary skill; exactly who was responsible for it is still not clear. As recently as the 1970's, the Wright sisters were interviewed on BBC television, and persisted in claiming, in their old age, the complete authenticity of the photographs. The whole story became as famous as the talking mongoose episode of the late 1930's, in which a family on the Isle of Man claimed to be in conversation with a mongoose through cracks in the walls of their house.

Conan Doyle was pilloried by the intellectual press for even tentatively—and he did say that this might be the greatest hoax in history—giving credence to this charming example of English dottiness. In a tolerably sympathetic review of his book *The Coming of the Fairies*, in *The Spectator*, the critic (anonymous in this instance) wrote that Conan Doyle had failed to prove that the fairies were not artificial figures set among the vegetation. The critic wrote, "One must freely admit that the children who could produce such fakes would be very remarkable children, but then the world, in point of fact, is full not only of very, but of very, very remarkable children."

Just before leaving for Australia, Conan Doyle had another personal psychic experience. He and Jean traveled to Merthyr Tydfil, in southeast Wales, to attend a séance given by the Welsh coal miner and medium Evan Powell. "For two hours," Conan Doyle wrote, "my wife and I sat listening to the whispering voices of the dead, voices which are so full of earnest life, and of desperate endeavors to pierce the dull barriers of our sense." Lights quivered and shook in the air, the medium's head sank down, and in the darkness Kingsley and Innes seemed to shimmer and grow large. Conan Doyle reached out to his brother and son, convinced that he heard their voices calling him, while outside the simple cottage windows the blaze of an ironworks lit up the night sky. When Oscar Hornung, the dead son of Willie and Connie, made an appearance, Arthur clutched Jean's sleeve and cried out through tears, "My God, if only people knew—*if only they could know!*"

Despite his involvement with ghosts, gnomes, and fairies, Conan Doyle continued to devote himself to his wife and family. It would be futile to search for Strindbergian quarrels, seamy undercurrents, extramarital romances, or disruptions at Windlesham. To all intents and purposes, his life and household were run with the proper regularity to be expected of a highly moral country squire. Breakfast was always served punctually at the same hour, and was typically English: porridge, bacon and eggs, toast in a rack, marmalade, and plenty of well-brewed tea. Conan Doyle spent most of the day writing, and when he was inspired, still had his meals left at the door on a tray. In the afternoon, when possible, he would walk or play golf at the links which he could see from his study window. In the evening, after the solid British dinner with its mutton or beef and substantial pudding, he would join his political and literary friends for brandy and cigars, discussing the urgent topics of the day while the ladies adjourned to the drawing room.

Yet the life at Windlesham, for all its warmth and good cheer, was not precisely what one would expect in the average middle-class home. Many nights, the family would hold séances in the nursery; and the children were steeped in the concept of communication with the dead from their earliest consciousness. Clairvoyants and mediums visited as frequently as sportsmen and scholars. At the same time, Conan Doyle made sure that the children had a healthy upbringing, with plenty of outside activity, sensible hours, and good food.

Before he left for Australia, Conan Doyle gave a farewell talk at the Holborn Restaurant. Fully booked three weeks in advance, the lecture was attended by peers, dons, clergymen, and military officers. He showed the work of four spirit photographers—pictures in which the faces of the departed seemed to hover in small clouds around those of the living. Even though these faces looked suspiciously like cutouts from magazines made into collages, or like models constructed of wax and cotton wool, they fascinated their audience. There was loud applause when Conan Doyle condemned critics of spiritualism, and announced that he had spoken to eleven relatives on the Other Side.

The Conan Doyles left for Australia on the P. & O. liner *Naldera* on August 13, 1920. The long voyage, through the Mediterranean and the Suez Canal, and by way of India and Ceylon to Fremantle, in Western Australia, was almost unendurably hot and exhausting, and the old campaigner was frequently forced to take to his bed. In his depressed state he even had doubts about survival after death, doubts he quickly disposed of. The children hugely enjoyed themselves on board, organizing games of cricket, quoits, deck tennis, and forming English teams to defeat the Australian children at tug of war. Silent movies and swimming were further diversions; Conan Doyle was unable to use the pool because he had neglected to bring a bathing suit, and none could be found large enough to fit him.

The weary journey at last was over, and at Fremantle, crowds of spiritualists came on board to bedeck the Conan Doyle family with flowers. Lectures in Perth proved successful, and the family sailed through a surprisingly calm Great Australian Bight to Melbourne. There they met the most important figure in Australian spiritualism, Charles Bailey. High-strung, Bailey was a former bootmaker who specialized in apports—the production of objects in the séance room from supposedly spiritual points of origin. In Bailey's case, these included coins, Babylonian clay tablets, live birds in their nests, an eighteen-inch baby shovel-nosed shark (fortunately dead), a crab dripping seaweed, a defanged rock python, a turtle, a jewel in a palm leaf, and a small bust of John the Baptist.

In February, 1910, Bailey's trustworthiness had been seriously impugned; during a séance in Grenoble, France, he had produced two singing birds in pretty nests, apparently from mid-air. Unfortunately, a local birdshop proprietor disclosed that a gentleman answering Bailey's description had bought those very feathered friends from him only two days before. The psychic investigators revealed that Bailey had hidden the birds and their nests in a portion of his anatomy they were too discreet to specify. It was, apparently, unusually commodious. In 1911, he was accused of hiding birds in his boots at a séance in London. In March, 1914, a sitter caught him pulling a Babylonian tablet out of his mouth.

Despite these disasters, Conan Doyle was determined to give Bailey a chance. Oddly, for a doctor, he thought it "absurd and obscene" that Bailey should be rectally searched. He arranged a séance at his hotel in Melbourne. A spirit hand appeared, with a shirt cuff which had a distinct resemblance to those worn by the medium. A spirit head was slightly more convincing. Conan Doyle was left with a vague feeling of discomfort, and nothing more happened.

At a second sitting, Bailey was stripped naked by the sitters and sewn up to the neck in a large canvas bag. The "absurd and obscene" place was, predictably, not examined. The medium went into a trance and began talking in a language which one sitter insisted was Hindu, but another declared to be a Welsh dialect. A moment later, Bailey, his head twisting in the bag, said, "Ah! Here it is!" and asked for the bag to be loosened. He was holding in his right hand a large bird's nest with a speckled egg in it. The egg broke open, and a tiny chick danced in the nest. Conan Doyle asked Abdullah, the medium's control, where the nest came from. "India, of course," Abdullah replied, most impertinently and in perfect English.

"What bird is it?"

"Ignoramus! It's a jungle sparrow," Abdullah snapped.

Conan Doyle, somewhat irritated, took the nest to the Museum of National History in Melbourne and was told that it was not a jungle sparrow's; it might possible be that of an Australian bird.

At the next séance, Bailey, again in the bag, produced an Assyrian tablet. Conan Doyle took it to London on his return, and had it analyzed at the British Museum. He was told that it was a forgery, made by Jews in Baghdad and purchasable for a shilling. Questioned about this by the press, Conan Doyle defended its spiritual origin, saying, "The forgery, steeped in recent human magnetism, was more capable of being handled by spirits than an original taken from an Assyrian mound."

Conan Doyle was widely acclaimed in Sydney, where he was given a lavish luncheon by the Press Club, and ran into a former patient from Southsea, who told him he was "alive despite the fact that he had been under Conan Doyle's care." He was treated with kid gloves by a highly skeptical Sydney *Morning Herald*. Toward the end of his stay, he ran into some opposition: one of his Town Hall lectures was picketed, by antiwitchcraft groups. There were cries of "Anti-Christ!" in the hall. One hysterical woman accused him of being Jack the Ripper, and when he talked about conversing with Kingsley across the Great Divide, a member of the audience shouted, "It must have been through the Devil!"

He was appalled by what he said was the "spiritual deadness" of the city, which still managed to raise a welcome for the author of Sherlock Holmes. He attended cricket matches, met Gallipoli veterans, and enjoyed the spectacle of lifeguards marching with banners along Manly Beach. An old woman gave him a stone which, she said, had been apported at a séance from her dead son in Gallipoli. He accepted it gratefully.

A great sadness of the Australian trip was the death of the Ma'am at eighty-three in Crowborough, where she had moved to be closer to the family. Conan Doyle was very distressed that he had not been with her, and could not attend her funeral. They had grown closer with the years. On his way back to England, Conan Doyle went ashore at Marseilles, and with Denis and Jean, headed north to tour the old battlefields. In Paris, the family stayed at the Hôtel de Louvre, and Conan Doyle went over to the Institut Metapsychique, at 89, Avenue Niel, to see the much-admired Dr. Gustave Geley. He gave a lecture there, and saw a medium named Georges Aubert, who could play a Mozart piano sonata blindfolded, apparently under the control of the composer, and could perform Beethoven while slowly and attentively reading aloud from a volume of Spinoza on the music stand. It was believed that he had not studied any aspect of music. Conan Doyle also watched the performance of the poet-essayist known as Franek Kluski, who was able to make the spirits dip their hands in boiling paraffin to produce glovelike casts, the fingerprints of which were—perhaps fortunately—not analyzed. At one of Kluski's séances a strange anthropoid creature made an appearance, and crawled like a monkey round the room. At another, a very large black bird flew in and settled alarmingly on the medium's head.

In addition to observing these marvels, Conan Doyle attended a private sitting with none other than Eva C. It was his first experience of this famous medium. The séance was held in daylight, in midafternoon. Eva C. was in a kind of Punch-and-Judy box; her hands protruded from the purple-velvet curtains and were held by the Conan Doyles. Above the curtains was a flap in the cloth through which the sitters could peep occasionally. For an hour nothing happened. Conan Doyle was beginning to lose his patience when Mme Bisson, Eva C.'s friend, invited him to stand up and peer into the cabinet. He was startled to see sitting on the medium's blouse a white object about six inches long and as thick as a human finger. He touched it gingerly, and it pulsed and shrank at his touch. He was told by Mme Bisson that it was authentic ectoplasm, and extremely sensitive.

After this brief and rather unsatisfactory demonstration, Conan Doyle questioned Mme Bisson about the mysterious substance. Geley had said that ectoplasm was a solidified thought-form. She maintained that it was a visible air current which Eva made material.

Puzzling over these strange experiences, Conan Doyle sailed back to England and into a new controversy.

Spirit photography had been in the news for several years, and had generally suffered a very bad press indeed. In 1909, Thomas Bedding, an authority on photography, had condemned this peculiar art form as "of all the impostures ever palmed off upon a credulous world, the most shameful and the most shameless." Writing in the scientific journal *Knowledge*, Bedding explained that there were three ways to create spirit photographs taken in daylight. The plate could be prepared ahead of time with specific images, or a transparency could be interposed between the plate and the sitter before exposure; or at the moment of exposure a fake spirit could glide into view. Bedding added, "The purely photographic part of the matter is so simple that spirit photographs in all styles and in all quantities can be ordered and dealt with just like other articles of commerce. The success of the business is only limited by the fatuity and banking account of the dupe."

Photographs of séances, at night, were taken by magnesium flare. Bedding referred to a séance at which, it had been announced, John Knox, the great Scottish divine was to appear for photographs. He materialized, but unfortunately a colleague of Bedding's managed to smear the spirit's hand with aniline violet. John Knox posed for his pictures, bowed three times, and disappeared. It was remarked by a sitter that "this showed an unusual degree of politeness in that contentious churchman." When the lights were turned up, an old gentleman, a sitter in the circle, was discovered to have violet stains on his hands, white hair, and beard.

Despite this and other episodes, Conan Doyle was fascinated by spirit photography. He was convinced that certain spirit photographs were genuine, and since 1918, he had been friendly with the spirit photographer William Hope, a carpenter from Crewe. Hope claimed to have discovered his psychic power in 1905, when he photographed a friend and upon developing the plate, saw the transparen. figure of a woman standing behind the subject. His friend identified the mysterious lady as his sister, who had died many years before. A séance circle of six people was arranged with the help of the Crewe Spiritualist Hall organist. The venerable former Archdeacon of Natal and rector of Stockton, Thomas Colley, unhesitatingly accepted the authenticity of the resulting photographs, in which disembodied heads were seen floating around the ceiling above the six members of the circle.

Trouble brewed in 1908, when a peculiar episode took place. Archdeacon Colley announced that he had seen his mother as an "extra" in a photograph taken by Hope; unfortunately, a Mrs. Spencer of Nantwich announced with equal firmness that it was a picture of her grandmother. In April, 1921, James Douglas, editor of the London *Sunday Express*, decided to investigate Hope's powers. Douglas sat for a photograph taken by Hope, which, when developed, disclosed a face hovering near his own. Douglas unhesitatingly identified the face as having appeared in a picture in a rival newspaper. Had the image been clipped from his own paper, he said, he might have been a little happier about it.

Douglas decided to have a professional photographer on the *Sunday Express* concoct spurious spirit photographs, to demonstrate that they could be created by natural means. Telling them his intention, he invited Conan Doyle, Hewat McKenzie, founder of the British College of Psychic Science, and the art editor of *Pearson's Magazine* to attend the sitting at his office. Douglas would act as referee and his decision would be final. He signed all the plates to be sure there would be no substitutions. The *Express* photographer, Marriott, took three pictures—of Douglas and Conan Doyle together, of the whole group, and then of Conan Doyle alone. Conan Doyle and the other members of the committee went into the darkroom to see the plates developed. They also searched Marriott thoroughly to be sure he was not secreting a substitute slide. When the plates were developed, Conan Doyle was shocked to see that a woman with upcast eyes appeared next to him in the picture taken with Douglas, and a ring of dancing spirit figures circled him in the one taken of him alone.

Astonishingly, several reporters for spiritualist publications claimed that Marriott's achievement proved that "Hope was right," and that spirits had made their way onto the plates, without Marriott knowing about it. Marriott pointed out that he had dressed up some *Sunday Express* office girls in ballet clothes, photographed them separately, and then simply superimposed their images on the original pictures, in the darkroom. He showed Conan Doyle how sleight of hand could easily deceive the eye in a subdued light, even when the observer thought he was watching every movement.

Because the report on the matter in the *Journal of the Society for Psychical Research* was extremely muddled and badly written, Hope escaped ruin. Then Harry Price, an investigator for the Society, made arrangements to settle the matter once and for all. He set up a séance at the British College of Psychic Science in February, 1922. He obtained four plates from the Imperial Dryplate Company, in Cricklewood, and asked the company laboratory experts to devise a method of catching Hope out. By means of a device which passed X rays through a stencil, they printed one-quarter of the company's trademark—a crowned British lion rampant—on each of the four plates. If one portion of the trademark was missing when the plates were developed, Price would immediately know that substitutions had been made. The plates were delivered in a wax-sealed parcel to show that there had been no interference before the séance began. Hope unwrapped them with Price. Then Hope and another sitter, the psychic photographer Mrs. Buxton, accused Price of having tampered with the parcel. He denied this.

The sitters sang hymns, and the séance began in pitch darkness. Hope took the photographs with magnesium flares. Afterward, Hope took Price into the darkroom. As they entered it side by side, Price noticed Hope, with amazing swiftness, slip one of the plates into his inside pocket and substitute another for it, all the while drawing his companion's attention to the excellence of his photographic equipment. When Hope developed the plates, Price saw a face come up on one of them. Price had the plates examined at Cricklewood, and on the one with the extra face, the portion of the lion trademark was missing.

Despite another prolix and muddled report by the Society for Psychical Research, Hope was severely affected by this setback. Attempting to defend him, spiritualists examined and re-examined the packet wrapper, and charged Harry Price with interference. One of the plates that did retain the lion trademark turned up mysteriously at the offices of the Society, with a spirit face on it. Shortly afterward, Conan Doyle published *The Case for Spirit Photography*, in which he expressed his conviction in Hope's genuineness and the certainty that he had been double-crossed. He insisted that he had taken photographs in Hope's presence, that they had never left his possession for an instant and that spirit pictures had appeared on them. The psychic investigator and magician Hereward Carrington declared that he had obtained excellent results with Hope; and it was stated that Dr. Allerton Cushman, a well-known American supporter of spiritualism, had called unannounced upon Hope's colleague Mrs. Ada Emma Deane (a former charwoman), who had produced a spirit picture of his dead daughter. It is uncertain how Mrs. Deane could have obtained a picture of the girl, and Dr. Cushman insisted that this photograph was unlike any of the girl taken during her lifetime.

The noted physicist Sir William Barrett was impressed with Hope. Later, Harry Price retracted some of his charges against Hope, indicating he believed some of Hope's photographs were genuine. The photographer continued his career, charging four shillings and sixpence for a dozen spirit photographs, and keeping

Archdeacon Colley supplied with a constant flow of pictures of his family in the Other World, until, after the Archdeacon's death, he produced portraits of the Archdeacon himself; after Hope's own death, and that of Mrs. Deane, they appeared frequently in spirit pictures taken by others.

10

ADVENTURES IN OTHER WORLDS

IN 1922, Conan Doyle decided to set out on his first spiritualist pilgrimage to the United States. With Jean, Denis, Malcolm, Billy, a tutor, and a governess, he arrived in New York on the S.S. *Baltic* on April 9. Tired after a rough crossing, Conan Doyle gave a rather irritable press conference, not responding as well to the cameras as he had in 1914. He told the reporters that life after death was free of all physical pain, that marriage in the Other World was strictly platonic, and that children were not born there. He swore that the Toledo medium Ada Besinnet had materialized the Ma'am in England. He said that Ada had brought him a letter from the Ma'am, with his pet name on it, and an apology for being skeptical about spiritualism and life after death. Discussing ectoplasm, he denied that it was made of cheesecloth, rejecting a report that someone had snipped some off with a pair of scissors at a séance and examined it under a microscope. He said that it was originally vapor, but the spirits made it into a kind of bag in which the head was formed, the residue dripping down rather like the plant called old-man's-beard. Professors Geley and Richet, he declared, had broken down estoplasm into its components, and found that it contained phosphates, carbonates, and sulphates.

The editorial in *The New York Times* the following day was brutal; it said that Conan Doyle had become a pathetic figure of fun, and an object of pity, and added, "With each of the interviews he gives it becomes harder to be patient with him." Conan Doyle was not in the least distressed by this display of materialist thinking. He enjoyed hobnobbing with Houdini, going to see a new Chaplin film, attending a Raymond Hitchcock revue, taking his children for an automobile ride along Broadway at night to see the bright lights, and luxuriating in a splendid suite at the Ambassador.

Conan Doyle was delighted with his tour manager, Lee Keedick, who, clean-cut and smiling, was the exact opposite of the shaggy whimsical Major Pond. He caught up with old friends —Melville Stone, Hamlin Garland, Edward Bok; he went with his family to the top of the Woolworth Building; and he noted the hooligan gangs in the street. New York was in the grip of a crime wave, and at one stage Conan Doyle succeeded in terrifying a cab driver. Alighting from a taxi, he discovered that he had left pages of his diary in it. Waving his umbrella mightily, he chased the cab headlong down Fifth Avenue, crashed into several pedestrians, knocking them over, and at last saw the cab stopped in a traffic jam. With his usual extraordinary memory, he had remembered the license number. No sooner had he made his way through the crush of vehicles in the middle of the street than the cab moved off. With one flying leap, Conan Doyle jumped on the running board. The driver looked at him in horror, convinced he was a criminal, as Conan Doyle poked an umbrella through the window and tapped him on the head with it. The cab stopped, Conan Doyle retrieved the papers, thrust a generous tip in the hackie's hand, and made off into the night.

Conan Doyle's first lecture at Carnegie Hall took place during a heat wave, the humidity so intense that it made his eyes swim. He struggled to the stage through swarms of people leaning out to touch him, and greeted Hamlin Garland, who was chairman, on the platform. There was a profound silence as he began his talk in a measured and calm voice of great power, presenting the evidence for psychic phenomena to the record-breaking audience of 3,500 people. He cited the many eminent scientists who had supported spiritualism, indicated how he had begun as a Catholic, gone on to atheism, reached a point of agnosticism, and then gradually been converted. He described many instances in which he had received personal proof of survival—conversations with Kingsley, messages from Innes in which he had indicated the name of a Danish healer for his wife, and other psychic communications. Many members of the audience were in mourning. Women wore gold stars on their black dresses, indicating that they had lost their sons in the war.

The next day, three of the five leading New York newspapers gave front-page spreads to the lecture. Heywood Broun, of the New York *World*, wrote:

> Sir Arthur Conan Doyle made an extraordinary impression last night at Carnegie Hall, in his attempt to prove the existence of life after death and the possibility of communication with the dead. The effectiveness of his talk depended on the fact that in spite of the imagination of his writings, he seems to be a downright person. He does not look a man who could be easily stampeded. His audience was profoundly attentive. Evidently it was a crowd which had its dead.

Reports in other papers were equally favorable. Conan Doyle delivered seven lectures in New York, all of which were rapturously received.

At a lecture in which lantern slides were shown, when Hamlin Garland introduced Conan Doyle and Jean, the audience, overcome, stood and prayed silently for several minutes. Occasional sobs and hysterical cries punctuated the quiet. Then, a strange, high-pitched whistle, eerie and unsettling, floated up to the ceiling, followed by several more. Someone called out from the stage, "There is a spirit manifestation among you, is there not?" The audience became hysterical. Everyone looked at everyone else. Conan Doyle called for a resumption of silence. A thin, quavering voice emerged from the depths of the hall, and an old man, leaning on a stick, rose to his feet. "No!" he cried. "It's not a spirit. It's my hearing aid!"

When this moment of grotesque comedy had passed, Conan Doyle excited the audience with a description of ectoplasm, recounting how it "thrilled" as he touched it in Eva C.'s cabinet in Paris, and "pulsed, viscous like putty." He described how Kingsley had come through Evan Powell and begged forgiveness for not being a believer. He told how a baritone voice of no known origin had resounded from the ceiling of the nursery–séance room at Windlesham, delighting the children with its song. He repeated his story of Ada Besinnet's resurrection of the Ma'am:

"I swear by all that's holy on earth I looked into her eyes." He discussed the nature of mediums: "They have something like an 'ear' in a musician. They are like telegraph boys bringing messages."

He showed a series of slides—of Katie King hand in hand with Crookes, smiling sweetly through her white veil; of Eva C. with ectoplasm pouring from her mouth; of paraffin "gloves" in Paris; and of the faces in William Hope's photographs, peering blankly through small gray clouds. Women fainted when the strange faces glowed on the screen, accompanied by the eerie strains of a Victrola. Others called out, begging for word of their sons. Every new slide brought a hubbub of excitement, screams, and faintings. Distracted people wandered up and down the aisles, sobbing uncontrollably. When the lecture had ended, Conan Doyle's dressing room was jammed with well-wishers. He gave a particularly warm greeting to a tired-looking woman in late middle age—the great medium Leonora Piper.

Newspaper reports of Conan Doyle's seven New York lectures caused an extraordinary rush of suicides by people who wanted to see the "next world" immediately, since it was obviously so very preferable to this one. Several of these made front-page news. Even *The New York Times* gave a three-column front-page spread to the Maude Fancher matter. This hysterical woman, after hearing Conan Doyle's speech referred to on the radio, murdered her two-year-old son and then consumed the contents of a bottle of Lysol because she believed that on the Other Side she could be of greater help to her husband, Harmon Fancher, of the Guaranty Egg Company. Before swallowing the poison, which took a week to kill her, she wrote a letter indicating that Sir Arthur Conan Doyle and spiritualism had "inspired" her to her act. She left minute instructions to her husband, specifying the bizarre details of her burial: she was to be placed sitting up, inside a tomb, with her baby in her arms.

A Brooklyn potter, Frank Alexei, who stabbed his wife in the forehead with an ice pick, explained that he had seen an evil spirit, which had flown directly from Carnegie Hall, sitting there like a raven while she slept. A young man killed himself and his roommate because, he said, there were "no gas bills in the Here-after." Conan Doyle, confronted with these and several other peculiar incidents, said they were the result of a "misunderstanding of what spiritualism is meant to be."

On May 1, 1922, a maid named Mildred Pecsyc, employed by Harold Vanderbilt, was discovered pallid and unconscious in a garage near Flushing, apparently overcome by drugs. She revealed that in response to the inspiring spiritualist messages in Carnegie Hall, she had taken the trolley car to St. Michael's Cemetery, between Flushing and Astoria, to confer with her dead mother at a grave. Finding the cemetery securely locked, and the last trolley car gone, she had wandered distractedly through the night, caught in the rain, and finally had found refuge in the open rumble seat of an automobile in the garage, where she had simply fallen asleep.

On April 14, Conan Doyle went to a séance at which the medium was the Italian Nino Pecoraro, a thin, prematurely wizened youth just under twenty years of age. He was the protégé of a psychic specialist, Dr. Vecchio. The other sitters were Dr. Allerton Cushman, Hereward Carrington, and three friends of the medium's. The séance was held at the Psychical Institute. The medium sat in a curtained cabinet, the room lit only by red light. A thin scream emerged from the cabinet, a vibrant call of "Aïda! Aïda!" so sudden that everyone jumped. The sitter of that name moaned with fear as she heard the voice, and when it commented, "Come to the cabinet," she flatly refused. As though impatient, the table danced about; a cold breeze emerged from the cabinet; and the medium's collar and belt spun across the room. While Aïda remained close to fainting, the spirit control announced that Eusapia Paladino was present. A grating voice vibrated through the room, saying, "I who used to call back the spirits now come back as a spirit myself."

Conan Doyle replied, "Paladino, we send you our love and our best encouragement." But despite his most earnest efforts, Eusapia refused to make an appearance.

During that week, Conan Doyle had a sitting with a young medium he later refused to name, whose spirit control continually addressed him through a silver trumpet as "Sir Sherlock

Holmes." When he declined to respond, the trumpet banged him impatiently. Finally, he shouted out, "MY NAME, SIR, IS CONAN DOYLE!"

At another séance, the medium was a Mr. Ticknor, a fat, Pickwickian little man. His control was Black Hawk, the same as Evan Powell's in Wales. Black Hawk talked for two hours, introducing practically the entire Conan Doyle family as he did so, including John Doyle, Richard Doyle, Arthur's father, the Ma'am, and Kingsley. Conan Doyle accepted their appearances as genuine, and was greatly impressed when John Doyle said, correctly, "I saw you last when you were a little boy in 1868, a few months before my death."

The shrewd reader will have noticed the irony in Conan Doyle's being taken in by spirit photographs obtained through the switching of photographic plates; it was the switching of photographs by Irene Adler in *A Scandal in Bohemia* that for once outfoxed Sherlock Holmes. An even harsher irony can be noted in relation to his stay in New York. A certain Alice Moriarty was partly responsible for his being made the victim of a widely reported hoax. In May, he attended a séance with various reporters at which the mediums were Eva and William R. Thompson, Ana Hartman, and Alice Moriarty. After a singing of hymns—"Nearer, My God, to Thee," "In the Sweet Bye and Bye," and "Somebody's Waiting for Me"—the lights were dimmed and the séance began.

The three women were fully visible, and controlled by the sitters. Thompson was in the cabinet. A figure emerged from the cabinet in spectacles, a shawl, and a long, flowing lace dress. It approached Conan Doyle. The face was identical with the Ma'am's. Overcome, he embraced the figure. He was appalled to discover a pair of exceedingly muscular shoulders under the lace, and knew at once that this was William R. Thompson. But he decided not to expose him on the spot, to spare the feelings of the others. This act of kindness caused him to be crucified by the yellow press, which accused him of being duped. When he protested that he knew Thompson was faking, no one would believe him.

He was also not believed in the matter of psychic sport. He

himself wrote in his book *Our American Adventure* about a young girl reporter who asked him at a press conference whether there was golf in the next world. He replied that there was no reason to believe that there was. She asked if the spirits had spoken of golf. He said that they had not. She reminded him that he had said dead people had amusements. He confirmed this. "Well," she added, "maybe golf is among them."

"I never heard them say it," he replied. The next morning, the headline read:

DOYLE SAYS THEY PLAY GOLF IN HEAVEN

In reviewing this episode, *The Spectator* commented, "The press had no easy time in trying to exaggerate the writer's views," and added that it was not surprising that Conan Doyle suffered from exhaustion on the tour, since in addition to participating in the activities of this world, he had been obliged to keep in constant touch with the next. Reviews in this vein of his popular account of the trip, *Our American Adventure,* were unhappily common on both sides of the Atlantic.

Mayor John Hylan, at a tenth-anniversary dinner of the Broadway Association, suggested a séance "to find out how much money Arnold Rothstein is making in the real estate racket."

The highlight of the trip to America was a visit to Ada Besinnet in Toledo. The Conan Doyles were delighted as dazzling lights danced up to the ceiling and flickered around the sitters; the Victrola gave out an odd whistling sound; a soldier, Dan, "who had died in the Philippines for Dewey," sang in a rich baritone; a somewhat cumbersome Spanish dancer called Lenore whirled around the room banging a tambourine; an Indian, Black Cloud, rather similar to Evan Powell's control Black Hawk, made several guttural announcements, followed by comments from a piping moppet called Pansy, who answered his reproving "Squaws talk too much," with an equally sharp "Some chiefs talk too much some time."

While Pansy and Black Cloud quarreled, various faces glimmered through the dark. Conan Doyle's tour manager, Lee Keedick, thought he recognized the explorer Ernest Shackleton, brother of the ill-fated Francis; then, wonder of wonders, they saw a very famous face. Jean cried out, "It is the same face, the same dress, the same drapery: it is Katie King!" The table rapped three times in assent. What may or may not have been William Crookes appeared, complete with white beard; he had died just three years ago. The séance ended with the arrival from the ceiling of spirit letters, seemingly written by Kingsley. One of them said, "It is bully to be here with you on the trip. Oscar and Uncle Willie [Hornung] are both here with you."

Conan Doyle told *The New York Times*, "It was impossible for Ada to know that Kingsley had an Uncle Will, or that Kingsley was dead." This must have been a lapse of memory: the death of Hornung, famous as the creator of Raffles, had been widely reported on both sides of the Atlantic, with all the obituaries mentioning his marriage to Conan Doyle's sister Connie; and everyone knew Conan Doyle had been bereaved by Kingsley's death at the end of the war.

A few days later, Fulton Oursler, the famous journalist who was later to be the editor of *Liberty* magazine, attended one of Ada Besinnet's séances. His account of what happened was very different from Conan Doyle's. He said that as the medium closed her eyes, breathed deeply, and went into a trance, he heard spirit voices—basso profundo, baritone, contralto, mezzo-soprano, tenor, coloratura soprano. The tambourine danced violently through the air, banged the side of his head, made some eccentric spirals, and somersaulted over the chandelier. The dining-room table floated up to the ceiling, and Black Cloud instructed the sitters to stand. Forty successive faces of varying age, from cherubic baby to ancient crone, floated before them. Suddenly, a hand grabbed his and tied it to the medium's. The lights went up and he discovered he was bound to Miss Besinnet, who was fastened to her chair with a complex of ropes. The lights went out again. The lamps danced, the tambourine banged, the bells rang. Hands released him, and a silver trumpet spun through the air. Black Cloud instructed him to put his ear to it. He did so, and a woman's voice told him that everything was fine and his loved ones were watching him from the Other Side.

The Victrola started up. A letter from a lost uncle fluttered down from the ceiling. It did not have a postage stamp. Little Pansy appeared, a pretty girl who tiptoed over to the buffet and brought people fruit. Oursler was offended because she left him out. He said, "I am surprised, Pansy. I'm a guest here. You bring fruit to everyone but me. Why don't you give me an apple?"

Pansy said coyly, "I'll try."

He heard a rustle of organdy, and without more ado stuck out his foot. A figure tripped over it and fell into a chair; it appeared decidedly buxom, and Oursler reached out and touched an ample bosom. He wrote later, "If the lady was not Miss Besinnet, then it was a thoroughly materialized apparition and a pretty hefty one at that." After this unfortunate accident, Black Cloud said sternly, "Mr. Oursler will change his place and move to the other end of the table." A few seconds later, the séance ended, and Miss Besinnet was seen to be more than a little disheveled.

Oursler unhesitatingly declared that the Spanish dancer Lenore, so far from being a spirit, was the somewhat cumbersome medium doing an elephantine tarantella around the room. He said that the hand of the so-called spirit wore Miss Besinnet's rings, that the table had gone up on wires, that any amateur magician could get free of the ropes, that the faces in the dark were masks and the spirit lights made with a simple device, and that he got a rather sharp response when he remarked at the séance, "It would be wonderful if I could go back to New York and say that I had seen two faces at once."

In Washington, Conan Doyle saw Julius Zancig and his wife, the mentalists who had created a sensation at the London Alhambra and at the offices of the London *Daily Mail* in 1906. He was convinced that their performance was psychic, not simply based on an ingenious code. One of them would stand blindfolded while the other passed through the crowd, pausing at times to pick out an object belonging to some individual. Obtaining clues about the nature of the object from the phrasing of the question, the mentalist on the stage would identify it.

In New York at his apartment, Houdini tried to explain to Conan Doyle how the glovelike paraffin casts, supposedly of spirit hands, were made. A rubber glove could be blown up with air, its wrist packed with wood; then it would be dipped in paraffin. If fingerprints were needed, the first step would be to get a mold of a hand in dental wax or plaster of Paris; an impression would be made of the palm side of a hand, and then of the back, and the two halves would be fitted together. Next, the entire hand would be duplicated in rubber, with the fingerprints preserved by a special process. Then one had only to dip the whole in paraffin and—hey, presto!—the job was done. Conan Doyle completely rejected this explanation.

On June 2, Conan Doyle appeared as a guest of honor at the American Club of Magicians at the McAlpin Hotel. He announced solemnly that he would show something which was "psychic" and "preternatural" only in the sense that it was "not nature as we can now observe it." After building up a tremendous atmosphere of excitement and expectation, Conan Doyle ordered the lights put out. Suddenly, the audience was astonished by films of primitive creatures, including an iguanodon, a tyrannosaur, and a brontosaur, struggling in primeval forests and slime. The next day, *The New York Times* ran a story:

DINOSAURS CAVORT IN FILM FOR DOYLE

SPIRITIST MYSTIFIES WORLD-FAMED MAGICIANS WITH
PICTURES OF PREHISTORIC BEASTS—KEEPS ORIGIN A
SECRET—MONSTERS OF OTHER AGES SHOWN, SOME
FIGHTING, SOME AT PLAY, IN THEIR NATIVE JUNGLES

Motion pictures of extinct monsters at play and in battle were shown by Sir Arthur Conan Doyle last night. . . . monsters of several million years ago, mostly of the dinosaur species, made love and killed each other in Sir Arthur's pictures. Prehistoric groups that resembled rhinoceroses magnified many times, equipped with enormous horns that pointed forward like those of the unicorn, drove dinosaurs away from feasting on one another. One monster, like a horned toad of monumental proportions, presented an impenetrable surface of armor plate to attacking reptiles and moved along in safety.

Whether these pictures were intended by the famous author and champion of spiritism as a joke on the magicians or as a genuine picture like his photographs of fairies was not revealed.

The next day, Conan Doyle wrote a letter to Houdini, which he also released to the press. He revealed that the films had come from sequences in a motion-picture version of *The Lost World* being produced by Watterson Rothacker in Chicago, the animation of the creatures done by the skillful Willis O'Brien.* The innocuous joke had an unfortunate repercussion. A man named Herbert M. Dawley claimed he had patent rights to the animation process used in making the films Conan Doyle had shown, that he had used the technique in his productions *The Glory of Slumber* and *Along the Moonshine Trail*, and that Rothacker had no right to make the picture at all. He added that O'Brien had been his assistant and had made off with the process. The case was settled out of court.

While Conan Doyle was in New York, the railroad tycoon Arthur E. Stilwell came to see him at the Ambassador. Stilwell told him that he had been advised by spirits in the building of every inch of his three thousand miles of railroad. He announced that he had never made a move in his endless business dealings without special instructions from the Other World.

Stilwell was again with Conan Doyle when he inspected the monster amplifier just installed in Atlantic City to receive radio messages from Newark and Pittsburgh, and he supported Conan Doyle's assertion that "since spirits exist in the ether, along with radio waves, they will soon be able to broadcast radio messages to the world." In this way, Conan Doyle stated, Gladstone, W. T. Stead, Kitchener, Lord Roberts, William Crookes, and Katie King would find it possible to address the world at large.

On June 17, the Conan Doyles were still in Atlantic City. Conan Doyle had dropped Houdini a line suggesting that he come down for a short vacation, and Houdini had enthusiastically accepted. At the hotel swimming pool, Conan Doyle, bobbing about in the tank and snorting happily, found it fascinating to watch the magician spend long periods under water, holding his breath. Houdini explained to Conan Doyle the secret of his endurance— extraordinary breath control.

* The film itself, seen today, seems very slight; it lacks the imaginative force and inspired humor of the novel. Its one good feature is the performance of Wallace Beery as Professor Challenger, a fine interpretation drawn accurately from the pages of the book.

While Jean and the children played with a beach ball, Conan Doyle and Houdini sat in deck chairs, looking out at the blue Atlantic and discussing aspects of spiritualism. Conan Doyle described the work done by Mrs. Deane in London, while Houdini, who knew that Mrs. Deane had been caught substituting a photographic plate out of her handbag for one exposed during a séance, maintained a stoical silence. Conan Doyle showed his friend a new photograph of a coffin draped with white roses, the pallid and staring face of a dead woman emerging from under it. Two solemn figures, a man and a woman looking straight ahead, stood one on each side of the coffin. Shubbery could be seen through the folds of their garments.

The children ran over and began telling Houdini that they firmly believed in survival after death, and were completely unafraid of personal extinction. They were affectionate, warm, and happy, and Conan Doyle was delighted to see them playing with the great magician. On Saturday evening, Houdini joined the whole family in attending a swimming contest. Conan Doyle became bored and wanted to leave, but Houdini urged him to stay, saying that it would distress the swimmers for the rest of their lives if the English author were seen to walk out.

On Sunday, Bessie Houdini, the magician's wife, joined the happy group. The couple was sitting at the beach one afternoon when a young lifeguard's son came running along hand in hand with Conan Doyle to tell Houdini that Lady Conan Doyle would like to give him a private mediumistic sitting in her suite at the Ambassador, sister hotel of the Ambassador in New York. Houdini, who was impressed by Jean Conan Doyle's obvious sincerity and decency, was thrilled. Perhaps at last he could obtain genuine proof of survival after death. When Arthur said that Jean would try to obtain a message from his adored mother, he was beside himself. The ambition of his life was to communicate with his dead mother. The savagery of his attacks on mediums stemmed from the fact that they dared to pretend that they could materialize her when in fact they could not.

Houdini went up to the suite with Conan Doyle, and Jean greeted the magician with great affection and tenderness. She sat down at a large mahogany table, where a pile of paper and a sharpened pencil lay ready. Conan Doyle took his place next to his wife, and Houdini sat at the other side of the table. Conan Doyle uttered a solemn prayer, calling on the help of God, and asked Jean whether she was ready. Her hand struck the table three times, in the spiritualist code for Yes. She sank into a deep trance. Houdini wrote later, "I had made up my mind that I would be as religious as it was in my power to be, and not at any time did I scoff at the ceremony. I excluded all earthly thoughts and gave my whole soul to the séance. I was willing to believe, even wanted to believe. It was weird to me and with a beating heart I waited, hoping that I might feel once more the presence of my beloved Mother. . . ."

Jean began to breathe deeply, and her eyes fluttered and seemed to sink in her head. Her hand, as though driven by a separate volition, dashed with amazing speed across the sheets of paper, Conan Doyle handing them one by one to the magician. Houdini was pale, and trembled violently. The message began, "Oh, my darling, thank God, thank God, at last I'm through. I've tried, oh so often—now I am happy. Why, of course, I want to talk to my boy—my own beloved boy—friends, thank you, with all my heart for this." The message continued with an expression of joy in Mrs. Houdini's new life, the beauty and sweetness of the Other World. After the writing of the words, "I wanted, oh so much—now I can rest in peace," Conan Doyle asked Houdini if he would like to ask her a specific question. "Her reply will prove," Conan Doyle said, "that your mother is at your side."

Houdini looked extremely anguished, and could not bring himself to reply. Conan Doyle suggested the question, "Can my mother read my mind?" Houdini silently nodded his assent.

Jean's hand began to move again. The following words appeared: "I *always* read my beloved son's mind—his dear mind—there is so much I want to say to him—but—I am almost overwhelmed by this joy of talking to him once more—it is almost too much to get through—the joy of it—thank you, thank you, thank you, friend, with all my heart for what you have done for me this day—God bless you, too, Sir Arthur, for what you are doing for us—for us over here—who so need to get in touch with our beloved ones on the earth plane——"

The message continued for over a hundred more words. At the end of the séance, Houdini sank back utterly drained and exhausted. Jean sat forward, her hair falling over the pages. Then, unseen by the Conan Doyles, Houdini scribbled with a fragment of pencil concealed in a fingernail a tiny marginal note on the first sheet of paper: "Message written by Lady Doyle claiming the spirit of my Dear Mother had control of her hand—my sainted Mother could not write English and spoke broken English."

A moment later, he picked up a piece of paper and scribbled boldly on it the single word "Powell." He looked at Conan Doyle challengingly. He had been thinking of his friend Powell, a well-known magician. Conan Doyle stood up as though an electric current had run through him. A warm acquaintance, Ellis Powell, editor of the London *Financial News,* had just died, and he had received the news by telegram only three days earlier. He was convinced that Houdini, with the gift of a medium, was trying to tell him that Powell was in the room. Houdini was much too fond of the couple to disillusion them on the spot. But in a letter to Conan Doyle a few days later, he indicated that he had been thinking of his own friend Powell.

Houdini left the Ambassador Hotel after a warm farewell to the Conan Doyles, and returned to New York to wrestle with his conscience. Should he disclose the truth—that his mother had not come through, that this had been her birthday and she had made no reference to it, that he had felt no instinctive sense of her presence in the room, that when he examined the message he could not smell her favorite perfume, that when the outpouring in perfect English ended, he felt more blankly and desolately than ever the hopeless impermanence of human love? If he were to reveal what he knew, the Conan Doyles would not only be hurt, they might be ruined. Their enemies would accuse them of trying to bring about the greatest triumph of the spiritualist cause—the conversion of a well-known disbeliever—by fraudulent means. On the other hand, if he kept quiet, he would be allowing the spiritualists a false victory. With his great decency of character, he withheld a statement until long after the Conan Doyles had left America. On December 19, 1922, he issued a release through Bronx notary public Agnes P. R. Boyd, in which he said that there was not the slightest evidence that his mother had "come through" Lady Conan Doyle, that his mother could not read, speak, or write English, and that when he wrote "Powell" on a piece of paper, he was simply reminding himself to attend to a matter connected with his magician friend of that name.

The Conan Doyles never suspected the blow that awaited them. Houdini remained extremely friendly; they went to the theater together, and attended a performance of a new Houdini film, *The Man from Beyond*. Houdini went down to see his friends off on the S.S. *Adriatic* on June 24. Raymond Ditmars, curator of reptiles at the Bronx Zoo, presented the boys with a five-foot king cobra, its poison sacs removed, which they insisted on swathing around their necks, delighting the Houdinis but causing the reporters and cabin stewards to disappear with lightning speed. The farewells were tender, and the Conan Doyles promised to return the following year.

There can be no question that Conan Doyle's visit to New York and other American cities was not only a major inspiration to American spiritualists, but also a source of consolation and joy to the parents and brothers and sisters of the American war dead. Despite much initial sniping, press coverage was generally fair, correctly giving the impression that his tour had been perhaps the most successful of any author's since Twain's, that the Americans' love of the Conan Doyles virtually knew no bounds. Even his sternest critics had to admit the warmth and sincerity of this man, his care and kindness, his goodheartedness and thoroughness, and the absence of evangelical zealotry in the way in which he put his most central convictions before the public.

Back in England, he moved into new and dangerous storms. A Canadian, James Black, published a letter in *The New York Times* asserting that the elder of the Wright girls, of fairy fame, had worked as an assistant in the darkroom of her photographer father, and had ample opportunity to fake the fairy photographs; and that the other girl was her cousin, not her sister. Clifton D. Wells, president of Bates College, announced that ectoplasm was simply fabricated of cheesecloth or animal tissue, and challenged Conan Doyle to produce it in a box Wells had prepared.

Wells wrote, "When the father of Sherlock Holmes succeeds in doing for ectoplasm what Madame Curie has done for radium, the colleges of this country will be no less ready to acknowledge his contribution to scientific knowledge."

In the late fall, *The Blue Island* appeared, a book supposedly consisting of communications, recorded by Estelle Stead and Pardoe Woodman, which were received from W. T. Stead after his death on the *Titanic*. Conan Doyle had supplied a special introductory letter of approval. Many papers discreetly ignored the publication. But *The New Statesman*, heading its review "A Childish Swindle," published a ferocious attack, calling it "a preposterous book, incredibly puerile in style and matter alike," and continuing, "It could no more have been written by W. T. Stead than the novels of [Ethel M.] Dell could have been written by Jonathan Swift." The review went on to discuss the book's graphic description of Stead's spiritual journey following the famous sinking. Hundreds of the dead were carried through air vertically, and went rushing up into the sky until they arrived at a kind of celestial aerodrome on a large blue island.

On arrival, Stead was supposed to have taken a walk by the sea with his father, who had remained the age he was when he died. Activities on the island included horseback riding, swimming, cricket, soccer, and all other sports. Travel was so swift that it was possible to be in two places almost at the same time. On reaching the island, each soul was interviewed alone by an Advanced Spiritual Instructor, in order to avoid embarrassment. In a special building was a kind of central telephone exchange for communication with earth; the officials were "entirely business-like" and in recognition of Stead's efforts at his end of the line on earth, he was "given unlimited assistance at this end of the line."

Spirits retained their national costumes, which was "particularly interesting and amusing, also instructive," and "patriotism still holds with me, as with most of us." There were Rest Houses, and those who had suffered on earth were given lavish palaces to live in. *The New Statesman* reviewer remarked that the Blue Island resembled Ellis Island, with rather less stringent formalities. He added, "If the writer be indeed Mr. Stead, it is a Mr. Stead whose mental and moral qualities went utterly to wreck with his body on the *Titanic*."

At the end of the article, the critic savaged Conan Doyle, accusing him of lending his name to an outright swindle by Estelle Stead, Conan Doyle wrote an infuriated letter, threatening to sue the paper for defamation. In a note to this communication, the editor bluntly stated that he could sue away; and there the matter was allowed to drop. But correspondence on the subject continued in other publications, causing the Conan Doyles acute distress, though not in the least shaking their loyal friendship with Estelle Stead.

The Conan Doyles managed to weather the release of Houdini's statement about the Atlantic City séance in December. They even remained friendly with Houdini, convinced that he was too nervous at the encounter with his mother to admit that it was genuine. They also said that an additional message had been received at Atlantic City, indicating that Houdini would die very soon, and they believed that this was another reason he had denied the authenticity of the communication.

On December 10, 1922, a remarkable event occurred at Windlesham. As Jean's pencil moved over the paper, a guide named Pheneas announced himself. Right then, the Pheneas Circle, consisting of Arthur, Jean, and the three children, was formed for sittings in the nursery. Pheneas declared that he was an Arab, that he had lived in the Ur of the Chaldees before the time of Abraham, and that he was in touch with the Conan Doyles' dead relatives and friends. He lived in a house built by his grandfather, and frequently visited Mesopotamia. His messages were consoling, and Conan Doyle put some of them into a book, *Pheneas Speaks*. At one séance, another control appeared, who lived in a version of the New Forest which was devoid of all ugliness.

Later a man named Josephus was heard from. He disclosed that Pheneas, his cousin, was a chief and a great warrior, beloved by all his people. At one stage, Conan Doyle appears to have had a moment of skepticism; remarking on the names Pheneas and Josephus, he said, "These are Eastern, but hardly Arab names."

The reply was sharp: "We care nothing for our old earth names." And the speaker added, "Time is as a puff of wind over here. It *is* not. Your own time will very soon be the same."

Conan Doyle began to have strange dreams during those months. He started collecting information on dreams, describing later in his book *The Edge of the Unknown* (1930) the contents of various letters he had received from people recounting their dreams. A captain in Ireland received in his sleep images of horses which were going to win races; Conan Doyle wrote, "He is not a betting man and makes no use of his information, which is just as well for the bookies." An Englishwoman living in Finald wrote that she had seen a vision of her brother killed in Flanders, and had been taken by a radiant spirit along a poplar-lined road to see his body. A correspondent in California, who frequently wrote to Conan Doyle, described a dream in which he commanded the bodyguard of a sultan, and was killed. He subsequently wrote to the Sultan of Oman and offered to enlist in his private guard.

A solicitor wrote from Bath to say that one of his clients had learned in a dream the location of a land grant which had been lost in an old box. A woman in Germany said she received messages in dreams about lost articles, as though by wireless. Conan Doyle himself had a vivid dream. He found himself in a suburb rather like those he had known in Edinburgh as a child. He looked around at broken buildings and weed-covered lots. Suddenly he was transferred to a large public hall. He looked up through pillars to an ornamental ceiling. A man in plum-colored doublet and hose stood next to him, and Conan Doyle said, "Well, if you fellows are going to dress like that, we poor moderns have no chance." Next, Conan Doyle was in a vehicle, a kind of horseless coach carried on air. He floated up a broad road to a hillside with ancient ruins. He looked down at a great gray expanse, with buildings and towers as far as the eye could see. Then he woke, wondering.

Conan Doyle's most remarkable psychic experience had occurred some five and a half years earlier, on April 3, 1917. He arose in the morning with a strong feeling that something very important had been conveyed to him in his sleep. All he could remember was one word, "Piave." It kept repeating itself in his head. During his visit to the Italian front, he had crossed the Piave River, but had thought little of it. He jumped out of bed, walked in his pajamas to his study, and looked up Piave in the gazetteer of his atlas. He placed it about fifty miles behind the front. He immediately wrote a letter describing his experience, carefully sealed it, and sent it to the Society for Psychical Research, with a covering note asking that it should be opened only at the writer's request. The letter, dated April 4, 1917, remained in the Society's possession until Conan Doyle authorized its opening fifteen months later. In the meantime, the Piave had become famous; the Italian army had halted there, and had held the river in a brave stand until June 17, 1918, when the first battle of the Piave was fought. Conan Doyle maintained that "the Allied victory at the Piave marked the final turning point of the War against the Germans."

In December, 1922, at just about the time Houdini's famous critique of the Atlantic City séance appeared, the *Scientific American* announced a very important competition to determine the authenticity of psychic phenomena. In a circulation-building stunt, the magazine's publisher and editor, O. D. Munn, announced that $2,500 would be paid to the first person producing a satisfactory spirit photograph, and $2,500 to the first person producing a genuine psychic manifestation in a séance room. A committee was set up, including the psychologist Professor William McDougall, Hereward Carrington, Dr. Daniel Frost Comstock, pioneer developer of Technicolor, the minister and psychologist Dr. Walter Franklin Prince, and Houdini.

Conan Doyle was asked to assist with the quest for a genuine medium, and he invited an associate editor of the *Scientific American*, the journalist and mathematician J. Malcolm Bird, to come to England for a preliminary investigation. Bird arrived early in 1923, and Conan Doyle liked him at once. Thin and beak-nosed, he fitted the name "Bird" perfectly; and in many respects, he was quite like Sherlock Holmes. The difference was that he was extremely impressionable, and had a somewhat emotional response to spiritualism.

Conan Doyle entertained Bird frequently at his London home, a spacious flat at 15, Buckingham Palace Mansions. It was comfortable, filled with Victorian furniture, and for a train lover like Conan Doyle, offered a splendid view of the Victoria Station railway tracks. On February 27, the Conan Doyles sat with Bird at a séance at the British College of Psychic Science. The medium was John Sloan, whose control, White Feather, was known familiarly as Whitey. Through a silver trumpet sounded the voices of various individuals: a lady who failed to give her name, but appeared to be Lily Loder-Symonds; Joseph Bell; a man named Robert Leckie, who claimed to be Jean Doyle's father (actually, her father's name was James); Malcolm Leckie, who gave the exact location of his death as "three miles and four furlongs from Mons"; Oscar Hornung, who warned of much opposition on the next American tour; and Ellis Powell. Neither the Conan Doyles nor Bird was impressed by this séance.

Soon after, they attended another séance, at a grocery store just outside London. There was no medium, just thirteen sitters. Sleigh bells tinkled; the shrill, piping voice of a little girl called Iris who had died many years before echoed through the room. She laughed with an unpleasant piercing sound, trumpets sounded, and a psychic concert began, in which bells rang, a mandolin thrummed, a drum beat, a mallet hit a stool, and a whistle blew. A music box fell down with a deafening clang; a stool flew about and banged on the table.

The Conan Doyles' old friend John King, spirit control of Florrie Cook and Eusapia Paladino, spoke; Iris produced spirit messages, very badly spelled; the spirit lamp flew about. "The entire evening," Bird wrote later, "was one prolonged three-ring circus."

On March 12, shortly after holding a séance at Windlesham, Evan Powell appeared as medium in a séance at the College, attended by the Conan Doyles and Bird. Black Hawk was the control. Powell stripped to his underwear, and had Bird search him; but he did not submit to an oral or rectal examination. Then Bird and a minister tied him to a chair; he sat in a cabinet that also contained a small table with a round top, upon which were sleigh bells, a trumpet, and a vase of flowers. The curtains remained open. The light went out; Black Hawk called for hymns. He addressed Conan Doyle as "Big Chief." The bells rang when Black Hawk ordered someone called Sweet Heart to ring them; the flowers moved around the circle, touching faces and hands; the sitters were caressed, petted, and sometimes impatiently slapped. Bird was convinced that the cords binding the medium had been broken and replaced.

After investigating the psychic photographers William Hope and Mrs. Buxton, Bird traveled to Paris and Berlin for further work. At the beginning of April, he and Conan Doyle, now fast friends, sailed to New York together, accompanied by the whole family, all most eager to revisit the United States.

While they were crossing, on Conan Doyle's old favorite the S.S. *Olympic*, news came over the wireless that the Earl of Carnarvon, leader of the expedition which had unearthed Tutankhamen's tomb, was ill and on the danger list. The official report was that he had been stung by some dangerous insect, and that he had a severe case of pneumonia. Conan Doyle was convinced that a diabolic force, protecting the dead Pharaoh, had lingered in the tomb from the moment of the interment, and was reaching out to destroy the Earl.

Conveniently for the press, Carnarvon died on the day Conan Doyle arrived in New York, so front-page news could be made of his announcement that the Earl was the victim of an ancient curse. Actually, there was one aspect of the story which was genuinely newsworthy, not merely hokum: the Earl had had a lifelong terror of insects, and was deeply afraid of any creature's biting him; like a character in one of Conan Doyle's ghost stories, he died in the fulfillment of a premonition.

On April 16, Conan Doyle gave an extraordinary new lecture at Carnegie Hall. He presented a slide taken by Mrs. Deane during the two-minute silence at the Cenotaph in Whitehall on November 11, 1922. This photograph showed faces floating in mist over the crowd of men and women in mourning and the various soldiers standing with bowed heads. As Conan Doyle presented the slide, several women screamed hysterically, and had to be carried out. The effect on the audience was overpowering. "Heads without necks, stern, grim . . ." *The New York Times* reported. "A woman cried, 'Don't you see them? Don't you see them?' "

The presentation of the Cenotaph picture was followed by Conan Doyle's description of the séance with Franek Kluski in Paris. He described the figures of the ape man and the strange bird, and a spirit which dipped its hand in boiling paraffin. At a second lecture, he recounted conversations he had had with W. T. Stead, confirming the findings published in *The Blue Island* by Estelle Stead and Pardoe Woodman.

The lectures again caused a considerable stir. While Conan Doyle departed for a nationwide tour, the *Scientific American* committee proceeded to make its first examinations of mediums. Just before he left New York, Conan Doyle recommended that the committee look at the work of a medium he had met briefly— Mina Crandon, a Canadian beauty who was married to celebrated Boston society doctor and surgeon, Le Roi Goddard Crandon.

Conan Doyle was even more interested in the first medium the committee investigated, George Valiantine. An obscure manufacturer of razor strops, swarthy in appearance and unreliable in temperament, he had been quite disinterested in mediumship until, at a New York hotel, he heard a loud rap at his door, ran out into the corridor, and discovered that no one was there. A woman he knew told him this experience proved he had mediumistic powers. He immediately held a séance, at which his dead brother-in-law, Bert Everett, apparently came through. By the time the *Scientific American* was ready to investigate him, he had several controls, including Hawk Chief, Kokum, Black Foot, Bert Everett, and Dr. Barnet, who gave medical prescriptions. Valiantine failed the committee's test, since an electrical control apparatus was shown to have been released during his séance indicating that he had left his chair. The authenticity of other mediums was equally brought into question, and the committee concentrated all its efforts on Mina Crandon.

On his tour, Conan Doyle ran into Houdini in several places, the first being Denver. There, the Conan Doyles attended Houdini's performance at the Orpheum Theatre, and talked to him extensively about the spirits, and the Houdinis attended Conan

Doyle's lectures. At that time, Conan Doyle also began work on a history of spiritualism, which appeared later in the twenties. Throughout the tour, he kept in constant touch with Houdini in order to obtain information about the *Scientific American* hearings. He continually urged the committee to give all serious attention to Mina Crandon.

Conan Doyle enjoyed his visits to Los Angeles, San Diego, and San Francisco. He was especially pleased with Los Angeles. He toured the Goldwyn studios, and had the delightful experience, which he described in *Our Second American Adventure* (1924), of seeing a picture set in the time of Mary Tudor: "The sulky king glowered. The queen picked daintily at her plate. It was a wonderful vision, and then in a moment we were back among town lots and chewing gum once more, with great hoardings [billboards] which implored me to preserve that schoolgirl complexion."

Conan Doyle lectured at the Trinity Auditorium to a very responsive audience. On May 24, the Conan Doyles, together with Denis, attended a séance held by a Mrs. Iñez Wagner, a pastor of the Los Angeles Spiritualist Church. She had an Irish control, who promised there would be no civil war with Ulster ("all will unite in time"). But he added a note of caution: "I have never looked upon prophecy as one of the certain gifts of the spirit. Even the early Christian circle went sadly astray upon that, for they foretold the immediate end of the world."

Conan Doyle received messages from his grandfather John Doyle, his Uncle Richard, his father, and the Ma'am. A spirit revealed that it had met Kingsley at Oceanside. On May 24, a Dr. and Mrs. Carl Wickland held a séance. Wickland had a psychiatric clinic, with a machine for static electricity with which demoniac spirits were driven from his patients. Conan Doyle observed, "I sat on the platform, received a shock, and entirely sympathized with the spirits in their desire to quit." Mrs. Wickland went into a trance and suddenly began acting all the roles in a play in Russian. She was apparently being controlled by a band of strolling players, who presented the play "before the undeveloped dead in order to teach them the moral." Later, this subdued and gentle woman became violent and used filthy language, giving the name of Jacky Williams, and behaving as a rough man alarmed to find himself wearing female clothes. Conan Doyle was intrigued when Mary Baker Eddy "came through," saying she regretted not having supported spiritualism in her lifetime.

On May 25, the Conan Doyles watched the shooting of scenes for Mary Pickford's new film, *Rosita*, directed by Ernst Lubitsch. Douglas Fairbanks came by, and Arthur and Jean posed for pictures with Doug and Mary. The Conan Doyles fondled Jackie Coogan on their knees, and Conan Doyle, as he reported in *Our Second American Adventure*, told the little boy "a gruesome Sherlock Holmes tale . . . the look of interest and awe upon his intent little face is an excellent example of those powers which are so natural and yet so subtle."

On May 26, Conan Doyle was entertained at the City Club by a large number of Los Angeles business leaders. He caused roars of laughter when he said, "A Los Angeles man was admitted to heaven, but Peter whispered to him as he passed, 'I'm afraid you'll be disappointed.'"

Conan Doyle then headed east by way of Oregon and Washington, and visited an old stomping ground, Jasper National Park, in Canada. In Vancouver, he attended a séance at which the medium was a Clarence Britton. While the medium sat in a cabinet, there appeared in the curtains a series of faces—black-bearded, white-bearded, and female. Among the visitors from the Other World was the Ma'am, but Conan Doyle was not totally convinced it was she. He did not rule out the possibility that a clever mask was being used. On August 4, an exceptionally hot day, the Conan Doyles, their mission done at last, sailed for England on the S. S. *Adriatic*.

Back home, Conan Doyle entertained Dr. and Mrs. Crandon, on leave from the *Scientific American* committee hearings, and held a séance with Mina, known popularly as "Margery," at the Buckingham Palace Mansions flat, controlling her by gripping her feet in his lap. He was greatly impressed with the messages her dead brother Walter brought, and with her ability to cause a bell box to ring seemingly without touching it. A dried flower fluttered from the ceiling and landed at Jean's feet.

He was devastated when Mina was discredited, at least temporarily, by the *Scientific American* investigators. At the séance attended by the committee, she had produced whirling psychic lights; a luminous curtain rod, which balanced on her megaphone; disembodied pinching, tugging, scratching, and licking; a psychic pigeon with a carrier number, which left unspiritual droppings on the carpet; and a tame bat, Susie, which tobogganed up and down the curtain rod, to loud approval from all present. As she shot down the rod, Susie had made a swishing sound that rose in pitch until she hit the table; then she had given a series of visible jerks and audible clicks as she climbed laboriously back up. The curtain rod had been threaded miraculously through a maze of arms and legs, while a ukulele had risen off the floor, jumped over a table, and cuddled in a sitter's arms like a baby. Later, something resembling an arm emerged from an unspecified portion of the medium's lower anatomy, and moved objects within several feet of her. It appeared to be rather like a tentacle, and somebody suggested that it was made of animal intestines stuffed with cotton and stiffened with wire.

Houdini helped to discredit Mrs. Crandon by tying an elastic band around his calf, making his ankle so swollen and sensitive that he was able to detect her foot sneaking out to press the bell box. He also caught her throwing things around with her head. Not surprisingly, the committee refused to award her a prize; later, when she produced Walter's thumbprint, it turned out to be that of her dentist.

Conan Doyle was convinced she had been much maligned and sprang to her defense, but the *Scientific American* committee refused to reverse its decision. However, Hereward Carrington for many years continued to believe that at least some of her phenomena were genuine.

Conan Doyle was soon faced with another shock. On November 20, 1924, the London *Daily Sketch* revealed that Mrs. Deane's Cenotaph ghost photograph was, undoubtedly, a "cruel fraud, designed to deceive credulous people and bereaved relatives of the glorious dead." The paper claimed that Mrs. Deane, Felicia Scatcherd, and Estelle Stead had jointly manufactured the pictures; that the faces were those of "the famous sporting figures Battling Siki, Jimmy Wilde, and several well-known foot-ballers." Conan Doyle strenuously denied this, but the subjects wrote in to confirm it. Next to a reproduction of the Cenotaph picture, the *Sketch* ran one made up by its photographic depart-ment, of several members of the Gaiety Theatre chorus floating over the entrance of the theater in a cloud, greeting the audience as it came through the doors. The *Sketch* offered a thousand pounds to anyone who could produce ghost pictures. There were no applications.

As if this were not enough, Conan Doyle had to endure the calumny which followed yet another public scandal. The maga-zine *John Bull* published an article headed "How Conan Doyle Was Tricked." The reporter, Sidney Mosely, revealed that in 1919, he had invited Conan Doyle, a Scotland Yard inspector, and the editors of two spiritualist magazines to the Criterion Restau-rant to see a demonstration by the famous Masked Medium. The sitters had placed certain possessions in a black-velvet bag, which had been tied up and locked away in an iron box. The Masked Medium, dramatically dressed in black, with a heavy veil, had sat in the dark with the box in her lap and announced its con-tents; she had revealed that Conan Doyle had placed Kingsley's signet ring in it, with the initials A. (for "Alleyne") K. C. D. Conan Doyle had unhesitatingly declared the Masked Medium genuine.

Mosely disclosed in the article that the Masked Medium had been working in collaboration with the magician P. T. Selbit. Selbit, while introducing the veiled lady, had somehow substi-tuted the box for another exactly like it. Then, behind the stage, he had opened the box, examined its contents, and sent the neces-sary information along a thin wire which was threaded up through the medium's dress and into small radio earphones con-cealed behind her heavy veil.

Angered by the article, Conan Doyle said that the statement that she had received her information by wireless was patently absurd. Instead, he asserted, she had received it telepathically. He asked for a test séance with the Masked Medium. She arrived with Selbit at the *John Bull* office, and objects were again placed in the box, among them a small brooch brought by Conan Doyle. Once again, the identification was correctly made, but the radio wire was shown to Conan Doyle, who was forced to admit his mistake.

Conan Doyle's life in those years, despite all of his problems, continued to be well balanced between work and play, between hours at his desk and enthusiastic bouts of golf or long walks across the Sussex Weald, between attending countless committee meetings and enjoying the happiness and consolation of his family. He remained utterly devoid of pretense, mentally youthful, enjoying good eyesight and hearing, and refusing to tolerate insincere and calculating people. He was passionately absorbed in all aspects of politics, religion, science, painting, and literature, and despite grave misgivings about the future of the world, and his fascination with the future life, he remained very much a practical man, never foolish about what he believed to be a pursuit of the eternal verities. Oliver Lodge, the scientist and great friend of Conan Doyle's, was to say of him after his death that he "lacked the wisdom of the serpent," and this was true now and then in his encounters with blasphemous fake mediums; but one can only marvel at his sense of wonder, the purity and almost childlike inquisitiveness of his approach to experience, characteristic also of his fellow Irishman William Butler Yeats, who similarly loved stories about ghosts and fairies.

His friendship with Balfour continued happily. During the war, Balfour had served as First Lord of the Admiralty, succeeding Winston Churchill, and later as Foreign Secretary, having moved from supporting Asquith to supporting Lloyd George. Though the importance of this office was somewhat reduced by the concentration of power in the War Cabinet, he emerged strongly in 1917 in his position in favor of the creation of a Jewish national state in Palestine. In 1922, he became both a Knight of the Garter and an earl. He joined Baldwin's second cabinet in 1925, and in the 1920's helped reconstruct the complex relationship between Great Britain and the Commonwealth.

Balfour's continuing passion for the Holmes stories, and his love of German music, were unbreakable bonds between him and Conan Doyle. In 1928, when he experienced the beginnings of circulatory failure and moved to his brother Gerald's house, Fisher's Hill, at Woking, Conan Doyle frequently visited him, along with Winston Churchill, Baldwin, and Lloyd George. Balfour read Holmes stories right up until the last months of his life, and they provided a great consolation. The friendship was a profoundly meaningful one to Conan Doyle, and although Balfour never finally accepted spiritualism, Conan Doyle wrote after his death in 1930 that he was convinced he had "some undeveloped psychic gifts of his own, and had obtained some results in an experiment in crystal-gazing." It is perhaps fortunate that because of his final illness, Balfour was unaware of Conan Doyle's break with the Society for Psychical Research, of which his sister, the widow of Henry Sidgwick, was an official.

In 1924, Conan Doyle turned his mind toward material matters. He became fascinated by a murder that had occurred only a step from his home in Crowborough. It was very similar to a killing, also in 1924, which had fascinated him: a Patrick Mahon had murdered and decapitated his girl friend, placed her head on a fire, and fled in horror into a storm when the heat caused her eyes to open. The local killing was that of an insipid girl named Elsie Cameron, presumably by her lover, Norman Thorne. Conan Doyle's chauffeur knew Thorne and liked him, but never doubted his guilt. Thorne, who owned a small run-down farm, reported Elsie's disappearance to the police, and showed them all over his property in an apparent attempt to find her. But a woman who lived next door disclosed that she had seen Elsie enter the premises on the night of her disappearance, and Scotland Yard closed in. Thorne said that he had found the girl hanged, and had panicked, cutting her to pieces with his hack saw, and burying her in the chicken run.

Conan Doyle was convinced that Thorne's explanation was correct, and that Elsie had committed suicide because she was jealous of Thorne's relationship with another woman, seeking by the manner of her death to destroy both of them. This interpretation exactly reflected the theme of a Sherlock Holmes story he had written in 1922—*Thor Bridge*. The law took a different view, and much to Conan Doyle's distress, Thorne was hanged.

Conan Doyle returned to the subject of Holmes in a new series of stories, written in late 1924 and in 1925 and published in *The Strand* the following year. Dismissed critically at the time, these tales are in many ways among the most interesting of his entire oeuvre, and are still undervalued by Holmes scholars. Holmes now seems tired and vaporous, and Watson is apparently so exhausted that he steps back from his role of narrator on three occasions, Holmes taking over in two of the stories and an anonymous narrator in a third. No doubt the falling off after 1923–1924 in Conan Doyle's health and energy, which was drained by his touring on behalf of the spiritualist cause, brought into being this valetudinarian portrait of two great figures in decline. But the imagination was as fresh and fertile as ever.

One of the stories, *The Lion's Mane*, narrated by a somewhat enfeebled Holmes, harks back yet again to that extraordinary year of 1874, when Conan Doyle first came to London. It concerns a man attacked by a vicious jellyfish, *Cyanea capillata*. In his invaluable book *Out of Doors: A Selection of Original Articles on Practical Natural History* (1874), the Reverend John Wood described this creature in alarming detail for the benefit of Victorian children who might wish to venture rashly onto an infested local beach. It is amusing to note that John Wood was also responsible for the instructive pages of *Bees: Their Habits and Management* (1886), a book which Holmes must have assiduously studied before writing a similar work and retiring to Sussex to keep those insects which Maurice Maeterlinck also loved.

The Blanched Soldier, a feverish reflection of *The Woman in White*, is the story of an unfortunate youth, son of an irascible army man, who lurks in the garden of Tuxbury Old Park, his face looking ghostly, convinced he is a leper. James M. Dodd, who brings Holmes word of the apparent disappearance of the youth, has served in the Middlesex Yeomanry, just as Conan

Doyle had wanted to do, and as Archie Langman had done; Colonel Emsworth, the crusty father, is clearly based on Lord Roberts; and his son, once handsome, the finest man in his regiment, is in his new ghostly guise oddly reminiscent of Kingsley Conan Doyle. References to the Boer War throughout are intensely personal. The theme of leprosy recalls Conan Doyle's visits to the white leper colony in Norway with Connie and Jerome K. Jerome, and to the leper island off Capetown, which must have been his first sight on steaming into port on his arrival in 1900.

In *The Mazarin Stone*, unique in the Holmes canon in that it is narrated in the third person, Holmes confronts the wicked Count Sylvius, who, big and swarthy, with a formidable dark mustache, reminds one of Major Pond. Sylvius has made off with the Mazarin crown diamond. Once again, one can only marvel at the extent of Conan Doyle's reading. The Mazarin Diamonds were among the French crown jewels stolen at the time of the French Revolution. There were eleven of them, including two which were originally part of the British crown jewels, and were given as surety by Queen Henrietta Maria, widow of Charles I, for a loan of 427,566 livres by the Duc d'Épernon. When she was unable to repay the loan, he sold them to Cardinal Mazarin, who willed them to the French Crown, on condition that they be known as the Mazarin Diamonds.

These jewels, with nine others not willed to the crown and valued at 556,000 livres, were stolen during the French Revolution—apparently by Royalists determined to prevent their sale for paper money. The most famous of the Mazarin stones, the 53¼-carat Sancy, which Count Sylvius had evidently stolen to the great despair of Lord Cantlmere (read Lord Salisbury), Holmes's client, was at the time the story of *The Mazarin Stone* was set, in the possession not of the keeper of the Tower of London, but of the Maharajah of Patiala. The fact that it originally came from the crown of Charles I links it, of course, with the crown discovered in *The Musgrave Ritual*.

The Three Gables, with its story of an urgent effort to discover and destroy an incriminating manuscript, recalls the Oscar Slater affair, while *Shoscombe Old Place* recalls the case of Hawley Harvey Crippen, whose trial Conan Doyle had attended at the invitation of Edward Marshall-Hall in 1910. Crippen, an American chemist, had fled England on the S. S. *Montrose* after murdering his wife, known as the Belle Elmore, and burying her in a cellar; he had arranged for his mistress, Ethel LeNeve, who had previously been seen wearing Mrs. Crippen's jewels, to dress up as his son for the transatlantic journey. Crippen had been arrested when a Scotland Yard inspector turned over a brick in the cellar floor and discovered the body; in the first use of wireless telegraphy for this purpose, the captain of the S. S. *Montrose* was asked to surrender his passenger to the police.

In *Shoscombe Old Place*, a squire who for financial reasons must conceal the death (caused by illness) of his sister buries her in a crypt, arranging for her maid's husband to dress up as the dead woman and go careering around the country to deceive the local gentry. This masquerade could also be a sly reference to the medium William Thompson's dressing up as the Ma'am at the séance in New York and to Ethel LeNeve's wearing Mrs. Crippen's jewels. There is a splendid moment when Holmes sets the sister's dog on the transvestite as "she" hurtles along in her carriage:

With a joyous cry [the spaniel] dashed forward to the carriage and sprang upon the step. Then in a moment its eager greeting changed to furious rage, and it snapped at the black skirt above it.
"Drive on! Drive on!" shrieked a harsh voice.

As always, Conan Doyle supplies numerous abstruse references to his own reading. At one stage, Holmes discovers a leaden coffin standing on end before the entrance to the vault. This is a reference to a famous real-life mystery known as the Shifting Coffins of Barbados, which fascinated Conan Doyle: the coffins of the Chase family were repeatedly found set on end despite their being locked in. The Governor's seal was placed over the keyhole, and sand strewn all the way down the steps into the vault in order to show the slightest footprint, but the cause of the disturbance was never found. Entertaining theories ranging from the growth of giant mushrooms to the effects of subterranean earthquakes were put forward to explain the mystery, all entirely without success.

The Creeping Man, alive with an antic humor reminiscent of the Challenger stories, embodies a theme based on the hullabaloo over the recent Voronoff monkey-gland experiments in the early 1920's. An eccentric professor returns from Europe, having secretly undertaken a course of medication similar to the Voronoff rejuvenation program. Periodically, he behaves like the langur, from which—it turns out—the serum he uses is obtained, and capers around his country estate, climbing up trees and vaulting over walls with all of the abandoned craziness of Mr. Hyde in Stevenson's story. Holmes's comment is typical: "When one tries to rise above Nature one is liable to fall below it."

In *The Sussex Vampire*, Conan Doyle agreeably satirizes Bram Stoker's *Dracula*. A woman is suspected of sucking a baby's blood when in fact she is saving its life by drawing curare from its neck. A vicious stepson, experiencing homosexual and incestuous affection for his father and jealousy of his new half brother, has tried to kill the baby with a poison-dipped arrow. An even more distant reference is also contained here. In the 1860's, England had been shaken by an extraordinary case in which a young girl, Constance Kent, had been accused of murdering her baby half brother, the child of the marriage of her father and a hated governess. She had been released for want of evidence, and had retired to a convent; years later, she astonishingly disclosed that she was the murderess. Many people had believed that she was shielding the actual killer, her father; that when the child had awakened in the nursery and started to scream while the father was making love to a nursemaid, he had smothered it accidentally with a pillow.

The slightly earlier *Thor Bridge* contains echoes of the Constance Kent case, along with its aforementioned prefiguring of the Norman Thorne affair (the resemblance between the words "Thor" and "Thorne" scarcely needs stressing). In *Thor Bridge*, we are introduced to an eccentric American Gold King, now resident in England, whose wife has been murdered. The portrait of the gold tycoon Neil Gibson is another of Conan Doyle's long-delayed acts of vengeance against Major Pond:

If I were a sculptor and desired to idealize the successful man of affairs, iron of nerve and leathery of conscience, I should choose Mr. Neil Gibson as my model. His tall, gaunt, craggy figure had a suggestion of hunger and rapacity. An Abraham Lincoln keyed to base uses instead of high ones would give some idea of the man.

An exchange takes place between Gibson and Holmes which has an authentic echo of the Conan Doyle–Pond relationship. Referring to the possibility of Holmes solving the mystery of Mrs. Gibson's death, Gibson says, ". . . if dollars make no difference to you, think of the reputation. If you pull this off every paper in England and America will be booming you. You'll be the talk of two continents." Though one wishes Holmes had replied, "Only two?" his response is very characteristic: "Thank you, Mr. Gibson. I do not think that I am in need of booming."

Thor Bridge has its clear parallels in life. For many years, Conan Doyle had been fascinated by an episode which took place in the country near Ightham Knoll, in Kent. A Major-General Luard, who had been in the army in India, had been walking with his wife Margaret in the woods. Leaving her, he had returned to his house to enjoy tea with a woman friend. He had subsequently been disturbed to discover that his wife had apparently disappeared. After a search, she was found near a summerhouse in the woods, shot dead. Luard was suspected of having murdered her, although there was no apparent motive. Some gossips did suggest that he had been having an affair with another woman in Ightham. Luard was so anguished by public criticism, and by the relentless needling of the Scotland Yard detectives sent to investigate the case, that he committed suicide by throwing himself in front of a train.

Conan Doyle did not believe, as *Thor Bridge* might indicate, that Mrs. Luard had shot herself in order to implicate her husband in her "murder." Instead, his view was that the killing had been an act of vendetta performed by an Indian who had for some reason stored up hatred for Luard, and had journeyed from the Orient to destroy him. In fact, an Indian had been seen mysteriously prowling about in the woods near Ightham, but the police had rejected the suggestion that he might be responsible.

Only a year before *Thor Bridge* was written, Conan Doyle had paid several visits to a friend, the Reverend B. T. Winnifrith, whose daughter Anna, later to become the well-known actress

Anna Lee, was to be a schoolmate of Billy Conan Doyle's. Winni-
frith showed him the Tithe Book for 1908, covering events at
St. Peter's Church in Ightham at the time of the crime. Conan
Doyle questioned Winnifrith closely on the matter, and the Tithe
Book for 1921 clearly discloses these conversations.

Just as Conan Doyle's earlier stories *The Ring of Thoth* and
Lot No. 249 are echoed loudly in the film *The Mummy* and its
sequels, and *The Silver Mirror* is recalled in "The Haunted Mirror," an episode of the famous omnibus ghost movie *Dead of
Night*, so *Thor Bridge* is reflected in two famous novels, both of
them filmed, Ben Ames Williams' *Leave Her to Heaven* and James
Hilton's similarly titled *Rage in Heaven*. In the former, a jealous
woman takes poison to ruin her husband and send her innocent
sister to her death; in the latter, a man throws himself on a knife
fixed in a doorjamb and marked with the fingerprints of his wife's
suspected lover.

The best of this valedictory group of Holmes stories, the
admirable tale *The Illustrious Client*,* presents us with one of the
most alarming villains in Conan Doyle's rogues' gallery: Baron
Adelbert Gruner, a poisonous male beauty with dark, languorous
eyes, who seduces and destroys women until a victim flings vitriol
in his face and ruins his major asset and source of income. He becomes something horrifying, a portrait of decadence "over which
the artist has passed a wet and foul sponge." It is worth noting
that in Paris Conan Doyle had recently attended performances at
the Grand Guignol, where vitriol throwing was a feature of the
stage presentations.

Gruner has small mustachios like an insect's antennae, a fine
figure, and exquisite clothes; like Thaddeus Sholto, he is a dandy
and an aesthete, but with a difference. On whom was he based?
There are hints in his character of Henri Landru (executed on
circumstantial evidence for murdering several women in February, 1922), and stronger ones of Henri Girard, a dashing and
wax-mustachioed toxicologist and *boulevardier*, whose method of
killing was exceptionally bizarre: he destroyed his victims with
germ cultures. In May, 1921, he himself escaped the guillotine by

* Once again, quite clearly Edward VII.

swallowing bacillus-infested water. Both of these cases were very recent; Conan Doyle was aware of the second of them because of his friendship with H. Ashton Wolfe, a detective-author attached to the Sûreté in Paris.

A closer parallel to Gruner can be found in a person who was extremely active during the crucial Doylean year of 1874. Henri Pineau was a handsome, dark-eyed, and thin-mustachioed decadent of extraordinary murderous propensities. He began as a waiter in Paris. There he seduced a wealthy Englishman named William Cotton, murdered him, and obtained his fortune. Having moved to England, he lived in splendor, posing as the Comte Henri de Tourville. He maintained homes in London and Scarborough, collected priceless porcelain—like Baron Adelbert Gruner—and dressed in the height of fashion. His Apollo's figure and delicately chiseled face ensured him a flock of male and female admirers.

He married an impressionable heiress, Edith Ramsden, whose mother held most of her fortune in trust. Then he killed the mother, making her death look like suicide, and poisoned his wife. Now a millionaire, he became a glittering figure of London society, wining and dining with authors, painters, and Members of Parliament.

Early in the story, Holmes refers to the fact that Gruner's wife has died in a so-called "accident" in the Splugen Pass, in Czechoslovakia. Pineau's second wife, Madeleine Miller, died in a so-called "accident" at Spondinning, in the Austrian Tyrol. Like the Baroness, she was flung off a precipice; like the Baron, Pineau benefited from her death, and traveled to London immediately after the crime.

Holmes is brought in to capture Gruner in order to avoid a scandal which would have affected the Throne. When Pineau was arrested, following the discovery of the latest murder, the Prime Minister, the Queen, and many highly placed people were relieved to hear that the person they had received so openly as a man of culture and position would not be tried in England. Pineau's death was scarcely less gruesome than the presumed end of Baron Gruner. Narrowly escaping the guillotine, he was condemned to the salt mines for life. This precious decadent, with a fortune of fifty thousand pounds lying unclaimed in a London bank, was forced to toil at hard labor without a break, until he died of blood poisoning in the 1880's.

After *Shoscombe Old Place*, Conan Doyle announced Holmes's retirement in several newspaper interviews. Watson settled down to a comfortable late middle age with (presumably) his second wife. The public protests were much fainter on this occasion. Conan Doyle's unpopularity with the solidly conservative elements in the middle class of Britain and America, following his espousal of the spiritualist cause, was largely responsible for this new indifference. The intellectual journals' coldness toward the final collection, *The Case-book of Sherlock Holmes*, was due to the contempt their editors felt for his spiritualist activities. He had, sadly, become a laughingstock in Bloomsbury, and the excellence of his later work in fiction was largely overlooked. The reviews of Holmes's valedictory appearances hurt Conan Doyle acutely, making him more aware than ever of the fickleness of fashion.

Looking back over the stories as a whole, one can find innumerable personal references in addition to those already discussed in these pages. The Charing Cross Hotel, near the hotel where Conan Doyle first met George Edalji, is the meeting place which Holmes, pretending to be Colonel Walter in *The Bruce-Partington Plans*, suggests to the spy Hugo Oberstein. "St. Oliver's" school in Yorkshire in *The Hound of the Baskervilles* suggests "St. Omer's" (the original name of Conan Doyle's school, Stonyhurst). Conan Doyle's visit to the Coptic monastery in Egypt is recalled by Professor Coram's treatise in *The Golden Pince-nez*, with its analysis of documents found in the Coptic monasteries of Syria and Egypt. The title of this story refers to the Ma'am's favorite spectacles, as well as to the *Chambers's Journal* article "My Detective Experiences." Favorite authors of Conan Doyle's crop up in various places. Gustave Flaubert, writing to George Sand, is quoted in *The Red-headed League*. Ronald Firbank has a set of villas named after him in *The Disappearance of Lady Frances Carfax*. H. G. Wells is subtly referred to in the

"Artesian Wells" of *The Three Garridebs,* and "Vernon Lee" has a lodge named after her in *The Illustrious Client.* Jules Verne becomes Dr. Verner in *The Norwood Builder.* Countless other examples could be cited. There is more than one reference to Queen Victoria. She rewards Holmes in *The Bruce-Partington Plans* with an emerald tiepin for his efforts on behalf of the Crown.

11

THE GREATEST JOURNEY

CONAN DOYLE'S home life in the middle 1920's was very happy indeed. A chauffeur, William Latter, joined his staff in 1925. Latter would drive him to the Crowborough golf course in the morning. Conan Doyle would hit a dozen balls on the links, leave Latter to pick them up, and walk back to the car. While they were driving, he might see an old tramp, join him on the road while Latter cruised alongside, give him five shillings, and learn the story of his life. On one occasion, Conan Doyle gave a tramp his shoes, and appeared on his doorstep shoeless, in the snow. Often, Latter would drive him to his old tricycling grounds at South Norwood or Croydon, and he would say, "I've had enough . . . I want to write, and I can't write in the car." Instead, he would return by train, writing furiously throughout the journey, and Latter would meet him at the station at the other end. To be free of interruption, Conan Doyle would write in a summerhouse in the garden, or in a local hotel room. He almost never worked in his study.

Apart from the emphasis on séances, the life of the family was completely normal; entirely healthy and happy. Outings of the entire family and staff were quite frequent. On one occasion, they all went to see the film version of *The Lost World* in London; on another, they went to see a revival of *The Speckled Band* on the stage. At Christmas and on birthdays, conjurers or jugglers would appear, to delight the children; Christmas Day was always spent at home, but on Boxing Day the family would visit Jean's father, about five minutes' drive away. The staff would be left behind to enjoy their own celebrating.

On one occasion, Denis and Malcolm staged a mock battle of

the family against the staff. The two sets of combatants gathered on the lawn next to the tennis court, running around with revolvers and shooting at random. Conan Doyle appeared, and said to Bassett, the second gardener, "Would you mind me having a look at those guns?" When they were brought over to him, he was shocked to discover that they were his Boer War revolvers, and still contained live ammunition. Bassett recalls, "Some of us might have been killed. I never forgot it."

Bassett also never forgot something which Major Alfred Wood told him about Conan Doyle. In an interview with Tony Rayns in 1975, he said:

[Sir Arthur] went out for a stroll one morning from his flat in Victoria, and it came on to rain, so he went into a shop and asked for a cheap umbrella. The assistant produced one that cost half a crown. When he came home he had his umbrella up and another five under his arm: he'd bought six! What on earth for, I wouldn't know. These celebrities, that's the sort of thing they do!

In this period, Conan Doyle bought a new house, Bignell House, Bignell Wood, in Hampshire at Wittensford Bridge, near Minstead. He needed a second home where he could find total seclusion, holding séances without fear of interruption. He had loved the New Forest ever since the walks in the 1890's which had inspired *The White Company*. He enjoyed the garden, which, with its clayey soil, offered many small rivulets, streams, and springs. He used the well near the house, and he channeled one of the springs underground for a distance beneath the garden to the north, also diverting it to create a little waterfall into a larger stream. The amphora set in the middle of the garden served to conceal a manhole through which the channel was cleaned.

He knew that the site was extremely historic; it was filled with Saxon relics, and had been inhabited continuously for thirteen centuries. A small, two-story cottage, dated 1700 A.D., was attached to the greenhouse, which in turn led into a Saxon barn/cottage. The Saxon part of the building had a thatched roof, which, though highly inflammable, was retained.

He rebuilt the house in red brick, facing it with white plaster and wooden beams, favored since the South Norwood days. The eighteenth-century cottage was turned into a west wing of the house with some of the vestigial walls of the Saxon barn incorporated into what became a living room. He had the exterior covered with ivy and Virginia creepers to make it look more romantic.

After a flood which caused a tree to fall across the stream which wound through the garden, Conan Doyle built a bridge, giving main access to the house from the west. Once this was accomplished, he made it a strict rule that tradesmen and others should always approach the house from the south, out of the household's sight. The reason for this fanatical desire for privacy was the deep local hostility of Conan Doyle's spiritualist activities, intensifying so sharply by 1926 that postmen refused to deliver mail to the door. Gypsies at nearby encampments were forbidden by their leaders to allow their eyes to fall on the building at all. Evil entities were reported in the nearby village, and a priest exorcised them—these were incorrectly thought to emanate from Bignell House.

Conan Doyle converted the 85-by-35-foot attic into a divided water tank, drawing drinking water from the well and water for other uses from the stream. He also, as in previous houses, supervised the preparation of a satisfactory private electric generator, set up in a little shed and run on gasoline obtained in London. He installed an electric heating system in the cellar, an adaptation of a similar system he had designed and introduced at Windelsham.

As his sons grew up, Conan Doyle rigorously taught them the three old-fashioned requirements of a gentleman: chivalry toward women, courtesy to social inferiors, and uprightness in financial dealings. He would forgive the mischievous Malcolm his accidental shooting of the gardener in the leg, his crashing of a seven-hundred-guinea automobile into an oak tree, and his strange spring gun's exploding and setting fire to the billiard room. But he would not forgive him his rudeness to a second housemaid.

Malcolm never forgot how his father vanished into his new study for days on end, while a maid tiptoed to the door and left trays of food which remained untasted for seventy-two hours at a stretch.

The children liked to listen to their father's fantastic schemes for investing in expeditions to recover buried treasure or sunken galleons; and enjoyed long walks with him across the Sussex Downs. He talked irresistibly about the strata of the Weald, and sang old sea chanteys in a roaring, still-Scottish burr, caught and carried away by the salt wind from the sea.

Early in 1924, Conan Doyle was asked to supply a tiny Holmes story for the library of Queen Mary's Doll House, which was exhibited at the Wembley British Empire Exhibition before being lodged in royal quarters. Among the other contributors were G. K. Chesterton, John Masefield, Arnold Bennett, H. G. Wells, Father Ronald Knox, Frank Swinnerton, George A. Birmingham, and Gilbert Frankau.

The title of the minute volume, written in ink by Conan Doyle in what appeared to be ants' footsteps, is *How Watson Learned the Trick*. The story opens at breakfast, when Holmes glances up and catches Watson's eye. He asks him what he is thinking about. Watson replies that he thinks Holmes's tricks are superficial, and he is amazed that the public takes them so seriously. Holmes concurs, observing that he himself was the first to make the remark. He then asks Watson how he can prove that the methods of deduction are easily copiable, and Waston proposes to do so by using them himself. Watson deduces that Holmes was very preoccupied when he rose that morning: he forgot to shave. He next deduces that Holmes has a client named Barlow, whose case he has failed to solve, for he has observed Holmes groaning and frowning as he puts into his pocket a letter signed "Barlow." Watson also points out that Holmes must be taking a special interest in financial speculation, since he exclaimed over something in the financial page of the morning paper. And he says that Holmes must be expecting an important visitor, since he has replaced his dressing gown with a black coat.

Holmes listens to these remarks patiently, and then disposes of them one by one. He discloses that the reason he did not shave is that he has sent his razor to be sharpened. He has put on his black coat because he has an early appointment with his dentist, whose name is Barlow; the letter is a confirmation of the appointment. The financial page faces the cricket page, which he turned to in order to determine if Surrey was holding its own against Kent. Holmes concludes with the words, "But go on, Watson, go on! [Deduction from observation] is a very superficial trick, and no doubt you will soon acquire it."

During the 1920's, several films were made of the Holmes stories, and Conan Doyle took a keen interest in them. He particularly liked the fact that the two most famous Holmeses in pictures had names ideally suited to the canon: Eille Norwood, bringing to mind Upper Norwood and South Norwood, and John Barrymore, sharing the name of the pair of servants in *The Hound of the Baskervilles*. Eille Norwood made a series of pictures with the Stoll Company, and Conan Doyle wrote of the star, "He has that rare quality which can only be described as glamor, which compels you to watch an actor eagerly even when he is doing nothing."

In 1923, Eille Norwood appeared in a new version of the Holmes stories in play form, *The Return of Sherlock Holmes*. It opened at the Princes Theatre, London, on October 9, 1923, and later went on tour. Conan Doyle enjoyed it very much, and was intrigued by the ingenious blending of the plots of *The Empty House, Charles Augustus Milverton*, and, most notably, *The Disappearance of Lady Frances Carfax*. The story concerns Lady Carfax, played by Molly Kerr, who, rather like Alice Faulkner in Gillette's play, is being kept prisoner by a villainous couple, who are gradually poisoning her. When Holmes attempts a rescue, her captors, a fake minister and his wife, call on the aid of Colonel Sebastian Moran, played by Lauderdale Maitland. There are curious elements imported bodily from Gillette's plays, and from the French revision of the last act of that play. Holmes dresses up as Moran's German valet, and discovers the gang in what is essentially a duplicate of the Stepney gas chamber. Finally, Holmes succeeds in decoying Moran with a replica of his head. At the end of the first night's performance, Conan Doyle received a standing ovation, along with Norwood, and he said to the audience, pointing at the playwrights, J. E. Harold Terry and Arthur Rose, "I am but the Grandpapa; these are the parents."

Conan Doyle enjoyed John Barrymore as Holmes in a Hollywood concoction, *Sherlock Holmes*, based squarely on the Gillette play, with the sinister Gustav von Seyffertitz as Moriarty, dressed up like Dr. Caligari in the old German silent film with long, flowing, white hair under a tall hat. Shot in London, the movie starred Hedda Hopper as the villainess, a role she played with considerable conviction. Another German version of *The Hound of the Baskervilles* was made at UFA studios in Berlin in 1929, with Carlyle Blackwell as Holmes; the results were entertainingly Gothic, but unfortunately Conan Doyle was not sufficiently well to see the picture when it was shown in London in 1930.

Conan Doyle's imagination flourished as powerfully as ever in the twenties. He wrote several remarkable stories which were precursors of today's science fiction, and which lost nothing by a comparison with his earlier efforts in the genre. The novel *The Land of Mist* presents the strange, comical, and harrowing adventures of Edward Dunn Malone and Professor Challenger among spiritualists in London. The account of séances, and the apparitions which accompany them, reaches into extraordinary realms of fantasy, achieving a fine conclusion as Challenger is converted from skepticism to conviction by the discovery that two people whom he believed he had killed have returned through his mediumistic daughter to inform him of his mistake. By implication, the book charts Conan Doyle's own progress toward belief, except that the characters do not exhibit the vibrant love of the mysterious that drove him forward even at his least credulous. Mr. and Mrs. Hewat McKenzie, the Reverend Vale Owen (a leading spiritualist), Dr. Geley, Felicia Scatcherd, and Conan Doyle himself appear in disguise in the book, Conan Doyle as "Algernon Mailey."

Most impressive, *The Maracot Deep* contains the story of the adventures of Captain Maracot, who combines elements of Captain Nemo (in Jules Verne's *Twenty Thousand Leagues Under the Sea*), Captain Sirius (in Conan Doyle's story *Danger!*), and Professor Challenger himself. Maracot and his companions travel by diving bell into a profound abyss under the ocean. There is a close parallel with Jules Verne's *Mysterious Island* as they are conveyed to what is left of the lost city of Atlantis. Atlantis becomes an odd symbol of the world's future. It is ruled by stunted blacks who have enslaved a tall, Caucasian people. Everyone is in uniform, and all food and drink is synthetically prepared. There is television and nuclear energy; transportation is by balloon. Conan Doyle, like H. G. Wells, was looking ahead, inspired by recent discoveries, including pioneering developments in television by John Logie Baird. The last part of the story is very odd: it is suggested that monsters live near Atlantis, ruling it in a sense, and threatening disaster. This adjoining world is run by the horrific Lord of the Dark Face. Here, as in the indication that blacks have enslaved whites, is a high-temperature recurrence of Conan Doyle's old terror of the colored peoples' emerging from Africa to dominate and destroy their traditional enemies.

Both of these works were quite well received, but not with the adulation which had greeted *The Lost World* and to a lesser degree *The Poison Belt*. Meanwhile, Conan Doyle was still busy with the spiritualist cause. On August 29, 1925, he opened his Psychic Bookshop, Library and Museum on the ground floor and in the basement of Abbey House, 2, Victoria Street, very close to Westminster Abbey. There, he exhibited numerous books, apports, including Charles Bailey's notorious "Assyrian tablet," photographs of Eva C. with her ectoplasm, pictures of Daniel Dunglas Home, the famous pioneer medium, and of other celebrities in the history of spiritualism, a piece of white cloth from Katie King's drapery, given to him by the late Sir William Crookes, and numerous other objects. He financed the Museum and its accompanying Library with his own money, and spent every spare minute attending it himself, but it was too modest in scope and too unsensational in content to be a success, and it lost him a great deal of money.*

* The contents of the Museum were stored during World War II, and destroyed by enemy action.

On September 5, 1925, Conan Doyle arrived in Paris to appear as Acting President of the International Spiritualist Congress. He was saddened because his beloved friend Dr. Gustave Geley was not present. On July 15, 1924, Geley had been killed in a mysterious accident. He had left Warsaw with a pilot in a small twin-engined monoplane, after giving a séance with Franek Kluski. He had apparently fallen out of the plane because of a freak wind current after undoing his safety belt, and moments later the plane itself had crashed, burning the pilot to death.

The Conan Doyles had considerable difficulty in entering the first public meeting of the Congress, at the Salle Wagram, not far from the old house of his granduncle Michael Edward Conan. A crowd of four thousand fought and kicked its way through heavy police cordons, and almost broke down the doors to get in. Thousands more caused a riot in the street outside, screaming to be admitted. Inside the Salle Wagram, Conan Doyle found much the same mass hysteria he had experienced at Carnegie Hall. He ordered the lights turned down, and the lantern-slide lecture began. The projectionist was inexperienced; Conan Doyle would announce a picture of Mina Crandon, yet Kluski would appear; he would describe a psychic "glove," and ectoplasm would be seen. The result of this muddle was that the audience became divided; the spiritualists literally fought with the nonbelievers, who hooted with laughter every time an incorrect slide was shown. During one brief pause, a man yelled out in English, "Look out, you're treading on my ectoplasm!" Conan Doyle tried futilely to deliver a lecture in French (he could read and write it well, but he spoke it clumsily). He said that Abraham Lincoln, Victor Hugo, and John Ruskin all believed in spiritualism, which was more than "a question of rapping tables and floating chairs." But he gave up before the end, and walked off the stage in a fury.

He gave a second lecture on September 10. Before he began, he announced that perhaps the "malicious spirits" which had ruined the previous session would not now be heard from. But once again the crowd stormed through the police cordons, knocked down the barricades, and made an earsplitting hubbub in the hall. The noise was so bad that the lights, which had been switched off, had to be turned up. Conan Doyle asked Jean to open one of the doors to let some more people in. She did so; the people ran in, kicking her, elbowing her in the ribs, and knocking her to the wall. Conan Doyle, announcing that he would never speak in Paris again, picked up his papers and started down the platform steps to assist her. Noticing his annoyance, the crowd at last settled itself, and after he had helped Jean to the stage, the lecture went on; but he never returned to France.

He was much happier with a meeting at the Albert Hall on Armistice Day, November 11, 1926. Previous Armistice Day spiritualist meetings had been held at the Queen's Hall, but because five thousand people wanted to hear him, a larger auditorium was necessary this time. There was a dramatic moment when, on the great concert platform before the high tiers crowded with his admirers, he shouted, "I ask all who are sure they are in touch with their dead to rise and testify!" In the solemn silence which followed, three thousand stood. Conan Doyle cried, "Thank God there are so many! I prophesy that within five years to such an appeal every man and woman in this great hall will arise. We are not testifying to faith, but to fact." He added, "We feel we are addressing those we have lost, and hold out our hands to them, not as shadow beings in an unknown life, but in a happy light—they are nearer to us than ever before." After he had spoken, the leading spiritualists Vale Owen and Estelle Stead joined him and the crowd in silent prayer.

A great shock in 1926 was the death of Harry Houdini. Conan Doyle had corresponded with him, on and off, since their time together in America, and their relationship, though it had deteriorated a great deal, had not been firmly ended. In mid-October, Houdini gave a lecture at McGill University, in Montreal, violently attacking spiritualism. After a show that night, a young admirer asked him whether he could tolerate body blows. The magician gave a qualified affirmative, and the youth struck him several times in the abdomen. Within hours, Houdini was in agonizing pain; his appendix had been injured. Like Rudolph Valentino in the same year, he died painfully of peritonitis.

Conan Doyle followed with utmost interest the various attempts by mediums to bring Houdini back; he placed most credence in Arthur Ford, who appeared to have produced a code which Houdini had supposedly given to Mrs. Houdini alone. Critics suggested that Ford need not have obtained the code from a spirit source, since it had already been published in the Brooklyn *Eagle*. But Conan Doyle insisted to everyone that despite this fact, he believed Ford was sincere.

In August, 1927, Dr. and Mrs. Carl A. Wickland, friends of the Conan Doyles from California, came to stay at Windlesham. Conan Doyle took them on a tour of the local sights, including the sinister moated grange called Groombridge, used as a basis for the Douglases' house in *The Valley of Fear*. While they were walking along, Mrs. Wickland said that they were being followed by an earth-bound spirit, of a hunchback dressed in a striped waistcoat and knee breeches. When they went to Crowborough for afternoon tea, Mrs. Wickland insisted that the man was sitting beside them. Back at Windlesham, Mrs. Wickland, before Conan Doyle's eyes, suddenly humped over, bared her teeth, and behaved like the man she said she had seen. Questioned by her husband, she identified herself as David Fletcher, who, she declared, was a hostler in charge of the horses at Groombridge, and had been alive in 1809. Conan Doyle later confirmed that the hostler had in fact existed then.

Conan Doyle was also busy with more important matters that year. The Oscar Slater case, for so long apparently a dead issue, preoccupied him again. The Scottish journalist William Park published through the Psychic Press in 1927 a new account of the case, which undoubtedly established Slater's innocence once and for all, and named a nephew of Miss Gilchrist's as her murderer. The book criticized the Glasgow police, the judge who had conducted the trial, and the various witnesses. It made mincemeat of the so-called inquiry into the case.

Conan Doyle supplied a devastating introduction to the book, reiterating his earlier charges of gross malpractice. *The Law Journal*, *The Solicitor's Journal*, and *The Police Gazette* all cried out for a new inquiry, but the Scottish authorities refused to do anything about releasing Slater. In September, 1927, Conan Doyle talked to Ramsay MacDonald, the leader of the Opposition, asking him to take action. MacDonald made a thorough investigation. The London *News Chronicle* published an important series of articles by E. Clephan Palmer, known as "The Pilgrim," tearing the original trial apart.

On October 23, the *Empire News* printed an extraordinary interview with Helen Lambie, who now lived in the United States, indicating that she had identified the man who had passed her in the corridor as someone who was a frequent visitor to her mistress, and that the police had flatly refused to accept her identification. She also indicated that the police had forced her to identify Slater as the one she saw. Her admission of perjury came as a shock to many people. It was followed by a statement from Mary Barrowman, whom Park had unearthed in Scotland, to the effect that she had told the police Slater "only resembled" the man she had seen, but that she had been compelled to identify him positively. She now definitely stated that Slater was not the person who had collided into her in the street.

On the strength of this information, and of more material accumulated by Ramsay MacDonald, Slater was temporarily released from Peterhead after eighteen years of imprisonment at hard labor. While waiting for the subsequent inquiry, he was to be kept in the charge of his friend Rabbi Phillips. Slater's arrival at the Rabbi's home in Glasgow was headlined in the press. He was astounded by the sight of a tablecloth, which he had not seen for almost two decades; he broke down in tears when he saw a bed with fresh sheets, a clean pillow, and a hot-water bottle ready for him. Conan Doyle wrote to him, expressing grief at his suffering. Slater replied:

Sir Conan Doyle, you breaker of shackles, you lover of truth for justice's sake, I thank you from the bottom of my heart for the goodness you have shown toward me. My heart is full and almost breaking with love and gratitude for you, your dear wife, dear Lady Conan Doyle and all the upright men and women who for justice's sake (and that only) have helped me, *me an outcast.* Till my dying day I will love and honor you and the dear Lady, my dear, dear, Conan Doyle, yet that unbounded love for you both, makes me only sign plainly,

Yours,

OSCAR SLATER

Conan Doyle dashed off a new version of *The Case for Oscar Slater*, reasserting Slater's innocence. Alive with all the fire and indignation that had characterized his Congolese manifestoes, it was sent to every member of Parliament and to the Prime Minister, Stanley Baldwin. On November 30, a special bill was passed by the House of Lords, allowing the Secretary of State to institute an appeal. A preliminary hearing was held at the High Court on June 8, 1928, under five judges. The Conan Doyles attended, along with Slater; Craigie M. Aitchison, the remarkable Scottish King's Counsel, acted for the appellant.

The judges agreed in principle to permit a re-examination of the earlier witnesses, and to admit any new evidence that might be called for. The appeal was fixed for Monday, July 9; it was indicated that Slater would not be allowed to give evidence himself. He was infuriated by this decision, and to Conan Doyle's horror sent telegrams to everyone, including Conan Doyle and William Park, saying that if he could not present his own case in court, he did not wish to proceed with the appeal. Conan Doyle was distressed and begged him to reconsider. Privately, he was so annoyed that he almost wanted to send him back to jail. Fortunately, Rabbi Phillips was able to calm Slater, and the appeal proceeded on schedule.

The greatest disappointment was that Helen Lambie refused to cross the Atlantic and give evidence. Apparently, she was afraid of charges of perjury, and even more afraid she would be forced to name the murderer. She was not heard from again. Her *Empire News* interview was admitted as evidence, however, together with Mary Barrowman's statements to reporters. Conan Doyle covered the appeal for the London *Sunday Pictorial* with his customary flair. He described Slater:

It is not an ill-famed face nor is it a wicked one, but it is terrible nonetheless for the brooding sadness that is in it. It is firm and immobile and might be cut from that Peterhead granite which has helped to make it what it is. A sculptor would choose that this is no ordinary man but one who has been fashioned for some strange end. It is indeed the man whose misfortunes have echoed round the world. It is Slater.

Craigie Aitchison argued most reasonably that the witnesses had been proven false, and that since they had lied, there could be no possible case against the appellant. Despite some demur among the judges, the decision, handed down on July 20, was favorable to Slater.

Conan Doyle shook hands coldly with the appellant. He was annoyed by Slater's attempt to withdraw the appeal, and he also deplored his background—his pimping, his prostitute mistress, his evident dealing in stolen goods. For Conan Doyle, Slater, like Casement, was simply a symbol of the oppressed; he was not a person worthy of respect. When Slater sent him the most generous gift he could afford, a silver cigar cutter, Conan Doyle returned it by the next mail.

But despite his feelings, Conan Doyle was not satisfied that the case was closed. He insisted that Slater seek compensation, and named the sum of ten thousand pounds. For himself, he asked only reimbursement for the legal fees he had advanced. He also suggested a small remuneration for William Park for the superhuman efforts in raising the appeal, which had broken his health and soon were to kill him. The Scottish Office offered six thousand pounds to Slater. Conan Doyle thought the sum insufficient, but Slater accepted immediately. On August 9, Conan Doyle wrote, insisting that Slater meet his obligations to those who had helped him. When Slater proved reluctant, Conan Doyle flew into a temper and told him in a letter that he "seemed to have taken leave of his senses," that he was "the most ungrateful as well as the most foolish person whom I have ever known." It is a bitter irony that the knight and the rescued man should thenceforth have become involved in an unseemly squabble over money.

On May 5, 1929, Conan Doyle wrote to the *Empire News* giving a breakdown of his expenses and demanding that Slater recompense him for his share of the payment to the lawyers. Slater still refused; he retired to a quiet existence first in Glasgow, and then in a bungalow in Ayr. There he married a waitress, Lina Schad, with whom he lived happily. Ironically, during World War II he was interned again, as an alien. He died in February, 1948, at the age of seventy-five.

Conan Doyle persisted in believing Miss Gilchrist's nephew murdered her. It was generally overlooked, however, that Helen Lambie was cut out of the will shortly before Miss Gilchrist's death.

One further footnote to the case is necessary. A bloody handprint had been found on the back of Miss Gilchrist's chair. William Roughead, in his preface to the Slater volume in the Notable British Trials Series, makes the statement that in 1908 fingerprint detection was not in use in the British Isles. The assertion is absurd. Fingerprint detection had, in fact, been employed since the turn of the century.

Having visited Australia, the United States, and France in the cause of spiritualism since the war, Conan Doyle decided to undertake an African mission in the same cause. At the end of 1928, the family sailed on the S.S. *Windsor Castle* from Southampton to Capetown, experiencing violent storms in the Bay of Biscay. The ship followed almost exactly the route taken by the S. S. *Oriental* during Conan Doyle's voyage in 1900. It was a journey full of nostalgia. Conan Doyle filled his time with lectures to the passengers of psychic experiences, and lessons to improve his French. He also read the Reverend C. Drayton Thomas' book *Life Beyond Death, with Evidence.*

At Capetown, the Conan Doyles, greeted by their friend the music critic Ashton Jonson and by spiritualists bearing flowers, happily checked into the Mount Nelson Hotel, where Conan Doyle and the Langman Hospital had stayed twenty-eight years before. He made local radio broadcasts, visited museums and galleries, and looked at primitive cave paintings. He held séances, including one with a Mrs. Kimpton, in the company of the actress Zena Dare. He also saw the medium Mrs. Butters, whose control was the Italian opera singer Sabatini. The Conan Doyles were amazed when Mrs. Butters suddenly stood up and sang an aria in a full baritone voice, and Ashton Jonson declared the voice to be "not only undoubtedly male, but of quite exceptional quality."

The Cape *Times* and *Argus* were as violent in their attacks on Conan Doyle as *The New York Times* had been. The Conan

Doyles brushed aside their complaints and steamed off on the S.S. *Aramadale Castle* to Port Elizabeth. There, they enjoyed the Snake Park, and chatted with Mrs. Fitzsimmons, its remarkable keeper. While they were looking at the snakes, Mrs. Fitzsimmons brought out a spirit photograph taken by William Hope, which showed her dead sister peeping over her husband's shoulder. The Conan Doyles left after a few days for Bloemfontein. On the train, Malcolm, asked by Denis if he found a certain woman attractive, said, "No! She's ugly!" Before he knew it, Conan Doyle had given him a backhand so violent he almost fell over. "*No woman is ugly!*" he shouted.

It is easy to imagine Conan Doyle's thoughts as he walked over the cricket ground at the Ramblers' Club and remembered his experiences in the typhoid epidemic. Very few of the people he had known at Bloemfontein were still there. The family enjoyed Durban, with its wide streets and magnificent bay, and Johannesburg, a vigorous boom town bursting with vulgarity and money. The tour continued into 1929. Conan Doyle, armed with a formidable umbrella, braved an extraordinary variety of climates. At one stage, the boys wanted to shoot a sleeping rhinoceros. Since Conan Doyle was opposed to killing sitting game, he advanced on the beast, opening and shutting his umbrella to try to waken it. But it simply opened one eye, closed it again, and went back to sleep. Conan Doyle also attacked a two-legged beast, a reporter who had accused him in an interview of exploiting Kingsley's death for money. He thrashed him heartily.

He loved the Kalahari Desert, Rhodesia (notably Bulawayo, the Zimbabwe ruins, and Victoria Falls), the Pungwe marshes, Tanganyika, Kenya, and Nigeria. On the way back to England, the family stopped in Malta. Perhaps the highlight of the trip was a visit to the grave of Cecil Rhodes, where Jean set down an automatic message from Rhodes himself: "This way I came and I went to my destiny, partly of happiness and partly of regret. But here one makes up for missed opportunities."

Back at Windlesham, Conan Doyle was filmed for a Fox Movietone newsreel, pottering about with an Airedale and discussing Sherlock Holmes and spiritualism ("I do not think, I *know*"). He also made a phonograph record for H.M.V., with virtually identical wording. He worked on a new story, *The Disintegration Machine*, based on the idea that it is possible to dissolve a human being into his component atoms and reassemble him elsewhere, a concept still seriously under discussion in the 1970's.

Another story, *When the World Screamed*, is the extraordinary account of Professor Challenger's attempt to drill a hole deep into the earth—Conan Doyle's version of an idea first put forward by the spiritualist astronomer Camille Flammarion in *The Strand*. Characteristically, Conan Doyle adds a sexual element to the tale. In his narrative, the world is a woman, or at least a female animal, that Challenger wants to penetrate to her "sensory cortex." As the phallic shaft reaches her cortex, the penetration causes a tremendous world scream, followed by tremblings and spoutings from one end of the earth to the other. It is hard to imagine a more extreme revelation of decayed Victorian psychology: the scream is one of pain, not of pleasure; the earth is seduced, and does not delight in the experience.

During 1929, the Conan Doyles strengthened their earlier friendship with a young airman and musician, Robin Sanders-Clark. Tall and handsome, genial and highly intelligent, Robin came to be like a third son to them.

Sanders-Clark recalled in an interview with me in Los Angeles in 1975:

> I had met Denis and Adrian [Malcolm] at a party, and they were very interested in motor-racing; I was doing a lot of flying at the time in a DeHavilland Moth, and had learned to fly when fifteen, a fact which interested Sir Arthur. I had loved Conan Doyle's books, and had become interested in psychic research through reading *The Land of Mist*. They invited me down to Windlesham on a Saturday, and I met the whole family. Sir Arthur didn't come down to lunch. They had tea at about four in the afternoon; he came down to high tea at six or six-thirty. He was wearing a blue blazer with insignia on the breast pocket, a soft collar, a loose-knotted tie, and wearing white flannels with a very thin stripe.
>
> My first impression was of his size. He was a huge man. He was a marvelous host. The meal was very good and typically English: steak and kidney pie, and pudding. The boys had told him I was a pilot; he started to question me, and I wanted to hear him. He asked

me about the difficulties I would meet on a flight I was planning to South Africa. I told him that the first problem would be the comparatively short range of the aircraft.

Having described the aeroplane to Sir Arthur, I noticed his intense interest. He asked me if it would be possible to take the front seat out, and have an extra petrol [gasoline] tank put in. I told him I already had planned on doing that. He asked me, "Would it not be possible to have the petrol tanks under the *lower* wings?" I said, "It probably would, Sir Arthur. It would cut down the air speed, of course." He replied, "That being the case, would it not be possible to arrange to drop the fuel tanks when they became empty?" I was amazed. Today, this method in propeller-driven aircraft is standard; in those days it was unheard of. I knew at once, and I know even more today, what a remarkable mind I was dealing with.

The evening I went to a movie with his sons; and we returned soon after eleven. My bedroom was almost exactly opposite Sir Arthur's study door. I saw a light under the door. It was ajar. Adrian said he thought I should know my room was badly haunted. Sir Arthur overheard this; he came to the door to reassure me there was no ghost in my room at all. I went into his study and sat down. We talked until two or three in the morning, about Challenger, Holmes, Brigadier Gerard, psychical research and so on. I would like to explode the fallacy that he did not want the name of Holmes mentioned in his presence. It was nonsense.

The family held séances frequently, contacting Kingsley, Innes, the Ma'am and other family members through raps from the table, or through Jean's automatic writing. At one time, an entity came through which gave the name of a society woman. Sir Arthur questioned her and she said she had recently passed on. He asked her "How?" She replied that it was through an accident in the hunting field, in Northern Ireland. The horse had refused a jump; she had fallen off, and the horse had rolled on her. That was at four-thirty in the afternoon. The *Evening Standard* was delivered at about six. The stop press news gave details of the death of the selfsame woman that morning in exactly the fashion described.

Sir Arthur, like Sherlock Holmes, had at the time an extraordinary range of dressing gowns. These, like his pipes and tobacco, were perfectly in keeping with his authorship of the character.

Sanders-Clark helped the Conan Doyles when, on August 15, 1929, a spark from a chimney set fire to Bignell House's thatched roof. He, Denis, and Malcolm, followed closely by Jean, ran up to the study and seized all the papers they could find, handing them down to Conan Doyle at the foot of the stairs.

Most of the manuscripts were recovered, but the house was severely damaged. With remarkable composure, Conan Doyle immediately set about rebuilding it. He was very absorbed at the time in studying the alleged posthumous writings of various authors, including Dickens, Jack London, and Oscar Wilde, who were supposed to have come back through mediums. He was particularly impressed by one of Wilde's reported remarks: "Being dead is the most boring experience in life. That is, if one excepts being married, or dining with a schoolmaster."

Conan Doyle was fiercely proud of his grown-up boys. Denis was strikingly handsome, rather like Kingsley in appearance, and Malcolm, though not a looker, was strapping and athletic. Their education had been somewhat scattered, because of their frequent travels, but both sons inherited their father's intelligence; and they never ceased to share his passion for spiritualism. Mary, who came down for weekends from Richmond, Surrey, was also a spiritualist; and so was Billy, who had developed from a pudgy little girl into a handsome young woman.

With Jean, Conan Doyle rushed off to Scandinavia in the autumn of 1929, about the time of the stock-market crash. He was not drastically affected by the crash, and was eager to preach in Denmark, Norway, and Sweden. He was most warmly received in all three countries. He is only disappointment was that his weakening health and tight schedule did not permit him to visit the fjords which he had seen with Louise, Connie, and Jerome K. Jerome so many years ago.

He longed to give his annual address on Armistice Day at the Albert Hall, but severe heart pains threatened to make this impossible. When his doctors forbade him to speak, he characteristically disobeyed them. His talk to the spiritualists was painful and halting, and he returned to Windlesham feeling weak and exhausted. He drew a sketch of himself which he called "The Old Horse"; it showed him weighed down with all of his enormous commitments—to justice, to Holmes fanatics, to politics, and to spiritualism. He never stopped working, and ironically, like the protagonists of *The Poison Belt*, he was kept alive largely by oxygen, in a room similar to Professor Challenger's. In those last

months of his life, suffering from angina pectoris, he was alter-
nately Challenger, Holmes, and Watson—sometimes irascible and
unpredictable, sometimes logical, sometimes bluff and hearty.

Despite his grave physical condition, the old campaigner's
spirit could not be dampened. With doctors giving him only
weeks to live, he traveled to London and began agitating for a
repeal of the Witchcraft Act, which forbade fortunetelling and
mediumship in England; when the London Spiritualist Alliance
refused to support him, he immediately resigned. His efforts toward repeal proved futile, and he was deeply distressed by this
failure.

The beginning of 1930 was marked by one of the most tragic
events in Conan Doyle's life. The *Journal of the Society for Psychical Research* published in its January issue a review by the Society librarian, Theodore Besterman, of *Modern Psychic Mysteries, Millesimo Castle, Italy*, by Gwendolyn Kelley Hack. The
review was extremely unfavorable. The book dealt with a series
of peculiar events at Millesimo Castle. The Marquis Scotto, whose
son had recently died, had held several sittings, in which trumpets
whirled about, knocking the sitters on the head, icy currents
were felt, a mysterious instrument called a "flexaphone"—a
stranger to any book of reference—appeared and disappeared,
swords and other objects were seen, and a doll turned up, looking almost human. Besterman pointed out that the descriptions of
the séances in the book showed the precautions against fraud to
have been inadequate, since the sitters and the medium had not
been searched, the windows had not been sealed, and the room
had not been checked for hidden devices.

Conan Doyle knew the Marquis Scotto through his friend
the author H. Dennis Bradley, at whose home at Dorincourt,
Kingston Vale, Surrey, the medium George Valiantine had produced the voice of Scotto's dead son. Rushing to the defense of
an admired associate and colleague, Conan Doyle precipitately resigned from the Society. He circulated a letter to the members
and associates attacking Besterman's review on the grounds that
Besterman had not not been present in Italy, and that it was inconceivable that an Italian nobleman could have faked the phenomena

described, levitated by means of wires, and imitated the voices of dead relatives. It was equally absurd, in his view, to believe that a female confederate could have concealed under her skirt a doll, a matador's sword, and a long medieval rapier, and helped the Marquis produce a large balloonlike object which hovered over the sitters and released blasts of ice-cold air. He added, commenting on Besterman, "Can we dignify such nonsense as this by the name of Psychical Research, or is it not the limit of puerile perversity?" Conan Doyle also observed that the Society had been extremely critical of disastrous experimental séances held in Berlin by George Valiantine, without having subjected them to an appropriate scientific examination.

Following the letter, Conan Doyle's subsequent manifesto, sent at the same time, charged that since the death of F. W. H. Myers and the end of the Leonora Piper sittings, the Society had done no constructive work of any importance, and that for a generation it had employed its energies in hindering and belittling those who were engaged in psychic research. He tackled various points in Besterman's review, claiming that Besterman had not read the book correctly. His resignation was final.

The reply by the President and the Honorable Secretaries, Sir Lawrence Jones, Eleanor Sidgwick, and W. H. Salter, was prefaced with the observation that in view of Conan Doyle's illness the Society would have preferred to avoid a controversy. However, the signators were forced to point out that in fact the Society had never ceased to deal constructively with matters connected with spiritualism. They reminded their members that the Society had frequently examined the celebrated medium Mrs. Osborne Leonard, and that it had commented favorably on the Naples Hotel sittings of Eusapia Paladino and on the Willi Schneider sittings at Tavistock Square in 1924. Sir Lawrence and his colleagues could have added that the Society had found unfavorably on George Valiantine at a sitting attended by the lesbian novelist Radclyffe Hall, and recorded by her friend Una, Lady Troubridge, who was also an investigator.

Theodore Besterman referred to Conan Doyle's criticism in yet another document circulated to the members, pointing out that in many instances his observations had been misunderstood.

The fault in this unhappy controversy appears to have been on both sides. Besterman, a librarian and amateur researcher, clearly did not have sufficient knowledge to review the book in question, and it should have been given to a more informed scientific critic. But while Conan Doyle's criticism of the review was basically cogent, he misquoted some of Besterman's remarks and acted far too rashly in wrongly accusing the Society of having failed to lend a sympathetic ear to mediums over the years. He had unquestionably been upset by the disastrous Valiantine séance with Radclyffe Hall and Lady Troubridge. When Valiantine's current control Feda (also Mrs. Leonard's control), insisted that Mrs. Wooley, one of the sitters, was a Mrs. Walker, and banged her with the trumpet because she would not respond, Mrs. Wooley firmly announced her correct identity. H. Dennis Bradley, as the host, was horrified, apologized, and became severely critical of his close friend Valiantine.

In her report, published in the proceedings of the Society, Lady Troubridge hinted that Bradley might have been an accomplice of Valiantine's, and Conan Doyle told the Society members in the manifesto that he took the gravest exception to this view. Whatever one may think of his rejection of the Society's work as a whole, one can only be touched, yet again, by his defense of the underdog, and his intense loyalty to old friends.

In the weeks following his resignation from the Society, Conan Doyle experienced considerable physical distress. His chest pains grew more and more agonizing, and he began to suffer from kidney trouble, which caused pain in his back. Nevertheless, his mind remained as acute and searching as ever. Even in his sickness, he managed to travel to London to visit the Psychic Bookshop, Library and Museum to try to help his daughter Mary and her assistant (Holmes specialists will be pleased to note that her name was Miss Faulkner). He took a constant interest in the work being done at the British College of Psychic Science. He still went to his favorite club, the Reform. He bombarded the London *Times* with letters on numerous subjects. He studied in detail Vladimir Zworykin's iconoscope, the device which transmits television images.

He was, to the end, a man ahead of his time. He ventured

into realms which are only now being fully explored. His misfortune lay in the character of the mediums whom he investigated, a problem he was the first to admit among friends. By counterfeiting their phenomena at the least a large percentage of the time, they effectively reduced the confidence of the uninitiated even in those phenomena that were perhaps genuine.

Having abandoned the London Spiritualist Alliance and the Society for Psychical Research, Conan Doyle retired to almost complete seclusion at Windlesham. He read, slept fitfully, and tried to keep up with the cricket results. He made his will, settled his affairs, and waited confidently for his release from the prison of his large, sick, confining body.

In the first hours of the morning of July 7, 1930, Denis and Malcolm had to obey a Challenger-like command: BRING OXYGEN. They came back from Tunbridge Wells with the precious cylinders, but it was too late. Shortly after dawn, Conan Doyle sat surrounded by his loving family in a large basket chair looking out across Jean's rose garden to the golf links and the rolling South Downs: Challenger's view. He was tired, and ready to undertake the greatest adventure of all.

In accordance with spiritualist principles, the funeral was not marked by shows of grief. The body in its heavy wooden coffin was carried across the lawn and through the rose garden to a grave beside the summerhouse where Conan Doyle had liked to work. The service was conducted by the Reverend C. Drayton Thomas, assisted by Conan Doyle's brother-in-law the Reverend Cyril Angell. Special trains were run from London, and for days afterward local villagers and laborers arrived with armfuls of flowers for the grave. Mary played spiritualist hymns on the piano. Simple and subdued, the ceremony gave ample proof that despite his many controversial activities, Conan Doyle was most widely beloved. On the grave marker of solid British oak were inscribed the words:

STEEL TRUE,
BLADE STRAIGHT

It was a perfect epitaph for the son of the Ma'am.

EPILOGUE: SÉANCES, MYSTERY, AND MURDER

A CROWD OF eight thousand people, not all of them spiritualists, filled much of the Albert Hall for the memorial service on July 13, 1930. The medium Estelle Roberts said she saw Conan Doyle's figure in evening dress, walk to the specially placed empty chair between Jean and Denis and sit down. After crying out, "He is here!" she moved over to Lady Conan Doyle and whispered a message to her which began, "Sir Arthur tells me that one of you in the family went into the summer house this morning. Is that correct?"

Lady Conan Doyle replied softly, "Yes."

Estelle Roberts continued: "Sir Arthur says, 'Tell Mary—,'" and at that moment the pipe organ drowned out the rest of the words for those nearby. Jean refused to disclose the nature of the message later, saying that it was too personal to be discussed.

Within twenty-four hours of Conan Doyle's death, the family was convinced it had received messages from him. Scores of mediums across the world claimed they also had received messages. On Thursday, July 10, a group of fifteen people gathered at 342 East 167th Street, in the Bronx, to attend a séance held by Nino Pecoraro. Pecoraro was swathed in bags and blankets; his hands, in gloves, were tied to his sides with wax-sealed ropes. His host, Dr. Salvatore Ajello, carried him into a small room, lit by a single red bulb under a heavy cloth shade. He was placed in a six-foot-high wire cage, and locked in like an animal. After ten minutes, a glistening figure came through the apartment door, posed for a picture, and sat down at a desk with the words, "How do you do everyone; I am Conan Doyle and I am glad to be here."

The magician Joseph Dunninger, head of the Science Investigating Committee of Psychic Phenomena, responded, "How amazing."

The figure replied, "You don't know nothing yet! Paper and pencil please, I want to write a book while I'm here."

Dunninger gave the visiting presence the items requested. An expert mentalist, Dunninger had grave doubts about the apparition, and in particular about its quite un-Doylean grammar. Just as the spirit took the pencil and paper, the phone rang; a patient was calling Dr. Ajello. The doctor left. After this mundane interruption, the phantom announced that it was making this appearance "through the courtesy of Harry Houdini and Madame Eusapia Paladino." It posed for two more pictures, and supplied a message for Lady Conan Doyle: "Four years I live in a castle. Remember our light never dies."

The lights were turned on and the cage opened. The seals on the medium's neck and hands were broken, but he lay completely cold and silent, like a corpse, seemingly not breathing. A *New York Times* reporter picked up the top sheet of the papers on the desk. The figure had simply scrawled three letters and four numerals on it: "SPR 3100." A sitter said that the message must refer to the Society for Psychical Research, and to Conan Doyle's membership number. The *Times* reporter corrected him. "It's the phone number of police headquarters," he declared.

Shortly thereafter, Pecoraro held another séance, in which a voice purporting to be Conan Doyle's announced from the ceiling that his fingerprints would be impressed on a paraffin-coated plate to prove to the sitters that he was present. Unfortunately, the Bureau of Criminal Investigation disclosed that whereas nine of the fingerprints were too blurred to be identified, the remaining one came from Pecoraro's left index finger.

The same night as the second Pecoraro séance, a Vancouver clairvoyant named Mrs. Cottrell claimed to have received a message from Conan Doyle, saying, "Already I have received an astonishingly warm welcome here from immense numbers of spirit folk." The family instantly rejected both the Pecoraro and Cottrell séances as absurdities. For some time, they accepted as genuine only messages sent through Jean herself in automatic writing.

On July 28, 1930, Jean announced to the press that her late husband had definitely established communication with her through a spirit photograph. She told the London *Daily Herald* in an interview that the Reverend Charles L. Tweedale, rector of Weston, in Yorkshire, and a well-known investigator of psychic phenomena, had sat for the photograph, and that Sir Arthur's face had appeared floating over that of the vicar. Also, the Welsh medium Evan Powell had told her what was contained in a sealed envelope which Conan Doyle had left with her, but she could not open it until she received direct instructions in automatic writing from her husband to do so. She added that the family had already received several messages from Sir Arthur, the first of them through her own hand only a few hours after his death.

In February, 1931, Lady Conan Doyle and Malcolm (now known as Adrian) attended a séance at the home of H. Dennis Bradley in Kingston Vale. The medium was George Valiantine. The lights were turned off, and the unpleasant piercing voice of Valiantine's control Bert Everett was heard from the ceiling uttering the words, "Good evening, souls." He was followed by another control, Dr. Barnet, who announced that Conan Doyle was ready to be heard. The trumpet flew into the air and Conan Doyle's voice came through it, recognized at once by Jean and Adrian. For an hour and a half he discussed family affairs with them. Occasionally the voice failed and the trumpet sank to the floor; then the voice would resume. On one occasion, the voice said to Adrian, "I am ready to go in the 'chitty' any time with you." This remark, which was taken to be a reference to Adrian's chitty-chitty bang-bang racing automobile, was regarded by Jean as convincing, and she accepted unhesitatingly the authenticity of the voice.

Unfortunately, in that same year, Valiantine was affected by a serious scandal. Bradley asked Valiantine to produce spirit fingerprints and thumbprints, including those of Conan Doyle, Lord

Dewar, and Sir Henry Segrave. In order to test Valiantine's veracity, the paraffin had been specially stained, and a mark was found on the medium's elbow revealing that he had tampered with it. When Conan Doyle's supposed thumbprint was checked, it was found to match that of the big toe of Valiantine's right foot. When the head of the Scotland Yard fingerprint department, Detective Inspector Bell(!), declared that "in a court of law this would be enough to condemn a man for murder," Valiantine broke down in tears. Nevertheless, his supporters continued to believe that Valiantine produced genuine spirit voices, including Conan Doyle's.

Early in 1935, John Goldstrom, author of *The History of American Aviation*, DeWitt MacKenzie, foreign editor of the Associated Press, and several others, including the Princess Lora Rospigliosi and Mrs. Chauncey Olcott, widow of the famous Irish tenor, set out in an American Airways Douglas airliner to attend an aerial séance over New York. Maina Tafe, the radio medium who carried messages from Station Astral, was to bring back Conan Doyle's voice through a silver trumpet. The plane was darkened for the occasion, and tested to see that it would be free of "etheric vibrations." It circled around Manhattan, while the sitters sat enthralled. Miss Tafe, described in the press as "a buxom blonde who rather resembles Miss Mae West," sank into a trance while the trumpet flew around the cabin and a voice purporting to be Conan Doyle's spoke through it in a piping intonation. One or two of the sitters rudely remarked that Conan Doyle had a deep voice, and that this one sounded more like that of the radio singer Kate Smith; others insisted that the voice was his and was saying several things "of great importance," one of which was: "Talking with persons in an aeroplane is more fantastic than death itself." The medium Arthur Ford, who was one of those present, swore that Conan Doyle's own intonations were heard.

Then Conan Doyle's voice was replaced by that of the explorer Roald Amundsen, who described the circumstances of his mysterious death on a rescue flight in the Arctic. As moonlight streamed into the cabin, and the passengers looked out at the dazzling lights of Manhattan and the black waters of the Atlantic, the voice of Conan Doyle was heard in a final salutation. "Dear friends, I am happy here. Wilbur Wright is standing beside me, and so is Amundsen. Farewell, Farewell."

Messages from Conan Doyle continued for years. In 1936, when Jean was ill with cancer, he was supposed to have diagnosed the disease before the doctors could. Until her death in 1940, Jean continued to be convinced that her late husband communicated through her, saving the lives of members of the family by warning of approaching illness, or alerting his sons to possible mishaps to their racing cars which might result from undetected mechanical faults. She also believed that he guided the family in the matter of business investments.

After Jean's death, other members of the family received spirit messages from her.

In 1955, the family finally sold Windlesham, and moved Arthur's and Jean's bodies to a grave at Minstead Churchyard, near Bignell House. Because of the Conan Doyles' dislike of publicity, the press was decoyed and the coffins were taken to their new resting place in a laundry van, and buried very late at night. Bignell House itself was subsequently sold, and is now being used as a clinic; Windelsham and Undershaw were both turned into hotels.

The great collection of furniture, armor, books, paintings, and manuscripts was divided among Denis, Adrian, and Billy (now known as Jean). Adrian became something of a professional eccentric; he staged a joust in medieval armor for *Life* magazine. Feeling disaffected with the Labour Government in Britain after World War II, he moved to Tangier, and then to Switzerland. He wrote several books, including pastiches of the Holmes stories with John Dickson Carr. He tended to live beyond his means, supplementing his earnings as an author with lecturing, shark fishing, and dirt-track racing. When Denis, a big-game hunter and racing driver, died in 1955, Adrian was left virtually in charge of the estate.

The bulk of the papers were held by Adrian in Switzerland. With flair worthy of one of his father's heroes, he conceived a romantic idea in 1962. He proposed to take over, with government assistance, the Château of Lucens, a beautiful twelfth-century castle near Lausanne, and to set up in it an Arthur Conan Doyle Museum, which would be a tourist attraction for visitors to Switzerland. The suggestion was accepted and the Château opened to tourists. On June 12, 1965, the Sir Arthur Conan Doyle Foundation was established under a council of five, including François Lugeon, consul general for Brazil and a wealthy coffee importer. For the rest of his life, Adrian lived surrounded by the objects in his father's grandiose collection, in baronial splendor reminiscent of the set for Orson Welles' *Citizen Kane*.

Tourists did not seem to be greatly interested in visiting the Château. According to the London *Sunday Times*, Adrian, apparently still short of money despite an arrangement whereby the Foundation would be tax free, took an extraordinary step. Although he had no title to the Château, he attempted to sell it privately to the University of Texas as a European campus. The University of Texas library of the Humanities Research Center in Austin owned the largest existing collection of Doyle manuscripts, sold by the broker Lew David Feldman, and acquired more manuscripts later from Adrian himself. In mid-1967, the Governors of the University of Texas agreed in principle to purchase the Château and its contents. The price had been reduced, after some haggling, to one million dollars.

The Swiss government was still completely unaware of these negotiations. While they continued, in April, 1968, a group of Holmes enthusiasts headed by Sir Paul Gore-Booth appeared at the Château in Victorian dress. They toured the castle, and were alarmed to discover that only a few of the important letters and manuscripts supposed to be contained in a special room were there. Professor Neale, director of the International Office of the University of Texas, was similarly disappointed, arriving only to learn that Adrian had left for the south of France and taken the key to the manuscript room with him. When the room was entered with a duplicate key, very few manuscripts were found.

Subsequently, Neale decided not to go ahead with the purchase. Adrian began arrangements to sell half a million dollars' worth of papers, apparently retained at his apartment in Geneva, through Lew David Feldman's House of El Dieff in New York; he had already, without consulting his relatives, sold certain others.

These extraordinary facts were published in the London *Sunday Times* in 1969. The officials of the canton of Vaud, in charge of the administration of the Conan Doyle Foundation, were dismayed by the *Sunday Times* "Insight" team's revelations. Adrian began a lawsuit against the paper, then dropped it. He also accused a secretary of stealing documents from the manuscript room and trying to peddle them on the international market. In turn, Adrian was accused by several interested parties of having tried to sell film rights to certain stories without consulting the other heirs. A committee of the canton of Vaud conducted a full investigation, expressing its dismay at Adrian's attempt to sell the Château without having a free title to it. Adrian died while these proceedings were going on. His widow, Anna, retained his flat in Geneva and a penthouse at St. Paul de Vence, in the south of France. The Château was taken over by the Foundation, and subsequently sold to a dealer in Zurich. The collection was broken up, and passed into various hands.

Meanwhile, the papers that Adrian had offered for sale through the House of El Dieff were returned to London. The Princess Mdivani* and Jean Conan Doyle, now Lady Bromet, disagreed radically on the disposition of this material. In the subsequent legal battle, negotiations broke down completely, and the great numbers of Conan Doyle manuscripts and letters, including fifteen hundred letters to his mother, were placed under lock and key, without provision for public access.

Another element in this complex matter was the question of the disposition of the published copyrighted material. After considerable differences, the heirs finally agreed to a sale, the proceeds of which they would share. The highest bidder, Booker Brothers, a well-known copyright-holding company, offered £172,000. This sum was apparently not acceptable to the Princess Mdivani, but was to the others, and acting on legal advice, the Princess and her husband, Anthony Harwood, decided to buy the copyrights themselves for £182,000. The rest of the family reluctantly

* Widow of Denis Conan Doyle.

agreed. Anna and Lady Bromet were to benefit equally from the sale, but so far as the Harwoods were concerned, the purchase proved to be a problem. They extended themselves too far, obtaining a loan from the Royal Bank of Scotland; as a result, the literary copyrights were taken over by the Bank and administered by a receiver. It is now estimated that about a third of the income of the Doyle estate since 1930 has been absorbed by litigation.

There is an appropriately bizarre footnote to the story. Certain Conan Doyle materials were retained in Switzerland after Adrian's death: family letters, scrapbooks, manuscripts. These were to be placed in the public library of Lausanne in a permanent Conan Doyle exhibition. In 1971, Anna Conan Doyle handed them over to the Foundation to be lodged temporarily in a bank in Lausanne. After I wrote to M. Dessemontet of the Foundation, and M. Clavel of the library, asking about the whereabouts of these materials, a small party representing the Foundation went to the bank to obtain them. The gentlemen were told that the papers had vanished into thin air. It seems only appropriate that Lausanne should have been the scene of *The Disappearance of Lady Frances Carfax.*

Either the papers had in fact been deposited there and were subsequently stolen, or they were never lodged in the bank in the first place. When I arrived in Lausanne in July, 1975, I walked into the middle of a Sherlock Holmes mystery. In September my hunch proved to be correct; it turned out that the Foundation had kept the papers all along, stored in a box with various items from the estate. It is perfectly in keeping with the mood of the story that, in the last analysis, the material proved to be insubstantial and scarcely worth the bother of inspection.

Three more bizarre footnotes must be added to this chronicle. After their ownership of the Conan Doyle copyrights was assumed by the Royal Bank of Scotland, the Princess Mdivani and Anthony Harwood lived on at the Park Lane Hotel in New York. At the beginning of 1976, they moved to the Stanhope Hotel. Soon after, the almost blind Princess Mdivani found her husband lying dead on the floor of the hotel room. He may have been murdered by an intruder or died as the result of a heart attack. At time of writing, this Doylean mystery remained unsolved.

A major event of late 1975 was the death of Dame Agatha Christie. Her passing brought a curious fact to light. In the Atticus column of the London *Sunday Times*, it was suggested that there might be a new explanation for the novelist's famous disappearance in 1926; she had vanished from her house, causing a major search which made headlines across the world. The police and the public joined in combing a wide area, and airplanes were used to scan the countryside. Her car was located, with its motor still running on the edge of a chalk pit. A note purporting to come from her indicated that she would be found in Yorkshire. Yet no trace of her could be discovered. Lord Ritchie-Calder, at the time the young journalist Ritchie Calder, recalled for Atticus that he was convinced, in 1926, that Agatha Christie had intended to stage a suicide which would implicate her husband and his girl friend. She was later found in a hydro, or health spa, suffering from complete loss of memory. Ritchie-Calder remembered that he, like most other journalists, had searched in her own detective fiction and that of her contemporaries for any possible inspiration for the suicide plan. No such source of inspiration could be found.

I have been advised by someone who wishes to remain anonymous that Conan Doyle, still retaining the position of Deputy Lieutenant of Surrey, was called in by the Chief Constable of Surrey to give his advice in the matter. It seems that by a process of analysis he was able to assist the police in locating the missing author. And isn't it very possible that she was inspired by *Thor Bridge*?*

The strangest footnote of all concerns Bignell House, Bignell Wood, in the New Forest. The present owner of Bignell House, Dr. R. K. McAll, a psychiatrist and former missionary in the Orient, runs it as a private psychiatric clinic, with no more than ten patients in residence at any one time. When he set up the clinic in the 1950's, he and his family and patients underwent

---

* Conan Doyle's daughter Lady Bromet asks me to say she knows nothing of this matter.

a series of extremely disquieting experiences, and thought at one stage that they would have to leave. It appeared that Conan Doyle was haunting the house restlessly. McAll hit on the idea of an exorcism, which was carried out late in 1961. He has experienced no repetition of the trouble since that time.

Almost a week after the exorcism was successfully carried out, Dr. McAll's attention was drawn to an item in the London *Daily Mail* reporting a statement by Estelle Roberts that she had achieved contact at a séance with Conan Doyle, and received the message that he was greatly distressed at having disturbed people during his lifetime. McAll interpreted this message to mean that Conan Doyle's spiritual existence was anguished because of his dabblings before death in matters that should not concern mortal man, and he believes that it was only his exorcism of the house that released Conan Doyle's spirit from its sufferings.

It is difficult to give credence to this view, since Conan Doyle, if he did survive death, would undoubtedly not have been tormented by memories of having brought so many people so much comfort during his lifetime. But McAll is entirely sincere in his belief.

Today, some forty-six years after his death, Sir Arthur Conan Doyle is still one of the most popular authors in the world. The collections of Holmes stories sell in enormous quantities in England and America, rivaling Dr. Spock and the Bible, and are available in almost every language; over 150 films have been made of his work; William Gillette's play recently returned to Broadway; each year brings its new shoal of books discussing the characters of Holmes and Watson, and arguing over such delicious problems as how many wives Watson had. Each new generation reaffirms the glory of the stories which Conan Doyle himself tossed off so cavalierly, but into which he poured the best of his genius. As at the beginning of this narrative, let us consider these words, possibly the five most exciting words in the English language:

"Dr. Watson, Mr. Sherlock Holmes."

And so we are brought back to the tales.

APPENDIX

THE SOLUTION to the cryptogram appearing in the
May, 1874, issue of *St. Nicholas* was published the next month. It is
as follows:

> Little drops of water,
> > Little grains of sand,
> Make the mighty ocean,
> > And the beauteous land.
>
> Little acts of kindness,
> > Little deeds of love,
> Make this world an Eden,
> > Like the Heaven above.

Also included was "the alphabet of the language of the Restless Imps":

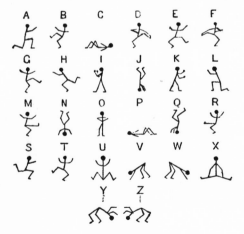

SELECTIVE BIBLIOGRAPHY

UNPUBLISHED SOURCES

The large collections of letters from Sir Arthur Conan Doyle to his literary editor, H. Greenhough Smith, at *The Strand Magazine*, to various publishers, to correspondents discussing details of his books, and to his family and friends, have been split up and scattered across the world in the past twenty years. A proportion of the family papers are inaccessible, and are being held in the offices of a firm of lawyers in London, for reasons described in the last pages of this book. Many other papers are to be found in the collection of the Central Library of Toronto, Ontario, Canada; the Berg collection of the New York Public Library; the University of Texas library of the Humanities Research Center in Austin; the library of Yale University; and the Huntington Library, Pasadena, California. Certain scrapbooks, red-bound séance notebooks, and other materials are held by the public library of the canton of Vaud in Lausanne, Switzerland. The book collections of the British Museum reading room and the Los Angeles Public Library have also been consulted. The Guymon collection of the library of Occidental College, Los Angeles, California, has the unique advantage of offering to the scholar both the *Beeton's Christmas Annual* of 1887, in which *A Study in Scarlet* originally appeared, and the first book edition of the novella published in 1888 by Ward, Lock, and illustrated by Charles Doyle. By a happy coincidence, just as I completed the passage on the Holmes story *Thor Bridge*, connecting it with the Luard murder case, Mrs. Robert Nathan (Anna Lee)—the daughter of the Reverend B. T. Winnifrith—supplied me with the Tithe Book of St. Peter's Church, Ightham, Kent, establishing Conan Doyle's interest in the killing.

PUBLISHED SOURCES
Magazines Consulted

Academy, American Magazine, American Mercury, Annales des Sciences Psychiques, Art Journal, Atlantic Monthly, Beeton's Christmas Annual, Book Buyer, Bookman, Chambers's Journal, Christian Century, Collier's, Contemporary Review, Cornhill, Cosmopolitan, Critic, Current History (*a magazine issued by* The New York Times), Current Literature, Eclectic Magazine, Everybody's Magazine, Fortnightly Review, Galaxy, Golden Book, Good Housekeeping, Good Words, Green Bag, Harbinger of Light, Harper's Monthly, Harper's Weekly, Idler, Illustrated Times, Independent, International Review, Irish Review, John Bull, John O'London's Weekly, The Illustrated London News, Lippincott's Monthly Magazine, Living Age, London Society, Melbourne Harbinger of Light, McClure's Magazine, Nation, National Magazine, New Statesman, Nineteenth Century, Outlook (*later* New Outlook), Pearson's Magazine, Play Pictorial, Psychic News, Punch, Quarterly Review, Review of Reviews, Revue des Deux Mondes, Revue Scientifique et Morale de Spiritisme St. Nicholas, Saturday Evening Post, Saturday Review (*London*), Saturday Review (*New York*), Scientific American, Scribner's, Society for Psychical Research: Journal and Proceedings, Spectator, Sphere, Spiritualist, Strand Magazine, Umpire, Westminster Review.

Newspapers Consulted

Conan Doyle's hundreds of letters to the London *Times* have proved an important source. *The New York Times* exhaustively covered most aspects of his career after the turn of the century. Other newspapers referred to are the Melbourne *Age* and the Sydney *Morning Herald*, both exhaustively researched by my appropriately named colleague and friend Colin Baskerville; the Cape *Argus* and *Times*, in South Africa, researched by Glendon Davies; the London *Daily Chronicle, Empire News, Daily Express, Daily Herald, Daily Mail, News Chronicle, Observer, Daily Sketch, Sunday Times, Westminster Gazette*, and—of most value—the *Daily Telegraph;* the New York *Daily Chronicle, Herald, Herald Tribune*, and *World*, and the Brooklyn *Eagle;* the San Francisco *Chronicle* and the Los Angeles *Times;* the Chicago *Tribune* and the Toledo *Blade*.

General Works Examined

Adams, W. S. *Edwardian Portraits*. London: Secker, 1957.

Asquith, H. H. *Memories and Reflections by the Earl of Oxford and Asquith*. Boston: Little, Brown, 1928. London: Cassell, 1928.

Bamford, F. and Banks, V. *Vicious Circle: The Case of the Missing Irish Crown Jewels*. New York: Horizon, 1965. London: Max Parrish, 1965.

Brereton, Austin. *The Life of Sir Henry Irving*. 2 vols. London: Longman Green, 1908.

Britton, John. *Modern Athens*. Edinburgh: Junes, 1829.

Christopher, Milbourne. *Houdini: The Untold Story*. New York: Crowell, 1969. London: Cassell, 1969.

Cocks, F. Seymour. *E. D. Morel: The Man and His Works*. London: Allen and Unwin, 1920.

Doyle, Richard. *A Journal Kept by Richard Doyle in the Year 1848*. London: Smith, Elder, 1885.

Forster, Joseph. *Studies in Black and Red*. London: Ward and Downey, 1882.

Frohman, Daniel. *Charles Frohman, Manager and Man*. New York: Harper, 1918.

Geley, Gustave. *Clairvoyance and Materialization*. New York: Harper, 1927. London: T. Fisher Unwin, 1927.

Gordon, W. J. *How London Lives*. London: Religious Tract Society, n.d. (?1885).

Gruggan, George. *Stonyhurst: Its Past History and Life in the Present*. London: Kegan Paul, 1901.

Hall, Peter. *Oscar Slater: The Great Suspect*. London: Carroll and Nicholson, 1951.

Hall, Trevor. *The Spiritualists*. London: Duckworth, 1962.

Hambourg, Daria. *Richard Doyle*. London: Art and Technics, 1948.

Hammerton, J. A. *Barrie: The Story of a Genius*. New York: Dodd, 1929. London: Sampson Low, 1929.

Holms, A. Campbell. *The Facts of Psychic Science and Philosophy Collated and Discussed*. New York: University Books, 1924.

Inglis, Brian. *Roger Casement*. London: Hodder & Stoughton, 1973.

Irwin, Francis. *Stonyhurst War Record*. London: Bernrose, 1927.

James, Robert Rhodes (ed). *Winston S. Churchill: His Complete Speeches*. New York and London: Chelsea House, 1974.

Jerome, Jerome K. *My Life and Times*. New York: Harper, 1929. London: Hodder & Stoughton, 1926.

Joyce, Michael. *Edinburgh: The Golden Age*. London: Longman Green, 1951.

Kellock, Harold. *Houdini: His Life Story*. New York: Harcourt, Brace, 1928. London: Heinemann, 1928.

Kennedy, Aubrey. *Salisbury, 1830–1903: Portrait of a Statesman*. London: John Murray, 1953.

Kingston, Charles. *Dramatic Days at the Old Bailey*. London: Stanley Paul, 1923.

Lambert, Gavin. *The Dangerous Edge*. London: Barrie and Rockliff, 1975.

Lilley, H. T. *Guide to Portsmouth, Southsea and Neighbourhood*. Portsmouth: Charpentier, 1899.

Madame Tussaud's Waxworks catalogues. London: Madame Tussaud's, 1869–1880.

Magnus, Sir Philip. *Kitchener: Portrait of an Imperialist.* London: John Murray, 1958.

Malcolm, Sir Ian. *Lord Balfour: A Memory.* London: Macmillan, 1930.

McGrath, William J. *Dionysian Art and Populist Politics in Austria.* New Haven: Yale University Press, 1974.

Morel, Edmund Dene. *Great Britain and the Congo.* London: Smith, Elder, 1909.

Myers, F. W. H. *Human Personality and the Survival of Bodily Death.* London: Longman Green, 1903.

Oursler, Fulton. *Behold This Dreamer.* Boston: Little, Brown, 1964.

Peters, Madison C. *The Great Hereafter.* New York: Wilmore, 1894.

Pound, Reginald. *Mirror of the Century: The Strand Magazine.* Cranbury, N.J.: A. S. Barnes, 1972.

Richet, Charles. *Thirty Years of Psychical Research.* New York: Macmillan, 1923. London: Collins, 1923.

Stead, Estelle and Woodman, Pardoe. *The Blue Island.* New York: Doran, 1924.

Traill, Henry Duff. *Lord Cromer: A Biography.* London: Bliss Sands, 1897.

Turner, Arthur Logan. *History of the University of Edinburgh.* Edinburgh: Oliver and Boyd, 1933.

Villiers, Elizabeth. *Riddles of Crime.* London: Werner Laurie, 1928.

Williamson, M. G. *Edinburgh: A Historical and Topographical Account of the City.* London: Methuen, 1906.

Young, Kenneth. *Arthur James Balfour: 1848–1930.* London: Bell, 1963.

Youngson, A. J. *The Making of Classical Edinburgh.* Edinburgh: Edinburgh University Press, 1966.

Books about Conan Doyle and Sherlock Holmes Consulted

Baring-Gould, W. S. *The Chronological Holmes.* New York: Potter, 1955.

⸺ *Sherlock Holmes of Baker Street.* New York: Potter, 1962.

Bell, Harold W. *Baker Street Studies.* Morristown, N. J.: Baker Street Irregulars, 1955.

⸺ *Sherlock Holmes and Dr. Watson: The Chronology of their Adventures.* Morristown, N. J.: Baker Street Irregulars, 1953.

Blakeney, T. S. *Sherlock Holmes: Fact or Fiction?* Morristown, N. J.: Baker Street Irregulars, 1954.

Brend, Gavin. *My Dear Sherlock.* London: Allen and Unwin, 1951.

Carr, John Dickson. *The Life of Sir Arthur Conan Doyle*. New York: Harper, 1949. London: John Murray, 1949.

Dakin, E. M. *A Sherlock Holmes Commentary*. New York: Drake, 1972.

Doyle, Adrian Conan. *The True Conan Doyle*. New York: Coward McCann, 1946. London: John Murray, 1945.

Ernst, B. M., and Carrington, Hereward. *Houdini and Conan Doyle*. New York: Boni and Liveright, 1932. London: Hutchinson, 1933.

Hall, Trevor M. *The Late Mr. Sherlock Holmes and Other Literary Studies*. New York: St. Martin's Press, 1971.

Harrison, Michael. *In the Footsteps of Sherlock Holmes*. London: Cassell, 1958.

—— *The London of Sherlock Holmes*. New York: Drake, 1972. Newton Abbot (England): David & Charles, 1972.

—— *The World of Sherlock Holmes*. New York: Drake, 1973.

Harwick, J. M. D. *The Sherlock Holmes Companion*. London: John Murray, 1962.

Hoehling, Mary D. *The Real Sherlock Holmes*. New York: Julian Messner, 1965.

Holroyd, J. E. *Baker Street Byways: A Book about Sherlock Holmes*. London: Allen and Unwin, 1959.

Klinefelter, W. *Sherlock Holmes in Portrait and Profile*. Syracuse, N. Y.: Syracuse University Press, 1963.

Lamond, John. *Arthur Conan Doyle*. With an Epilogue by Lady Conan Doyle. London: John Murray, 1931.

Littlejohn, H. D. *Report on the Sanitary Conditions of the City of Edinburgh*. London: Colston, 1865.

Locke, Harold. *A Bibliographical Catalogue of the Writings of Sir Arthur Conan Doyle*. London: Privately printed, 1928.

Nordon, Pierre. *Conan Doyle: A Biography*. New York: Holt, Rinehart and Winston, 1966. Contains a bibliography supplementing Locke.

Pointer, Michael. *The Public Life of Sherlock Holmes*. New York: Drake, 1975.

Roberts, Sydney. *Holmes and Watson:* A Miscellany. New York: Oxford University Press, 1953.

Rosenburg, Samuel. *Naked Is the Best Disguise: the Death and Resurrection of Sherlock Holmes*. Indianapolis: Bobbs-Merrill, 1974.

Sir Arthur Conan Doyle Centenary: 1859 to 1959. London: John Murray, 1959.

Smith, E. W. *Baker Street and Beyond: A Sherlockian Gazetteer*. New York: Pamphlet House, 1940.

—— *A Baker Street Four-Wheeler: Sixteen Pieces of Sherlociana*. New York: Pamphlet House, 1944.

Smith, E. W. *The Incunabular Sherlock Holmes*. New York: Morrison, 1957.

—— *Profile by Gaslight: An Irregular Reader about the Private Life of Sherlock Holmes*. New York: Simon and Schuster, 1944.

Starrett, Vincent. *The Private Life of Sherlock Holmes*. New York: Macmillan, 1933. London: Nicholson and Watson, 1934.

Warrack, G. D. H. *Sherlock Holmes and Music*. London: Faber and Faber, 1947.

Works by Sir Arthur Conan Doyle

(The date for each volume is that of the first printing)

An Actor's Duel, and the Winning Shot. London: John Dicks, 1894.

The Adventures of Gerard. London: George Newnes, 1903.

The Adventures of Sherlock Holmes. London: Georges Newnes, 1892.

Beyond the City. London: George Newnes, 1892.

The Black Doctor, and Other Tales of Terror and Mystery. London: Georges Newnes, 1919.

Brigadier Gerard: A Romantic Comedy in Four Acts. London: Rosenfield, 1906.

The British Campaign in France and Flanders. 6 vols. London: Hodder and Stoughton, 1916–19.

The Captain of the "Pole-Star" and Other Tales. London: Longmans, Green, 1890. This title appears in various forms in various editions.

The Case-Book of Sherlock Holmes. London: John Murray, 1927.

The Case for Spirit Photography. London: Hutchinson, 1922.

The Case for Oscar Slater. London: Hodder and Stoughton, 1912.

The Coming of the Fairies. London: Hodder and Stoughton, 1922.

The Crime of the Congo. London: Hutchinson, 1909.

The Croxley Master, and Other Tales of the Ring and Camp. New York: George H. Doran, 1909.

Danger! and Other Stories. London: John Murray, 1919.

The Dealings of Captain Sharkey and Other Tales of the Pirates. New York: George H. Doran, 1919.

Debate with Joseph McCabe. Girard, Kansas: Holdeman-Julius, 1922.

A Desert Drama, Being the Tragedy of the "Korosko". Philadelphia: Lippincott, 1908. The American edition of *The Tragedy of the "Korosko."*

The Doings of Raffles Haw. London: Cassell, 1892.

A Duet, with an Occasional Chorus. London: Grant Richards, 1899.

The Early Christian Church and Modern Spiritualism. London: The Psychic Bookshop, Library, and Museum, and the Psychic Press, n. d.

Edgar Allan Poe Shrine, The Old House. Richmond, Va.: Published by the Shrine, 1923.

The Edge of the Unknown. London: John Murray, 1930.

The Evidence for Fairies. New York: George H. Doran, 1921.

The Exploits of Brigadier Gerard. London: George E. Newnes, 1896.

Fairies Photographed. New York: George H. Doran, 1921.

The Field Bazaar: A Sherlock Holmes Pastiche. Summit, N. J.: Pamphlet House, 1947. Originally published in the Edinburgh University magazine *The Student*, November 20, 1896.

The Firm of Girdlestone: A Romance of the Unromantic. London: Chatto and Windus, 1890.

The German War. London: Hodder and Stoughton, 1914.

The Great Boer War. London: Smith, Elder, 1900.

Great Britain and the Next War. Boston: Small, Maynard, 1914.

The Great Keinplatz Experiment and Other Stories. New York: Rand McNally, 1894.

The Great Shadow. Bristol and London: Arrowsmith/Simpkin Marshall, 1892.

The Green Flag and Other Stories of War and Sport. London: Smith, Elder, 1900.

The Guards Came Through and Other Poems. London: John Murray, 1919.

The Gully of Bluemansdyke and Other Stories. London: Walter Scott, 1893.

His Last Bow: Some Reminiscences of Sherlock Holmes. London: John Murray, 1917.

The History of Spiritualism. New York: George H. Doran, 1926.

History of the Great War: The British Campaigns. 6 vols. New York: George H. Doran, 1915–20. (The American edition of *The British Campaign in France and Flanders*.)

The Hound of the Baskervilles: Another Adventure of Sherlock Holmes. London: George Newnes, 1902.

The Land of Mist. London: Hutchinson, 1926.

The Last Galley: Impressions and Tales. London: Smith, Elder, 1911.

The Last of the Legions and Other Tales of Long Ago. New York: George H. Doran, 1922.

The Lost World. London: Hodder and Stoughton, 1912.

The Man from Archangel and Other Tales. New York: Street and Smith, 1898.

The Maracot Deep. London: John Murray, 1929.

The Memoirs of Sherlock Holmes. London: George Newnes, 1894.

Memories and Adventures. Boston: Little, Brown, 1924.

Micah Clarke. London: Longmans, Green, 1889.

My Friend the Murderer and Other Mysteries and Adventures. New York: Lovell, Coryell, 1893.

The Mystery of Cloomber. London: Ward and Downey, 1889.

The New Revelation. London: Hodder and Stoughton, 1918.

Our African Winter. London: John Murray, 1929.

Our American Adventure. London: Hodder and Stoughton, 1923.

Our Second American Adventure. London: Hodder and Stoughton, 1924.

The Parasite. London: A. Constable, 1894.

Pheneas Speaks. London: The Psychic Press and Simpkin, Marshall, 1927.

The Poison Belt. London: Hodder and Stoughton, 1913.

The Refugees. London: Longmans, Green, 1893.

The Return of Sherlock Holmes. London: George Newnes, 1905.

Rodney Stone. London: Smith, Elder, 1896.

Round the Fire Stories. London: Smith, Elder, 1908.

Round the Red Lamp, Being Facts and Fancies of Medical Life. London: Methuen, 1894.

Sherlock Holmes. New York: Samuel French, 1922. A play, written with William Gillette.

The Sign of Four. London: Spencer Blackett, 1890.

Sir Nigel. London: Smith, Elder, 1906.

Songs of Action. London: Smith, Elder, 1916.

Songs of the Road. London: Smith, Elder, 1911.

The Speckled Band: An Adventure of Sherlock Holmes. London and New York: Samuel French, 1912. The play version.

The Stark Munro Letters. London: Longmans, Green, 1894.

A Study in Scarlet. London and New York: Ward, Lock, 1888.

Tales of Pirates and Blue Water. London: John Murray, 1921.

Three of Them. London: John Murray, 1923.

Through the Magic Door. London: Smith, Elder, 1907.

The Tragedy of the "Korosko." London: Smith, Elder, 1898.

Uncle Bernac: A Memory of the Empire. London: Smith, Elder, 1897.

The Valley of Fear. London: Smith, Elder, 1915.

A Visit to Three Fronts. London: Hodder and Stoughton, 1916.

The Vital Message. London: Hodder and Stoughton, 1919.

The Wanderings of a Spiritualist. London: Hodder and Stoughton, 1921.

The War in South Africa, Its Cause and Conduct. London: Smith, Elder, 1902.

Western Wanderings. New York: George H. Doran, 1915.

The White Company. London: Smith, Elder, 1891.

INDEX

Abbas Hilmi, 140–41
Abbey Grange, The, 186–87
Abdul-Hamid (Sultan), 208
"Adair, Honorable Ronald" (character), 183
Adams, Mr., 223–25, 227
"Adler, Irene" (character), 89–91, 95, 148, 281
Adler, Viktor, 91
Adventure of . . . , 69*n*
Adventure of the Hansom Cab, The (Stevenson), 69
Adventures of Sherlock Holmes, The, 106
Ahmed (medium), 210–11
Airplanes, 328–29
    Conan Doyle's short stories on, 177–78, 238–39
    séances in, 338
Aitchison, Craigie M., 324, 325
Ajello, Dr. Salvatore, 335, 336
Alexandria (Egypt), 97, 140
Alexei, Frank, 279
Alford, 105
Algiers, séances in, 210–14
Allen, Grant, 100
America (United States)
    Conan Doyle in, 127, 128, 133–38, 240–43, 276–90, 296–99
    Conan Doyle's longing for, 28
    pirating in, 84, 106
    "Sherlock Holmes" of, 219, 241
    Sherlock Holmes plays in, 168–69, 217, 344
American's Tale, The, 49
Ames, Julia, 257
Amundsen, Roald, 338, 339
Anderson, Mary, 105
Angell, Rev. Cyril, 165, 174, 207, 334
Angell, Norman, 250
Anglesey, Marquess of, 173
Annales des Sciences Psychiques (periodical), 210, 213
Anson, Hon. G. R., 200
Arctic, the, Conan Doyle's trip to, 50–53, 58, 97, 187
Argyll, Duke of, 206
Armstrong, Henry, 203–4
Arrowsmith (publisher), 75
Asquith, Herbert, 207, 231, 242, 245, 249–50
Athenaeum Club (London), 54, 81, 107

Atlantic City, 286–89, 292
Atlantis, Conan Doyle's story about, 319
Aubert, Georges, 270
Australia, Conan Doyle in, 256*n,* 264, 267–71
Australian troops, 253
Austria-Hungary, Conan Doyle in, 86–87, 90
Automatic writing, 233, 255–56
    of Jean Conan Doyle, 259, 263, 288–89, 292–93, 329, 337
Automobile race, Germany-England, 227–28
Automobiles, 337
    Conan Doyle's driving of, 181–82

Bagehot, Walter, 129
Bailey, Charles, 268–69, 319
Baird, John Logie, 319
"Baker, Henry" (character), 22
Baker Street, 12, 35, 70, 184, 190–91, 192
Baker Street irregulars, 38, 73, 172
Baldwin, Stanley, 302, 303, 324
Balfour, Arthur J. (Lord Balfour), 110–11
    as prime minister, 167, 171, 175, 176, 194–95
    in Society for Psychical Research, 117–18, 124, 128, 303
Ball, William, 140
Barbados, Shifting Coffins of, 306
Baring, Evelyn (Baron Cromer), 141, 143, 168, 208, 221, 222
Baring-Gould, Rev. Sabine, 263
Barr, Robert, 102, 104
Barrett, Sir William, 274
Barrie, James M., 102, 105, 107, 128, 129, 175
Barrowman, Mary, 225–27, 323, 324
Barrymore, John, 317, 318
Baskerville, Colin, 348
Baskerville, Henry, 240
"Baskerville, Sir Henry" (character), 171
Bassett (Conan Doyle's gardener), 314
BBC (British Broadcasting Company), 265
    Edalji case on, 203
Beauchamp, Lord, 221
Bedding, Thomas, 271

Beekeeping, 11, 304
Beerbohm, Max, 146
Beery, Wallace, 286n
Beeton's Christmas Annual, 75–76, 347
Bell, Detective Inspector, 338
Bell, Dr. Joseph, 9, 45–47, 58, 68, 81, 167, 235
  Conan Doyle's spiritualistic contact with, 295
Bellew, Mrs., 203
"Bellinger, Lord" (character), 184
"Bellingham, Edward" (character), 138–39
Bennett, Arnold, 249
Bentley Ltd. (publisher), 78
Beraud, Marthe, *see* "Eva C"
Bergmann, Geheimrath von, 85–86
Berlin, 318
  Conan Doyle in, 85–86
Beryl Coronet, The, 101–2, 109, 204
Besinnet, Ada, 276, 278, 282–84
Besterman, Theodore, 331–33
Bethmann-Hollweg, Theobald von, 228
Bettany, Professor, 75
Beyond the City, 97, 98
Bicycle tracks, 191
Bicycling, 181–82
Bignell House, 12, 314–15, 339
  fire at, 329–30
  "haunting" of, 343–44
Binnington, Fred, 216
Bird, J. Malcolm, 294–96
Bisson, Mme. Alexandre, 213–24, 271
Black, James, 290
Black Hand, the, 219
Black Peter, 187
Black Plague, 193–94
Blackheath, 147, 209
Blackwell, Carlyle, 318
"Blackwell, Lady Eva" (character), 185, 186
Blackwoods (publisher), 78
Blanched Soldiers, The, 304–5
Bloemfontein (South Africa), 158, 161–63, 210, 327
Blood, Thomas, 110
Blue Carbuncle, The, 22n, 99, 115, 204
Blue Island, The (book of communications), 291–92, 297
Boer War, 157–67, 174, 182, 184, 194, 210, 305, 314
Bohemia, 38
  "King of" (character), 11, 81, 89–92, 93, 95, 115, 129
Bok, Edward, 277
Booker Brothers, 341
Bookman, The (periodical), 135
Boot, W. H. J., 93, 94
Boraston, John, 166–67
Boston (Massachusetts)
  Boylestone bank robbery in, 113
  Conan Doyle in, 136–37
Botany, Conan Doyle's knowledge of, 79
Botha, Gen. Louis, 158, 161
Boxing, 50, 130, 139, 216
Boyd, Agnes P. R., 289
"Brackenstall, Lady" (character), 186–87

"Brackenstall, Sir Eustace" (character), 187
Bradley, H. Dennie, 331, 333, 337
"Brent, Alice" (character), 190 ·
"Bribb, John Alfred Napoleon" (character), 190
Brieger, Professor, 85
Brigadier Girard (play), 215
Brinvilliers, Marquise de, 179
Bristol Mercury, The, 76
British Broadcasting Company, *see* BBC
British Campaign in France and Flanders, 245, 253
British College of Psychic Science, 273, 295, 333
British Society for Psychical Research, *see* Society for Psychical Research
Britton, Clarence, 299
Bromet, Lady (daughter of Conan Doyle), *see* Conan Doyle, Jean Lena Annette "Billy"
Brooklyn *Eagle,* 322
Brougham, Lord, 23
Broun, Heywood, 278
Brown Hand, The, 176
Bruce-Partington Plans, The, 12, 81, 206–7, 311, 312
Budd, Dr., 54, 73
Buller, Gen. Sir Redvers, 158
Bülow, Bernhard von, 184
Burke, Sir Bernard, 204
Burns, William J., 241–43
"Burnwell, Sir George" (character), 102
Butler, Arthur, 126
Butters, Mrs., 326
Buxton, Mrs., 274, 296

Cabell family, 168, 169
Café Royal (London), 103
Caillaux, Joseph, 228
Caillaux, Mme. Joseph, 186
Caine, Hall, 102
Cairo (Egypt), Conan Doyle in, 141–46
Caithness, Earl and Countess of, 120
Calmette, Gaston, 186
Cambon, Jules, 228
Cambridge, Duke of, 160
Campbell-Bannerman, Sir Henry, 195
Canada, Conan Doyle in, 240, 243–44, 299
Canterbury, Archbishop of, 249
"Cantlmere, Lord" ((character), 305
Cape *Argus,* 326, 348
Cape *Times,* 326, 348
Captain of the "Pole-Star," The, 58–59, 61, 139, 180
Captain of the "Pole-Star," and Other Tales, The, 62
Cardboard Box, The, 43, 104
"Carey, Capt." (character), 187
"Carfax, Lady Frances" (character), 12, 233, 317
Caricature, John Doyle's, 22, 23
Carnarvon, Earl of, 296
Carnegie Hall (New York City), Conan Doyle's lectures in, 277–78, 296–97

Carr, John Dickson, 339
"Carrière, Eva," *see* "Eva C"
Carrington, Hereward, 274, 280, 294, 300
Case-Book of Sherlock Holmes, The, 311
Case for Oscar Slater, The, 227, 324
Case for Spirit Photography, The, 274
Casement, Roger, 220, 235, 248–50
Cassell's (publisher), 78
Cassell's Saturday Journal, 60
"Challenger, Professor George Edward" (character), 47, 234–37, 286, 318, 319, 328, 329, 334
  Conan Doyle dresses up as, 11, 236–37
Chamber of Horrors (Madame Tussaud's), 35–37
Chamberlain, Joseph, 157, 165, 176, 182, 184, 194
Chambers's Journal, 49, 71, 89, 311
Channel tunnel, 239–40
Chaplin, Charles, 173
Chaplin, Henry, 185
Charles I (King), 109, 110, 305
Charles II (King), 110
Charles Augustus Milverton, 185–86, 187, 317
Chesterton, G. K., 249
Chiaia, Dr. Ercole, 197
Chicago (Illinois), Conan Doyle in, 135, 137
Chicago *Times-Herald,* 136
Choate, Joseph H., 241
Christie, Dame Agatha, 343
Churchill, Winston, 167, 230, 261, 303
Clavel, M., 342
"Clay" (character), 103
Cleeve (butler), 160
Cocaine, 71, 81
  See also Drugs
Colley, Archdeacon Thomas, 272, 275
Collier's magazine, 244, 245
Collins, Wilkie, 83
  The Moonstone, 41, 67–68, 71, 99
  A Terribly Strange Bed, 101
  The Woman in White, 41, 124, 304
Comerford, John, 22
Coming of the Fairies, The, 264, 265
Comstock, Dr. Daniel Frost, 294
Conan, Marianna (wife of grandfather), 21*n*
Conan, Michael Edward (granduncle), 21, 41, 320
Conan Doyle, Adrian (Malcolm) (son), 220, 276, 313, 315, 327–30, 334
  career of, 339–41
  on father's ability at deduction, 10
  at séance after Conan Doyle's death, 337
Conan Doyle, Alleyne Kingsley (son), 107, 147, 164, 207, 233, 305
  Conan Doyle's spiritualistic contacts with, 258–59, 263, 266, 269, 281, 283, 298, 301, 327, 329
  in World War I, 251, 252, 258
Conan Doyle, Anna (daughter-in-law), 341, 342
Conan Doyle, Sir Arthur
  birth of, 21
  in Boer War, 159–67, 174, 210, 305, 314
  boyhood of, 20, 25–28
  death of, 334
    spiritualistic contacts after, 335–39, 344
  denied peerage, 261
  as Deputy Lieutenant of Surrey, 175, 251, 343
  descriptions of, 20, 48–49, 70, 98, 129–30, 328
  as detective, 173
    Bellew case, 203–4
    Christie case, 343
    Edalji case, 199–203
    Irish crown jewels mystery, 103, 110, 204–6
    Lloyd case, 247–48
    Slater case, 187, 223–27, 305, 322–26
    Thorne case, 343
  dogs, of, 170
  dreams and, 293–94
  education of, 28–32, 40, 45–49, 53, 58
  estate of, 339–43
  illnesses of, 167–68, 318
    angina pectoris, 330–31, 333
    dysentery, 163
    influenza, 96
    intestinal blockage, 214–15
    typhoid fever, 53, 70, 163
  investments of, 190
    in *McClure's Magazine,* 135, 181
  knighthood of, 10, 174–75, 192
  letters to, 191–92
    poison-pen, 203
  literary agent of, 17, 134, 189–90
  musical instrument played by, 40
  personal characteristics of
    absorption in work, 132–33, 176, 220, 315–16
    amateur photography, 98, 116
    buys six umbrellas at once, 314
    costumes, 11, 89, 107–8, 236–37
    deductive powers, 10
    did not take drugs, 11, 48
    favorite authors, 102
    filing system, 109, 130
    love of chivalry and heraldry, 26–27, 36, 293
    love of Scotch whisky and soda, 69
    model railroad fan, 154
    moodiness, 130
    obsession with supernatural, 58
    patriotism, 133
    resemblance to Sherlock Holmes, 9–11
    unhappiness, 131
    untidiness, 109
    Victorian morality, 74, 148–49
  as physician, 54
    becomes ophthalmologist, 86–87
    in Boer War, 159–63
    in Edalji case, 201
    in Portsmouth, 55–56
    ship's surgeon, 50–53
    treats Barrie, 105

Conan Doyle, Sir Arthur (*continued*)
  visit to Koch, 85–86
  and wife's illness, 111–12
  politics of, 165–67, 194
  reburial of, 339
  reform activities of, 239
  religion and
    belief in Nature, 61, 65, 72
    break with Catholicism, 40, 49, 53–54, 58
    Coronation oath, 217
    life after death, 177, 178, 257–58, 276
    marries as Protestant, 66
    See also Spiritualism
  residences of, 10–12
    See also specific places
  romances of, 53, 147–49
  spiritualism and, *see* Spiritualism
  sports and, 151, 187
    ballooning, 155
    bicycling, 181
    billiards, 151
    bowls, 98
    boxing, 50, 130, 139, 216
    cricket, 29–30, 67, 81, 98, 105, 128, 149, 155, 160, 209–10, 270
    fishing, 128
    football, 67, 81
    fox hunting, 155, 156
    golf, 136, 149, 282, 302, 313
    hunting in Africa, 327
    motoring, 181–82
    soccer, 98, 162–63
    at Stonyhurst, 29–30
    tricycling, 98–99
    watching baseball, 242
  works of, 20
    The Adventure of . . . in Holmes stories, 69
    Bell's influence, 9, 45–46, 68, 81, 169
    Collins' influence, 67–68
    first book and early stories, 57–61
    first published, 49
    first stories, 31–32
    Gaboriau's influence, 43–45, 171
    ghost stories, 217–19
    horror stories, 155–56, 176–79
    list of, 352–54
    manifestoes about people falsely accused of crime, 11, 227, 324
    method of writing Holmes stories, 72
    pirated, 84, 106
    play adaptation, 142, 152, 215
    plays, 104, 136, 215–17
    Poe's influence, 41–43, 81, 83, 101, 133, 184–85
    rate of writing Holmes stories, 99
    Reid's influence, 27–28, 73, 100, 112
    writing while traveling, 109, 220, 313
    See also "Holmes, Sherlock"; *specific works*
Conan Doyle, Denis (son), 220, 270, 276, 298, 313, 327–30, 334, 339

Conan Doyle, Jean Leckie (second wife), 155, 156, 160, 164, 174, 215, 216, 227, 237, 270, 321
  in America, 241, 242, 299
  children of, 220
  death of, 339
  marriage of, 207–8
  romance of Conan Doyle and, 147–49
  spiritualism and, 148, 259, 263, 266, 276, 283, 327, 329
    after Conan Doyle's death, 335, 337, 339
  Phineas circle, 292–93
  séance with Houdini, 287–89, 292
Conan Doyle, Jean Lena Annette "Billy" (Lady Bromet (daughter), 12, 220, 309, 330, 339, 341, 342
Conan Doyle, Kingsley, *see* Conan Doyle, Alleyne Kingsley
Conan Doyle, Louise Hawkins (first wife), 12, 65–67, 86, 89, 96, 109, 129, 146, 159
  and Conan Doyle's love affair, 148–49
  Conan Doyle's nickname for, 67
  in Conan Doyle's works, 77, 79–80, 155
  death of, 199
  in Egypt, 141–44, 146
  marriage of, 66–67
  tuberculosis of, 106, 108, 111–13, 116, 140, 146, 151, 164, 194
Conan Doyle, Malcolm, *see* Conan Doyle, Adrian
Conan Doyle, Mary Louise (daughter), 78, 97, 147, 207, 245, 330, 333, 334
Coney Island (New York City), 243
Congo Free State, 220–22
Constantinople, Conan Doyle in, 208
Coogan, Jackie, 299
Cook, David, 226
Cook, Florrie, 119–24, 196, 197
Cook, Henry, 119
Cook, Joseph, 253
Cook, Kate, 119
Copper Beeches, The, 100, 153, 170
Copyrights, 106
  after Conan Doyle's death, 341–42
"Coram, Professor" (character), 311
Corelli, Marie, 205
Corner, Edward, 110
Cornhill, The (periodical), 49, 59, 75, 84, 88, 99, 113
Cottrell, Mrs., 336–37
Courcelle, Pierre de, 190
Courvoiser (valet), 36
Craddock, Frederick Foster, 195–96
Crandon, Mina, 297–300
Crawford, Dr. J. W., 260
Creeping Man, The, 306–7
Cricket, 67, 81, 98, 105, 128, 149, 155, 160, 209–10, 270
"Stonyhurst," 29–30
Crime
  in Edinburgh, 21

Jack the Ripper, 77, 100, 104, 269
  in London, 37–38
  in Madame Tussaud's waxworks, 35–
    37, 106, 127, 186
  See also Conan Doyle, Sir Arthur—
    as detective; Scotland Yard
Crime of the Congo, The, 221–22
Crippen, Hawley Harvey, 305–6
Cromer, Baron, see Baring, Evelyn
Crooked Man, The, 133
Crookes, William, 118, 120–24, 129,
  198, 279, 283, 319
Crowborough, 11, 209, 244, 270, 322
Crown jewels, 39, 101–2, 110
  Irish, 103, 110, 204–6
Cruikshank, George, 22
"Cubitt, Hilton" (character), 188
"Cuff, Sergeant" (Collins' character),
  67–68, 95
Cunningham, Daniel, 47
Cunningham, Sir Henry, 137
Cushman, Dr. Allerton, 274, 280

"Dacre, Lionel" (character), 179
Daily Chronicle, 250
Daily Herald, 337
Daily Mail, 284, 344
Daily News and Leader, 229
Daily Sketch, 300–301
Daily Telegraph, 86, 111, 184, 202, 348
Dancing Men, The, 188
Danger!, 207, 230, 232, 319
Dare, Zena, 326
Dartmoor, 169–70
Davies, Glendon, 348
Davis, Richard Harding, 102
Davos (Switzerland), 112, 113, 116,
  117, 127, 129, 137, 139
Dawley, Herbert M., 286
De Profundis (Conan Doyle's story),
  139
Dead of Night (film), 309
Deaf and dumb, teaching of, 239
Deane, Mrs. Ada Emma, 274, 275, 287
  Cenotaph photograph of, 296–97,
    300–301
Delcassé, Théophile, 182
Denmark, 330
Denton, William, 178
Desborough, Lord, 103–4, 244
Dessemontet, M., 342
Devil's Foot, The, 233–34
Dewar, Lord, 338
Dialectical Society (Edinburgh), 57,
  117
Dickens, Charles, 24, 55, 330
Disappearance of Lady Francis Carfax,
  The, 81, 233, 311, 317
Disintegration Machine, The, 328
Ditmars, Raymond, 290
Divorce Reform Association, 239
"Dodd, James M." (character), 304
Doings of Raffles Haw, The, 86
"Don Murileo" (character), 219
Douglas, James, 272–73
"Douglas, John" (character), 103n, 246
Doyle, Adelaide (Adele) (aunt), 22,
  32

Doyle, Annette (aunt), 22–24, 32, 33
Doyle, Annette (sister), 25, 85
Doyle, Charles Altamont (father), 22,
  51, 124
  alcoholism and institutionalization of,
    25, 26, 49, 58, 66, 218
  Conan Doyle on, 26
  Conan Doyle's spiritualistic contact
    with, 281, 298
  death of, 71, 116–17
  in Holmes stories, 70–71
  personal characteristics of, 24–25
  A Study in Scarlet illustrated by, 76–
    77
Doyle, Connie (Mrs. Hornung) (sis-
  ter), 25, 67, 98, 100, 106, 117,
    149, 174, 175
Doyle, Dodo (Mrs. Angell) (sister),
  25, 164–65
Doyle, Francis (uncle), 22, 24, 32
Doyle, Henry (uncle), 22, 24, 32, 66–
  67
Doyle, Ida (sister), 25
Doyle, Innes (brother), 25, 49–50, 56,
  63, 64, 67, 72, 207
  Conan Doyle's spiritualistic contact
    with, 259, 263, 266, 277, 329
  on trip to America, 133–38
  in World War I, 251, 252, 258
Doyle, James (uncle), 22, 24, 32, 39
Doyle, John (grandfather), 12, 27, 32,
  97, 176
  Conan Doyle's spiritualistic contact
    with, 281, 298
  personal characteristics and work of,
    22–24
Doyle, Julia (sister), 25
Doyle, Lottie (Mrs. Oldham) (sister),
  25, 98, 100, 106, 129, 142–44,
    146, 207
  marriage of, 165
Doyle, Louise, see Conan Doyle, Louise
  Hawkins
Doyle, Mary Foley (the Ma'am)
  (mother), 24, 26, 54, 63, 66,
    160, 165, 181, 204, 311
  attitude toward séances, 117
  Conan Doyle's knighthood and, 174
  Conan Doyle's letters to, 147n
  Conan Doyle's spiritualistic contact
    with, 276, 278–79, 281, 298, 299,
      306, 329
  forbids Conan Doyle to kill Holmes,
    100
  personal characteristics of, 25
Doyle, Richard (uncle), 12, 22, 24, 27,
  53–54, 76
  Conan Doyle's 1874 visit to, 32–36,
    39–40, 73, 82
  Conan Doyle's spiritualistic contact
    with, 281, 298
  death of, 56
  spiritualism and, 56–57
D'Oyly Cartes, the, 107
Dracula (Stoker's novel), 307
Drayson, Maj.-Gen. A. W., 62, 79, 113,
  257
Dreamland and Ghostland, 57–58

Dreams, 293–94
"Drebber, Enoch" (character), 73
Drinkwater, John, 249
Drugs, 11, 35, 71, 81
Duet, A, 155
Dumolland, Mr. and Mrs., 36
Dunninger, Joseph, 336
"Dupin, Auguste" (Poe's character), 41–42, 68, 81, 83, 133
"Durham, Duke of" (character), 236
Dynamiter, The (Stevenson), 75

Eddy, Mary Baker, 299
Edge of the Unknown, The, 293
Edinburgh, 105
   Conan Doyle's boyhood in, 10, 12, 20, 39
   Conan Doyle's political campaign in, 167
   description of, 20–22, 26
Edinburgh University, 105
   Conan Doyle at, 45–49, 53, 58, 70, 79, 188
"Edricson, Alleyne" (character), 79, 107
Edward VII (King, *earlier* Prince of Wales), 23, 91, 114, 168, 171, 172, 184, 194, 195, 309*n*
   Conan Doyle knighted by, 174–75
   Conan Doyle's friendship with, 167, 207
   death of, 216–17
   Irish crown jewels case and, 206
   in Tranby Croft case, 92
Egypt, 296
   Conan Doyle in, 140–46, 147, 208, 215, 216, 311
Elbe (ship), 128, 133
Elmore, Col., 131
Empire News, 323–25
Empty House, The, 154, 181, 234, 317
"Elmsworth, Col." (character), 305
Encyclopedia Americana, 80
Engineer's Thumb, The, 101, 108
Etruria (ship), 138
Eugénie (Empress), 144
"Eva C" (Marthe Béraud), 210–14, 270–71, 278, 279, 319
Evening Standard, 329
Exorcism of Conan Doyle's spirit, 344
Exploits of Brigadier Gerard, The, 147
"Extra," definition of term in spiritualism, 10

Fairbanks, Douglas, 299
Fairies, photographs of, 263–66, 290
Fancher, Maude, 279
"Faulkner, Alice" (character), 153, 190, 317
Faulkner, Miss, 333
Fayrer, Sir Joseph, 101
Feldkirch, 40, 43
Feldman, Lew David, 340, 341
Fenians, 74, 75
Field, Eugene, 102, 135
Films, 309
   of *Lost World,* 285–86, 313
   newsreel, 327–28
   of Sherlock Holmes, 240, 317–18

Final Problem, The, 112, 153, 246
Fingerprinting, 188, 326, 336, 337–38
Firbank, Ronald, 311
Fires of Fate, The (play), 215–16
Firm of Girdlestone, The, 47, 78, 104
Fitzsimmons, Mrs., 327
Five Orange Pips, The, 91, 99, 246
Flammarion, Camille, 328
Flaubert, Gustave, 311
Flood, Solly, 49
Ford, Arthur, 322, 338
Ford, Ernest, 107
Forster, Joseph, 186
Fortnightly Review, The, 248
Fournier d'Albe, Dr. E. E., 260
Fox Movietone newsreel, 327–28
France, Conan Doyle in, 21, 41, 251–53, 270, 320–21
Frank, Leo, 241
Franzel, Dr., 85
Frederic, Harold, 102
Friston, D. H., 76
Frohman, Charles, 133, 152–53, 232, 247

Gaboriau, Émile, 43–45, 82, 171
Gabrielli, Gaspare, 22
Gainsborough's "The Duchess of Devonshire," 114
Galsworthy, John, 249
Gardner, Edward L., 263–64
Garland, Hamlin, 102, 277, 278
Gault, Julian, 173
Geley, Dr. Gustave, 270, 271, 276, 318, 320
Gemier, Firmin, 190
George V (King), 217, 231, 261
"Gerard, Brigadier" (character), 126–27, 129, 140, 147, 164, 189, 215, 329
Germany
   Conan Doyle in, 85–86, 227–28
   Holmes films in, 240, 318
   Moroccan crisis and, 228–29
   See also Wilhelm II
"Gevrol" (Gaboriau's character), 43
Gibbs, Dr. Charles, 159, 162
"Gibson, Neil" (character), 307–8
Gilbert and Sullivan, 80, 107
Gilchrist, Marion, murder of, 223–27, 322–26
Gill, Thomas Patrick, 80
Gillette, William, 152–54, 172–73, 173*n*, 174, 244, 344
Gillray, James, 22
"Gilroy, Professor" (character), 124–26
Girard, Henri, 309–10
Glasgow, Slater case in, 223–27, 322–25
Goethe, Johann Wolfgang von, 102
Gold Bug, The (Poe), 41
Golden Pince-Nez, The, 11, 89–90, 311
Goldstrom, John, 338
Golf, 136, 149, 282, 302, 313
Goligher family, 260
Good Words (periodical), 85
Gordon-Cumming, Sir William, *see* Tranby Croft affair
Gore-Booth, Sir Paul, 340

Gorst, Sir Eldon, 208
Grace, W. G., 128, 155
Gray, Capt. John, 50, 187
Gray, John, 103
Great Boer War, The, 164, 174
Great Brown-Pericord Motor, The, 177–78, 238
Great Shadow, The, 105–6
Great Wyrley, 199–203
Greek Interpreter, The, 81
Green, Harry, 200
"Green, Honorable Philip" (character), 81
Greenacre, James, 36
"Gregory, Inspector" (character), 170
Grey, Sir Edward, 229, 231
"Gruner, Baron Adelbert" (character), 309–10
Gurney, Edmund, 198
Gwenn, Edmund, 216
Guthrie, Lord, 226

Hack, Gwendolyn Kelley, 331
Haggard, Rider, 102
Haig, Field Marshal Douglas, 252
Hall, Radclyffe, 332, 333
Halves (stage adaptation), 142, 152, 155, 215
Hampshire Post, The, 76
Hanoi Shan case, 234
Harding, Lyn, 217
Harper's Weekly, 103, 104
Harris, Mrs., 124
Harris, Percy, 244
Harte, Bret, 49, 75
Hartman, Ana, 281
Hartopp divorce case, 185
Harwood, Anthony, 341, 342
Hastings, Marquess of, 185
"Haunted" houses
    Conan Doyle's investigations of, 131–32, 149, 171
    by spirit of Conan Doyle, 343–44
"Haw, Raffles" (character), 117
Hawkins, Mrs. (mother of Louise), 127
Hawkins, Emily, 65, 67
Hawkins, Jack, 65–66
Hawkins, Louise, *see* Conan Doyle, Louise Hawkins
"H.B.," 22, 76, 115
Henley, W. E., 105
Herne, Frank, 119
Hewlett, Maurice, 265
Higham, Sir Charles, 187, 244
Hilton, James, 309
Hindhead, *see* Surrey
His Last Bow, 22, 246
History of Spiritualism, 256, 298
Hitchcock, Raymond, 276
Hodder (preparatory school), 28–29, 188
Hodgson, Richard, 198
"Holden, Sir Dominick" (character), 176
"Holdhurst, Lord" (character), 110–11, 118
Holland, Mrs. (pseudonym), 198
"Holmes, Mycroft" (character), 81
Holmes, Oliver Wendell, 31, 68, 137

"Holmes, Sherlock" (character)
    "of America," 219, 241
    Conan Doyle's bust of, 210
    Conan Doyle's exasperation with, 100
    Conan Doyle's lectures on, 129, 160
    Conan Doyle's son's work on, 339
    death of, 112–16
    disguises of, 11, 89, 110, 311, 317
    files of, 109, 130
    films of, 240, 317–18
    gasogene of, 69
    illustrations of, 76, 77, 91, 94–95, 112, 153*n*, 189
    jokes about, 192–93, 242
    "knighthood" of, 175, 280–81
    knighthood refused by, 10
    later stories of, 304–12, 316–17
    personality of, 9–10
    philosophical essay by, 72
    plays on, 152–54, 168–69, 171–74, 190–91, 217, 317–18, 344
    on Poe, 43
    popularity of, 77, 96, 114–15, 191, 216, 311, 344
    pseudonym of, 22*n*
    resemblance to Conan Doyle of, 70–72
    revival of, 169, 174, 180–89
    smoking by, 68–69
    textbook use of, by Egyptian police, 143
    untidiness of, 109
    use of drugs by, 11, 35, 71, 81
    violin playing by, 33–34, 172
    World War I and, 246, 252
    See also Conan Doyle, Sir Arthur—works of
Home, Daniel Dunglas, 119, 121, 319
Homosexuality
    Casement's, 220, 248
    in Irish crown jewels case, 205, 206
    Jesuits and, 30
Hope (ship), 50–53, 58, 68, 70, 187
Hope, Anthony, 104–5
"Hope, Jefferson" (character), 187
"Hope, Lady Hilda Trelawny" (character), 185
"Hope, Right Honorable Trelawny" (character), 184, 187
Hope, William, 124, 272, 296, 327
Hopper, Hedda, 318
Hornung, E. W. (Willie), 117, 174, 149, 175, 191, 237, 283
Hornung, Oscar, 256, 266, 283, 295
Horror of the Heights, The, 238, 245
Houdini, Bessie, 287
Houdini, Harry, 261–63, 265, 276, 284, 297–98, 336
    Conan Doyle's wife's séance with, 286–90, 292
    death of, 321–22
    on *Scientific American* committee, 294, 300
Hound of the Baskervilles, The, 12, 126, 168–71, 174, 311
    film versions of, 240, 317, 318
House of Temperley, The (play), 216, 217

How the Brigadier Held the King, 126
How the Brigadier Won His Medal, 127
How It Happened, 182
How Watson Learned the Trick, 316–17
Howells, William Dean, 102
Hubel, Ludmilla, 90–91
"Hudson, Mrs." (character), 64
Hugo, Victor, 320
Human Personality and Its Survival of Bodily Death (Myers), 179
Husk, Cecil, 196
"Huxtable, Thorneycroft" (character), 188
Hydraulic press in Conan Doyle's story, 101
Hylan, John, 282

Ightham Knoll, 308–9, 347
Illustrious Client, The, 103, 309–11, 312
Imperial Dryplate Company, 273
In the Valley (Frederic), 102
International Review, The, 74, 84
International Spiritualist Congress (1925), 320–21
Irish crown jewels, *see* Crown jewels—Irish
Irish Review, The, 249
Irving, Henry, 39, 82, 104, 136, 175–76
Italy, Conan Doyle in, 252–53

J. Habakuk Jephson's Statement, 49
Jack the Ripper, 77, 100, 104, 269
James, Henry, 102
James, William, 118, 195, 197
Jameson Raid, 157, 185
Jane Annie; or the Good Conduct Prize (Barrie's comic opera), 107
Jarman, Herbert, 216
Jeffreys, Judge, 78
Jellyfish, 304
Jerome, Jerome K., 104, 107, 132, 175, 208, 219, 260
Jesuits, Conan Doyle educated by, 28–32, 40, 45
John Barrington Cowles, 60–61
John Bull (magazine), 301–2
John O'London's Weekly, 265
Jones, Sir Lawrence, 332
Jonson, Ashton, 326
"Joyce-Armstrong" (character), 238

Keedick, Lee, 277, 282
Kelly, Ned, 233
Kent, Constance, 130, 307
Kerr, Molly, 317
Kilderlen-Waechter, Alfred von, 228
Kimpton, Mrs., 326
King, Katie (apparitions), 119–23, 279, 283, 319
"King of Bohemia" (character), 11, 81, 89–92, 93, 95, 115, 129
King of the Foxes, The, 156
Kingsley, Charles, 107
Kingston, Charles, 183
Kipling, Caroline, 136
Kipling, Rudyard, 102, 129, 136, 175

Kitchener, Lord (Sir Horatio Herbert Kitchener), 141, 143, 146, 155, 182
in Boer War, 157, 158, 160, 164–66
death of, 253
Kluski, Franek, 270, 297, 320
Knowledge (scientific journal), 271
Knox, John, 271–72
Koch, Dr. Robert, 85–86, 111
Kohlsaat, H. H., 136
Kruger, Paul, 157–58, 165
Ku Klux Klan, 91, 99
Kubelik, Jan, 176

"Lady Ermyntrude" (character), 193
"Lady Mary" (character), 193
"Lady Maude" (character), 79
Laermann, Albert, 233
Lagos (Nigeria), 53
Lamb, Jack, 50
Lambie, Helen, 223–27, 323, 324, 326
Land of Mist, The, 318, 328
Landru, Henri, 309
Lang, Andrew, 78
Langham Hotel (London), 81, 82, 203
Langman, Archie, 159, 161, 208, 305
Langman, John, 159, 208
Lankester, Edwin Ray, 234
"Larrabee" (character), 190
Last Galley, The, 214
Latter, William, 313
Lausanne (Switzerland), 12, 340, 342
Law Journal, The, 322
Leather Funnel, The, 178–79, 189
Leckie, Jean, *see* Conan Doyle, Jean Leckie
Leckie, Malcolm, 209, 251, 255, 256, 295
"Lecoq, Monsieur" (Gaboriau's character), 43–45, 68, 81
Lee, Anna, 308–9, 347
Leech, John, 76
Le Fanu, Sheridan, 126
LeNeve, Ethel, 306
Leonard, Mrs. Osborne, 332
Leper colonies, 107, 305
"Lestrade, Inspector" (character), 43
Levitation, 119
Levy, Dr., 85
Lewis, Col. Henry, 144, 146
Lewis, Matthew, 125
Life magazine, 339
"Linchmere, Lord" (character), 156
Lincoln, Abraham, 320
Lion's Mane, The, 170, 304
Lippincott's Monthly Magazine, 80, 81, 84
Liverpool, 53
Lloyd, John, 247–48
Lloyd George, David, 195, 242, 261, 303
Loder-Symonds, Lily, 255–56, 258, 259, 295
Lodge, Oliver, 118, 128, 175, 257, 260, 302
London
Athenaeum Club, 54, 81, 107
Café Royal in, 103

Conan Doyle's Buckingham Palace Mansions flat in, 12, 299
Conan Doyle's Devonshire Place office in, 87
Conan Doyle's 1894 trip to, 128–29
Royal Lyceum Theatre, 82*n*, 104, 171–72
Tower of, 39–40, 109–10
See also Baker Street
London, Bishop of, 260
London, Jack, 330
London Dialectical Society, 120
London Society (periodical), 49, 60
London Spiritualist Alliance, 331, 334
Longmans, Green (publisher), 78, 84, 126
"Loring, Sir Nigel" (character), 79, 193
Los Angeles, Conan Doyle in, 298–99
Lost World, The, 47, 178, 234–37, 319
film of, 285–86, 313
Lot No. 249, 138, 309
Lowndes, Mrs. Belloc, 219
Luard, Maj.-Gen., 308, 347
"Lucas" (character), 184, 186
Lugeon, François, 340
Lusitania (ship), sinking of, 231–32, 247, 255
Luxmoore, J. C., 121
Lyttleton, May, 118

McAll, Dr. R. K., 343–44
Macaulay, Lord, 31, 35, 39, 50, 54
McBride, John H., 74
McClure, S. S., 134–35, 181
McClure's Magazine, 102, 181
MacDonald, Ramsey, 250, 323
McDougall, William, 294
Machen, Arthur, 255
McKenzie, Mr. and Mrs. Hewat, 272, 318
McLachlan, Jessie, 130
Maclagan, Andrew, 46
Maggs, Mrs., 62
Magicians, 261–63, 285
Mahon, Patrick, 303
Mahony, Peirce, 204–6
"Mailey, Algernon" (character), 318
Maitland, Lauderdale, 317
"Malone, Edward Dunn" (character), 234–37, 318
Man from Archangel, The, 60
Man with the Twisted Lip, The, 69, 99
Maracot Deep, The, 318–19
Marbot, Baron de, 126
"Margery," *see* Crandon, Mina
Marie Celeste (ship), 49
Mariette, A. E., 143
Marriott (photographer), 273
Marryat, Capt., 57
Marryat, Florence, 57, 121–22
Marsault (lawyer), 211, 213
Marshall, Mrs., 120–21
Marshall-Hall, Edward, 232–33, 306
Marvin, Charles, 110
Masked Medium, 301–2
Massingham, H. W., 249
Mazarin Stone, The, 305
Mdivani, Princess, 341, 342

Medal of Brigadier Gerard, The, 127
Medina Pomar, Count de, 120
Meinert, Rudolph, 240
Memories and Adventures, 191, 243
Meredith, George, 55, 105, 129
Merthyr Tydfil, 266
Metternich, Prince Paul von, 176
Micah Clarke, 75, 77–78, 81, 84, 106
Milner, Sir Alfred, 157–58
"Milverton, Charles Augustus" (character), 185–86
Missing Three-Quarter, The, 170, 187
Mitchel, John P., 242
Mongoose, talking, 265–66
Monkey-gland experiments, 307
Mons, battle of, 251, 255, 295
Monsieur Lecoq (Gaboriau), 43–45
Moonstone, The (Collins), 41, 67–68, 71, 82, 99
Moore, Adm., 195–96
Moore, George, 102
Moorlands, 147
"Moran, Col. Sebastian" (character), 183, 317
"Morcar, Countess of" (character), 115
Morel, Edmund Dene, 221, 222, 234, 248–51
Moriarty, Alice, 281
Moriarty, George, 34, 101, 113
"Moriarty, Professor" (character), 28, 112–14, 152–54, 172, 190–91, 246, 318
Mormonism in *A Study in Scarlet,* 73–75, 84
Morris, Dr. Malcolm, 86
"Morstan, Mary" (character), *see* "Watson, Dr." (character)—wife of
"Mortimer, James" (character), 170
Mosely, Sidney, 301
Movies, *see* Films
Mummy, The (film), 309
Munn, O. D., 294
Murders in the Rue Morgue, The (Poe), 41–43, 83
Murray, David Christie, 137
Murray, John, 190
Musgrave Ritual, The, 109–10, 204, 305
Myers, F. W. H., 118, 128, 179–80, 198, 332
Mystery of Sasassa Valley, The, 49

Nana Sahib, 36
Napoleon (Emperor), 35, 40, 106, 127, 140, 147, 189
Narrative of John Smith, The, 64, 111
Nathan, Mrs. Robert, *see* Lee, Anna
National Observer, The, 105
Naval Treaty, The, 10, 110–11, 118
Neale, Professor, 340
Necrophilia in Conan Doyle's stories, 59, 138–39
Neil, Inspector, 247, 248
"Neligan" (character), 187
New Forest, 79, 314
New Revelation, The, 61, 180, 256, 258
New Statesman, The, 291

New York City
    Conan Doyle in, 133–35, 137, 240–43, 276–86, 290, 296–97
    Harwood's death in, 342–43
    Holmes plays in, 168, 217
    Ocean Bank robbery in, 113
    séance over, 338
New York *Herald*, 133
New York *Herald Tribune*, 265
New York *Sun*, 134
New York Times, The, 232, 243, 276, 279, 285, 336, 348
New York *World*, 265, 278
Newbold, William Romaine, 197
Newcomb, Capt. W. E., 254
Newnes, George, 88, 140, 147, 166, 174, 190, 208
    Holmes stories and, 94, 100, 101, 114
News Chronicle, 323
Newton, Lord, 251
Nichols, Helen, 154
Nineteenth Century (magazine), 101
Ninon (medium), 211
Noel, Gen., 210, 213
Noel, Mme., 210–13
Nordon, Pierre, 203
Norway, Conan Doyle in, 106–7, 111, 187, 330
Norwood, Eille, 317
Norwood Builder, The, 147*n*, 188, 246, 312
Nouveaux Horizons, Les (magazine), 213

"Oberstein, Hugo" (character), 311
O'Brien, Willis, 286
O'Callaghan, Dr. Robert, 159, 162, 176
Olcott, Mrs. Chauncey, 338
Oldham, Capt. Leslie, 165, 256
"Olebarre" (character), 190
Olympic (ship), 240, 296
Oriental (liner), 160–61, 163, 326
Orth, John, 90–91
Oswald, Richard, 240
Our American Adventure, 282
Our Second American Adventure, 298, 299
Oursler, Fulton, 283–84
Owen, Rev. Vale, 318, 321

Padwick, Henry, 185, 186
Paget, Lady Florence, 185, 186
Paget, Sidney, 88, 91, 94–95, 112, 129, 153
Paget, Walter, 94, 96
Pain, Barry, 104
Painful Predicament of Sherlock Holmes, The, 173*n*
Paladino, Eusapia, 195, 197, 261, 280, 332, 336
Palmer, E. Clephan, 323
Parasite, The, 124–26, 218
Paris
    Conan Doyle in, 21, 41, 252, 253, 270, 320–21
    Sherlock Holmes play in, 190
Park, William, 322, 324, 325

Parker, Gilbert, 102, 105
Payn, James, 75, 84, 113
    Halves, 142, 152, 155, 215
Pearson's Magazine, 272
Peary, Adm. Robert E., 241
Pecoraro, Nino, 280, 335–37
Pecsyc, Mildred, 280
Peel, Sir Robert, 23
"Penclosa Helen" (character), 124–26
"Pericord, Francis" (character), 177–78
Peterhead, 187
Petrosino, Lt. Joseph, 219
"Phelps, Percy" (character), 110
Pheneas Speaks, 292
Phillips, Rabbi, 323, 324
Phillpotts, Eden, 105
Phonograph record, Conan Doyle on, 328
Photography, 98, 116
    of fairies, 263–66, 290
    spirit, 10, 124, 267, 271–75, 279, 281, 287, 290, 327
        Cenotaph photograph, 296–97, 300–301
        of Conan Doyle (as spirit), 337
        contests for, 294, 301
Piave, battle of the, 294
Pickford, Mary, 299
Pictorial Magazine, The, 177
"Pilgrim, The" (E. Clephan Palmer), 323
Pilgrims' luncheon, 241–42
Pineau, Henri, 310–11
Piper, Leonora, 118, 195, 197–98, 279, 332
Pirating, 84, 106
Plank, William, 94
Playing with Fire, 156
Plumage issue, 239, 243
Plymouth, 10, 54
"Pocket Venus," the (Lady Florence Paget), 185, 186
Podmore, Frank, 131–32, 149, 171, 176, 197, 234
Poe, Edgar Allan, 76, 111, 237
    influence of, on Conan Doyle, 41–43, 81, 82, 101, 133, 184–85
Poison Belt, The, 237, 319, 330
Police Gazette, The, 322
Pond, Maj. J. B., 127, 133–35, 138, 242, 305, 307–8
Portsmouth
    Conan Doyle's Southsea house in, 10, 19–20, 54–56, 62–67, 71, 101, 111
    in *Micah Clarke*, 77–78
    séances in, 62, 79
    in *A Study in Scarlet*, 55–56, 73
Portsmouth Literary and Scientific Society, 69
Powell, Sir Douglas, 111
Powell, Ellis, 289, 290, 295
Powell, Evan, 266, 278, 281, 295–96, 337
Price, Harry, 273–74
"Prince, Sidney" (character), 190
Prince, Walter Franklin, 294
Prince of Wales, *see* Edward VII
Priory School, The, 187–88, 191

Psychic Bookshop, Library and Museum, 319, 333
Psychic Press, 322
Psychical Institute (New York City), 280
Psychical research, *see* Spiritualism
Psychometry, 178–79, 234
Punch (magazine), Richard Doyle's work for, 24, 33, 53, 57
Purbrick, Father Edward Ignatius, 29, 188
Purloined Letter, The (Poe), 184–85
Purple Cloud, The, 194

Queensbury, Marquis of, 103
Quiller-Couch, Arthur ("Q"), 105

Radio, spirit messages by, 286
"Raffles" (Hornung's character), 117
Railroad accidents, 32–33
Ravaillac (assassin), 36
Rayns, Tony, 314
Reade, Charles, 127
Reade, Winwood, 72
Red Circle, The, 219
Red-headed League, The, 89, 92–93, 95, 98, 103, 113, 311
Redway, George, 57
Refugees, The, 94, 98, 100, 108
Reichenbach Falls, 28, 111, 112, 181
Reid, Capt. Mayne, 27–28, 73, 100, 112, 243–44
Resident Patient, The, 43, 113
Return of Sherlock Holmes, The (play), 317–18
Revue Scientifique et Morale de Spiritisme, 212
Rhodes, Cecil, 157, 327
Rich, Lt. Brackenbury, 69
Richards, Brinsley, 86
Richet, Dr. Charles, 210, 212–13, 276
Ring of Thoth, The, 59, 138, 309
Ritchie-Calder, Lord, 343
Roberts, Estelle, 335, 344
Roberts, Lord, 158, 160, 162–65, 176, 183, 210, 247, 255, 305
Robertson, Gen. William, 251
Robinson, Fletcher, 168, 169, 171, 233
Rodney Stone, 139, 146, 216
Rolland, Romain, 251
Roosevelt, Theodore, 241
Rose, Arthur, 318
Rospigliosi, Princess Lora, 338
"Ross" (character), 103
"Ross, Colonel" (character), 103
Ross, Robert, 103
"Rossiter, Sir Thomas" (character), 156
Rothacker, Watterson, 286
Rothenstein, William, 222
Rothstein, Arnold, 282
Rouby, Dr., 212, 213
Roughead, William, 326
Round the Red Lamp, 138–39
"Roxton, Lord John" (character), 235, 237
Royal Bank of Scotland, 342
"Royal Person" (character), 101–2
Royal Society, 123

Royce, Josiah, 195
"Roylott, Dr. Grimesby" (character), 101, 126, 217
Rudolf, Crown Prince, 90
Rush, James Bloomfield, 36, 186
Ruskin, John, 24, 320
Russell, Lord John, 23
Russell, Lord William, 36
Rutherford, William, 47, 234

St. Nicholas (magazine), 188–89, 345
Saintsbury, H. A., 217
Salisbury, Lord, 110, 129, 141, 167, 184, 305
Salter, W. H., 332
Sanders-Clark, Robin, 328–29
Santos Zelaya, José, 219
Scandal in Bohemia, A, 81, 89–92, 95, 97, 153, 184, 281
Scatcherd, Felicia, 263, 301, 318
Scharlieb, Dr. H. J., 159, 162
Schneider, Willi, 332
Schrenck-Notzing, Baron von, 214
Science fiction, 318–19
Scientific American contest, 294–98, 300
Scotland Yard, 338
Conan Doyle and, 202, 247
public clamor vs., 77, 115
Scotsman, The (periodical), 76
Scott, C. P., 249
Scott, Adm. Sir Percy, 231
Scott, Dr. Sydney, 131–32, 149, 171
Scott, Sir Walter, 31, 35, 50, 67, 75
Scotto, Marquis, 331
"Scrowrers," 246
Sealed Room, The, 177
Séances, 119–24
aerial, 338
in Australia, 268–71
Conan Doyle at, 62, 79, 249, 260, 266, 267–71, 278–84, 287–89, 295, 298–302, 306, 326
Conan Doyle's stories on, 124–26, 318
of "Eva C," 210–14, 270–71
fraud in, 195–98, 257, 260, 261, 268–69, 271–72
galvanometer at, 121
of Golighers, 260–61
in Irish crown jewels case, 205
Marquis Scotto's, 331
photographs of, 124, 271–75
Scientific American's contest on, 294–98, 300
silver trumpets in, 128, 280–81, 295, 333, 337
See also Spiritualism
Second Strain, The, 183–86
Segrave, Sir Henry, 338
Selbit, P. T., 301, 302
Sexual obsession, Conan Doyle's stories of, 58–61, 124–26, 138
Seyffertitz, Gustav von, 318
Shackleton, Ernest, 205, 282
Shackleton, Francis, 205–6
Sharp, Royden, 203
Shaw, George Bernard, 104, 229, 249

Sherlock, Alfred, 68
Sherlock Holmes (film), 318
Sherlock Holmes (play), 152–54, 168–69, 171–74, 190–91, 344
Shiel, M. P., 155, 194, 237
Shifting Coffins of Barbados, 306
"Shilling shockers," 75–76
Shinburn, Max, 183
"Sholto, Thaddeus" (character), 82–83, 103, 103n, 309
Shoscombe Old Place, 170, 305–6, 311
Sidgwick, Eleanor, 332
Sidgwick, Henry, 118, 303
Sign of Four, The, 36, 38, 69, 71, 80–84, 96, 103, 103n, 109, 126, 170
Silver, Christine, 217
"Silver, Long John" (Stevenson's character), 84
Silver Blaze, 102–3, 169, 170
Silver Mirror, The, 217–18, 309
Sing Sing prison, 242–43
Sir Arthur Conan Doyle Foundation, 340–42
Sir Nigel, 193–94
"Sirius, Capt. John" (character), 230, 319
Sitwell, Sir George, 122
Slade, Henry, 61, 120
Slater, Oscar, 187, 223–27, 305, 322–36
Sloan, John, 295
Smith, George Joseph, 248
Smith, H. Greenhough, 88, 140, 146, 208, 347
    Holmes stories and, 93–94, 100, 106, 112, 114, 181n
    revision insisted on, 189
Smith, Madeleine, 130
Smuts, Jan Christiaan, 158
Société Universelle d'Études Psychiques, La, 210
Society for Psychical Research, 117, 118, 124, 128, 176, 198, 272–74, 294
    Conan Doyle as special investigator for, 131–32, 149, 171
    Conan Doyle's break with, 303, 331–34
    Journal of, 273, 331
Solicitor's Journal, The, 322
Solitary Cyclist, The, 189
South Africa, Conan Doyle in, 326–27
    See also Boer War
South Norwood, Conan Doyle in, 10, 96–98, 146
Southsea (suburb of Portsmouth), *see* Portsmouth
Speaight, William A., 255
Speckled Band, The, 99–101, 111
Speckled Band, The (play), 217, 248, 313
Spectator, The, 266, 282
Spencer Blackett (publisher), 84
Spirit hands, Houdini on, 284–85
Spiritualism, 27, 61–62, 117–24
    The Blue Island, 291–92, 297
    of Conan Doyle, hostility to, 261, 311, 315
    Conan Doyle on life after death, 177, 178, 257–58, 276

    Conan Doyle's books on, 61, 180, 256–58, 264, 265, 274, 298
    Conan Doyle's bookshop of, 319, 333
    Conan Doyle's break with Society for Psychical Research, 303, 331–34
    Conan Doyle's lectures on, 259–61, 268, 269, 276–79, 290, 296–98, 320–21, 330
    murders after, 279–80
    Conan Doyle's original skepticism to, 198
    Conan Doyle's study of, 117, 123, 128, 179–80, 198, 214, 257, 260
    his final conversion, 256
    special investigator, 131–32, 149
    Congress of (1925), 320–21
    Gillette's interest in, 154
    Houdini and, 262, 287–89
    posthumous writings, 330
    radio and, 286
    Richard Doyle's interest in, 57
    Stevenson and, 108
    World War I and, 253–59
    See also Conan Doyle, Jean Leckie—spiritualism and; Photography; Séances
Spiritualist, The, 123
"Stangerson, Joseph" (character), 73
"Stapleton, Jack" (character), 12
Star (London newspaper), 265
Stark Munro Letters, The, 25, 26, 65, 66, 80, 116
Staunton case, 153
Stead, Estelle, 291–92, 297, 301, 321
Stead, W. T., 229, 257, 291, 297
Steele, Frederic Dorr, 153n
Stella of the Tea-Cups (pseudonym), 62
Stevenson, Robert Louis, 49, 69, 75, 102, 108, 129, 138
    Treasure Island, 84, 105
Stillwell, Arthur E., 286
Stock-broker's Clerk, The, 104
Stoddart, Joseph Marshall, 80–81
Stoker, Bram, 104, 136, 208, 307
Stone, Melville, 277
"Stoner, Helen" (character), 100
Stonyhurst (college), 28–32, 40, 45, 58, 79, 170, 311
Story of the Beetle Hunter, The, 156
Story of the Brazilian Cat, The, 155–56
Story of the Japanned Box, The, 156
Story of Waterloo, A, 104, 136, 175
Straggler of '15, A, 104
Strand Magazine, The, 140, 146, 147, 265, 328
    Conan Doyle refuses to give spiritualist writings to, 190
    Conan Doyle's gentlemen's agreement with, 190
    Conan Doyle's reminiscences in, 51
    Holmes stories in, 89, 92–95, 98, 100, 102–4, 112, 189, 191
    death of Holmes, 114
    later stories, 304
    rate per thousand words, 181n
    revival of Holmes, 169, 171, 174, 181n, 182, 187
    The Voice of Science in, 88–89, 92

Study in Scarlet, A, 43, 71–77, 84, 134, 170, 219, 234, 246, 347
  house in, 55–56, 73
  pirated, 84
Submarines
  Conan Doyle's article on, 231
  in Conan Doyle's stories, 206–7, 214, 230–32
  Titanic and, 229–30
  in World War I, 231–32
Sudan, the, 141–42, 144–46, 155, 182
Suffragettes, Conan Doyle on, 242
"Summerlee, Professor" (character), 235, 237
Sunday Express, 272–73
Sunday Pictorial, 324
Sunday Times, 340, 341, 343
Surrey
  Conan Doyle as Deputy Lieutenant of, 175, 251, 343
  Conan Doyle's Hindhead residence in (Undershaw), 11, 140, 146, 150–52, 154, 160, 164, 170, 194, 209, 210
  Conan Doyle's wife buried in, 199
Sussex
  Conan Doyle's Windlesham residence in, 12, 109, 176, 209–10, 237, 315
  family life at, 313–14
  séances at, 267, 278, 292–93, 329
  sold by family, 339
Sussex Vampire, The, 147*n*, 307
Sweden, 330
Switzerland
  Conan Doyle in, 111, 124, 126, 129, 140
  Conan Doyle museum in, 340–41
Sydney *Morning Herald*, 256*n*, 269, 348
"Sylvius, Count" (character), 305

Tafe, Maina, 338
Television, 319, 333
"Temperley, Sir Charles" (character), 216
Temple Bar magazine, 58
Terribly Strange Bed, A (Collins), 101
Terror of Blue John Gap, The, 218–19
Terry, J. E. Harold, 318
Texas, University of, 340
Thackeray, William Makepeace, 24, 39
Thomas, C. Drayton, 326, 334
Thompson, Eva, 281
Thompson, William R., 281, 306
Thomson, Sir Charles Wyville, 47
Thor Bridge, 188, 304, 307–9, 343, 347
Thorne, Norman, 303–4, 307
Three Gables, The, 305
Three Garridebs, The, 312
Three Students, The, 188
Three of Them, 220
Through the Magic Door, 194
Ticknor, Mrs. 281
Times, the, 74, 82, 86, 99, 110, 158, 214, 232
  Conan Doyle's letters to, 127, 221, 239, 246–47, 333, 348
  crime in, 34–35, 37, 75
"Timewell, Ruth" (character), 77
Tirpitz, Adm. Alfred von, 207, 229, 230

Titanic (ship), sinking of, 229–30
"Toby" (dog character), 170
"Tonga" (character), 36, 83, 126
Tower, John Brown, 75
Tower of London, 39–40, 109–10
Tragedy of the "Korosko," The, 147, 215
Tranby Croft affair, 92, 95, 102
Treasure Island (Stevenson), 84, 105
Tree, Herbert Beerbohm, 152
Trench, Detective Lt., 226, 227
Trevelyan, Charles, 250
Tréville, Georgés, 240
Tricycles, 98–99, 106, 111
Troubridge, Una, Lady, 332, 333
Tuberculosis
  of Conan Doyle's wife, 106, 108, 111–13, 116, 140, 146, 151, 164, 194
  Koch and, 85–86
Turkey, Conan Doyle in, 208
Turvey, Vincent Newton, 263
Tutankhamen, 296
Tweedale, Violet, 263, 337

Umpire, The (newspaper), 199
Uncle Bernac, 147
Undershaw, *see* Surrey—Conan Doyle's Hindhead residence in
Union of Democratic Control (UDC), 250–51
United States, *see* America
Upper Norwood, 10, 69, 96

Valentino, Rudolph, 321
Valiantine, George, 297, 331–33, 337–38
Valley of Fear, The, 103*n*, 113–14, 246, 322
Vanbrugh, Irene, 91, 173
Vanderbilt, Harold, 280
Van Dyke, Dr. Henry, 137
Vecchio, Dr., 280
Verne, Jules, 75, 235, 312, 318–19
Verrall, Mrs. A. W., 198
Verviers mail-train robbery, 183
Vicars, Sir Arthur, 110, 204–6
Victoria (Queen), 11, 23, 92, 93, 97, 114, 129, 130, 167, 312
  Diamond Jubilee of, 155, 157
Vidicq, François Eugène, 44
Vienna, Conan Doyle in, 86–87, 90
Visit to Three Fronts, A, 252, 253
Vital Message, The, 256
Vitriol throwing, 309
Voice of Science, The, 88–89, 92
Volckman, William, 120
Voodoo, 219–20
Voronoff monkey-gland experiments, 307

Wagner, Mrs. Iñez, 298
Wainewright, Thomas, 185
Wainwright, Henry, 36
Wales, séance in, 266
"Walker, Clara" (character), 98
"Walker, Ida" (character), 98
Wallace, Alfred Russel, 118
Waller, Lewis, 215

War in South Africa, The: Its Cause and Conduct, 166, 174, 183
Ward, Herbert T., 222
Ward, Lock (publisher), 75–76
"Watson, Dr." (character), 42, 44, 52, 64, 99, 112, 217, 316–17
  birth of, 69–71
  bull pup of, 170
  first name of, 69
  illustrations of, 76, 95
  in later stories, 304
  personality of, 9
  resemblance to Conan Doyle, 70–72
  wife of ("Mary Morstan"), 80–82, 344
Watson, Dr. James, 69
Watson, Dr. John A., 9, 69, 96, 114
Watt, A. P., 117, 134, 138, 152
Webster, Ben, 216
Weiner, Bertha, 187
Welden, Elmore, 53
Wellington, Duke of, 23, 126
Wells, Clifton D., 290–91
Wells, H. G., 155, 175, 178, 311, 319
"West Cadogan" (character), 12
Westminster Gazette, The, 146, 265
When the World Screamed, 328
White, Eliza, 122
White Company, The, 79, 81, 84, 106, 107, 127, 134, 193, 314
Wickland, Dr. and Mrs., 298–99, 322
Wilde, Oscar, 80–81, 103, 330
Wilhelm II (Kaiser), 91, 129, 175, 184, 207, 228
Williams, Ben Ames, 309
Williams, Charles, 119

Williams, Mrs., murder of, 247–48
Willoughby, Sir John, 185
"Wilson, Jabez" (character), 92–93
Wimpffen, Count, 90
Winchester, Bishop of, 249
Windlesham, *see* Sussex
Wingfield, Miss, 233
Winnifrith, Rev. B. T., 308–9, 347
Wisteria Lodge, 219–20
Witchcraft Act, 331
Wither, George, 109
Wolfe, H. Ashton, 310
Woman in White, The (Collins), 41, 124, 304
Wood, Maj. Alfred, 159, 191, 209, 244, 252, 314
Wood, Rev. John, 304
Woodman, Pardoe, 291, 297
World War I, 229, 244–59, 294
  submarines in, 231–32
  Zeppelins in, 239, 247, 254
Worth, Adam, 113–14, 183
"Worthington bank gang" (characters), 113
Wright, Wilbur, 339
Wright sisters, 264–66, 290

Yeats, William Butler, 302
Yellow Book (periodical), 88, 95, 104
Ypres, battles of, 252, 253, 255, 256

Zancig, Julius, 284
Zangwill, Israel, 102, 104, 149
Zeppelins, 239, 247, 254
Zworykin, Vladimir, 333